Sportin' Life

OXFORD CULTURAL BIOGRAPHIES

Gary Giddins, Series Editor

Sportin' Life

John W. Bubbles, An American Classic

BRIAN HARKER

OXFORD
UNIVERSITY PRESS

OXFORD
UNIVERSITY PRESS

Oxford University Press is a department of the University of Oxford. It furthers
the University's objective of excellence in research, scholarship, and education
by publishing worldwide. Oxford is a registered trade mark of Oxford University
Press in the UK and certain other countries.

Published in the United States of America by Oxford University Press
198 Madison Avenue, New York, NY 10016, United States of America.

© Oxford University Press 2022

CIP data is on file at the Library of Congress
ISBN 978–0–19–751451–1

DOI: 10.1093/oso/9780197514511.001.0001

1 3 5 7 9 8 6 4 2

Printed by Sheridan Books, Inc., United States of America

For Sally

Contents

PART IV: SURVIVOR (1953–1986)

Foreword

A Tuesday afternoon in early December 1976: Bing Crosby, about to make his first Broadway appearance in forty years, was rehearsing a final run-through before opening night. Color markers were taped to the stage floor to facilitate the blocking. When a performer asked his color, and was told blue, Crosby, who didn't need a marker, sang a few notes of "Am I Blue" ("ahhh, Ethel Waters," he murmured to no one in particular), and walked over to his great pianist Hank Jones. "Remember Buck and Bubbles?" he asked. Of course he did. Crosby evoked a time when he heard Bubbles sing "Am I Blue," and raised his voice half an octave to suggest his style. Jones laughed and played a few chords. Crosby—the same age as Bubbles, who rarely appeared in public—told a story about him that I could not make out, but the reverence in tone was as unmistakable as the wistful smiles.

Crosby loved Bubbles. In 1965, he turned a portion of television's *The Hollywood Palace* over to him. They sang duets and Bubbles soloed on a gamut of songs from "Stranger in Paradise" to the Mickey Mouse Club theme song. But mostly, there was the dancing: the prodigious, cunningly rhythmic, emotionally expressive dancing. In his as-told-to memoir, Crosby wrote of working with him in an early-1930s stage show: "Five times a day, seven days a week, Bubbles never danced the same routine twice, but always an inspired improvisation." As Brian Harker explains in this delightful and revealing biography, he also stressed the admiration that Fred Astaire had for him, yet never stated quite so explicitly: Astaire, Crosby wrote, considered John Bubbles "to be the greatest soft shoe, buck and wing, or tap dancer who ever lived."

Most tap and other vaudeville-bred featured dancers smiled and focused on their steps, on the coordination of their body and limbs, their specialty turns and inventions. Bubbles was different. He imbued his dances with character-driven drama that defined the man, his confidence, his intransigent individuality. Famous for playing rogues, he is perhaps the only dancer to perfect a terpsichorean villainy, at once charming, witty, daring, irresistible. You can't ask for a better example than his celebrated solo flight in the 1943 Vincente Minelli movie *Cabin in the Sky*: a supremely ironic version of

"Shine," a song written in 1910 by Ford Dabney and Cecil Mack that plays with racial tropes and turns stereotypes on their head. Bubbles bounds around the set, menacingly inspired, flashing his derby, his eyes, his smile, and climaxing with one-legged spins and a perfect walk-off. He is accompanied by his partner of forty years, the pianist Buck Washington, and the orchestra of Duke Ellington, whose facial expressions reflect the joy that Bubbles invariably generated.

Seven years earlier, he had originated the consummate evildoer, Sportin' Life, in the 1935 debut of *Porgy and Bess*. George Gershwin created the role for him—a major role and the only one not played by an operatically trained singer: no one else had a tenor and an attitude as tantalizing and unyielding as Bubbles. Harker shows how Gershwin, determined to retain him, put up with his personal inclinations, which included a certain casualness about rehearsals. The composer ran interference between him and the rest of the cast, personally coaching Bubbles, who didn't read music. Yet he stamped the role for all time, creating a tradition of casting jazz and pop stylists in the part. When Leontyne Price and William Warfield recorded their version of the score in 1963, she convinced Bubbles to recreate it.

The Oxford Cultural Biographies series was launched with the idea of generating biographies of major figures whose stories had not been told. Even now, it's difficult to believe that no one had published a life of John William Sublett, aka John W. Bubbles. He endures as an irreplaceable artist, an unrivaled force in the development of the art of tap dancing, whose life spans the evolution of modern entertainment from vaudeville to television. His story also uniquely illuminates the ongoing struggle for racial parity in the world of show business. Teamed with Ford Lee "Buck" Washington, Bubbles broke down one color bar after another. In Professor Harker, we have an ideal chronicler of Bubbles, his art, and his times. As a teacher of music history, he has focused on Black musical idioms; for one example, his 1999 article, " 'Telling a Story': Louis Armstrong and Coherence in Early Jazz," is a standard work in contemporary musicology. A graceful writer and patient researcher, he has had access to a lengthy interview with Bubbles, an unpublished biography, and the personal archive of John Bubbles, housed at Brigham Young University. He has a riveting story to tell.

Gary Giddins,
Series Editor

Chronology

1903   John William Sublett Jr. is born in Nashville
1910   Performs at airdome; moves to Louisville
1914   Moves to Indianapolis; acquires nickname "Bubbles"
1917   Returns to Louisville; meets Buck Washington, forms Buck and Bubbles
1920   Goes to New York; meets Nat Nazarro, plays Palace Theatre
1922   Triumphs at Hoofers Club
1927   Sunset Café (Chicago); marries Viola Sullinger
1928   Held over second week at Palace
1929   Hugh Wiley comedy shorts for Pathé (films)
1930   First trip to England; *Blackbirds of 1930* (revue)
1931   *Ziegfeld Follies of 1931* (revue)
1933   Radio City Music Hall
1935   *Porgy and Bess* (opera)
1936   Second trip to England; BBC: first TV broadcast in history
1937   *Varsity Show* (film)
1938   Short-lived swing band
1939   "First colored act" on American TV
1943   *Cabin in the Sky* (film)
1944   *Atlantic City* (film)
1945   *Carmen Jones* (opera-musical)
1948   *A Song Is Born* (film); marries Mabel Roane
1949   Leaves Nat Nazarro
1952   Buck arrested; Buck and Bubbles split up
1953   Bubbles goes to Europe
1955   Buck dies of pneumonia
1957   Bubbles returns to the United States; *Peter Lind Hayes Show* (TV show)
1958   Marries Aysha De Festa
1959   *Judy at the Met* (revue)
1960   *American Musical Theater* (TV show)

1962   *The Tonight Show* (TV show)

1963   Tours with Bob Hope USO troupe

1964   Tours with Anna Maria Alberghetti

1965   Tours with Eddie Fisher

1967   Marries Ruth Redina Campbell; *Judy Garland at Home at the Palace* (revue); incapacitated by stroke

1969   Meets Wanda Michael

1979   *No Maps on My Taps* (documentary); *Black Broadway* (revue)

1980   *By Word of Foot* (documentary)

1984   Second stroke

1986   Dies in Baldwin Hills, California

Introduction

Fred Astaire needed help with his tap dancing. Not that his technique was rudimentary or undeveloped—far from it. For ten years he had danced in vaudeville and musical theater to great acclaim. At thirty-one he was an acknowledged veteran, a master of his craft, and in the view of some critics already the greatest "stage dancer" alive.

Nevertheless, Astaire recognized he had more to learn. It was 1930, and times were changing. In the previous decade Black dancers had begun developing a new style of tap. It was fast and complex, and seemed in sync with the new and exciting jazz music being cooked up by such rising stars as Louis Armstrong and Duke Ellington. It was a confrontational and intimidating style, one Astaire did not yet fully comprehend. With the economy sinking and rivals honing their routines, that had to change.

The most prominent Black tap dancer was Bill "Bojangles" Robinson, at fifty-two a relative old-timer in the world of show business who would shortly star alongside curly-headed Shirley Temple in movies sentimentalizing life in the Old South. In the Black community Robinson was still regarded as the king of tap. There was a time when Astaire himself looked to Robinson as a model. No longer. He needed to go to the source, by all accounts, of this dazzling new style.

He needed to contact a performer he likely knew only as "Bubbles."

The man who went by that name was best known to the public as the singing and dancing half of Buck and Bubbles, one of the most successful vaudeville acts of the day. (His partner, Buck Washington, played the piano.) Born John William Sublett Jr., he acquired the nickname "Bubbles" for his buoyant disposition, though he wouldn't be known as *John* Bubbles or John W. Bubbles, his full stage name, for another five years. He was a handsome man, six feet tall and lanky, with long arms and legs, close-cropped hair swathed in brilliantine, and a beaming smile distinguished by a wide gap in his lower front teeth. When Astaire tried to contact him that fall, he was performing with his partner in the all-Black revue *Blackbirds of 1930*. Astaire meanwhile was preparing for the premiere of an ill-fated Broadway show

Sportin' Life. Brian Harker, Oxford University Press. © Oxford University Press 2022.
DOI: 10.1093/oso/9780197514511.003.0001

called *Smiles*, which also featured his sister Adele and an erstwhile Ziegfeld beauty named Marilyn Miller with whom he may have been romantically involved.

As Bubbles told the story, Astaire asked him how much he charged for tap lessons. Ordinarily Bubbles didn't give "lessons," but this was Fred Astaire, after all. So, as with all business propositions, Bubbles referred him to his bumptious manager, a near-sighted ex-gymnast named Nat Nazarro, who pulled a figure out of the air: $400 an hour. It was quite a fee, especially in 1930, and reflected not only the value Nazarro placed on his man's talent but also, possibly, his interest in discouraging such a transaction from ever happening.

But Astaire never flinched at the price. The lesson—for there was only one—took place backstage at the Ziegfeld Theatre, where *Smiles* was due to open on November 18. Marilyn Miller was there as well, and Bubbles ended up teaching both of them, by turns. Years later he recalled Miller as the better student, the quicker of the two to pick up on his tricky new steps. But almost certainly Astaire was preoccupied with watching Bubbles's feet. Execution was not the problem; it was the conception he wanted. At the end of the session Astaire paid the $400 and in uncharacteristic magnanimity Nazarro did not take his cut. "I got [to keep] the money," Bubbles said.

What was the proximate cause of Astaire's reaching out to Bubbles? There's a good bet he was having technical difficulties with one particular scene in *Smiles*, the only one he was proud of in the end. As Astaire told the story, early one morning as he was lying in bed, he got an exciting idea for a dance sequence. Using his cane as a gun, he would "shoot" at a line of chorus boys, punctuating each hit "with a loud tap from my foot," and then mowing them all down with a "machine gun" of tap sounds. The machine gun part—a rapid-fire tattoo, like a stick dragged across a picket fence—might have stretched the boundaries of tap technique, prompting Astaire to seek help. In any case, he was so pleased with the result that he reprised the scene five years later in one of his greatest films with Ginger Rogers, *Top Hat*.

The critics panned *Smiles* but raved about Astaire's dancing. One interviewed a fellow dancer, who gushed that Astaire "can dance with or against rhythm, he can dance under and over it; he's rhythm itself and there's no dancer in the world who can touch him at it." Another critic, after lambasting the show, conceded that there were moments, "such as when Fred is shooting down chorus-boys with his stick . . . when the back of your neck tingles and you realize that you are in the presence of something Pretty

Darned Swell." "I don't think that I will plunge this nation into war," he added, "by stating that Fred is the greatest tap-dancer in the world."

That critic, Robert Benchley, wrote a theater column for the *New Yorker* for ten years, from 1929 to 1939. In that period, he never once addressed the dancing of Fred Astaire's teacher, the comparatively obscure and unheralded "Bubbles."

Such contempt for Black talent was commonplace in that era. Astaire himself didn't speak up until years afterward, and then only to praise Bubbles in general terms. About the alleged meeting at the Ziegfeld, he never said a word. So why believe Bubbles's story? For one thing, it fits a pattern. As fashion editor Diana Vreeland recalled, Astaire did the same thing earlier with Bill Robinson: "I went to Harlem one evening in the twenties with Fred and his sister, Adele. Fred was going to have a lesson from Bill 'Bojangles' Robinson, whom he admired tremendously. Bojangles taught Fred a shuffle: six steps up and six steps down." For another, the account has the ring of truth, from Nazarro's chiseling fee to the precise time and location of the lesson to the particular rhythmic problems Astaire was wrestling with at the time.

And yet, in the broader scheme, the literal truth of the story doesn't matter. Astaire's complex stepping in *Smiles* (and *Top Hat*) could only take place within a world informed by Bubbles's innovations. Whether by studying with the man privately or observing him from afar, the result was the same: Astaire borrowed ideas from Bubbles. Everyone did. Striking a comparison with a certain founder of jazz, tap teacher Henry Le Tang said of Bubbles, "He was our Louis Armstrong." Others made even grander claims. "Bubbles was the greatest tapper ever," said dancer Honi Coles. "Before him, tap dancers worked on their toes, like Bill Robinson. By using his heels, Bubbles added syncopation, changed the whole beat. Then the drummers listened to his feet, the other musicians listened to the drummer and a new style of jazz was born. All from him." The jazz connection in these tributes was hardly accidental: It was Bubbles, more than any other dancer, who bridged the rhythmic divide between ragtime and jazz. In recognition, he is known today as "the Father of Rhythm Tap" (or "Jazz Tap").

Bubbles's contributions to tap were only one dimension of his legacy. History will also celebrate his vaudeville act with pianist Buck Washington, a partnership that lasted thirty-six years. Almost from the moment of their arrival in New York in 1920, Buck and Bubbles conquered one white institution after another, shattering color barriers as they went: the Palace Theatre, the London Palladium, the Ziegfeld Follies, Radio City

Music Hall. They appeared on the first-ever television broadcast in 1936, a BBC production out of London. Known for their rollicking blend of singing, dancing, virtuoso piano playing, and comic repartee, Buck and Bubbles routinely "stopped the show," delivering encore after encore as audiences roared their appreciation. "They were an act no one wanted to follow," recalled a contemporary. "Those were two very classy guys." When vaudeville hit the skids in the early 1930s and longtime acts began dropping from view, Buck and Bubbles were able to keep going. As many critics observed, theater managers continued booking them because their act was a sure-fire draw, guaranteed to please the dwindling audience for live entertainment. They remained successful for another twenty years.

Of all Bubbles's achievements, however, the one that best captured the full range of his abilities was his central role in George Gershwin's classic "folk opera," *Porgy and Bess*. Handpicked for the 1935 premiere by the composer himself, Bubbles played the part of Sportin' Life, one of the most indelible villains in American musical theater. Despite being unable to read music, Bubbles stole the show with his arch portrayal of the sinister dope peddler who threatened all Bess's hopes. Mindful of Bubbles's special talents, the director instructed him to "make no move in the play except in the pattern of dance," and Bubbles obliged with a performance of great verve and ingenuity. As one critic put it, he combined "humor and heartiness and agility and grace into a rich and hilarious characterization that is a miracle of racy brilliance," producing "the most completely soul-satisfying [performance] of the year." Introducing, as vocalist, such evergreens as "It Ain't Necessarily So" and "There's a Boat Dat's Leavin' Soon for New York," Bubbles set the standard for all subsequent Sportin' Lifes, an illustrious lineage that included Avon Long, Cab Calloway, and Sammy Davis Jr. *Porgy and Bess* gathered all Bubbles's many gifts into a single magnificent performance, the highlight of his career.

Tap dancer, singer, actor, comedian—John Bubbles was the consummate entertainer. Yet despite a long and influential career, he is not well known today. Why?

The short answer is that he failed to appear in enough films, in strong enough roles, to ensure his immortality. Partly this was due to the extremely limited roles open to Black actors in the 1930s and 1940s. Equally detrimental, though, was his own potent sexuality. Bill Robinson and Stepin Fetchit showed that it was possible, at some cost to their self-respect, for a Black actor to succeed in movies. But unlike them, Bubbles wasn't willing or

able to hide his masculine allure behind a screen of self-abasement or buf-
foonery. Even his vaudeville act, film critic Pauline Kael recalled, smoldered
with "slinky sexy" menace, an unacceptable quality for a Black actor in 1930s
Hollywood. As a result, while his first role in a white feature film was predictably small, his later roles were even smaller. Such arbitrary restrictions, based
on considerations irrelevant to his ability, killed his movie career and any
chance of him joining Bill Robinson and Stepin Fetchit—or Fats Waller and
Count Basie—in the nation's collective memory of great Black performers.
Nor did these restrictions apply only to movies. A central theme of this book
will be the constant tension between Bubbles's surging performances—in any
domain—and the forces of racism pushing down on them. His own outraged
words about his treatment during the making of his last film say it best: "They
smother you, they smother you."

In the second half of his career, Bubbles tried to overcome his failure in
Hollywood. After his vaudeville career collapsed, he made a comeback as a TV
personality, appearing on talk shows with Perry Como, Steve Allen, and Johnny
Carson. Judy Garland snapped him up for one of her own comeback tours, as
did Bob Hope for his USO tours. Dean Martin, Bing Crosby, Lucille Ball, and
Barbra Streisand all enlisted Bubbles for their TV programs. In some ways he
was getting more attention from the entertainment establishment than he had
ever gotten. And yet. His role as second banana to Garland or Hope was a far
cry from the glory days of Buck and Bubbles, when—within his sphere—he
reigned supreme. His new patrons acknowledged those days, on camera, with
real affection. But they did so in the service of a gauzy nostalgia that pervaded
television in the 1960s: Here was a *gen-u-wine* relic of the vaudeville era, they
seemed to say, when "ethnic humor" was A-OK and everyone knew their place.
In the age of civil rights, tap dancing smacked of subservience and Uncle Tom,
enraging young Blacks but greatly comforting white Americans of a certain age
who regarded the agitation around them with bewilderment and dismay. By
reprising his old routines, Bubbles was part of the comfort brigade—and con-
sciously or unconsciously he knew it. When a massive stroke sidelined him in
1967, a tiny part of him might have been relieved.

The rest of him, however, girded for battle. Over the next nineteen years,
through a combination of his own strenuous letter-writing campaigns and
a growing outside interest in his work, he managed to pierce the public
consciousness one last time. In 1979 he staged a *second* comeback, giving
acclaimed performances—from his wheelchair—in the nostalgia-drenched
musical *Black Broadway*. A new generation of (mostly female) tappers

organized seminars and workshops to honor him and his aging colleagues in the tap fraternity. Bubbles received citations from the cities of New York, Los Angeles, and Louisville. He appeared on *Good Morning America*. His devoted companion tended his reputation, curating his archive and angling for a star on Hollywood's Walk of Fame. At his death in 1986, obituaries proliferated in newspapers throughout the land.

But without a rich film catalog, it wasn't enough. After a few years Bubbles dipped back into obscurity. He is regarded today as a "highly influential but mostly forgotten" figure. It is time to remember him.

PART I

PRODIGY (1903–1920)

1

Words to Live By

1

John W. Bubbles sat in a hotel bar near the Palace Theatre in Times Square, where he appeared every night with Judy Garland. It was the summer of 1967—the Summer of Love—and the air outside shook with the youthful sounds of political protest and electrified rock. Inside the Palace, however, a different kind of sound rose up. Drunk on sweet memories of an older, simpler time, middle-aged audiences cheered as Garland, in a sequined gold pantsuit, sang her repertoire of standards (ending of course with "Over the Rainbow"), while Bubbles, with patented derby and cane, performed his now antique song-and-dance routine on "It Ain't Necessarily So." Bubbles had first appeared at the storied old theater in 1920, so the Garland show represented a homecoming. Though no one knew it at the time, it was historic for another reason as well: The Palace date would be Bubbles's last job before a stroke ended his career three days after the final show. In the meantime, it was strangely fitting that a writer for *The New Yorker* should ask the great man for a summing-up. They met in the hotel bar.

Dressed in a dark suit with a red-and-blue striped tie, the sixty-four-year-old Bubbles struck his interlocutor as "tall, limber, stylish, and full of mischief." The reporter congratulated him on his enthusiastic reception at the Palace. Bubbles conceded the role played by the passage of time. "The ovation I get is not in the same vein as Judy Garland's," he said. "It's more like 'Well, I'll be damned! Here he is again!' Or—'Where did they get *him* from?'" Bubbles laughed. "Now, on that stage I'm not going to stand on my eyebrows with any great step, . . . but whatever I do is going to be pleasing, because 'Here I am again!'"

Clearly charmed, the reporter asked "how it all had started," and Bubbles launched into an auctioneer-like recitation of career highlights—*Blackbirds of 1930*, the Ziegfeld Follies, *Porgy and Bess*, a "command performance" for the Prince of Wales—slowing down only occasionally to recount an anecdote or paint a picture of the events passing in his mind. Many of these events

Sportin' Life. Brian Harker, Oxford University Press. © Oxford University Press 2022.
DOI: 10.1093/oso/9780197514511.003.0002

can be verified today. That doesn't mean they tell the whole story. Like most people, Bubbles was careful to omit episodes that for one reason or another he didn't want to address, especially from his childhood. "I remember everything!" he boasted to the reporter. "I remember saying to my mother when I was a year and a half, 'Put me down.'" (He added with a twinkle: "I've been down ever since!") But then, as in other interviews, he quietly skipped over the topic of family, home, and the conditions of his upbringing—for two possible reasons. One, he had long spread misinformation on a few key points, making it risky to discuss those years in detail. And two, he had no desire to revisit the grimmest period of his life.

2

About the most important facts of his childhood—when and where he was born—Bubbles repeatedly told deliberate falsehoods. "I was born on February 19, 1902, in Louisville, Kentucky," was his standard line. But there is no evidence the Sublett family lived in Louisville before 1911. Every census from 1910 to 1940 says John was born in Tennessee, and in an early profile from 1935, the reporter narrows that down to Nashville. Only when it began to appear professionally advantageous to do so did Bubbles claim Louisville as his birthplace. As to the year, according to two early press notices and the 1910 census he was born in 1903, a date confirmed by Bubbles himself on the certificate of his first marriage. As we shall see, he had professional reasons to fudge the truth about his birth year as well. Judging from the earliest facts on record, then, he was born on February 19, 1903, in Nashville, Tennessee, and named John William Sublett Jr., after his father. This would make him exact contemporaries with Bob Hope, Bing Crosby, and jazz pianist Earl Hines—not to mention the Wright Brothers' famous airplane.

According to the city directory, John and his family lived in a Black neighborhood in West Nashville known as Hell's Half Acre. Here, as in other Black parts of the city, residents huddled in tiny wooden shacks jammed together in meandering rows. In 1904, when John was a year old, a social scientist described his experience visiting these neighborhoods:

> In these sections of the city there is nothing that resembles a home in the true sense. Five women and a man were found preparing breakfast in a little one-room barber shop that was also used as an eating, sleeping, cooking, and

washing apartment. Two women were found preparing breakfast in a room so small that the two single beds in it nearly filled it. One of the women was also ironing on a board thrown across the foot of the beds. It is a common sight to see a woman washing at every door down a cramped and filthy alley.

Saloons, brothels, and gambling houses attracted a rough crowd, and street violence erupted regularly. In a futile search for a decent place to live, John's parents moved every year according to the city directory—and probably more often than that.

In these crowded spaces families drank from a water supply tainted by waste, unknowingly exposing themselves to disease. The mortality rate among the city's Black children reached a staggering 40 percent, and the rate in John's family was even higher: Of eight children his mother bore, only three survived. A doleful entry in the County Clerk's register for September 17–18, 1907, notes the birth and death of an unnamed baby girl whom John's parents buried in Greenwood, a Black cemetery four miles south of town. His older sister, Annie Gertrude, was born on August 26, 1900, and his younger sister, Carrie, on February 13, 1906. But to the end of his life, he told everyone he had *seven* sisters, never forgetting the little corpses he watched being carried out of the house year after year.

For comfort in a bleak world John looked to his mother, whom he worshipped with a lifelong devotion. Tall and thin, with slight shoulders and gentle eyes behind horn-rimmed glasses, Katie Sublett raised her children with a strict but loving hand. When John got in trouble with the law, it was Katie who sat with him before the judge, pleading for clemency. When he wanted to be an entertainer, she cheered him on. And John showed his gratitude by taking her into his own home after the death of his father, and caring for her until she passed away. A faded photograph shows the tall son, resplendent in a suit and tie, leaning to bestow a kiss on his mother's cheek, his hand gently touching her chin. She "helped me to do anything I wanted to do," he said. "She was always in my corner. Beautiful mother. Beautiful mother. Where she came from I don't know."

Little indeed is known about Katie's background, but she seems to have received a stable upbringing. She grew up in the small rural community of Milton, Tennessee, a thick patchwork of farms and forests some fifty miles southeast of Nashville. Born most likely on August 31, 1878, she was the youngest of seven children in a bustling household of girls. Her parents, Antony (or Anthony) Brown and Ruthey Ann Taylor, got married the

Bubbles and his mother, Katie Sublett.
Source: L. Tom Perry Special Collections, Harold B. Lee Library, Brigham Young University, Provo, Utah.

summer after the Civil War. Coming out of the shadow of slavery, they gave their children the dignity of middle names or initials (Katie's was K.) and made sure they learned to read and write. Antony was that rare ex-slave who did not farm for a living but supported his family with skilled labor as a house carpenter. After he became too old to wield a hammer he switched to farming and by the end of the century had done well enough to buy his own land.

In 1896, the year Katie turned eighteen—also the year *Plessy v. Ferguson* marked the height of Jim Crow rule in the South—a young man named John

Sublett came home from prison. Two years later, on July 31, 1898, Katie and John were married at the County Courthouse in Murfreesboro. But Katie had tied herself to a deeply troubled man. His behavior soon turned violent, rivaling hunger and disease as a plague on the Sublett household. To understand Bubbles's beginnings, it will help to contemplate the likely origins of his father's torment.

3

John Sublett Sr.'s immediate ancestors were owned by a white family that had immigrated from France in the year 1700. Over time they replaced their French name, *Soblet*, with an Americanized version: *Sublett*. In the early 1800s two brothers began to distinguish themselves among the restless settlers of Middle Tennessee. George and A. C. Sublett co-founded the first newspaper of Rutherford County and helped launch the presidential candidacy of Andrew Jackson. They also acquired a moderate degree of wealth. On the eve of the Civil War, A. C. owned a farm by a stream in Lascassas, eight miles west of Milton, and twenty slaves to work the land, growing corn, cotton, and other staples. Both brothers had sons who fought to preserve the Southern way of life. When the war ended, they came home to villages burned to the ground by Union forces. George's son committed suicide. A. C.'s took up the hand-to-mouth existence of a farmer in postwar Tennessee. And his twenty slaves emerged from their cabins to explore the possibilities of life under their own powers.

One of them was a smart and ambitious young man who in customary fashion took his master's surname: Robert Sublett. After a failed first marriage, Robert moved to Milton and began living with a single mother named Myra Bilbro. Myra had two sons: John, born probably in February 1874, and H. C., born three years later. As a breadwinner, Robert was a catch. Like Antony Brown, he would eventually claw his way up to the status of landowner, paying off his mortgage by his mid-fifties. A white judge praised him as "one of the most reliable and hard-working colored men of the community." Unfortunately, Myra and her children would not enjoy the fruits of his industry. In 1884 Robert left the family to marry another woman. Whatever sorrow, anger, or confusion ten-year-old John may have felt, he continued to see Robert as his father and took his name. Buffeted by family upheavals, he never learned to read or write.

John came of age during a time of escalating terror. In Tennessee, home of the Ku Klux Klan, vigilantism surged after Reconstruction. One summer night in 1875, between seventy-five and one hundred horsemen stormed the County Jail in Murfreesboro. Pushing past the jailer, they hauled a Black murder suspect outside, thundered down the hill, and hanged him from a tree on the Salem turnpike, where passersby would be sure to see the body. Other abductions followed. The tree on the Salem pike got so much use that reporters began referring to it as the "celebrated tree." As white citizens eagerly drank in the myth of the Lost Cause, segregation laws multiplied, Confederate monuments went up—and the violence accelerated. In 1890 there were 5 Blacks lynched in Tennessee and 85 lynched nationwide; in 1891 those numbers jumped to 13 in Tennessee and 113 nationwide. The following year reached an all-time high of 17 in Tennessee and 161 nationwide.

On Sunday, July 12, 1891, just as this rampage was nearing its peak, seventeen-year-old John Sublett made the mistake of being alone in a woodland clearing with "a very pretty young white girl." The next day the sheriff arrested him on a bombshell charge: attempted rape and murder. A conscience-stricken judge tried to dismiss the case, but when told "a mob was ready to take charge" of the boy's fate, he downgraded the crime to assault and battery and sent him back to jail for his own safety. Four months later John appeared before another judge to stand trial on a modification of the original charges. Attempted murder had been dropped, but he would still be tried for what many Tennesseans believed to be a more serious crime: attempted rape. He pleaded not guilty.

In a packed courtroom the prosecution called a single witness, the girl who made the accusation. According to her testimony, a reporter wrote,

> Sublett attacked her at a well, about 100 yards from the house where she was staying. She said that he did not make any improper proposal to her, but caught hold of her arm, and she screamed and that he then put his hand over her mouth and threatened to shoot her if she screamed again. She paid no attention to his threats, however, and screamed out twice more as loud as she could, and he immediately ran off into the bushes.

And that was it—the whole story. The defense attorney tried to raise doubts about the criminality of John's intentions (as opposed to the panicked threats of a boy who had just made a foolish miscalculation), but the all-white jury was unmoved. They found him guilty of attempted rape, and the judge pronounced his sentence: ten years hard labor in the Tennessee State Penitentiary.

4

The ordeal awaiting John Sublett can be fairly imagined on the basis of eye-witness accounts of the Tennessee prison system in the late 1800s. Given his race, he was almost certainly transported to one of several privately owned coal mines to labor in the state's infamous convict-lease program. Unlike slaveholders of an earlier time, prison clients had little financial incentive to keep their workers healthy. Indeed, since casualties could be easily replaced at little or no cost to the company, the incentive actually went the other way, en-couraging overseers to drive the men as hard as possible—to death, if need be.

At Coal Creek in northeastern Tennessee, state investigators found convicts crammed into three half-completed barracks with walls open to the elements. The men slept two-to-a-bed, without sheets or pillows, on long rough planks. In winter, they had to huddle together to stay alive. In such close quarters, the *Nashville Banner* alleged, "the practice of sodomy was open and notorious." Conditions were no better at Tracy City to the south-west, a camp "black with coal dust and dirt." Lights out at nine o'clock began a night-long battle against body lice and chinch bugs, which attacked the men in ravening hordes. One guard, holding up his lantern, saw "the walls abso-lutely black with the stinking vermin"; turning his gaze to the inmates, he estimated "five hundred body lice on one shirt."

In the morning the men repaired to the mines, where each prisoner toiled to complete a daily quota. If the workers fell short, they were whipped. The weapon of choice at one of the camps was a long, two-ply leather strap tied to a staff, the entire apparatus weighing some two-and-a-half pounds. At Tracy City, one ex-convict recalled, whippings occurred eight or nine times a day, not only for "work failure" but also for cursing, fighting, or talking in line. At the Star Coal Mine in Anderson County, a man died after being whipped. Some victims *wished* to die, were heard to "beg to die before day and beg to die before night."

In a world seemingly designed to inflict maximum pain, true comforts were rare—but they did exist. Prison clients, hard-headed capitalists who understood the value of a reward system, would, on occasion, allow some of the better-behaved inmates to enjoy the company of wives, girlfriends, or prostitutes.

And where carnal pleasures could not be had, the prisoners sang.

On any given day, digging crews would form a line, and as they swung their picks into the hard stone they sang to the beat, bellowing mighty refrains that echoed through the hills. This was much more than recreation. The legendary ethnographer Alan Lomax considered singing "essential" to Southern prisoners' spiritual and even physical survival, since the music "kept them 'normal' and humane," less likely to snap and harm themselves or others. When the men got to singing, he wrote, the music "cooled the souls of the toiling, sweating prisoners and made them, as long as the singing lasted, consolingly and powerfully one."

The prisoners sang keening, bluesy melodies in the overlapping call-and-response fashion of their ancestors on the plantation, and before that, in Africa. When the words did not tell of love or women—the inmates' favorite themes—they might address the bitter realities of prison life, as in this work song overheard at Tracy City about a year before John was incarcerated:

> He'll come down to the mine,
> He'll poke his head in the hole,
> The very first word you'll hear him say,
> Nigger gimme that coal . . .

> The foreman he was a bank boss,
> And he knows the rule,
> If you don't get your task,
> He's sure to report you . . .

> And after you are counted,
> Then they ring a bell,
> And from that to eight o'clock
> That Nigger catches hell.

As the men sang, they entered a kind of trance, losing themselves in the flow of the music. The singing, sometimes by scores of men in a line, could be unbelievably loud, "like a choir of trumpets and trombones." It brought violent men to a unity of purpose. It softened their hearts and toughened their minds. "These songs plumbed the depths of their despair," Lomax wrote, "yet also asserted their determination to endure."

Together with a brutalized body, mind, and spirit, John Sublett must have emerged from prison with something else: a deep knowledge of African American vocal style. The legacy to his only son—on both sides of the ledger, the good and the bad—is difficult to calculate. Nevertheless, when an early review praises Bubbles for his fantastic blues singing (the kind only a "real darky" could produce), and marvels at his "plaintive delivery of the mournful stuff," we might recall one likely source of this supposed authenticity.

5

After five years in the Tennessee State Penitentiary, in a ritual display of white magnanimity toward "the colored" of the state, John Sublett was pardoned by the governor and sent home in time for Christmas. He married Katie Brown and within a couple of years they moved to Nashville to build a better life.

It was an elusive dream. As a transplanted field hand, John Sr. was only qualified for unskilled labor, which paid better than farm wages but not always well enough to cover the expenses of raising a family in the city. Drifting from job to job, he worked as a porter, a stamper, whatever he could find. Katie helped by taking in laundry. But they lived on the edge, with little room for error. One day in December 1906, John Sr. came home with a serious injury: Somehow a nail had been driven through his hand. All his earnings came to a halt while he recuperated at home. It was weeks before he could return to work—weeks, no doubt, of hunger, deprivation, anxiety, and perhaps violent outbursts from the convalescent himself.

John Sr.'s toxic behavior was the family secret Bubbles most wanted to hide. Late in life, when an interviewer asked how he and his father got along, he responded, "We were all right. I wasn't as close to him as I was to my mother." Then, as if still afraid of his father's power, even in death, he added, "Anyway, I appreciated both of them. Both of them. My father and my mother." He spoke more frankly in private, confiding once to his third wife that his father had a nasty habit of beating his mother (this woman he worshipped) and then "making love to her"—Bubbles's euphemism, presumably, for spousal rape. In the confined dwellings of Hell's Half Acre, such horrors could not be concealed from childish eyes and ears.

How much Bubbles knew of his father's incarceration is impossible to say (he never spoke of it). But his own earliest experiences taught him plenty about the cruelty and capriciousness of life. The beauty of mortality was real, but fleeting. He made up his mind to live strictly in the moment, adopting a personal motto straight out of Isaiah: "Live it up, as tomorrow you may die." His path to "living it up"—to securing the good life as he saw it—was a successful career in show business. As if sensing the presence of a lovelier world, he reached for this prize early on, making his first public appearance, on his own initiative, at the tender age of seven.

2

The Soul of Minstrelsy

1

For most Americans the cares of life could be temporarily banished by a visit to the theater, where they might hear beautiful music, laugh at clowns, or marvel at a magician's wonders. In segregated Nashville, however, such transports were reserved for a privileged caste. As late as 1910 there was still no theater in the city designated for Black use. So when Nashville opened its first Black theater in the summer of that year, the project met with great excitement.

On the Fourth of July, 1910, an open-air theater, or "airdome," opened in the middle of Hell's Half Acre, only a few blocks from the Subletts' home. It was built, the city's Black newspaper noted, "especially for the Negroes of Nashville, who have no place to go . . . to spend the evenings in innocent amusements." Aimed at the working classes, the airdome offered bleachers under a tent at "popular prices." The inaugural attraction, a minstrel company called Allen's Troubadours, was greeted thunderously by a standing-room-only crowd—"the largest," a Black reporter wrote with exuberant hyperbole, "that ever entered a theatre in the history of Nashville." The troupe consisted of nine actors—five men and four women—and performed "seven big numbers . . . with a comedy afterpiece entitled 'Liza Way Down in Dixieland.' Each member of the company was applauded at every move they made, and were forced to take encore after encore."

But the undisputed highlight of the show was an event taking place that same day some two thousand miles away in Reno, Nevada: the prizefight between Jack Johnson, the first Black heavyweight champion, and James J. Jeffries, his white challenger. Billed as "the Fight of the Century," the Johnson-Jeffries bout divided the country along starkly racial lines, the stakes feverishly high on both sides. As returns of the fight reached the airdome in Nashville, the matinee was momentarily paused while someone stepped to center stage and read the results to the spellbound audience, "round by round." And when word came that Johnson knocked out his opponent in the

Sportin' Life. Brian Harker, Oxford University Press. © Oxford University Press 2022.
DOI: 10.1093/oso/9780197514511.003.0003

fifteenth round, pandemonium ensued. "The show stopped right there and the curtain went down, for the entire audience and performers shouted and yelled until they were all hoarse."

Whether seven-year-old John Sublett Jr. was sitting in the airdome on that auspicious day is not known, but the new theater became for him a bright light in a dark world. John attended as often as he could, selling bottles on the street to earn his ten-cent admission fee. As he watched the singers and dancers on stage—a new and magical experience—he felt a strange kinship with them. He began envisioning himself on that stage. He begged his mother to let him attach taps to the bottom of his shoes, and when she asked why he said, "I wanna dance wherever there's people happy and laughing so I'd like to see them smile, and they can hear the sound of my feet—that will make them smile more." Recalling the songs he had heard others sing, he began singing them himself.

One day after a show, John walked up to the man in charge and asked if he could sing with the company. "Who told you you could sing?" the man barked. "I told myself," John replied. Impressed, perhaps, by the boy's pluck, the man took him backstage for an impromptu audition. The two songs John later recalled singing—"Naughty! Naughty! Naughty!" and "I'm So Glad My Mama Don't Know Where I'm At"—were published too late to have been the ones he actually performed. But whatever he sang must have been convincing, because the man hired him on the spot, offering to pay the boy twenty-five cents a week plus free, unlimited admission for his entire family. "I used to bring my family and other people's family, too," he admitted. John was delighted, but, characteristically, not surprised. As he later put it, "I was what you call a born actor, born performer."

The news created a stir in the Sublett household. Apart from the obvious benefits of notoriety and free entertainment, John's achievement inspired a wistful, almost unimaginable hope. At one time John Sr. had wanted his son to be a doctor, but the boy, though intelligent, was not bookish. A more realistic ambition was a career in the service industry. For several years the *Indianapolis Freeman*, a Black newspaper, ran a column called "The Waiter." Every week the paper announced who had become head waiter at a hotel in Vicksburg, Mississippi, or Bloomington, Illinois. Given the racial barriers to professional advancement, the clean, respectable, indoor job of waiter, or butler, or Pullman porter was a highly coveted position to be lionized in the press. But as the Subletts quickly recognized, young people with performing talent had other options. In 1904 Black waiters in Nashville were paid $7 a week. Successful vaudeville artists, of course, earned many times that amount.

2

John Jr.'s stint at the airdome—his first professional engagement—ended when the show closed after two weeks. Almost immediately the Subletts packed up and moved 175 miles north to Louisville, Kentucky. Why Louisville? Although Kentucky had been a slave state it was never part of the Confederacy, and in the years after the Civil War its largest city on the northern border had become known for moderation on racial issues, safeguarding the Black vote and steering clear of mob violence. The Subletts arrived five years before the brutal logic of carrot and stick—wartime jobs in the North, a revived Ku Klux Klan in the South—drove Southern Blacks to begin heading north in large numbers.

The strain of the move weighed on the Subletts. The family of five had to make do, for a time, with a single room in a Black boarding house. Tensions mounted between father and mother, nearly capsizing the family. On September 25, 1911, John Sr. accused Katie of adultery—"or such lewd and lascivious behavior . . . as proves her to be unchaste"—and filed for divorce. For some weeks they lived apart. In the end, however, John didn't go through with the divorce and probably never intended to.

Caught in the maelstrom of their parents' conflict, John Jr. and his sisters, Annie and Carrie, developed an intimate bond of love and trust. Late in life he paid tribute to the women in his family in startling terms. "I don't think you could say that I've ever *loved* anyone or anything except God, my mother and my sisters," he said. Four wives, three children, a vaudeville partner of thirty-six years—John "cared for" them all. But he reserved his "love," a quality he equated with God, for the three individuals who watched over him during his years of greatest vulnerability.

One bright spot in Louisville was the steady job John Sr. landed almost immediately, working as a fireman in the basement of the Louisville Trust Company building just north of the courthouse in the center of town. Tasked with keeping the ovens burning, John spent his days shoveling coal. It was hot, filthy, exhausting, and dangerous work—one never knew when a boiler might explode, killing or maiming its human attendants. One day John witnessed a different sort of workplace tragedy when a Black window washer, his first day on the job, fell thirty feet to his death, crashing through a skylight and landing in a heap on the floor of the basement. John and another man rushed to his side, but there was nothing to be done.

If the Subletts moved to Louisville in part to capitalize on their son's promising start in show business, they arrived at a good time. In the past decade the infrastructure of Black vaudeville in the South had grown from a few saloon-theaters and parks to more than one hundred full-fledged Black theaters. When the Subletts arrived in late 1910, Louisville had recently opened two Black theaters, the Olio and the Ruby, rival venues located on West Walnut Street. In addition, unlike in Nashville, Black patrons were allowed to attend white theaters—as long as they entered from the rear and sat in the gallery.

To add variety to his act, John Jr. enlisted the help of his sister Annie (just as, 750 miles away in New York City, a young Fred Astaire teamed up with his sister Adele). On Valentine's Day, 1914, the Sublett children scored their first press notice. A vaudeville show at the Olio began with "Leon the great magician," the *Freeman* reported, followed by "lanky Phil Jiles, doing a soldier act." In the third slot was Salvator Floroer, "the world's greatest baritone" (who also played a mean "sliding trombone"). And the act that came second to last was identified as "the Sublett twins, Johnie and Anna B., the two little nine-year-old kids. They sing, talk and dance well. They are great." The children were not twins; John was ten and Annie was thirteen. But the published billing exaggerated their cuteness, boosting their appeal.

Seemingly emboldened by their children's success, the Subletts headed north again within a month of the Olio engagement. Almost 115 miles away, their destination this time was Indianapolis, a crossroads of big-time acts and traveling shows that dwarfed Louisville's more regional entertainment setting.

3

For starry-eyed migrants, Indianapolis was known as a "Negro Heaven." True, de facto segregation—segregation by custom rather than by law—put up rigid barriers in housing and employment. But the city boasted a vibrant Black community, with thriving businesses, good schools, and well-developed support networks for newly arrived Southerners.

Right away, Katie enrolled her son in School No. 24, a Black elementary school on the corner of North and Agnes Streets, where he excelled in the arts. Though not academically inclined, he strove to be "head of the class" in singing, drawing, and vocational training. His greatest pleasure came in putting on school plays for the other children. A popular scenario was Cowboys and Indians, for which he would don his favorite get-up, an elaborate Indian chief costume lovingly made by his mother.

As the Sublett children grew older, they shared the responsibility of supporting the family. "I was ready . . . to go to work anywhere, do anything," Bubbles recalled. "Make some money . . . Needed the money to pay bills . . . I kept myself busy at all times." John Jr., age eleven by this time, fell into a daily routine. Every morning before school he lit the ovens and washed dishes at a local restaurant. After school he might return to the restaurant to help wait tables, or sell newspapers for the *Indianapolis Star*, or stamp meat at Kingen's Packing House, or shine shoes, or sell rags—or any combination of these responsibilities.

Hard-pressed during the week, John lived for Friday nights when he could blow off steam at a Black theater called the Crown Garden, located at 521 Indiana Avenue, close to his home on the west side of town. Every Friday night the management held an amateur talent contest, and John was an avid competitor. The first night there were singers, dancers, instrumentalists, even a ventriloquist. But John won first prize, and continued to win for eight weeks running. One of his songs, he recalled much later (again, erroneously, given its late publication date), was "Georgia Rose": "That's a beautiful song, a lovely song. I did it holding a mirror, and it would reflect the spotlight to wherever I wanted. I'd sing, 'Sweet little Georgia Rose, from the land where the cotton blossom grows,' and I'd turn the light on different girls in the audience. I was a butcher in that theatre." Finally, when the other contestants refused to participate if John was in the lineup, he was politely asked to retire as undefeated champion. His reign had been profitable. One night he came home and spread before his beaming parents the munificent sum of $50.00— his contest winnings for the night. "I gave it all to my mother but a quarter," he said.

As John got ready to leave the Crown Garden on the last night, Riley Roberts, the theater manager, asked him a question: "How come they call you Bub?" John explained it was short for Bubber, a nickname used by his family (and common in Black families as a variant of "brother" as far back as slavery). "Well, I'm gonna change your name," Roberts said. "I'm going to start calling you Bubbles," because "you always wear a smile." John loved the new moniker and immediately adopted it, both onstage and off.

Sensing the boy's disappointment at having to quit the contest, Roberts gave him a job working in the theater, selling concessions, and doing errands—and adding to his endless round of odd jobs. John composed a sassy little pitch, and as the silent movies were playing he'd roam the aisles shouting it with gusto, as though he were at a ballpark:

Get your chewing gum and your Cracker Jack.
Get your double-jointed peanuts and don't bring 'em back.
Get your ice-cold pop, and don't hesitate.
Tell me, how long will I have to wait?

Sometimes the young teenager sat in for the film operator, cranking the machine by hand—"Just a moment," he called down between reels, "The operator is having a fit." By the end of the night, exhausted from the day's labors, he would collapse in a seat on the front row and fall asleep. Sometimes he awoke to find someone had stolen his concessions.

As a vaudeville performer John Jr. seems to have been increasingly active, far more than scattered news reports would suggest. Within a month of the family's arrival in Indianapolis, the *Freeman* announced he was already drawing "great crowds" in the city's Black theaters. Though still appearing with Annie, he had eclipsed her in the eyes of the public. For a news story promoting an upcoming bill at the Hoosier Theatre, John's name filled the headline. The article described him as a "comedian," a word which in that era meant not only a jokester but someone who sang and danced as well. This time the paper reported his true age:

Master Johnnie Sublett . . . is drawing great crowds by his cleverness as a singer and dancer. Johnnie is only eleven years old, but already shows a remarkable ability as a real artist. In fact, the lad has a great many of our adult performers "bested" when it comes to first class singing and dancing. Master Sublett will sing "Fifteen Cents" and "Pray for the Lights to Go Out" Saturday evening and Sunday at matinee and night [*sic*]. The little comedian will be assisted by his sister Annie.

Not everyone approved of the Subletts' performances. According to John Jr., a policeman came by the house one night and warned Katie to "get those kids offa the stage or you'll be in trouble." "What kind of trouble?" Katie asked. "Well, I'll just have to throw you in jail, that's what kind of trouble," the officer responded lamely, and left. John thought it was Katie's calm, beneficent gaze that disarmed the man. "She had a way with words, sometimes without any words at all," he recalled. "It was her eyes, I guess. It was the way she looked at you. No one could help but melt just a little when she looked at you."

4

During this period John Jr. came within the gravitational field of a cosmic force in the world of entertainment: the Ziegfeld Follies. Every winter in 1915, 1916, and 1917 the Follies came to Indianapolis and appeared at English's Opera House. The show was especially meaningful to Black theatergoers because since 1910 the originally all-white Follies had featured a single Black artist, the greatest Black comedian of his day—some said the greatest regardless of race—Bert Williams.

Williams was the last great exponent of blackface minstrelsy, a performing tradition dating back almost a hundred years. The tradition was based on a premise shockingly repellent by modern standards, namely, that white actors would darken their faces with burnt cork and parody the songs, dances, and jokes of slaves on the plantation. After the Civil War, Black entertainers applied the hated cork to their own faces, grudgingly accepting the shame and self-mockery the institution required. And yet, paradoxically, Black people came to see minstrelsy as a source of pride as well as shame. Audiences could tell the difference between white and Black minstrels, and increasingly they favored the latter. Proud of their "authenticity," Black minstrels advertised their race openly. Bert Williams and his partner George Walker, for example, billed themselves as "Two Real Coons." Walker played the fast-talking dandy, while Williams played the slow Southern darky. Investing these stock roles with humanity, expressiveness, and humor, Williams and Walker rose to the top of their profession, becoming the only Black artists to be mentioned in the same breath with leading white actors.

When Walker died prematurely, Florenz Ziegfeld hired Williams to join the Follies as a single. Like other principals in the show, Williams offered musical or comic relief from the troupe's well-known specialty—world-class feminine pulchritude in the form of lightly clad chorus girls. As Williams himself quipped, "I'm just out there to give the gals time to change." Corked up, with rings of white paint around his eyes and lips, and dressed in a ragged top hat and tails, he would amble onto an empty stage and perform pantomimes that left the audience gasping with laughter. In his most famous bit, "The Poker Game," he played the part of a hapless gambler, clutching an invisible hand of cards, alternating expressions of hubris, jollity, and paranoia as the game progressed, and finally despairing as he lost everything. During the 1917 season Williams appeared with a legendary roster of comedians: W. C. Fields, Fanny Brice, Will Rogers, and Eddie Cantor. Even in company this fast, Williams dominated according to Fields, who called him "the funniest man I ever saw." Yet when he returned to his hotel after every show, he had to use the service elevator. He was, after all, still Black.

Given the Follies' popularity, it was nearly impossible for Black patrons to see them. A Black reporter complained angrily that when the Follies came to Louisville there were only a small number of gallery seats reserved for Black patrons, who otherwise "were obliged to take standing room in the rear." John Jr. was not one of the lucky few who got to see the great Bert Williams in the flesh. But it was during this period that he first read about the Ziegfeld Follies in the newspaper. He was mesmerized by the company's glamour and prestige. The Follies, he noted, were from New York, a city he'd learned about in his geography class. An idea took root in his mind: Someday he wanted to go to New York, and once there, to perform, like Bert Williams, with the fabulous Ziegfeld Follies.

In the meantime, he was inching closer to his destiny as one of Williams's most distinguished heirs. In early 1917 a Black reporter named Billy Lewis wrote a lengthy tribute to a child entertainer identified only as "Bubbles" (surely the erstwhile "Johnnie Sublett"). Describing a recent performance at the Washington Theatre (formerly the Crown Garden), Lewis hailed the thirteen-year-old boy as a prodigy. Bubbles, he said, had absorbed and synthesized the great Black actors who came before him, while staking out a future surpassing them all:

> "Little old Bubbles" is the way one would like to speak of the boy Bubbles who bids fair to be the leading comedian of his race. He styles himself as Bubbles, the Star Comedian. Rather ambitious sounding, but one has only to see and hear this boy prodigy and he will give him whatever he wants, or call him whatever he wishes to be called. At this time he has no airs and frills, he is just old Bubbles whom no one would turn around to see. But he is the very soul of minstrelsy.

He has been a human sponge, absorbing the best that has been put over the footlights. . . . He is some of String Beans, some of Stovall, some of Jines, some of Higgins, some of Mills, some of the rest of them and done up so that he is wholly himself—a part of all of them, but imitating none of them.

Well, he was received with thunderous applause, and through it all he calmly collected the dollars, nickels, and dimes that flowed to him. Lord, keep Bubbles poor, keep him humble, if the greed for money, fine clothes, fine association and fine manners would away him from his present notion of life and things. Keep his head little.

Apart from this statement's remarkable prescience—from the prophecy of future greatness to the final prayer against the corrupting influence of money—what did Lewis mean by calling Bubbles "the soul of minstrelsy"? Clearly he intended it as a compliment. Rather than invoking burnt cork (which Bubbles did not wear in Indianapolis), *minstrelsy* here suggests a command of Black idioms that could not be matched by even the most talented white performers.

Authenticity, to be sure, came in many shades. Bert Williams may have outminstreled his white competitors, but as a native Bahamian performing exclusively in white theaters, he did not plumb the folkways of the rural South. By contrast, the men Lewis identified as Bubbles's likely influences were all mainstays of the "colored circuit," playing only in Black theaters. Their brand of entertainment mingled the traditions of minstrelsy with more up-to-date elements from vaudeville and popular music. Sometimes they wore blackface, sometimes not. Sometimes they used plantation settings, sometimes not. Rooted in the spontaneous delivery, ragged rhythms, blues sonorities, and off-color humor of Southern saloon culture, their art drew criticism from class-conscious Black reporters. But working-class audiences loved it. A performer like String Beans (aka Butler May Jr.), for example, electrified his hearers with the blues, a music relevant to their own lived experience.

We have reason to believe Bubbles admired String Beans. Recall that shortly after the Subletts arrived in Indianapolis, he sang "Pray for the Lights to Go Out," one of Beans's biggest hits—possibly in imitation of the older man. Beans was a natural idol in any case, the "greatest attraction" in Black vaudeville, a master of the unpolished but hypnotic vernacular. His dancing was said to be "eccentric," original. His singing was likened many years later to the soulfulness of Ray Charles. And his comedy—his talk, patter, and jokes—betrayed a compulsion to improvise:

[String] Beans . . . takes more chances [than other comedians of his race]. In fact he can't help himself. He couldn't repeat a show word for word to save his life. . . . He is original, because he is built that way. The beauty of it is that he is good in his originality, saying things that produce a different kind of laughter, the kind that seizes one all over—makes you laugh until it hurts.

As modernizing as these vernacular elements unquestionably were, Beans delivered them within the context of old-time minstrelsy. Performing customarily in blackface, he was regarded as "an excellent delineator of the ignorant, funloving, obstreperous levee or cotton field darkey." Thus, Beans typified the mix of old and new that made Black entertainment in the 1910s so exciting. The child Bubbles may have achieved a similar mix, updating minstrelsy in his own idiosyncratic manner—and drawing the attention of gatekeepers like Billy Lewis.

5

Months passed. The Subletts moved to 707 N. California Street on the west side, a poor, racially integrated neighborhood mingling Eastern European immigrants and Black families. And one hot summer night, John Jr. didn't come home.

Earlier in the day he had asked his mother if he and his friend J.B. could go to Military Park, a popular playground two blocks south of their house. Instantly concerned, Katie made her son promise he wouldn't get into trouble. John reassured his mother, and the two boys took off barefoot down the hot pavement toward the park.

Katie was right to be worried. Military Park, an old Civil War training ground, more than lived up to its combative name and history. In 1913 a "race riot," according to the newspaper, broke out among fifty Black and white youths. "Stones and clubs flew through the air and one of the negroes drew a knife." Two years later another "race war" took place. As the paper grimly acknowledged, "There has been trouble between the white and colored boys of the neighborhood for a number of years, and the park has always been chosen as the battle grounds [sic] of the young gangsters."

So on the night of July 9, 1917, when a neighbor appeared at the Subletts' door to inform them that their son had been arrested, Katie, though devastated, could not have been overly surprised. Her mind must have flown immediately to the vicious race riot that had torn apart the city of East St. Louis exactly one week before, leaving over a hundred Blacks dead and thousands homeless. She went down to the Juvenile Detention Home at 28 W. North Street where John was being held to find out what had happened.

John and J.B. had arrived at Military Park a little before noon. At John's urging, they had decided to challenge a park rule reserving the swing set for the exclusive use of white children. They hopped onto the forbidden swings and started pumping. As John recalled the experience, a handful of white boys began yelling: "Get down, nigger!" "You gonna get out of that swing, nigger?" Other boys ran over, all yelling, taunting, and threatening. J.B. jumped off his swing and ran from the park, but John dug in. Still swinging back and forth, he peered down at the park policeman and the other adults on hand (most of whom were white), hoping for assistance. They just stared back at him, and he realized, with rising panic, that these grown-ups were not on his side.

He finally agreed to get off the swing—but in a last-minute show of defiance decided to take his time. He would come down "when the cat dies," he told the boys, which meant when the swing stopped of its own accord. "So I let the swing calm down, calm down, calm down, calm down," he recalled, "and it finally gets down to where I can step out." As the waiting mob rushed toward him John somehow broke through the melee and ran behind the merry-go-round. He stood breathing heavily, tears streaming down his face.

Then he remembered something. He reached in his pocket and felt the cold metal of his pocket-knife inside his fist. As the white boys wheeled around to resume their attack, he whipped out the blade and brandished it in front of them. They paused, and he lunged at the group. The boys scattered— all but one straggler. John plunged the knife into the boy's forearm, opening a small river of blood. Then he turned and ran for all he was worth.

Enraged, the boys chased him out of the park and all the way home, where he jumped the fence of his next-door neighbors, a white family named Grant, and hid behind a piano box. When the white boys ran past, the Grants let him in the house. They were sympathetic—they liked John—but thought it best to call the police. Treating John as the aggressor, the police drove him to the hospital where the injured boy bitterly identified John as the one who stabbed him. Then they took him to the police station. Like his father twenty-six years before, John was charged with assault and battery and put behind bars.

As he sat in his cell in the Juvenile Detention Home the door opened and his mother came in, followed by a man whom he later took to be a judge.

Sitting on a wooden bench, Katie and her son discussed their options with the man. There weren't many. He advised Katie to take her family and leave town, as far away as possible. "But this is our home," she pleaded. "What if we decide not to move?" "I'll just have to send John to reform school," the man replied.

Faced with this unpalatable prospect, the Subletts chose to leave the state. They packed their belongings and boarded a train once more, this time heading south. Cutting their losses, they returned to Louisville.

Before 1917 John Sublett Jr. had developed a local reputation as a talented and hard-working young man with a puckish sense of humor and strong family loyalty. The Military Park incident revealed new qualities of character. He was, in addition, fiercely proud, brave, and pugnacious—a natural leader with a keen sense of injustice. The incident also marked a pivotal moment in John's education. He had learned the same hard lesson his father had learned: Do not transgress the code of white supremacy in this country. The lesson would be drilled home again and again, in subtler ways, for the rest of his life.

Although the return to Louisville must have been demoralizing, Bubbles remained forever grateful to the man who made it possible. If the judge had forced him into reform school, Bubbles figured, he might have grown up a violent criminal: "If this was only a kid, what will I do with a man that's 21 or a man that's 35? . . . I'm going to create more difficulty with the prejudice going on, I'm going to be a helluva Negro, man. That's common sense tells you that." Instead, he was allowed to turn away from the bad blood in Indianapolis and start over. In his mind the return to Louisville represented deliverance, and a second chance.

3

Buck and Bubbles

1

Louisville in the summer of 1917 was a proud city conceding nothing to powerhouses like Chicago or New York. As the Louisville Convention and Publicity League boasted in a pamphlet from that year, the town of 230,000 was "big enough to command world recognition and respect, but not big enough to . . . minimize the individuality of her sons and daughters." All the advantages of a big city, none of the drawbacks. A perfect place to live.

Families who chose Louisville, the League noted, would have access to 265 churches, 106 schools, more than twenty parks and playgrounds, ten branches of the public library, eleven streetcar lines (automobiles were not yet ubiquitous), and eleven theaters. Industry was booming, with over 1,200 factories pumping out the town's signature products. Pleasure-seekers could go to the Kentucky State Fair, or head to Churchill Downs to watch the world-famous Kentucky Derby. Picknickers might spread their blankets on the sylvan banks of the Ohio River, or in Cherokee Park on the eastern outskirts, "described by landscape artists as [the] most beautiful park in the world." And no city could rival Louisville's finest neighborhoods—"the avenues and boulevards of the Highlands, the shaded thoroughfares of Parkland, and the country home district along the River Road."

Praise came from the town's citizens as well, including its Black residents. "My Louisville was a strong and rich community," recalled Blyden Jackson, a Black English professor seven years younger than Bubbles. "I have never felt cheated because I grew up in it." And yet Jackson could not ignore the town's strict social hierarchy. He recalled as a teenager gazing as if "through a veil" at "the forbidden city, the Louisville where white folks lived."

> It was the Louisville of the downtown hotels, the lower floors of the big movie houses, the high schools I read about in the daily newspapers, the restricted haunts I sometimes passed, like white restaurants and country clubs, the other side of windows in the banks, and of course, the inner

Sportin' Life. Brian Harker, Oxford University Press. © Oxford University Press 2022.
DOI: 10.1093/oso/9780197514511.003.0004

sanctums of offices where I could go only as a humble client or a menial cus-
todian. On my side of the veil everything was black: the homes, the people,
the churches, the schools, the Negro park with the Negro park police.

Although Black Louisville offered many advantages, the halcyon world
described in the Convention and Publicity League pamphlet was the forbidden city spoken of by Jackson. For him—as for Bubbles and his family—
this world was a constant reminder of their second-class status, even in a city
known for its tolerance.

The Subletts arrived in late July well in time for school, but fourteen-year-
old John Jr. didn't enroll. As with most poor children of this era, his formal
education ended after eighth grade. Speaking to an interviewer late in life,
he regretted it: "I wisht I hadda finished school because I would have had
more brains . . . than I have, in all these crises. I'd have been one of them guys
up there on that there calendar, man,"—meaning U.S. presidents—"because
I know I've got the mind."

There were advantages, however, to being out of school. Now he could devote
full time to earning money for the family—and, as the opportunity arose, to performing. Just weeks after the Subletts' return, the *Freeman* previewed an appearance by "Tiny and Bubbles, incomparable juvenile comedians," at the Palace
Theatre in Louisville. Annie had left home (two years later she would pop up
again in North Carolina to get married), and Bubbles's younger sister Carrie had
now taken her place in the Sublett duo, appearing under the stage name "Tiny."
It was a role she cherished. To the end of her long life, she would sign letters to
her brother with that name (though she always spelled it "Tinnie"). Her time on
the stage was all the more precious because it was so short. Within a few months
Bubbles met a boy who would replace Carrie in the act, becoming his best friend
and closest collaborator. Over the next thirty-six years they would build one of
the most successful partnerships in the history of vaudeville.

Bubbles met his partner not in the theater but, fortuitously, in the course of
doing odd jobs. Most of his employers lay within a mile or so of his home on
the west side of town. He might begin a typical day at Wile's Grocery Store on
838 West Market, where he delivered to a route of twenty-five customers—
then head over to do errands for Van Dyke's Bicycle Repair Shop on 312 South
1st Street. At Hodges' Tobacco Plant away to the southwest, he laid tobacco
leaves out to dry. And in the middle of these establishments was his most
consequential employer, Grote's Bowling Alley, one of three such businesses

run by German immigrants. In the days before mechanized pinsetters, "pin boys" were employed to reset the pins after every turn and roll the ball back to the customer. The demand was unrelenting, and for bathroom breaks you'd have to get another pin boy to cover for you, then return the favor. That is what Bubbles did one day with a boy working the lane next to him, a diminutive youth named Ford Washington. They helped one another during their shift, and after work joined the other pin boys in a craps game on the hard cement floor.

As the boys got to know each other, they discovered several things in common. They were both middle children in families of five. Ford had a bicycle being repaired at Van Dyke's, where Bubbles worked (Bubbles helped him get it out of hock). Ford's nickname was Buck, a euphonious complement to John's nickname Bubbles. Most intriguing of all, Buck was a working musician, and a very talented one. In other ways, to be sure, they could not have been more different. Despite being the same age, for instance, Buck was much smaller than Bubbles, and people guessed him to be years younger. (As we shall see, in later years Bubbles peddled another glaring falsehood, telling interviewers Buck was four years his junior.) From the start, Bubbles took a paternalistic interest in his little friend. "He was a great kid, jolly all the time," Bubbles said. "He was hard to understand, for anyone but me."

Ford Lee Washington was born in Louisville, Kentucky, on October 16, 1903. His parents, Abraham and Jennie Washington, had two other children—a daughter named Ella and a son named Luther. They lived on the east side of Louisville, across town from the Subletts. Buck learned music from his father, who supported the family as a saloon pianist despite missing all four fingers on his left hand. Abe Washington began teaching Buck to play the piano at the age of six. The child showed prodigious talent, and by the time he met Bubbles was playing in saloons himself, drawing on a repertoire of light classics and show tunes such as the Sextet from Donizetti's *Lucia di Lammermoor*, Debussy's *Clair de lune*, and Victor Herbert's "Kiss Me Again." Although such pieces came from the Euro-American tradition of written music, Buck played everything by ear or from memory. It is doubtful whether his father could read music, and Buck never learned to do so. Most of his performances came highly individualized in any case. One of his specialties was a practice then known as "ragging the classics"—adding spontaneous syncopation to those classical warhorses he'd learned from his father.

The two boys began performing together under the name Buck and Bubbles, an inspired (if perhaps obvious) choice. Bubbles, who liked to be in charge, assumed the role of senior partner, handling the team's business affairs and taking the lead onstage. For most of their long career together, Buck seemed perfectly fine with this arrangement. The only problem was, since "Buck" appeared first in the team's name, people sometimes confused him with the tall singer and dancer who appeared to be the leader, and they sometimes mistook "Bubbles" for the piano player in the act. This problem could have been solved, Bubbles said, by calling the team "Bubbles and Buck," but that, of course, didn't sound as good. So they put up with the occasional misidentification and the confusion it entailed.

The kind of work they would do together over the next two and a half years differed radically from anything Bubbles had done in show business thus far. First of all, for reasons almost certainly related to World War I, they wouldn't perform in any Black theaters. The draft decimated the ranks of Black artists, and the government taxed or monopolized railroad lines, in some cases shutting down traveling shows entirely. This had the effect of cutting off revenue for already fragile Black theaters, making it difficult for some to produce shows in late 1917 and 1918. Shut out of the theaters, Buck and Bubbles began at the bottom of the ladder, performing in saloons, corner stores, truck beds, private homes—venues that paled by comparison with the heights Bubbles had so recently conquered in Indianapolis. On the plus side, the boys' audience for these performances was white. Bubbles had never performed for white patrons before. And although he had to start at the bottom to do it, his access to white audiences ultimately led him much higher up the ladder, from the world of String Beans to that of Bert Williams, with all the opportunities—and compromises—that implied.

2

The logical first move was for Buck to introduce Bubbles to his own musical environment—the saloons. In the fall of 1917, the United States had recently entered the war, and American soldiers were in desperate need of patriotic and sentimental songs. Bubbles watched his friend play for the soldiers and marveled. Buck was so short he couldn't reach the pedals if he sat on the stool, so he dispensed with a chair entirely and played the piano standing up. Despite this handicap, "Buck played the greatest piano you've ever heard," Bubbles said. "Why, he could play two numbers at one time—for instance, 'Dardanella' with one hand and 'Yankee Doodle' with the other." "Oh, he was

Buck and Bubbles, knockabout comics, ca. 1920s.

Source: L. Tom Perry Special Collections, Harold B. Lee Library, Brigham Young University, Provo, Utah.

a genius." Soon, Bubbles joined in to sing. As long as they didn't get kicked out by the police or—when the drunks got out of hand—the proprietor, the boys took their music from bar to bar, earning tips along the way. "We were as busy as cats on a tin roof at these different bars," Bubbles recalled.

To fill out their repertoire, the boys began hanging out at J. G. McCrory's Five-and-Ten-Cent Store, where Bubbles worked as a janitor. At a time when radio was nonexistent and the phonograph player was still a luxury, the best way for poor, non-note-reading musicians to learn new songs was to hear them performed live. Store managers would advertise sheet music by hiring someone to sing and play the songs on a piano as customers stood listening. Buck and Bubbles listened carefully, and when the regular pianist took a break Buck would step up to the keyboard and play what he had heard while Bubbles chimed in on the vocal part, singing the melody from memory and reading the words off the sheet music. In this manner they learned dozens of songs: "Darktown Strutters' Ball," "When You and I Were Young, Maggie," "Oh, You Beautiful Doll," "When The Midnight Choo-Choo Leaves for Alabam," "and, oh, I can't make head nor tails of all the different songs I sang," Bubbles said.

Some dated from long ago, such as "When You and I Were Young, Maggie," a Civil War–era song dripping in nostalgia that had attained something like folk status by 1917. Others were more lively and up-to-date, like the ragtime songs "Beautiful Doll" and "Midnight Choo-Choo." Still others represented the very latest developments. The previous May, "Darktown Strutters' Ball" had become one of the earliest recordings ever made in that riotous new idiom called "jazz." As Buck and Bubbles performed it at the five-and-ten-cent store—Bubbles singing joyously in his boy soprano and Buck pounding out that striding left hand—the white customers following along must have sensed they were witnessing something special, something *authentic*. Customers flocked around whenever the boys performed.

One of those fascinated observers was a thirty-two-year-old businessman named Humboldt Collins. A college-educated family man, Collins was a friendly fellow with an entrepreneurial flair. Watching the customers crowd around Buck and Bubbles in the five-and-ten-cent store, he had an idea. As a manager and salesman for the Indiana Truck Company, he persuaded the boys to do their act in the back of one of his trucks at the Kentucky State Fair. The live music attracted passersby, whom Collins would engage in conversation and, if he was lucky, a little sales talk. The idea proved so successful that Collins raised his sights and adopted the role of manager and impresario, ushering Buck and Bubbles into the inner precincts of the Forbidden City. Collins and the two boys would appear unannounced at a home where a party was going on, a home in one of those rarefied white neighborhoods celebrated in the Louisville Convention and Publicity League pamphlet. When the homeowner answered the door, Collins gave a curious pitch: "Let us niggers in and if you don't want us niggers here, we'll leave." Bubbles thought this introduction "superior, superior." By including himself with the boys, coyly blurring the line of who was "colored" and who was not, Collins neutralized what might have been an insurmountable barrier: "His saying nigger didn't mean nothing, 'cause we knew he was white. . . . What meant something was him telling this other white fella . . . that the word when he used it wasn't as harmful to us as it would be to George and Jim. . . . And they don't have to bring up the term at all, 'cause he's already introduced us as being one of us—us—he used the term, it was us." The elephant in the room—a white man allowing two Black teenagers to perform for his private party—was neatly overlooked by momentarily pretending there was no veil separating the races in Louisville. There was just *us*.

Humboldt Collins was the first in a long line of white patrons giving Bubbles sponsorship, training, and protection. Such patronage was essential. As an old-timer in New Orleans once told Louis Armstrong, "As long as you live, no matter where you may be—always have a *White Man* [who] can [and] will put his Hand on your shoulder and say—*This is My Nigger* and, Can't Nobody Harm Ya." Some of Bubbles's patrons were more exploitative than others, but he liked Humboldt Collins. "I enjoyed his friendship and everything and we were successful to his managerials," he said.

3

Another Louisville patron was the manager of one of the most luxurious hotels in town. Walking through the five-and-ten-cent store during his lunch break one day, he heard Buck and Bubbles performing for a crowd of some twenty or thirty people. Stunned by their appeal, he returned to his office and asked his assistant, Billy Maxie, what he thought about having them entertain in the hotel dining room. If guests objected to Black people in the hotel, that fact could be withheld from them. The men invited Buck and Bubbles for an audition, dressed them in borrowed tuxedos—with safety pins to adjust the capacious fitting and had them perform that very night, in burnt cork and white gloves. The boys' race was thus safely hidden.

There were drawbacks, however, to concealing their race. In doing so, the hotel was undercutting the act's biggest selling point: authenticity. Billy Maxie hatched an ambitious plan. He added another Black teenager to the team, a chubby singer known as Sugar Bailey (Buck and Bubbles called him Sugar Babe), and rechristened the act the Three Ink Spots, openly advertising the boys' race. In accordance with the new policy of racial transparency, they would perform in their natural complexion—no blackface. Maxie dressed them in unaccustomed finery: matching Norfolk suits with knickerbockers, high-topped shoes and spats, straw hats, kid gloves, and bamboo canes. He then paid to have the trio sit for high-quality publicity photos in rich sepia. With this act Maxie planned to leave behind the truck beds and private parties and hotel dining rooms. He was going to present them in white theaters, where the money was.

But the boys couldn't perform in Louisville—white theaters there would never allow it. So Maxie launched the act in Indianapolis, where Sugar Babe lived with his mother. During the week of February 18, 1918, the Three Ink Spots debuted at the Lyric Theatre. They specialized in singing three-part barbershop harmony, with Buck on the lowest part, Bubbles on the highest, and Sugar Babe in the middle, carrying the melody, while Buck accompanied the group on piano. Their feature number was "America, I Love You," a 1915 patriotic song in ragtime rhythms:

> *America, I love you,*
> *You're like a sweetheart of mine,*
> *From ocean to ocean, for you my devotion,*
> *Is touching each bound'ry line.*

In a preview of the act, Buck and Bubbles's new partner, an Indianapolis native, got most of the copy: "One of the 'spots' is none other than Sugar Bailey, the little, fat newsboy of dusky hue who sang and danced on local street corners for several years past to the delight of hastily gathered audiences. Sugar has turned professional now and is, perhaps, the most important member of the trio." During the team's first performance, however, it was Buck who won the audience's favor: "The 'ink spot' that stands up to play the piano . . . carries off the honors of the act of the three colored boys."

After their debut, "a man in the meat business" named William Poe, a short, fast-talking character sporting a vest and derby, offered to be the boys' producer and to set them up in the much larger entertainment market of Chicago. Elated, Maxie and the boys agreed. Poe got to work and arranged for a well-received performance at the Nerva Theatre on the west side of town. Then, disaster. A con man from the start, Poe took all the money and skipped town, leaving Buck and Bubbles and Sugar Babe and Billy Maxie and his wife stranded in Chicago. Sugar Babe's mother, outraged by the fiasco, came and hustled her boy back to Indianapolis. But the rest of them couldn't get home. "We didn't have a dime between the four of us," Bubbles recalled. "It was snowing and cold, and the wind was really blowing. We were so broke that we had to share an apartment, and I remember it was across the street from the mother of the famous prize fighter . . . Jack Johnson."

Hungry and without food, Maxie and his wife were desperate. But Bubbles, the odd-job king, knew what to do. Seeing a load of coal outside a woman's apartment, he offered to shovel it into her coal bin for three dollars. When he finished the job, he gave two dollars to the now jubilant Maxies and split the last dollar with Buck. They all did their own shopping. Bubbles bought five potatoes, a quarter pound of bacon, and ten cents worth of corn meal. Then he went home and cooked the dinner he'd been dreaming about all day. He fried the bacon and used the grease to make corn bread. Then he boiled the potatoes, threw in the bacon, and made potato stew. A simple but hearty recipe, and more than enough to feed them all. "And, boy, was it good," he said. "Nothin' has ever tasted better."

4

Somehow Bubbles and his party found a way back to Louisville, but things looked bleak. The Three Ink Spots had dissolved, and it appeared Buck and Bubbles might be next. They continued doing private parties, but there was no future in that. When Bubbles got a chance to hit the road with a carnival troupe, he took it—even though the manager wouldn't take Buck for fear he was underage. For the moment, Buck and Bubbles split up.

Bubbles got his opportunity when a carnival known as T. A. Wolf's Superior Shows came through Louisville. Superior Shows had rides—a Ferris wheel, merry-go-round, and whip—fortune tellers and weight guessers, games of chance. There was a wild animal show, a girlie show, a "midget" show, and a minstrel show. Every Monday the carnival set up in a new city and was open for business by 7:00 p.m. The minstrel tent was located at the end of the midway, right behind the open-air restaurant. In addition to a "jazz band," the minstrel show featured a dozen singers and dancers. Bubbles's job, he recalled, was to "come out on the ballyhoo platform in front of the tent where the big banner was, with the girls and the musicians, and I'd sing. I had a pair of pipes! I could turn a song every way but loose!"

The hardest part was the traveling. Southern trains were always a trial for Black passengers, who had to crowd into a single "Jim Crow car" together with a foul-smelling menagerie of livestock brought aboard by rural passengers, including "dogs, chickens, pigs, cats, coons, and 'possums." Superior Shows had a private train, so Bubbles's experience may have been somewhat better, but the segregation persisted. There was a "privilege car," well-stocked with food and drink for white performers, but this was off-limits to the Black minstrels, who were only allowed to procure refreshments through Bubbles, their messenger boy. "Anything you wanted to eat, you had to go up to the privilege car and carry it back to the colored car," he recalled. "I was the one who had to go where the others couldn't go—to get them things to eat and drink, and keep them in good spirits." Bubbles probably took abuse on both ends. As he himself put it, "I went through hell on the train."

After several months with the carnival, Bubbles became restless. News from home that his mother had come down with the Spanish flu, the dreaded disease then killing millions, filled him with worry and he yearned to see her again. The skimpy carnival wages were hardly worth it in any case. One of his friends, an American Indian named Kid Fox, "wanted to see me get a better break than this carnival. . . . The man that run the carnival, he was a nice guy, nice guy, but he'd give you peanuts instead of chocolates. If you take the peanuts . . . you don't know . . . what the chocolates tasted like." So when Buck sent a telegram asking him to come home, Bubbles was receptive. Buck had incredible news: There was a job for Buck and Bubbles at B. F. Keith's Mary Anderson Theatre, a white theater on 612 South 4th Street. In the fall of 1919, Bubbles returned to Louisville to see what chocolate tasted like.

5

Bubbles's first priority was to see his mother, who had been sick in bed for two weeks. He had a home remedy for the flu, he said, that he'd gotten from his friend Kid Fox. Brewing a potent mix of whiskey, rock candy, and glycerin on the family's coal-burning stove, he gave it to Katie, who after some initial hesitation drank it up. "And the next day my mother was up and out, you know? I never forgot about that as long as I live. I said the good Lord brought me back there with my mother then."

Next Bubbles sought out his old pal Buck. What about the job at the Mary Anderson? Alas, it turned out not to be a performing job after all—it was a job working as ushers in the gallery, Buck confessed sheepishly. Buck's good news had sounded incredible, because it was. After two and a half years of hacking through the ignominy of saloons and truck beds and hotel dining rooms, they were now apparently giving up, leaving show business to take service jobs, the usual endpoint for talented Blacks who had taken a chance on dreams. Such might have been Buck and Bubbles's fate, too, were it not for one final and unexpected opening.

Bubbles told the story many times during his long career. It has become part of the John Bubbles legend. One night the manager of the Mary Anderson Theatre, H. C. Carter, came to Buck and Bubbles with a problem. One of his vaudeville acts was sick, and he wondered if the boys would like to fill the spot? The boys were ecstatic, though disappointed on one point. Carter had assigned them a "tutor"—an old dresser experienced in the traditions of blackface to teach them how to properly apply facepaint. As in the hotel dining room, the good patrons of the Mary Anderson couldn't be trusted to accept Black performers. "We had to wear cork and gloves so that the white people didn't know we were colored," Bubbles said. The racist nature of this opportunity, however, should not obscure its importance: The boys were performing for the first time—as Buck and Bubbles—in a white theater. The ramifications would be significant.

Opening night was a cold evening in late December 1919. Bubbles grandiosely recalled the Mary Anderson Theatre as "the biggest in the South," but with only 1,475 seats it was not even the biggest in Louisville. Even so, it was a beloved venue, "a cozy, intimate theater in the very heart" of the theater district. Chilled patrons taking their seats that night were enveloped in a sophisticated ambiance—"elegance without ostentation and brilliance of coloring without gaudiness," as one observer described the interior.

Buck and Bubbles were first on the program. The orchestra played an introduction, and Buck walked to the grand piano at center stage and tossed off an arpeggio. Still offstage, as if from afar, Bubbles started crooning "When You and I Were Young, Maggie," the sentimental parlor song he had learned at the five-and-ten-cent store. As he continued singing, doing his best imitation of a blackface Irish tenor, he walked onstage dressed to the hilt—black felt hat, Eton shirt, Buster Brown collar, butterfly tie, white gloves, patent leather shoes, and spats, his face safely shrouded in cork. By the time he reached the climax he was standing beside Buck, similarly attired, who now added a rich, full accompaniment.

And now we are aged and gray, Maggie,
Our trials are nearly done,

Let us sing of the days that are gone, Maggie,
When you and I were young.

Their song melted the audience, which exploded with applause. "Man, the building like to come down at that," Bubbles recalled. For the rest of the act, as one eyewitness said, the boys "really worked [their] hearts out," and "the audience loved it."

In the first news article to print the name "Buck and Bubbles," a reporter for the *Louisville Courier-Journal* gave a slightly different version of the story. He suggested this may not have been the boys' first outing at the Mary Anderson, while at the same time confusing their identities, comparing Buck (instead of Bubbles) with Bert Williams's one-time partner, the late singer and dancer George Walker. After H. C. Carter had gone to such lengths to conceal Buck and Bubbles's race, the writer immediately let that cat out of the bag:

> An act which has a distinct local interest is that which is presented by the impish little negro, Bubbles and his partner Buck, the former a talented instrumentalist, the latter an embryonic George Walker. Bubbles and Buck have been "hanging around" the Mary Anderson in official positions, but they have been called upon "many a time and oft" to help when a vacant spot on the programme needed filling.

"Frequently the filling of a thing is better than the thing it fills," the reporter noted pointedly, "and Buck and Bubbles prove one of the amusing parts of the bill this week."

H. C. Carter hired the boys to perform for one week—the standard contractual unit in vaudeville—but audience response was so enthusiastic that he extended their engagement for a second week. Then things took a surreal turn. Carter sat the boys down and asked the question every aspiring show person dreamed of hearing: How would they like to audition for a powerful white producer coming into town with a big show from New York? The producer was Irwin Rosen, and the show, *Kiss Me*, was a musical comedy starring a cast of twenty singers and dancers. According to the *Courier-Journal*, Buck and Bubbles played the Mary Anderson over New Year's, and *Kiss Me* opened the week of January 5, 1920. Somewhere along the way the boys got their chance to audition. Standing on an empty stage, they did four or five of their best numbers while H. C. Carter and Irwin Rosen sat watching.

When they finished, Rosen stood and applauded: "By heaven, you boys ought to be in New York!" What about the *Kiss Me* company? they asked. Rosen said he didn't want them in *Kiss Me*, an all-white show in the middle of a tour. He wanted to send them to New York on their own. But at sixteen their age could be a problem. It may have been this offer that compelled both boys to falsify their age by a single year—though even at "seventeen" they were still minors and would need their parents' permission. Here Rosen sweetened the deal. If they could get their mothers to sign off on the plan, Rosen said, he would pay each mother $35 a week—double the average working-class wage—plus room and board for their sons.

Buck and Bubbles raced home to tell their families of their head-spinning good fortune. Their lives would change forever. Buck, who had been attending a vocational training school in sensible anticipation of one day having to make a living as a laborer, now told the principal he would not be coming back. In response to the man's protestations, Bubbles pointed out that his friend "has such marvelous hands on the piana, there ain't nothing he's going to learn in this school that's going to do him as much good as his talent in the field." As for Bubbles himself, school was not a barrier and neither were his parents. "I was one of the boys [whose] parents wanted to be what he wanted to be," he said. John and Katie Sublett lived vicariously through their son. His dreams were their dreams, his success their success. Both mothers signed Rosen's papers.

Buck and Bubbles packed their belongings into a single trunk, laced up their roller skates, and sped off to the train station, the trunk swaying between them, their minds chaotic with the thrill of possibilities. Rosen's offer, though unexpected, was not foreign to them. Bubbles had dreamed about going to New York, the world's entertainment mecca, ever since he first read about the Ziegfeld Follies. There was one thing, however, that should have given the boys pause. What exactly they would be doing in New York was never explained.

PART II
INNOVATOR (1920–1931)

4

A Find of Finds

1

Within a few weeks of their arrival in New York City, Buck and Bubbles found themselves trapped by their new patron in what seemed an odd and useless charade. Bubbles couldn't figure it out. What on earth was the man up to?

Every Monday morning the boys headed to the office of Irwin Rosen, where a thuggish bruiser of a man known to them only as "Martin" would peel off precisely $28 and hand it to them. The boys would spend the rest of the week doing not a single thing to earn the money. No shows, no parties, no performances of any kind. So why were they getting paid?

After leaving Irwin Rosen's office, they returned to their flat at Reese Dupree's, a Black boarding house on 241 W. 41st Street, near Times Square. Ten years earlier, Dupree had come north from his home in Georgia to try for a career in show business. By 1917 he had scaled back his ambitions to run a boarding house for other aspiring entertainers. He offered modest accommodations. The rooms were so small that, as Bubbles put it, "you had to step out in the hall to turn around, and then you could go back inside." The two boys shared a single bed and the only piece of furniture was the large trunk that contained all their earthly belongings. Rent was due every Monday morning, which is why Martin always gave them precisely $28—just enough to pay for their room and board for another week (at two dollars a day), no more and no less. Their bellies were full, and they had a place to sleep, but life was more than that. They needed meaningful work, and they needed spending money. But if they walked away from Mr. Rosen's barebones allowance, what would become of them? They didn't know anyone in New York. Where would they go—how would they survive?

As they pondered their dilemma, there was meantime plenty to distract them between Mondays, starting with the most exciting entertainment district in the world.

A few blocks south of Central Park in midtown Manhattan, two great thoroughfares—Broadway and Seventh Avenue—intersect to form a

Sportin' Life. Brian Harker, Oxford University Press. © Oxford University Press 2022.
DOI: 10.1093/oso/9780197514511.003.0005

tall, slender X, like a giant electrified chromosome. Known since 1904 as Times Square, this glittering sector was home to banks, hotels, restaurants, ballrooms, and, at one point, *The New York Times* (hence the name). Above all, it was home to the premier theaters in the city. Most of the action lay on the west side of Broadway in venues lining the cross-streets: 42nd Street, 43rd, 44th, etc. As soon as they arrived, Buck and Bubbles raced to 42nd Street to see the magnificent New Amsterdam Theatre ("beyond question the most gorgeous playhouse in New York," exclaimed the *Dramatic Mirror*), where Ziegfeld had installed his Follies seven years before, and where Bert Williams had performed many times since. (When the boys asked for an audition, they were told to come back when they weren't under contract.) The ghosts of history echoed even louder across the street at the Rialto, a movie house that before 1915 was known as Hammerstein's Victoria, "America's greatest vaudeville theater," according to Buster Keaton, where larger-than-life performances inspired endless tales of theatrical heroism. East of Broadway and a block north stood a somewhat newer venue, the George M. Cohan Theatre, named for (and run by) the famous composer of "Give My Regards to Broadway" and "You're a Grand Old Flag." Back on the west side and still farther north stood the Shubert Theatre, a bastion of elegance from whose stage Mae West had recently introduced—to white audiences—the dreaded shimmy. And up near the top of Times Square, on the corner of 47th and Broadway, loomed every vaudevillian's dream and nightmare: the Palace Theatre. The most elite and competitive vaudeville theater in the country, the New York Palace represented the ultimate test.

Some of the acts appearing in these and other theaters are still familiar today. When Buck and Bubbles arrived, in mid-January 1920, the Marx Brothers were knocking 'em dead at the Colonial ("without a doubt the best comedy tabloid vaudeville has ever seen"), while up in Harlem Sophie Tucker was holding forth at the Alhambra. The Strand and Rivoli were showing new silent films by Harold Lloyd, Mary Pickford, and Will Rogers. Most theaters, however, featured performers that are now long forgotten. Some acts sounded like law firms (Clayton & Clayton), some were garishly offensive by later standards (Midgetland, Oriental Oddities), and some were more enigmatic or mysterious (Stop, Look, & Listen). There were singers and dancers, jugglers, wire walkers, clay modelers, strongmen, and animal acts. And the crazier the better. One improbable act, Swain's Trained Cats and Rats, elicited an astounded "Very good!" from the critic on hand.

From Buck and Bubbles's wide-eyed perspective, vaudeville must have appeared superbly robust, an industry in its prime. Box office receipts had just hit an all-time high, according to the *New York Star*: "Prices for admissions were up . . . [bringing] the totals away beyond any record set for the big time vaudeville houses." This sanguine report, however, masked hidden weaknesses, like a champion athlete unaware of the cancer growing inside her. In the case of vaudeville that cancer was talking pictures, a technology in its embryonic stages, microscopic but no less deadly for that. In little more than ten years it would overwhelm its host (movies often played in vaudeville houses), scattering a generation of performers to a life of bitter prospects.

A career in vaudeville was hard enough, even before the collapse. Every week *Variety* listed about twenty major vaudeville theaters in Manhattan, each of which produced nine or ten acts apiece, around 190 total. In the week of January 19, 1920, these theaters introduced forty-two new acts, which, like all the other acts, hoped to rotate into new theaters (in or out of New York) at the end of the week. If they were lucky enough to be a "hit" (and a *big* hit at that), they might be held over for a second week. More likely, they would have to scramble just to keep working. Under the constant scrutiny not only of theater managers and competitors but also of critics (some of whom literally counted the laughs in a turn), every act faced great pressure to succeed, knowing their career was only as viable as their last performance. One "Bee Palmer" and her "Six Kings of Jazzapation" had the good fortune to play the Palace, where she "finished fine," noted a critic approvingly. But a few weeks later Palmer had to be carried out of the Royal Theatre in an ambulance, "having broken down from overwork. She is at present resting in a clinic."

For Buck and Bubbles, the picture was even worse. Since racial integration in vaudeville exceeded that of the general population, it is possible to overstate the discrimination suffered by Black actors. Yet in vaudeville's highly stratified world, Black performers faced unique barriers. "Big-time" vaudeville—consisting of two circuits; Keith-Albee in the East and Orpheum in the West—offered the biggest salaries, the best working conditions (two shows a day rather than three), and the most prestige. "Small-time" consisted of all the other circuits—Loew's, Pantages, Fox, and so on. Below small time, at least in respectability, was burlesque (which did not yet feature striptease but rather comely chorus girls and low comedy). And at the bottom of the totem pole was the all-Black theater circuit (soon to be known as

T.O.B.A., the Theater Owners Booking Association), which Bubbles played in Nashville, Louisville (the first time), and Indianapolis.

Although Black performers found success at every level of this hierarchy, their numbers settled disproportionately near the bottom. Of some twenty thousand vaudevillians estimated to be hawking their routines in 1919, less than half were able to fill the available jobs. Of that remainder, less than 10 percent—about eight hundred—made the big time. Inside Manhattan the competition intensified, devouring all but the most talented and determined souls. And here, as the rewards thinned out, racism flared up to guard the plum spots for white performers. Among the forty-six acts for the week of January 19 in New York's top five big-time theaters—the Palace, Colonial, Riverside, Royal, and Alhambra—there was only one Black act. In the same theaters over the next four weeks—126 acts later (not including repeat performances)—there were only two Black acts. One of those, a reporter wrote, succeeded in planting themselves on the big time "with 'spot' appearances." Such acts could be tolerated, in other words, but only in miniscule numbers—in this case, about 1 or 2 percent of the total.

In bringing Buck and Bubbles to New York, Irwin Rosen was betting he could squeeze the boys if not into that tiny minority at least into the larger share of small-time jobs. Right away he booked them into a Staten Island theater where the stakes were low. "The manner in which they were received by the audience," a reporter wrote, implying racial animus, "was not so good." This experience may have spooked Rosen, causing him to sequester the boys until he could figure out what to do next. In late January there were rumors he had booked them into Poli vaudeville, a small-time circuit, but that was false. Week after week went by. The boys waited for something to happen, but it never did.

2

After a month of lolling around New York, Bubbles's initial excitement had dissipated. Discouraged by prolonged unemployment, the sixteen-year-old boy was also terribly homesick, missing his mother especially. Nevertheless, he made a decision and sold it to his partner. It was time to stand up to Irwin Rosen. On Monday the boys walked into Rosen's office as usual. Martin whipped out a roll of bills ("enough to choke a horse," Bubbles said) and began counting out the $28. Bubbles stopped him, and his composure broke.

"It isn't enough, Mr. Martin," he said, tears rolling down his cheeks. "I mean, where's any extra money for Buck and me? You give us twenty-eight dollars a week. Our room and board costs exactly twenty-eight dollars a week. Where's some extra for Buck and me?" Martin extended his hand, proffering the allowance. "You keep your money, Mr. Martin," Bubbles said. "Buck and Bubbles don't work for you and Mr. Rosen any more."

The boys returned to the Reese Dupree and asked the landlady to spot them a few days' rent. Then they laced up their roller skates, and, as Bubbles grabbed on to the bumper of a passing car and Buck held on to Bubbles, they sped up Seventh Avenue. Their destination was Leo Feist Music, a block north of the Palace, where Martin had once taken them to audition for some show business fat cats; perhaps they could renew those contacts and see about getting a job. On the way they got sidetracked. Back in Louisville they had developed a repertoire of roller-skating tricks—jumps, turns, spins—befitting their role as entertainers. Now, they marshalled these skills for an improvised street ballet, as Bubbles recalled:

> I told Buck to hang on, and we did a spin in the middle of the street, caught a car headed the other way, just long enough to give us some speed, and then we let go. We headed for the other side of the street, and we did another spin. Then we spread the eagle, you know, where your skates are headed different directions . . . and we skated right up the gutter, and we ended up sitting down on the curb right in front of [a] police officer.

Pedestrians who had stopped to watch crowded around to congratulate the boys. "Some skating, kid." "Do you teach skating?" "Thanks for the show." As the crowd dispersed, a well-dressed man stepped forward and introduced himself as Nat Nazarro. He was stocky and well built, with black, slicked-back hair, steel-rimmed glasses with extra thick lenses, and a resonant voice. He complimented the boys (whom he later recalled wearing matching fur coats) and told them he wanted to see what else they could do.

Nat Nazarro was a thirty-three-year-old veteran performer who had built a successful big-time career as a strongman. He usually had a small boy help him with his act, and lately he had groomed some of these assistants, as they got older, to branch out on their own while staying on the payroll. When Nazarro saw Buck and Bubbles skating in the street, he recognized their broad appeal and began calculating the potential advantage of folding them into his expanding operation. He was especially interested in capitalizing

"WHAT A BREAK"
BUCK and BUBBLES
Held over 2nd week Orpheum,
Los Angeles.
"HURRAY"
Direction **NAT NAZARRO, N. Y. C.**

Buck and Bubbles, ca. 1920. In this ad (published in 1929) they appear to be
wearing the "short fur coats" Nat Nazarro recalled seeing on the day he met
them.
Source: Variety.

on the new enthusiasm for jazz and blues, with which he had already been
experimenting via a jazz band led by one of his white protégés. What could
he do with a couple of Black kids?

Nazarro followed Buck and Bubbles to Leo Feist Music, where they found
a room with a piano in it. For two hours he watched them perform every
song and dance they could think of. Nazarro was enthralled. He immediately
offered them a spot in his act at the Columbia Theatre, a burlesque house on
the corner of 47th and Broadway, directly north of the Palace, the following
Sunday. (To their relief, he also paid their rent.) Though impressed, he harbored the standard reservations about the boys' race. A racially integrated act
was not unprecedented. For almost thirty years white performers, especially
women, had enlisted "picks" (short for "pickaninnies," i.e., Black children) to
give their acts "a sock finish." But such acts were not common, and Nazarro
needed to proceed cautiously. Start at the bottom, in a burlesque house, and

if that went well, move up from there. His apprehensions were well founded. When Buck and Bubbles showed up for rehearsal Sunday morning, Bubbles overheard Nazarro arguing with the theater manager. "I don't want any damn niggers in my theater," the manager said. Although Nazarro stoutly defended the boys, Bubbles was deeply depressed by what he heard. He expected such attitudes in Louisville but thought New York would be different. He did not tell Buck.

Despite the theater manager's resistance, Buck and Bubbles performed their first show in Manhattan on Sunday, February 15, 1920, in a matinee at the Columbia Theatre. Nazarro attempted to ease them on with a little sleight of hand. First, he beguiled the audience with a missed stunt, in which he tried to raise his boy assistant above his head and failed. Then, the audience's interest piqued (since failure in an act was almost as fascinating as success), he told a story about two highfalutin "gentlemen" he had met at Carnegie Hall, classical virtuosos who wanted to perform in vaudeville. "Are the gentlemen here?" he called in stentorian tones. "Bring them on!" When Buck and Bubbles walked onstage, they were dressed not in the expected tuxedos but in "vagabond clothes," Bubbles said—"yella shoes, brown pants, blue coat, brown cap and gray cap."

The misdirection worked. The sight of the boys caused a ripple in the theater as the audience exhaled—"Ohhhhhhhhhh!"—and Buck and Bubbles went into their lively opening number. They sang, danced, and told race-based jokes ("colored gags," Bubbles called them). Delighted by the boys' comical high spirits, the audience applauded with gusto; then it was time for a change of mood. "Bubbles," Nazarro called out, "tell the audience about that letter you got from your mother." The appeal to a mother's love was an old ploy in vaudeville, with its immigrant-heavy audience, yet it remained powerful. For Bubbles, Nazarro's cue brought all the disappointments and worries and homesickness of the last month to the surface. As he began singing "Mammy O' Mine," a sentimental ballad published the previous year, he wept openly:

I've read your letter, Mammy O' Mine,
Now I feel better, Mammy O' Mine,
Still, I'm kinda homesick, too,
No one can cure me but you.

Mammy O' Mine,
Below that old Dixon line,

Oh, how I'm longing to kiss you,
I miss you all of the time.

"When I sang that verse you could hear a pin drop," Bubbles recalled. "When I got to the part, 'Mammy of mine, I long to kiss you, I miss you all the time,' the tears are just pouring down my cheeks, man, 'cause I'm heartbroken from what I'm going through, I was really overloaded."

When he finished, the audience leapt to its feet. They shouted and whistled and wouldn't stop clapping. In this response Bubbles saw shock and recognition. "At that time," he said, whites seemed to believe "the most important things in the Negro world were a crap game, a bottle of gin, and a pair of dice—understand? Anything concerning the appreciation of life or your mother or father could not occur to the mind of a Negro." Bubbles's searing performance demonstrated that Black people worked and sorrowed and lived and died just like anyone else. The audience applauded his abject humanity.

When Buck and Bubbles had finished their bows, Nazarro returned to his failed gymnastics stunt and this time succeeded in spectacular fashion, triumphantly lifting the boy above his head and putting a dynamic exclamation point on everything that had come before. Again, the audience erupted.

After the show, hardly able to believe his good fortune, Nazarro locked the boys in their dressing room. He brought them dinner, made sure they were comfortable, but kept the door locked—he was not about to let them saunter out the back alley. In a touching change of heart the theater manager rushed backstage, asking, "Where's the two colored boys?" But Nazarro was not interested in a return booking at the Columbia. He had set his sights much higher.

From there things moved quickly. It was Sunday night—too late to book Buck and Bubbles for the next day but *not* too late for the second half of the week. As it happened, there was an open spot for Thursday, Friday, and Saturday at the Audubon Theatre, a small-time venue located on 165th Street and Broadway known for its beautiful polychrome terra-cotta façade and English Renaissance-style interior. (Long after its heyday, the Audubon became notorious as the site of Malcolm X's assassination, in the second-floor ballroom, in 1965.) Nazarro booked the Audubon and apparently began reaching out to his high-level contacts in the entertainment world, telling them about the sensational new addition to his act. It was important the right people be on hand to witness their next performance.

On Thursday, February 19, 1920, Buck and Bubbles opened at the Audubon as part of the Nat Nazarro act. (By a happy coincidence, it was Bubbles's seventeenth birthday.) Nazarro used the same gambit to introduce the boys, who seem to have caused even more commotion than they did at the Columbia, according to the act's first New York review:

> Following the routine of stunts, Nazarro now announces that he recently met two "gentlemen" at Carnegie Hall. . . . The "gentlemen" . . . prove to be two colored lads—a short one, who appears to be about fourteen years old, and the other, a few inches taller, and about sixteen. Both are attired in misfit clothing. Following some great comedy between the two, the smaller of them seats himself at the piano and the other does a song and dance. . . . The lad at the piano plays "blues" about as wickedly as possible. The kid is a wonder. The other sings, dances, does comedy—in fact, is an all-round performer. What he can't do in the line of "coon" dancing and tap work isn't worth doing.

The reporter closed with a boffo endorsement: "With the two colored lads, Nazarro has one of the best comedy singing and dancing offerings to be seen and can hold his own on any bill. . . . These lads can cope with the best black-faces on the big time." And the audience? According to the reporter, Buck and Bubbles stopped the show *four times*—meaning, on four separate occasions during their twenty-minute act the sustained applause prevented the boys from continuing. The rarity of this achievement can be judged by what happened next: Nazarro immediately signed a contract to present Buck and Bubbles at the Palace Theatre the following Monday.

But no sooner did the supreme prize come within reach than it was yanked away.

Suddenly an irate Irwin Rosen came out of the woodwork to protest the whole sordid business. Nazarro had stolen his act, he claimed, and now stood to benefit from the talent Rosen himself had nurtured so carefully as far back as Louisville. To which Nazarro countered that Rosen, far from offering support and encouragement, had so neglected the boys that they voluntarily left him to find work elsewhere. To add to the drama, somehow the Gerry Society (The Society for the Prevention of Cruelty to Children) had heard about the upcoming Palace date and filed an injunction against Nazarro for child endangerment. The whole mess landed in court and the Palace contract was canceled. (The bill on which Buck and Bubbles were supposed to appear became historic for another reason: It was Helen Keller's vaudeville debut.)

After hearing the case, a judge canceled Rosen's contract and ordered that Buck and Bubbles be returned to Louisville, at Rosen's expense. On February 27, in the custody of H. C. Carter (who had midwifed the Rosen deal in the first place), they returned home on the train. One can only imagine the joyous reunion as the boys arrived in triumph to break bread again with their families. Nazarro came down a few days later, met the boys' parents, and got their mothers to sign new contracts committing Buck and Bubbles to his exclusive representation—and to his care. They started out at $90 a week each, a staggering windfall. The boys were back in New York in time to fill an engagement at Fox's Bedford Theatre the first week of March.

Thus began a professional relationship that would last, for good or ill, for almost thirty years. Buck and Bubbles, in fact, would be the first of many

Nat Nazarro, 1921. For a man so obsessed with publicity, Nazarro went to great lengths to avoid the camera. The few extant photos of him all show him without his glasses, about which he was apparently self-conscious.
Source: Indianapolis Topics.

Black acts represented by Nazarro, who more than any other single person, perhaps, pioneered the entrée of Black performers into white show business. During these heady early days, Bubbles loved Nazarro like a father, believing he had "a heart of gold." He later revised that opinion. Nat Nazarro was a complex man, and his relationship with Buck and Bubbles was complex. Without question he taught them a lot. At times he could be kind, at times generous. But over the years his pattern of exploitation and duplicity poisoned their relationship beyond saving. Long before Buck and Bubbles cast their lot with him, this pattern had become a matter of public record.

3

Nat Nazarro was born Notel Itziksohn on May 7, 1887, in Pompiani, Lithuania, the second of five children in a devout Russian-Jewish family. In 1890 the family came to America and settled in Philadelphia, where they anglicized their names. The parents became Harry and Yetta Isaacson, and Notel became Nathan Isaacson. Whereas his father was a rabbi and his older brother was a tailor, Nathan chose a more exciting—and American—career in show business. Casting about for an appropriately exotic handle, he changed his legal name to Nat Nazaroo; then, fearing, perhaps, it lacked dignity he changed it again—to Nat Nazarro.

His life took off in 1909 when he married a girl named Queenie, also an entertainer, and launched his vaudeville career. Possessed of unusual strength and agility, he put together a troupe of acrobats featuring himself, another man, and two young boys, to be billed as "a distinct Herculean novelty." For reasons that are difficult to fully grasp from the fragmentary descriptions of news reports, the act dazzled audiences from the beginning. Critics especially lauded the grand finale when Nazarro lifted one of the boys above his head in a "one-arm hand-to-hand stand with the youngster lying full length" (the same stunt he later did at the Columbia with Buck and Bubbles). The trick looked "perilous enough to [the child's] wrists," fretted one reporter, "to reflect that bones may snap if somebody bungles." In between hair-raising gymnastic feats, the children performed comical antics to break the tension. Touring the West Coast with the small-time Sullivan-Considine circuit, Nazarro painstakingly built a reputation, as one paper put it, for "one of the most startling [acts] ever staged."

Yet there were already signs, no doubt common enough in his field, of the dark path Nazarro had taken to success. During a stopover in Butte, Montana, in 1911, Nazarro was hauled into court over allegations that he had beaten one of his child performers, a seven-year-old boy named Jimmy whom he and Queenie had "adopted" back in Philadelphia, in an attempt to compel him to bend his body in half. All the performers on the bill testified to Nazarro's cruelty. At one point, when he took the stand to defend himself, one of the actors yelled "Liar!" and was jailed for contempt. It is not known how the judge ruled, but two months later Nazarro was back on the road, resuming his upward trajectory.

On March 25, 1912, a year to the day after the trial in Montana, Nazarro opened at Chicago's Majestic Theatre, the first stop in a thirty-eight-week tour with the big-time Orpheum circuit. The reviews were glowing, especially for an acrobatic act. Most acrobats in vaudeville were dismissed as little more than woolly-headed filler for the more serious performers—the singers, dancers, and comedians: the *artistes*. But Nazarro was different. "Nat Nazarro and his company have the most entertaining acrobatic act in vaudeville," wrote one critic. "Not only do they perform apparent impossibilities, but they have bright touches of humor lightly applied and a clean appearance of professionalism." Another added, "For once an acrobatic number comes close to headline quality." Not just close. Six months later Orpheum made "a radical departure from set house rules" by making Nazarro a headliner. Feeling his oats, he began picking fights with both artists and theaters, in the process showing an astute grasp of self-promotion and an instinct for the jugular. He began taking out ads: "Nat Nazarro (an acrobat) <u>REFUSES</u> to play on the same bill with Mme. Sarah Bernhardt," went one volley. In the same month a theater canceled his act for going too long. But he got his revenge, since "the audience clamored for 15 minutes" after he left the stage, "refusing to allow the next act to go on." Nazarro published another ad: "Nat Nazarro Cancelled!! For the first time in the history of Show Business an act is cancelled because applause is so great nothing can follow."

In the late 1910s Nazarro moved his operations to New York, where he appeared regularly at the Palace Theatre. There he received the respect he had long craved: recognition as "a genuine artist" (in the words of one critic) and a master showman. As their adopted son Jimmy came of age and began showing top-line ability, the Nazarros sent him out to perform under his own name—or rather the stage name they had given him: Nat Nazarro Jr. Recognizing that past age thirty his acrobatic days were numbered, Nat Sr.

opened a booking agency to make the gradual transition from performer to manager, from building an act to building an empire.

At the same time, old sins were catching up with him. In 1919 Queenie filed for divorce, alleging multiple infidelities. Husband and wife became locked in a vicious custody battle over their two children—their adopted son Jimmy and their biological daughter, three-year-old Dorothy—a battle he ultimately lost. In Jimmy's case there was more at stake than the relationship. Queenie was now advising the boy, directing his career. Nazarro was losing control over his greatest protégé, and he had no one to blame but himself. The boy he once beat into submission had turned his back, choosing Queenie over him.

When Buck and Bubbles met Nazarro the following year, they saw none of this. All they saw was a powerful and charismatic figure twice their age and experience, who knew big-time vaudeville and had shown himself willing to fight for their interests. After Rosen, he seemed a godsend.

As soon as Buck and Bubbles got back from Louisville, Nazarro booked them into a new theater every week for a month. Then they took a breather. He brought them home with him to Philadelphia, where his mother still lived. Another packed schedule in May, then a summer spent performing on and off in theaters around southern Pennsylvania. The critics' buzz shifted to his new recruits, "two phenomenal pickaninnies who are said"—by Nazarro himself, no doubt—"to be the find of finds."

In September Nazarro paid a visit to his friends in the Keith office and signed Buck and Bubbles to a honey of a contract: one hundred weeks on the Keith circuit, starting October 1. He lined up a formidable fall season. In quick succession Buck and Bubbles would play the six leading theaters in Manhattan: the Riverside, the Royal, the Orpheum, the Alhambra, the Colonial, and to cap it off—*finally*—the Palace. By weaving the newspaper reviews of this period into a single composite account, we can envision—despite the jarring mix of critical praise and flamboyantly racist language—what the act had become after six months of experimentation and coaching:

> The act is announced—"Nat Nazarro and Company, in 'A Variety of Varieties'"—and Nazarro walks onto an empty stage accompanied by "a nice looking blond boy." (The act is performed "in one," meaning in front of the curtain with no props or scenery.) They perform various hand-to-hand stunts, for which the audience applauds. Finally they simulate a failed lift, setting in motion the artifice that brings out Buck and Bubbles.

"A voice offstage announces the 'arrival of the folks.' The two ragamuffin colored boys walk on and for the next 25 minutes take possession of the center."
They look as though they have "just come from the river, or some hangout
where clothes are nothing more than a habit." One of the boys "is a short,
tough looking young smoke, the other a string bean brunet." For a few
minutes, as prompted by Nazarro, they engage in a little insult comedy—"the
familiar negro crossfire about what they will do to each other, and so on." The
biggest laugh comes when the lights go out. "I can't see you, Buck," the tall one
says. To which the little fellow replies, "Well, yuh ain't no electric light sign."

Then Buck, "who looks about eight years of age," goes to the piano "and
tears off a yard and a half of rag, leading up to a snappy bit of stepping by the
pair, the tall boy being a top notch eccentric hoofer."

After some more comic banter, Buck "is announced to offer a piano solo,
for which he plays 'Dardanella' with one hand, 'Yankee Doodle' with another, chews his gum in time to another melody, and keeps time with both
feet." The gum chewing is not incidental. "The little chap at the piano must
spend a small-sized fortune on chewing gum, judging from the manner
in which he masticates it. But he should worry, as every time he clicks his
ebony jaws he gets a laugh."

The two boys again trade barbs, after which "the runt goes back to the keyboard to furnish the accompaniment for one of those 'blues' numbers delivered
by his tall partner. That long, absurd looking smoke can deliver 'blues' to the
queen's own taste. It takes a real darky to get this style of song across, but this
particular boy leads the procession in plaintive delivery of the mournful stuff."

At this point Nazarro, "who has stood aside during all this, announces
'Buck,' the short kid, will play any selection called for. Buck does just that
for ten minutes, playing selections as they are called from the audience, first
straight and then with the rag twist." It doesn't matter "whether you call
'Humoresque' or any classical number that may be difficult to do in ragtime, the little colored fellow 'rags' it."

"The two boys get together again for a song and dance finale and the act
closes with another hand-to-hand formation which Nazarro and his boy
assistant had missed just before the arrival of the Gold Dust Twins."

As this account demonstrates, the act in 1920 already contained the basic
elements of Buck and Bubbles's lifelong routine: an easy back-and-forth between set-pieces for the two principals, mediated by comic racial chatter. At
this point audiences admired Bubbles for his blues singing and "eccentric

hoofing," Buck for his ragtime piano and party tricks—playing two songs at once, ragging the classics—and both boys for their outlandish stage personalities. Little Buck might have made a slightly bigger impression in these early days. At the Colonial, it is reported, "the raggedy, gum-chewing piano playing of Buck was greeted with cheers and shrill whistling from the gallery."

One critic thought the act needed polishing. It was too long, for one thing, and Bubbles's blues number—the high point in his view—should have been reserved for the end. Nevertheless, in the first five theaters, without exception, the boys were a hit. If Nazarro had extracted the best blurbs for one of his ads, it might read as follows:

Riverside: "The turn is what is popularly called a 'knockout.'" (*Variety*)

Royal: "Buck and Bubbles are humdingers. . . . They completely stopped the show." (*New York Dramatic Mirror*)

Orpheum: "The real worth of the act lies in the ability of Buck and Bubbles." (*New York Clipper*)

Alhambra: "There was no let-up once Buck and Bubbles, the two young colored entertainers, came on." (*New York Clipper*)

Colonial: "Nat Nazarro with the two colored boys, Buck and Bubbles, kept the house in an uproar." (*New York Dramatic Mirror*)

With these conquests under their belts, Buck and Bubbles had only to finish their New York sweep with a cracking good show at the Palace.

4

The Palace Theatre was constructed in 1913 on the ground floor of a narrow, ten-story office building on the corner of 47th Street and Broadway. Squeezed between smaller buildings housing a café and a pool hall, it looked faintly ridiculous from the street, an oblong tombstone jutting skyward. Performers came in by an iron gate on 47th Street, through a courtyard and onto the stage where they gazed on the lavish *beaux arts* interior hung with two balconies and sixteen boxes cascading toward the ceiling. Showtime often brought a packed house, excited patrons filling every one of the 1,736 seats.

By the time Buck and Bubbles came to New York, the Palace was already legendary. After a disastrous opening (sabotaged by powers hellbent on its failure), the theater had quickly recovered and began siphoning up all the best talent. Within a few years it became known as the flagship theater of the entire Keith-Albee circuit. Audiences fell under its spell. "For those who are too young to remember the Palace in its heyday, it is hard to convey its magic," recalled one theatergoer. "The richness of Palace bills at their best was a marvel, . . . drawing forth immeasurable laughter and occasional tears." Performers were, if anything, more intoxicated. "Only a performer can describe the anxieties, the joys, the anticipation, and the exultation of a week's engagement at the Palace," recalled Jack Haley, the Tin Man from MGM's *Wizard of Oz*. "This was a dream fulfilled; this was the pinnacle of variety success."

Nazarro booked Buck and Bubbles to open the week of December 6, 1920. They would share the bill with eight other acts, a colorful mixture of experience and naivete. The headliner and biggest star was Kitty Doner, one of vaudeville's best-known male impersonators, who did quick wardrobe changes to show she could be just as convincing as a strapping he-man or a feminine ingénue. The grand old man of the bill was fifty-two-year-old Jimmy Barry, a beloved veteran with experience as a dramatic actor dating back more than twenty years. In the role of hayseed, he made gently comic observations as his wife fed him the prompts.

Another performer with "legitimate" credentials was Marie Nordstrom, a former opera singer turned actress. Appearing alone before elaborate sets, the beautiful and elegant "Miss Nordstrom" delineated tragic or comic characters—the "heartbroken woman at the telephone receiving calamitous news," the female executive "running her office, smoking cigars, telephoning home imperiously to a submissive spouse." To add mystery to the bill, Harry and Emma Sharrock would present, according to one critic, "the most extraordinary display of mind-reading ever witnessed in public." And rounding out the old guard was Henrietta De Serris, who treated vaudeville audiences to "living reproductions of famous works of art" using fifteen female models from the Academy of Sculpture in Paris.

The neophytes were led by Corinne Tilton performing "character studies" of young female archetypes—a flapper, a "love pirate" (dressed fetchingly in "pirate knickers, cocked hat, and boots"), and a "souse"—all through catchy original songs. Others included the team of George Wilson and Ben Larson, comedy acrobats, and Adelaide Bell, a dancer who specialized in "legomania"—high kicking and contortions.

Inevitably, Nazarro stood alone in his presentation of Black performers. As Bubbles later put it, "There ain't no two black acts on no bill."

The show ran about three and a half hours, 2:00 to 5:30 in the afternoon and 8:00 to 11:30 at night. The three younger acts went first, while the audience was still arriving and settling down. Thereafter the old hands held sway. A couple of wobbles were noted by critics: Adelaide Bell was hampered by her miserable onstage pianist, and at the Monday night show Emma Sharrock became flustered and almost misidentified one of the hidden objects (a stone from the Washington Monument) during her mind-reading trick. But none of the acts bombed; all were to varying degrees a hit. The biggest laugh-getters at the Tuesday matinee were Mr. and Mrs. Jimmy Barry (forty laughs), followed by Nat Nazarro and Co. (thirty-six) and Harry and Emma Sharrock (thirty-one). The others got two, three, or none.

After the Monday night show, *Variety* awarded top honors to two acts: Nat Nazarro and Kitty Doner. Then, to Buck and Bubbles, the "show business bible" gave perhaps the best possible compliment: "The Nat Nazarro act [is] a rough and ready variety turn, with two of the best natural negro comedians in the persons of Bubbles and Buck that have flashed across the theatrical horizon since Williams and Walker hove into view 25 years ago." This flattering comparison set Buck and Bubbles apart, casting them as a "Williams and Walker" for the next generation. The writer continued: "Bubbles is a tall youth with a pair of educated dancing feet, a husky voice containing a peculiar Ethiopian sweetness and a real knowledge of comedy values. Buck plays the piano, not as it is usually played in vaudeville but in real rag style. A great combination, these two youths. They should quickly climb the ladder."

One review stood out from all the rest. *Billboard* scribe J. A. Jackson wrote, "'Buck' and 'Bubbles' . . . were the outstanding surprise of the Palace bill. . . . The real names of the boys are Ford L. Washington and John W. Sublett. They are natives of Louisville, Ky., and have come thru the minstrel ranks." A Black man himself, Jackson was the only reporter to identify the boys by their real names.

When they returned home to their families at Christmas, Buck and Bubbles had reason to crow. Going from the bush leagues to the Palace, they had accomplished in less than a year what thousands of vaudevillians toiled a lifetime to achieve. But of course it had not been less than a year—it had been *less than a week*. From their debut at the Columbia on February 15 to their first (canceled) contract with the Palace five or six days later, they had gone from penniless no-names to hot properties that showbiz kingpins fought over in court. What Humboldt Collins and Billy Maxie and H. C. Carter and Irwin Rosen and Nat Nazarro had seen in their act had been endorsed by the most powerful people in show business, despite their handicap of age and race. For Bubbles, barely seventeen, it was the first in a lifetime of landmark achievements.

Bubbles's year of triumph ended on a sad note. Three months after the Palace date he got word from home that his father had died. John Sublett Sr. had been struck down by "general paralysis of the insane," a complication of syphilis. Victims showed a gradual disintegration of mind and body, bringing memory loss, disorientation, delusions of grandeur, violent rages, muscle collapse, and finally debilitating seizures. (Since the symptoms could appear up to thirty years before death, it is possible John Sr.'s abusive episodes stemmed, at least in part, from his illness.) Had he lived during the age of penicillin, he might have been saved. As it was, John Sublett Sr. died on March 7, 1921, at about age forty-seven.

A few days later, Bubbles went home for the funeral. The service was held in the family home, where his father's body lay in a casket. During the sermon, "Everybody was cryin' and yelling," Bubbles recalled, but not him— he felt nothing at all. Then the preacher reached his climax: "Christ was on the cross, and there was a liar on one side and a thief on the other who were askin' the Lord to save them. And just as Christ turned his head to die, he says, 'Oh, Death, wait.'" Bubbles was thunderstruck. "My father couldn't ask death to wait, no matter how good he was or how fine he had been, he couldn't ask death to wait. Then I started crying."

John Sr. was buried under a tree in the Louisville cemetery. Returning to the house with his mother and sisters, Bubbles sat down at the family piano and started playing the blues. Thinking his selection inappropriate at such a time, Annie Gertrude told their mother to make him stop. But Katie said, "Go ahead and let him play." No wonder. As a musical epitaph for John Sublett Sr., the blues made perfect sense.

5

Reinvention

1

Although John Bubbles did not hesitate to propagate falsehoods about the mundane details of his early life—notably the year and location of his birth—he was remarkably forthright about the facts of his career, often nailing specific episodes with surprising accuracy. His account of Buck and Bubbles's stint with the Three Ink Spots, their debut at the Mary Anderson Theatre, the arrival of Irwin Rosen, the dead time during their first weeks in New York, their encounter with Nat Nazarro and their breakout performance at the Audubon Theatre, even the fact that they opened there on Bubbles's birthday—all can be verified in news reports.

But there was one big exception to this candor: the matter of how and when he learned to dance. The story went like this. As a teenage prodigy, Bubbles was primarily a singer. "I didn't dance in those days," he recalled, with characteristic bravado. "You don't dance with the voice I had." On the strength of his singing alone he made it to New York, and, with his partner, Buck, quickly began climbing the entertainment ladder. Then, during the Audubon engagement, his voice cracked as he went for a high note (his voice had not yet broken), and he realized he had better acquire a back-up skill to supplement his singing, just in case. It was only then, in a quest for versatility, that he started dancing. After honing a few sharp moves, he dropped by the Hoofers Club in Harlem and tried them out on the veteran Black dancers. It was a disaster. The old bulls laughed him out of the club. Determined to get his revenge, he practiced for months during a tour of the West Coast, and when he returned to New York, armed with a clutch of revolutionary new steps, he went back to the Hoofers Club and dazzled the naysayers into penitential silence. That was the story Bubbles always told.

The truth is more believable and more interesting. The truth, as we have seen, is that Bubbles had been a dancer from the beginning.

As a child, he had begged his mother for permission to put taps on his shoes. At age eleven he earned praise in Indianapolis for his "cleverness as

Sportin' Life. Brian Harker, Oxford University Press. © Oxford University Press 2022.
DOI: 10.1093/oso/9780197514511.003.0006

a singer *and dancer.*" By the time he got to New York it was clear that white critics, at least, considered dancing to be his strong forte: "Bubbles sings, but his dancing pleased more than anything else." "What he can't do in the line of 'coon' dancing and tap work isn't worth doing." "An exceptionally clever dancer." "A top-notch eccentric hoofer." "When it comes to stepping [he] can hold his own with the best of them." High praise, indeed, coming from hard-bitten New York reporters. But to go from *that* to rank humiliation at the Hoofers Club was too much to own up to—so Bubbles dissembled, painting himself as a novice who could barely tie his shoes. "I didn't dance in those days . . ."

The rest of the story, however, was apparently true. He did flop at the Hoofers Club. He did redeem himself through innovation. And, according to posterity, he parlayed that innovation—those fancy new steps—into something much bigger, forever transforming the art of tap and possibly jazz music as well. That is a story worth telling.

2

Buoyed by their success at the Palace, Buck and Bubbles roared into the new year a name act with influence and connections. At Philadelphia's New Standard Theatre, they were billed as the "Sensation of the Season." Music publishers trumpeted their endorsement of new songs. At top dollar, no doubt, Nazarro even "loaned out" the boys to another impresario, a hard-driving comedian named Frank Fay, one of the most successful and—at $17,500 per week—highest paid vaudevillians of the decade (who also became Barbara Stanwyck's first husband).

Clearly, they had won over the white establishment. In the years ahead it would be equally important, though for different reasons, to prevail in Black circles and to do so outside the context of vaudeville. Buck would seek validation within the fraternity of jazz pianists, while Bubbles craved the respect of the Black dancers of Harlem. It was not just a matter of winning the favor of his own people. Tap dancing, like jazz, was a predominantly Black creation. As much as he appreciated the acclaim of white critics, their approval didn't count for nearly as much as that of known experts on the matter. He went to the Hoofers Club to seek that approval (or to demonstrate his dominance, which amounts to the same thing). In his recollection, he made the visit just before Buck and Bubbles began a West Coast tour on the Orpheum circuit.

Since, according to news reports, that tour began in September 1921, he must have gone to the Hoofers Club sometime in July or August.

With a population only 33 percent Black in 1920, Harlem was not yet the Black mecca it would become. It was not yet the Harlem of Duke Ellington at the Cotton Club, Louis Armstrong at Connie's Inn, or Lindy Hoppers at the Savoy Ballroom. It was not yet the playground of wealthy whites seeking Black and Tan fantasies. In short, the entertainment district of Harlem—the area north of 131st Street between Seventh Avenue and Lenox—was not yet the Black counterpart to Times Square. But young entertainers nourished dreams worthy of that brilliant future. During the dead weeks with Irwin Rosen, Buck and Bubbles had made regular pilgrimages to Harlem's Tree of Hope, grasping its trunk and wishing for that lucky break that would catapult them to fame. The tree stood near the Lafayette Theatre on the corner of 132th Street and Seventh Avenue, at that time the most important Black venue in the city. Two doors down, at 2237 Seventh Avenue, was the Hoofers Club.

The Hoofers Club was neither a nightclub nor a dance studio nor a club requiring formal membership. It was, rather, a back room in the basement of a pool hall that had been commandeered over the years by *hoofers*—tap dancers—as an informal gathering place to practice, experiment, joust, and learn. No photographs exist. The place lives today only in the written memories of the original participants. As you entered from the street and walked downstairs you immediately heard tapping (an indulgent landlord replaced the floor every six months). At the bottom of the stairs was a lunch counter, to the left a couple of card tables where men played poker or blackjack, and dead ahead was a small room, an upright piano in the corner, benches along the wall, and a "good floor" for dancing. Regulars included characters with names like "Piano," "Happy," "Slappy," and "Motorboat." ("Piano" could only dance if he hung on to the piano with both hands.) They often dueled for supremacy in the same competitive spirit as jazz pianists or trumpeters. Tricks were passed around and new ideas were born. Occasionally one of the greats would come in. At such times an unwritten code required absolute deference from the rank and file. No talking to the great one; no distracting movements as he flashed his signature steps. Only after the master had left could the regulars get back to their trash talk, jokes, dances, and challenges. This was the atmosphere—part celebration, part ritual, informal but with unforgiving protocols—that Bubbles encountered when he walked into the Hoofers Club (probably not for the first time) in the summer of 1921.

As Bubbles recalled the experience, the regulars were mixed with heavyweights on that day—Eddie Rector, for example, "and a bunch of other experts"—all fixing their eyes on this eighteen-year-old kid from Louisville. "I was only doing a strut and turn then," he said with the false modesty he needed to sell his false narrative. "I did my little steps, and they laughed me out of the club. 'You're hurting the floor,' they said. I just couldn't class with them." We must wonder what actually happened. Could the dancer who had just conquered vaudeville with his "top-notch eccentric hoofing" really have been laughed out of the club—for his *dancing*? Or was it something else? Given Bubbles's well-known haughtiness, it seems more likely he failed to show proper respect for the chiefs, who might have found it necessary to humble this cocky upstart. Whatever the reason, Bubbles came away hurt, angry, and determined to get even.

3

In September 1921, Buck and Bubbles got on a train to Chicago, where they kicked off a six-month Orpheum tour with a week at that city's Palace Theatre. Chicagoans received them, if possible, even more rapturously than New Yorkers had. When the boys came onstage, "the audience just howled to see these be-ragged colored urchins step forth, with their hair liberally coated with brilliantine. The boys lost no time in getting to work." Buck added a new trick to his comic repertoire, doing hilarious impressions of Nazarro and his boy assistant. "The act furnished 30 minutes of entertainment," noted *Variety*, "and left the house gasping and applauding for more—but there was no more."

Leaving Chicago, the boys, in the company of Nazarro, hit the usual western stops, receiving enthusiastic coverage wherever they went: Peoria, Davenport, St. Paul, Duluth, Minneapolis, and finally a long jump to the coast, starting in Vancouver, Canada, and working their way south. By late January 1922, they were in San Francisco, by February Los Angeles, and by March they were back in Chicago, where the reception was again so positive, apparently, that they stayed in the area for three more months before returning home to New York in July. Reviewing a show at Chicago's Majestic Theatre, a *Tribune* reporter directed the bulk of his praise to the boys— starting with the headline: "Welcoming Messrs. Buck and Bubbles"—and made an observation increasingly common in reviews of the Nat Nazarro act: that Buck and Bubbles were overshadowing their patron:

> Reporting the current festivities at the Majestic resolves itself chiefly into a matter of words about two amazing pickaninnies named Buck and Bubbles. These blithe gamins take possession of an act supposed to be presided over by one Nat Nazarro, and before they are through with their ministrations make themselves easily the hit of the bill. Clad as if they had just stepped in from the alley, they sing, dance in whirlwind fashion, and play the piano with rollicking zeal and genuine skill. Withal, they have a sly sense of comedy, seemingly somehow to be born entertainers. Mr. Nazarro's offering, originally something acrobatic, is quite eclipsed by his ubiquitous assistants, but nobody minds, apparently—least of all the complaisant Mr. Nazarro.

Despite the nice things people were saying about him in the newspapers, Bubbles had not forgotten what had happened at the Hoofers Club. He stewed about it all year and plotted his strategy to redeem himself and shame his detractors. Originality was what counted, he knew. To live down his last appearance he had to do something undeniably new and difficult. The question was, what would it be? Put another way: Whose legacy would he need to challenge?

For ambitious young tappers, the industry standard and man to beat was forty-four-year-old Bill "Bojangles" Robinson. Born and raised in Richmond, Virginia, Robinson was orphaned at seven and sent to live with his grandmother, a reluctant guardian who actually went to court in an effort to escape legal responsibility for the boy. Young Bill often had to steal in order to get enough to eat. He also started dancing on street corners for pennies. In time he took a job as a "pick" with a traveling show headed by a white performer. By 1900 he was in New York, hustling for jobs in the nation's top vaudeville market. He became the junior member of a comedy duo, his only option according to an unofficial "two-colored" rule banning solo Black performers in white vaudeville. With this team he became a fixture on the Keith circuit, first as a singer and comedian but increasingly over time as a remarkable tap dancer. His reputation increased to such an extent that when he split with his partner a few years later, he was able to break the "two-colored" rule and work as a single without any diminishment in salary or prestige. By the time

Buck and Bubbles came to New York in 1920, Robinson was easily the most successful Black tap dancer in the business.

According to a longtime friend, Robinson didn't smoke or drink but had a favorite food: ice cream. As if to make up for all the times he was denied such a delicacy as a child, he ate it constantly as an adult. For breakfast, a late-in-life profile confided, he typically had muffins and vanilla ice cream. For lunch, a heaping bowl of vanilla ice cream. And for dinner, meat, vegetables, muffins—and vanilla ice cream. In its pristine simplicity, vanilla ice cream—plain, without adornments or contaminants—was the perfect dish, impossible to be improved upon. Robinson took a similarly pure approach to his dancing.

When he arrived in New York in 1900, the hot new trend in popular music was ragtime. Initially an idiom for solo piano, ragtime quickly invaded every corner of the publishing industry—songs, concert band arrangements, even orchestral works. It was the accompaniment to which Robinson danced in vaudeville. Tap, indeed, with its happy syncopated rhythms, was the dancer's counterpart to ragtime music (or vice versa, since the tap-ragtime relationship is a classic chicken-egg problem). Not surprisingly, Robinson confined his stepping to a repertoire of simple ragtime rhythms: down beats and mildly erratic eighth-note syncopations, enlivened with occasional triplets (three taps to a beat). Robinson is known for one important innovation: He danced "up on the toes" rather than in the flat-footed manner of his predecessors. After that, however, he "didn't change his style for sixty years," continually recycling a few basic steps. Why, then, was he so celebrated? In addition to his winning personality and brilliant showmanship ("Bo's face was about forty percent of his appeal," remarked one dancer), Robinson executed those basic steps with unmatched perfection. His dancing, a critic wrote, was "indescribably liquid, like a brook flowing over pebbles." Yet every tap sounded with individual integrity; every tap, a fellow dancer marveled, "was a pearl."

Unable to improve on this level of perfection, young tappers tried to distinguish themselves in other ways. As Bubbles recalled, most of his peers "tapped a little, and then went into Wings, splits, and Russian kicks— anything to be flashy. . . . Body movement was the big thing, not taps." Thus, Ulysses S. Thompson, according to Marshall and Jean Stearns, combined "somersaults, cartwheels, and tap dancing with knee-drops and kazotskys [Russian kicks]." A few dancers, like Willie Covan, aspired to complicate the art of tap itself. But no one, apparently, took it as far as Bubbles did while touring the West Coast in 1922.

4

For the first time in his life, Bubbles "got crazy with practicing." On the road he practiced day and night, "in hallways, backstage, in hotel rooms and train vestibules," anywhere he could find. "One of the best places . . . to practice was in an empty grain car," he said. "The grain polished the floor better than any stage I've ever been on." He experimented again and again. And one night shortly after returning to New York he achieved a breakthrough. Beginning around eleven o'clock he took off his shoes (so he wouldn't wake the neighbors) and danced all night in his stocking feet. By six in the morning, he had invented a new step (or combination of steps, it's not entirely clear). To celebrate, he went to a diner for coffee and a donut. "And I cried like a baby 'cause I'm so happy for learning the step that I stayed up all night to get." "I can remember thankin' God for letting me stay at it that long." The next day he went back to the Hoofers Club, loaded for bear. "Man, I was really forti-fied, like a fellow with a double-barreled shotgun—who's gonna stop me?" Nobody did, and nobody laughed this time, either. Now the dominant emo-tion was fear. "Don't go in there 'cause Bubbles is in there," people said after seeing his new routine.

At this distance it is difficult to know exactly what steps Bubbles unveiled on that particular day. Since no extended footage of his dancing exists be-fore 1937, anything prior must be imagined through a fog of retrospective accounts, whether the self-serving memoirs of Bubbles's rivals or the equally biased judgments of his followers. Even Bubbles's own recollections are in-consistent. On one occasion he claimed his game-changing step was the now standard "Over the Top," on another occasion "*double* Over the Top," and on still another "a double Wing with a top Figure Eight with the Trenches." The truth is lost to the ages. The best we can do is extrapolate backward from the later testimony of peers who were clearly convinced he had done *some-thing, somewhere* to set in motion a dramatic new approach. That doesn't mean his story lacks merit. To the contrary: We might think of his triumph at the Hoofers Club, however shrouded in myth, as a promissory note on his mature style.

What do we know about that style?

It was fast and complex, audacious and unpredictable. In contrast to Bill Robinson's immaculate perfection, Bubbles questioned the very idea of per-fection, the idea that there was no more progress to be made, nothing more to be learned. For Bubbles, that notion was antithetical to tap. After developing his new routine, he explained, "I didn't look back. . . . I kept multiplying to it all the time, changing steps so fast that each step was mounting the next." It was a matter of stasis vs. change. If Robinson was Apollo, then Bubbles was Dionysus. If Robinson was Classic, Bubbles was Romantic. And if Robinson's dancing was a bit vanilla (so to speak), Bubbles's was the flavor of the week—with an endless array of toppings.

John Bubbles tap dancing, ca. 1960s.

Source: L. Tom Perry Special Collections, Harold B. Lee Library, Brigham Young University, Provo, Utah.

The foundation of his new style involved breaking up Robinson's convivial eighth notes into smaller, more rambunctious subdivisions. But that was hard to do at the bright tempos favored by the older generation. So Bubbles cut the tempo, opening up the space he needed to really explore the possibilities. Next he began dropping his heels, rejecting Robinson's practice of always dancing "up on the toes." The heel drops disrupted the even flow of tapping. "By using his heels," Honi Coles explained, "Bubbles added [new] syncopation[s], changed the whole beat." Bubbles apparently got this idea while watching a white act called Doyle and Dixon, possibly during the 1921–1922 Orpheum tour. Harland Dixon specialized in Lancashire clogging, a British cousin of American tap that employs a lot of heel drops. "By combining the Lancashire Clog with Buck dancing," Dan Healy said, Bubbles "started a new style." (Bubbles himself put it in racial terms: "I took the white boys' steps and the colored boys' steps and mixed 'em all together so you couldn't tell 'em, white or colored. I made it *me*.") The new style exploded with fast combinations, such as the now standard Cramp Roll, a rapid alternation between heels and toes—like a drumroll. According to Ralph Brown, Bubbles "created" the Cramp Roll, though, as Brian Seibert points out, it may be more accurate to say he accelerated it.

Thus armed, Bubbles forged a style of high invention, improvising variations on steps and variations on the variations. This is the quality that most impressed Fred Astaire, who found Bubbles's dancing "always new, always fresh." The great teacher and choreographer Buddy Bradley recalled a cutting contest at the Hoofers Club: "A fellow named Detroit Red was scaring everybody to death doing variations on Over the Top. Then somebody said, 'Here comes Bubbles.' . . . Well, Bubbles started working out on the same step, and before he was through, Toots Davis, who was in the audience, said to me: 'I invented that step, but I never knew there were so many ways to do it.'" The improvisatory aspect also set him apart. Although Robinson was capable of improvising, he preferred highly rehearsed routines such as his signature Stair Dance, a tap journey up and down a small flight of stairs in which every nuance—in old-school vaudeville fashion—was carefully planned and polished. Bubbles, by contrast, thrived on spontaneity. In his vaudeville act he would change his dancing from one show to the next. "I could never steal a step from Bubbles," Nick Castle lamented, because "he never repeats—he's the greatest *ad lib* dancer in the world."

This thirst for invention gave birth to a new phraseology. Again, Robinson provides a clarifying foil. Like ragtime composers of his era, Robinson organized his rhythms into symmetrical patterns. In a 1932 film of his Stair Dance, for example, he begins by alternating two contrasting rhythms (which we will call *a* and *b*). Alternating simple ideas every one or two bars, Robinson continues as follows:

```
| a | b | a | b |
| a | a | b | b |
| c | c | b | b |
| c | c | b | b |
| d | b | d | b |
```

The balance and regularity of this design made his dancing comprehensible to audiences already predisposed to approve of this ingratiating performer.

Now consider Bubbles's janitor routine in the 1937 film *Varsity Show*. In a dazzling display of tap artistry, he presents his ideas not in short contrasting phrases but in a flowing river of variations, punctuated by random explosions along the way. Before long he makes stark changes in rhythm and step, juxtaposing lightly swinging eighth notes, for instance (a^1–a^9), with an extended barrage of triplets and even faster rhythms (c^1–c^5):

$$| a^1 | a^2 | a^3 | a^4 |$$
$$| a^5 | a^6 | a^7 | a^1 |$$
$$| a^1 | a^4 | b^1 | b^2 |$$
$$| c^1 | c^2 | a^8 | a^9 |$$
$$| c^1 | c^3 | c^4 | c^5 |$$

Rather than creating a comforting regularity, this kind of dancing challenges the audience to keep up with the performer's ever-changing ideas. In this respect Bubbles's dancing resembled the free-wheeling solos of the great jazz artists of his time. As dancer Baby Laurence put it, Bubbles "was like [tenor saxophonist] Coleman Hawkins in sound."

These, then, are the elements of Bubbles's mature style. Today that style is called *rhythm tap* or *jazz tap*. With its speed and complexity, swinging rhythms, improvisation, and constant invention, rhythm tap bore an obvious kinship to jazz. Less clear was the priority between the music and the dance, another chicken-egg problem which jazz historians have mostly ignored. For this reason, Bubbles's fellow dancers called for the recognition they felt was due to him, loudly proclaiming his influence on the music. While their claims may appear overstated or difficult to prove, they are not unreasonable. We will address them in future chapters.

Bubbles's innovations were not universally appreciated. Reviewing his dancing a year later, J. A. Jackson, the Black *Billboard* critic, felt the need to take him down a notch: Bubbles "moves with grace," he wrote, "but he had nothing to offer . . . that all the other dancers have not done in Harlem." This rebuke sounds like an injured defense of the old guard, as if Bubbles or his boosters had been making proprietary claims. Clearly, revolution would not come easily.

6

Beautiful Days

1

In the summer of 1922 Nat Nazarro made an abrupt change of strategy. After two years of triumph on the big time, he suddenly swerved in the opposite direction, booking Buck and Bubbles (and himself) mostly into small-time theaters. Given the unappealing nature of small time—"no one played it by preference," an old trouper once said—how is this move to be explained? Quite simply: Nazarro's motivation was money, and by 1922 the money situation had changed. Big time was declining, and everyone knew it.

For more than a decade, silent movies had surpassed vaudeville in popularity. And yet E. F. Albee, the head of the Keith circuit, refused to abandon the expensive and antiquated model of first-class, two-a-day vaudeville. Sensing weakness, his small-time competitors pounced. By building larger theaters and charging less for admission, they discovered that they could outbid Keith for "name" acts that were once beyond reach. And by adding a feature film after the vaudeville part of a program, they could double their audience appeal. Circuits like Loew scrambled the categories, becoming known as "big small time."

Nazarro embraced the anti-Keith trend. Lured by higher paydays and in some cases the potential for huge returns, he booked Buck and Bubbles on road tours with Shubert, Poli, Loew, and Pantages, plus an all-Black musical and a burlesque show. Since he kept his employees on a fixed salary, Buck and Bubbles wouldn't benefit directly from his financial schemes. Nor would they continue to enjoy the cushy working conditions that came with big-time employment. Still, they were young and carefree. They used the time to pay their dues, mastering the art of showmanship and hammering out the framework of a permanent routine. In the process they accumulated a rich stockpile of memories of life on the road.

Nazarro's first gambit was to join forces with Lee Shubert, Albee's biggest foe in 1922. Previously specializing in musical comedies, Shubert now moved aggressively to capture a large share of the big-time vaudeville market.

Sportin' Life. Brian Harker, Oxford University Press. © Oxford University Press 2022.
DOI: 10.1093/oso/9780197514511.003.0007

Unveiling his plan for what he called "Advanced Vaudeville," Shubert announced a series of traveling shows pairing a vaudeville bill with a musical revue, hoping to achieve the best of both worlds. In casting he spared no expense, hiring the best talent at rates exceeding big-time salaries. Despite Albee's furious threats to blacklist anyone who signed up, many vaudeville headliners joined Shubert, including Will Rogers, Fanny Brice, Fred Astaire, Fred Allen, and the Marx Brothers. In September 1922, Nat Nazarro also joined, bringing Buck and Bubbles with him.

They were assigned to a show called *Frolics of 1922*, featuring Herman Timberg, a violin-playing comedian, as the headliner. For the next seven months the troupe toured as far north as Boston, as far south as Washington, DC, and as far west as Chicago, garnering positive reviews along the way. One critic placed the company "among the leaders of the Shubert units." In keeping with standard journalistic protocol, critics tended to be politely deferential to the headliner, but one doesn't need to read too far between the lines to discern the true stars of the show: Buck and Bubbles. As one reporter put it, Timberg's turn "paved the way nicely" for Buck and Bubbles, who closed both the first and second halves of the show. As if simply including a Black act weren't novel enough, someone decided to dramatize their entrance by having them charge onto the stage from the audience. Everywhere the show went the duo "mopped up" or "had things their own way." In Boston they took *nine curtain calls*. In Cincinnatti a critic did not mince words: "Buck and Bubbles . . . were the shining lights of the Frolics."

Unfortunately, the larger project didn't fare as well. Through a combination of "exorbitant salaries," low admission prices, and mismanagement, Shubert's traveling units ran out of money by early 1923. (One historian considers this "one of the worst fiascos in show business.") When the *Frolics* started withholding wages, Nazarro showed his worth. On April 5, the night of the last performance, he entered Philadelphia's Chestnut Street Opera House five minutes before curtain time, and with two lawyers and two deputy sheriffs in tow, impounded all the orchestra music, some of the sets and costumes, and even Timberg's violin. For an hour, "while the house was in tumult," Nazarro argued with officials. Only after he and everyone else in the cast had been paid back wages did he allow the show to begin.

The Shubert disaster didn't dissuade Nazarro from taking risks. In the summer of 1923 he gambled a great deal by mounting his own show. Perhaps he had noticed that Sissle and Blake's *Shuffle Along*, the first successful all-Black musical since the days of Williams and Walker, was still making headlines two years after its Broadway premiere. This show had been the surprise hit of 1921, launching the careers of Josephine Baker, Florence Mills, and Paul Robeson. It also inspired a generation of would-be producers eager to duplicate its success, among them Nat Nazarro. He decided to stage his own all-Black revue with Buck and Bubbles as headliners. Box-office receipts for this sort of enterprise would be modest, but if the show were successful, Nazarro himself—as sole producer—could make a killing.

Hiring Jo Trent to write the book and Frank Montgomery to do the staging, Nazarro assembled a cast of thirty singers, dancers, and comedians. Trent fashioned a time-honored storyline that began in Africa and ended in Harlem, tracing the rise of Black Americans from the jungles to twentieth-century urban life. To reflect this progress Nazarro called the show, with a nod to Genesis, *Raisin' Cain* (after an abortive first title, *Hot Chops*). But his efforts were no more successful than those of a dozen others trying—and failing—to follow in Sissle and Blake's footsteps. After opening in Washington, DC, to "poor business," the show had its New York premiere at Harlem's Lafayette Theatre the second week of July. It received mixed reviews. Whereas the Black *Amsterdam News* regretted "extremely our inability to say we think it is great," *Variety* was more generous, noting "plenty of entertainment" and predicting that, with some judicious cuts, "it'll go over."

It didn't. After only two weeks at the Lafayette, the show "was reduced to tabloid size and put on the Fox circuit" without the headliners. Now it was Nazarro who had to answer the angry protests of unpaid cast members. The *Pittsburgh Courier* summed up the whole affair: " 'Raisin' Cain' Raises Cain— And Goes Broke."

How much Nazarro himself lost on the venture is not known. But, characteristically, he had taken steps to cushion himself in the event of just such a calamity. Simultaneous with his plans to produce *Raisin' Cain* he had signed Buck and Bubbles to appear in a traveling burlesque show in September. (If *Raisin' Cain* had taken off, presumably he would have broken his burlesque contracts, just as those contracts now saved him in the wake of its demise.) Why did he choose burlesque, an institution not known for its cultivation of famous stars? Again, it came down to money. As *Billboard* reported, after watching a rival circuit sign Fatty Arbuckle, the popular silent film comedian, for the fall season, the Columbia burlesque circuit began courting "big acts" for its own shows. Somewhat panicked, company executives spread word that they were "willing to pay the price for topliners, anything from a big name single to a big act of many people who have sufficient prestige to draw exceptionally large attendance." Buck and Bubbles were cast in a show called *Dancing Around*, where they received "special billing" together with headliner Harry Steppe, a "Hebrew comedian."

Dancing Around consisted of a series of sketches by a "comedian" (the headliner), a "prima donna," a "soubrette," a "juvenile," an "ingenue," and various specialties, including Buck and Bubbles. For the latter, the show must have felt like a replay of *Frolics of 1922*. Like the *Frolics*, the company toured the East Coast. As before, Buck and Bubbles made their entrance from the audience. And their work inspired similar reviews, which preferred Buck and Bubbles to the headliner. One reporter grumbled that "the only really bright and sparkling bit in the show is supplied by Buck and Bubbles." Another, *Billboard*'s J. A. Jackson, enjoyed the whole show but also named Buck and Bubbles the "best" of the troupe. They "literally stopped the finale," he exulted. "Three encores for them tells the story."

For Bubbles, an unexpected encounter made this show unforgettable: While on tour he fell in love for the first time. The thundering ovations for him and Buck attracted the attention of a chorus girl named Eleanor Heinemann. She invited Bubbles to a party, and their relationship blossomed. (Around the same time, Buck began dating Josephine Baker, one of the standouts of *Shuffle Along*.) "She was the first one who told me I was going to be a star," he recalled. "I didn't know this. Hadn't the slightest idea." For his part, he considered Eleanor "too good for anybody I know." Bubbles gave her a ring, then went home to Indianapolis where his family had recently moved, to ask his mother for her blessing. He was hopeful, but also worried. His sweetheart, he knew, had a potentially fatal flaw: Like everyone else in *Dancing Around* except Buck and Bubbles themselves, Eleanor was white.

Bubbles bared the feelings of his heart to his mother, and, sure enough, she opposed the union. The nightmare her husband once experienced for flirting with a white girl had planted in Katie a lifelong aversion to interracial couplings. But as she and Bubbles continued talking, she eventually made a concession: If Bubbles could get the girl's father to agree to the marriage, Katie would agree as well. The "concession" was actually a crafty flanking maneuver—a way of getting what she wanted while still appearing reasonable. Katie knew that no white father in 1923 was likely to approve of such a match. On reflection, Bubbles realized this as well, which is why in the end he didn't bother asking. He dropped the girl, she married a nice white boy, and Bubbles walked away with a broken heart.

It was just as well. At the party she invited Bubbles to attend, Eleanor had placed her guest in an awkward and even dangerous position. When he and Buck arrived, they found themselves the only males in a room full of females, all dressed in negligees and "smelling like a rose garden." Suspecting a "setup," Bubbles avoided direct contact with the girls. ("What shall we do?" he asked himself. "Keep a cool head.") Predictably, some of the male cast members found out, and the next day Buck and Bubbles escaped violence only through a combination of grandstanding, appeasement, and pure dumb luck. In pulling this stunt Eleanor probably acted out of naivete, for her love of Bubbles seems to have been genuine. After they broke up, she kept in touch, following the developments of his career and sending cards and letters—under her married name, Eleanor Gross—for the rest of her life.

When Buck and Bubbles left *Dancing Around* in March of 1924, Nazarro put them back into straight vaudeville. Rather than booking a Keith or Orpheum route, however, he sent them out on the small time. He wasn't the only manager to do so. "Vaudeville acts are selling their services to the highest bidders," wrote *Variety*. Few bidders were as aggressive as Loew. Lillian Shaw, a character actress who had worked for Keith for twenty years, for example, could not get the company to raise her salary of $750 a week. Loew offered her a whopping $1,250 a week and she gladly left Keith to take it. *Variety* listed thirteen other "name" acts signed by Loew, including Nat Nazarro with Buck and Bubbles.

From the spring of 1924 to late 1926, they performed a marathon run of small-time vaude, mostly the Poli, Loew, and Pantages circuits, hitting forty cities in seventeen states or provinces, and spending lots of time in the New York area. With Loew they made a stop in Indianapolis, where Buck and Bubbles received a hero's welcome. Guided by Nazarro's fact-challenged publicity release, a local reporter hailed them as hometown boys made good. Back in 1918, he reminded readers, they had performed at Indy's own Lyric Theatre, with Sugar Bailey, as the Three Ink Spots. "At that time Buck, the pianist, was eleven years old, and so small that he had to stand up while playing the piano," he wrote, exaggerating their youth and much else. "Bubbles, the dancer, was twelve years old but he was as agile as he is now. Both are from Indianapolis." After coming to New York, he continued, they met their current manager. "Within twenty-four hours Nazarro introduced them to Broadway and they made a hit."

2

In later years Bubbles looked back on his touring days with fondness. Summing up his many experiences, big time, small time, road shows, burlesque, he recalled (through somewhat rose-colored glasses, probably for the benefit of his white interviewer):

> Buck and I went out on the Keith circuit—twenty-six weeks—as far as Winnipeg, Portland, Seattle, San Francisco, Los Angeles, Phoenix, and back through St. Louis to Chicago and New York. No one-nighters, and Pullman all the way. Beautiful days! Life was great. The package was one big family, all traveling together. We might have Mel Klee, the comedian; Frances White, the singer; a bicycle act—Joe Jackson, a great comedian. He was crazy! People like Doyle & Dixon, Rae Samuels. Buck and I went out on the Pantages circuit, too, and Loew's, the Poli, and the burlesque circuit.

Occasionally Bubbles acknowledged hard times as well—waiting on freezing platforms at 3 a.m. for a train to the next city, for instance. "It's funny to think about now but it wasn't then," he said. "I can still feel the cold breeze hitting my shoulders once in a while when I think about it." Then, of course, there were the troubles, inconveniences, and indignities all Black performers faced on the road. The need to seek lodgings on the other side of town from the rest of the company; to stay in rundown boarding houses instead of the comfortable hotels enjoyed by their white counterparts; to order food from the back door of white restaurants rather than being allowed to sit in the dining room; to accept the worst dressing room in a theater—"usually on the top floor, a billion miles up from the stage, next to the dog act," as Eubie Blake recalled—even when they were the most popular act on the bill. Bubbles didn't like to talk about those things. "We just persevered the best we could," he said. "One distraction we took with us everywhere . . . was our collection of electric trains. Buck and I were nuts about 'em and we had a trunk full of them. We used to lay track all over our dressing room."

The biggest solace came under the bright lights of a packed theater. There, for a brief moment, their color didn't matter. Or rather it did—but in a "good" way. Audiences loved their seemingly unconscious display of racial authenticity. "Their dress and manner are so natural," a Chicago critic wrote, that "one suspects Nat Nazarro of having suddenly rushed down

South State street, grabbing the first two crap-shooters he laid eyes on and yanking them into a taxi and onto the Palace stage sans makeup, sans stage dress." Under Nazarro's direction, Buck and Bubbles played the part expected of them, peppering their sensational dancing and piano playing with "colored gags." As Bubbles put it, "We looked poor, we talked like we didn't know nothing, and we danced like we didn't care." In the 1920s they developed a repertoire of jokes and banter that would form the core of their lifelong routine.

When they first arrived in New York, Buck and Bubbles had looked so young that people thought they were children. One critic said Buck, in particular, appeared to be "about eight years of age." Nat Nazarro had no desire to correct this misperception. On the contrary, he seems to have crafted the boys' public biographies to exaggerate Buck's youth and therefore his appeal as a child prodigy. Although early news accounts state that the boys were the same age, at some point Bubbles started telling interviewers (presumably at Nazarro's bidding) that he was actually four years *older* than Buck, a falsehood he maintained to the end of his life. Buck played along, even to the point of giving the bogus birth year to authorities when traveling to

Buck and Bubbles in performance. "They were an act no one wanted to follow," recalled a contemporary.

Source: L. Tom Perry Special Collections, Harold B. Lee Library, Brigham Young University, Provo, Utah.

and from Europe. Later in life, however, when asked to give some biographical information to an encyclopedia, he gave his true date of birth. Perhaps with an eye toward history, he felt free to come clean. The point, in any case, is that Nazarro clearly believed the act's success depended on maximizing the differences between his two stars. Their size, their age, their skills—everything glowed more brilliantly in the light of contrast.

Now in their early twenties, Bubbles had grown to his full height of six feet and Buck to five foot four, the tallest he would ever be. Handsome in a devilish sort of way, an ever-present gleam in his eye, Buck "not only infatuated his audiences but drew women like flies to the stage door to see him." With a long torso and short, bandy legs, he nevertheless boasted an appearance that was well adapted to comedy. He was the funny man to Bubbles's straight man. Bubbles was tall, he was short. Bubbles was dignified, he was crass. Bubbles was serious, he was funny. But once he sat down at the piano, the laughing stopped. Then even Bubbles had to pay homage, listening appreciatively, bobbing his head, or rubbing his hands together as if before a roaring fire (this was some *hot* piano playing). By the same token, Bubbles contributed his share of comic asides. Like all great comedy teams, the two performers indulged an easy give-and-take, making full use of their multifaceted personalities.

Buck and Bubbles's comedy routine was documented on film only once, in a 1938 movie short called *Beauty Shoppe*. By mingling jokes from this brief footage with recollections from those who saw the act in person, we can recapture the flavor of their routine in its maturity. Buck would come onstage, pushing a piano on wheels. Bubbles, with the easy job, guiding the instrument from the front end, would badger him:

BUBBLES: Push the piano!
BUCK: Ain't I pushing on the piano?
BUBBLES: No you ain't. You're leaning on it.
BUCK: You just pull your end.
BUBBLES: You push your end, my end will follow.

This little sketch encapsulates the basic posture of the team in their various exchanges: comically antagonistic, with Bubbles forever picking on Buck. In this sense they continued the venerable Black tradition of insult comedy (aka the dozens), or as one early admirer of the team put it, "the familiar negro crossfire about what they will do to each other, and so on."

Once situated on stage—dressed in "vagabond clothes," mismatched and mis-sized—they immediately went into a song. After the applause, Bubbles began mocking Buck for his short stature and long clown shoes:

> BUBBLES: Get outta that hole!
> BUCK: I ain't in no hole.
> BUBBLES: [scrutinizing Buck] You sure is a low man. . . . And look at those shoes!
> BUCK: You look at 'em. I'm tired of looking at 'em.
> BUBBLES: Are them skiis you got on? How do you get your pants off at night?
> BUCK: I pull them off over my head.

Sometimes they told jokes adaptable to any comedy team, Black or white:

> BUBBLES: I passed by your house last night. Why didn't you put your window shades down? I saw you kissing your wife.
> BUCK: Ha! Ha! Ha! Ha!
> BUBBLES: What you laughing about?
> BUCK: I wasn't even home last night.

But often they involved stereotypes of Black laziness or cowardice:

> BUBBLES: What was you runnin' down the street for?
> BUCK: I was runnin' to stop a fight.
> BUBBLES: Who was the fight with?
> BUCK: Me and another fella.
> BUBBLES: Well, why was you runnin'?
> BUCK: You don't think my legs is gonna stand around and let the rest of my body be abused?
> [pause for laughter]
> BUBBLES: You was runnin' because you is a coward.
> BUCK: I'm no coward.
> BUBBLES: Yes you are. You're scairt t' death of lightnin' and thunder.
> BUCK: I'm not scared of lightnin' and thunder.
> BUBBLES: What are you talking about? The other day when there was lightnin' and thunder you went down in the basement and hid.

BUCK: Of course I did.

BUBBLES: Why?

BUCK: Well, if lightnin' is gonna strike me, then let it come lookin' fo' me.

In addition to these dialogues, Buck and Bubbles stocked their routine with punchy one-liners. One observer recalls Bubbles singing dreamily, "Am I blue? Am I blue?" while the team made their stage entrance. "You ain't blue, you black," Buck deadpanned.

We must remember, of course, that in comedy delivery is everything and mere words on a page cannot possibly reproduce the humor that sent 1920s audiences into tizzies of laughter. The facial expressions, the tone of voice, the play of hands, the timing—all contributed. White reporters tended to credit the team's effective delivery less to intelligence, forethought, or rehearsal than to their race. With the *Frolics*, one wrote, "They just acted natural and had little difficulty in provoking shrieks of laughter."

Recognizing their audience's expectation of "naturalness," Buck and Bubbles acted excessively relaxed and nonchalant. Even when performing his hurricane dance steps, Bubbles tried to create the illusion of effortlessness so as not to agitate his viewers:

> I thought I'd fix a step in a rhythm more in keeping with a person sitting out there in the audience. He doesn't really know what I'm doing—whether it's difficult or easy—but I can make it relaxed to suit the average rhythm of the average person. . . . When an audience is sitting down, they're relaxed and they want to stay that way. So I fixed my dancing to keep them relaxed, and they liked it.

After finishing his dance, he and Buck switched places and the latter took his own uproarious turn at dancing, relaxed to the point of somnolence (here's the "laziness" trope), while Bubbles provided a rudimentary piano accompaniment. In the words of Buck himself, "I pretend that I'm an amateur. I watch Bubbles do a step, then I repeat it, but listlessly as if I were tired. The biggest applause comes when I stub my toe." They switch roles again and Bubbles dances again as Buck, now flat on his back, accompanies "in the laziest manner imaginable," recalled Paul Draper, "remembering to reach up from the floor just in time to plunk one note every sixteen bars." Surveying his prone partner, Bubbles asks, "What's the matter with you? You tired?" Buck: "No, I'm just resting so that I won't *be* tired."

When they saw Buck and Bubbles's stage routine, long-serving critics instinctively thought of Williams and Walker. After several rounds of this comparison, Nazarro finally had the team do a Williams and Walker imitation in both *Raisin' Cain* and *Dancing Around*, billing them as "successors to Williams and Walker." In some ways the comparison has merit. Walker, in top hat and tails without blackface, was the straight man, and Williams, blacked up and wearing the same clothes but tattered in outrageous parody, was the comedian. Their sketches depicted the smooth talker taking advantage of the bumbling hick. One can see in Buck and Bubbles an echo of this dynamic, with Bubbles channeling the domineering Walker and Buck recalling the vulnerable (but funny) Williams. But in one significant way the comparison falls short. Unlike Williams and Walker—or other older Black teams like Miller and Lyles or Greenlee and Drayton—Buck and Bubbles had a secret weapon: virtuosity. When audiences weren't laughing at their comical antics, they were marveling at an expertise in music and dance that the old teams, for all their comic ingenuity, could never compete with. In their virtuosity, Buck and Bubbles heralded a new age of Black achievement.

3

Despite their outward success, by late 1926 the team had reached a crossroads. In many ways Nat Nazarro had been good to them. He kept them busy and paid them a salary that initially seemed generous. Over time, however, Buck and Bubbles became aware of a stubborn disconnect between their audience popularity and their professional rewards, particularly as compared with their white peers. Instead of trying to remove this disconnect, Nazarro increasingly seemed bent on preserving it. After six years was it time to leave him?

It had become clear early on that Buck and Bubbles could equal or outperform just about any act, despite the disadvantages of their race. In their second engagement at New York's Palace Theatre in March 1921, they played back-to-back on the same bill with the Marx Brothers, with "Julius" (i.e., Groucho) "running wild." Yet it was Buck and Bubbles, a reviewer noted, for whom the audience gave a "reception" (applause on entrance) and who "could have been there yet according to the demonstration accorded them at the finish." As we have seen, they repeatedly upstaged the headliners in *Frolics of 1922* and *Dancing Around*. Their small-time tour inspired rivers of plaudits: "Buck and Bubbles . . . just walk away with the honors"; "swept everything before [them]"; "stopped the show"; "ripped 'em loose from their seats"; "scored heavily"; "brought the offering to a deafening ovation at the close."

Their popularity (and Nazarro's sponsorship) allowed them to bypass the fate of other Black acts, who were typically consigned to the "deuce spot," the second position on a bill also known as the "graveyard" for the difficulty of commanding audience attention so early in a show. Instead, they were bumped around, from the third spot to right after intermission to the last spot in the first half and finally, of necessity, to what *Variety* called "the honor spot": the penultimate position in a program, aka *next-to-closing*. This was the spot normally reserved for the headliner, but Buck and Bubbles's dominance made their fellow actors—even the headliners—eager to go first. "They were an act no one wanted to follow," recalled one contemporary. "Those were two very classy guys." The honor of next-to-closing was not unprecedented among Black acts, but it was rare. Nevertheless, Buck and Bubbles were assigned that spot frequently after 1924.

They also appeared as headliners, but this honor didn't mean as much with Nazarro's name in larger letters, outshining their own. Their subordinate billing especially rankled in view of Nazarro's rapidly dwindling relevance. "Here is an act," wrote one critic, "where the one whose name is in largest type, does the least, and might just as well be spending his vacation [*sic*] . . . Buck and Bubbles assisted by Nat Nazarro and Co. would be the correct billing." Another review went further: "Nazarro was on stage during most of this turn and hindered, rather than aided, his colored proteges." Perhaps stung by this sort of criticism, Nazarro by 1926 had dropped the acrobatic part of the program, serving only as master of ceremonies to his two phenoms. It was crucial that he preserve ostensible control of the proceedings to maintain the devious game he was playing: By remaining on stage he could justify paying Buck and Bubbles as employees in *his* act instead of functioning as a true agent by representing them in their own. The difference amounted to hundreds of dollars a week.

When Nazarro first hired Buck and Bubbles, as we have seen, they each signed a contract for a salary of $90 a week. In coming years, he gave them two small raises, but by late 1926 they were still only making $125 a week and their expenses had greatly multiplied. Bubbles had recently brought his mother and sister Carrie to the East Coast so he could take better care of them. He took them first to Philadelphia, Nazarro's hometown. "I couldn't take them directly to New York," he explained. "The shock of that place would have been too much for my mother. I eased 'em into it by taking them to Philadelphia." Although Carrie soon got married, she still called upon Bubbles from time to time to pay her rent. As for his mother, she eventually moved into his apartment in New York, adding to his responsibilities but also providing a stabilizing influence to offset the effects of Bubbles's growing gambling habit. At some point, he and Buck fell into a pattern of asking Nazarro for advances on their salary. Over time, of course, these loans only deepened their distress.

In Bubbles's mind, the solution became obvious: Like other successful vaudevillians, he and Buck deserved to be paid what they were worth. Somehow, he discovered that Nazarro was charging $750 a week for his act, the going big-time rate. That meant that after paying Buck and Bubbles $125 each, he was pocketing $500 for himself. For some gigs Nazarro may have earned much more, depending on what he negotiated with Loew and others. And yet while Buck and Bubbles paid for Nazarro's big contracts by living on the road, traveling constantly, and enduring the grueling small-time regimen of three or four (or more) shows a day, their salary did not change. That was wrong, and Bubbles was ready to do something about it, given the right circumstance. One more provocation was all it would take.

7

Dancing in the Dark

1

At the end of the Pantages tour, Buck and Bubbles got into a huge fight with Nat Nazarro. In Toronto, it seems, they ran out of money and couldn't pay their boarding house bill. Promising the landlady to send the money from the road, they went on to Boston. As he had done many times before, Bubbles asked Nazarro for money to pay the bill, but for some reason, this time he refused. Bubbles implored him. He had promised the woman! It would ruin his reputation! It was only $26! But Nazarro said no. He wouldn't even loan him the money. Something snapped. At curtain time Buck and Bubbles refused to leave their dressing room until the matter was resolved. The theater manager threatened to blackball them, but they held firm. Furious, Nazarro called the police and impounded their trunk. It contained everything they owned: their clothes, costumes, music—everything.

Buck and Bubbles bolted. They ran out of the theater and tracked down a lady friend who loaned them $350. They caught a train to New York and used the money to order new music and new costumes. They were going to try to make it on their own, without Nazarro. They bought a suitcase to hold their new possessions, but when they got back to their room Bubbles realized—to his horror—that he'd left the suitcase on the running board of the cab that had dropped them off. "We were right back where we started. No music, no clothes, and very little money." In desperation, Bubbles borrowed $200 from a loan shark to *again* replace all their belongings. Then he contacted a theater in Philadelphia and booked a job. With the earnings, he paid back his Boston friend and the loan shark. He and Buck were just starting a show in Newark when Nazarro caught up with them. Citing a contract they'd signed three years before, he filed an injunction forbidding them from working in any theater in New York or New Jersey. By this time their money was gone,

Sportin' Life. Brian Harker, Oxford University Press. © Oxford University Press 2022.
DOI: 10.1093/oso/9780197514511.003.0008

and they had no way of earning more. "We were dead broke," Bubbles said, "and that was a rough Christmas on Buck and me. We really suffered."

They needed to get out of town, somewhere Nazarro wouldn't be able to find them. They went to the office of William Morris, one of Nazarro's competitors, and offered to work for $350 a week, half what Nazarro charged. Just send us anywhere in Chicago, they said. Unaware of Nazarro's continuing contract, Morris booked the team for a series of "presentation houses" (movie theaters that included a vaudeville program) run by Balaban & Katz. Their first engagement was at the Uptown Theatre the week of January 17, 1927. They played the Tivoli a week later. The Oriental a week after that. Then the Harding, the Senate, and the Uptown again. And audiences loved them. Bubbles recalled being told at the Oriental Theatre, where they joined a bill headed by the popular bandleader Paul Ash, that as the first Black team ever to play the theater they had to cut their fourteen-minute act down to eight minutes. But once they got on stage the audience wouldn't let them go. Twenty minutes passed. Thirty minutes. They finally extricated themselves from the swelling ovations after *fifty-eight minutes* on stage. "We got under the skin of that audience," Bubbles said. "Man, we're putting them into the aisle. And do you know what happened after that? They built the whole unit around Buck and Bubbles, and we played all the Balaban & Katz theaters with the show built around us."

There is no account of this epic feat in local newspapers. But it turns out Buck and Bubbles played for not one but three bandleaders during their first month in Chicago. Calling up memories from forty years earlier, Bubbles may have confused Ash with another bandleader named Bennie Kreuger, with whom Buck and Bubbles played in "a huge stage celebration" their second week in town. "It will be fast, snappy and peppy, with jazz at its utmost," a reporter wrote. Kreuger's orchestra will play "American music—jazz. His dancers [will do] the black bottom, buck and wing and other typical American jazz dances." The centerpiece of all this jazzmania was Buck and Bubbles. Kreuger gave them their own special presentation called "Jazz à la 1927." They were so well received that he called them back for four more (non-consecutive) weeks. He hardly had a choice. "These two colored singers and dancers have been booked back by popular and insistent demand," the *Suburbanite Economist* informs us. Buck and Bubbles asked William Morris for a fat raise, from $350 to $1,000, and Morris gave it to them. They had proved themselves eminently capable of thriving without Nazarro.

2

The year 1927 was indeed an important one for jazz, but not the kind being performed in downtown theaters. The white musicians who played that music couldn't wait to get off work so they could rush down to the South Side and soak up the real McCoy, as they saw it, in the Black nightclubs. Paul Ash was among them, probably Bennie Kreuger as well. Then there were the hungry young wannabes: Benny Goodman, Tommy and Jimmy Dorsey, Gene Krupa, and others now recognized for their own contributions to jazz in later years. (In Chicago they were still apprentices, studying at the feet of the masters.) Whatever their background, these white devotees might have gone to the Nest Club to hear clarinetist Jimmie Noone or the Plantation Club to hear cornet player King Oliver. Most often, however, they headed for the Sunset Café, a Black and Tan (racially mixed) cabaret on 35th Street just across from the Plantation. There they could hear trumpeter Louis Armstrong and pianist Earl Hines holding forth on a nightly basis. Together with Duke Ellington in Harlem and a few others, Armstrong and Hines were then in the process of bringing jazz out of its formative years and into its full maturity as an art form. The Sunset was ground zero for these historic developments.

About a month after their arrival, Buck and Bubbles took a job at the Sunset, where they performed every night after finishing their work downtown. They had played cabarets before, but never anything so high-class. The Sunset opened onto a large room with symmetrically arranged tables and stately square columns from floor to ceiling. Black waiters served food and illegal liquor (clandestinely, in teacups), while mostly white patrons danced, caroused, or sat with eyes riveted to the entertainment on stage. The shows started at 10 p.m. and went until the hilarity faded around three or four in the morning. As Louis Armstrong and his Sunset Stompers supplied fiery accompaniment, a parade of Chicago's hottest Black talent passed for review: Mae Alix, "the pachydermatous mistress of the splits"; Dotty McClendon, "a beautiful long-haired girl" who sang "I'd Love to Have Somebody to Love Me"; Slick White, "the little man with the big voice"; Chick Johnson and Sammy Vanderhurst, "whirlwind dancers"; Georgie Staten, a "midget dancer"; and a chorus of ten "Dancing Dimpled Darlings." To this lineup Buck and Bubbles added their talents on Friday, February 18, and threw everything into commotion. As vaudeville celebrities straight from New York, they "were compelled to respond to their wild admirers" for no less than forty-five minutes straight. Over the next two months they ran riot at the Sunset, "stopping the shows . . . nightly."

In late February they got word that Nat Nazarro had sued them for $20,000 for breach of contract. When asked about it by a Black reporter, they laughed it off, adding with relish that they had countersued Nazarro for $100,000 for back pay. Far from being worried about such legal entanglements, they were "having the time of their lives."

The Sunset interlude raises a question posed earlier in this book, one of great importance for the history of entertainment: What was the relation between jazz and tap dancing? Marshall and Jean Stearns stated, without elaborating, that "the rhythms of tap dance influenced jazz." Among historians, musicians, and dancers alike, there appears to be a vague consensus that this is probably true, but how did it happen? Some have implicated Bubbles. His faithful disciple Honi Coles claimed that "by using his heels, Bubbles added syncopation, changed the whole beat. Then the drummers listened to his feet, the other musicians listened to the drummer and a new style of jazz was born. All from him." In a later chapter we will have occasion to examine the role of drummers. For now, let's turn to another possible catalyst, unmentioned by Coles, the most consequential figure in jazz history: Louis Armstrong.

In the early 1920s jazz was not what it is today, an art of solo improvisation and individual self-expression. It was instead a grab bag of contrasting styles and approaches. There were big bands turning out dance music, orchestras presenting classical-sounding scores like Gershwin's *Rhapsody in Blue*, and comedy outfits making funny noises on their instruments and shouting jokes from the bandstand. Jazz historians believe Louis Armstrong cut through this chaos with a vision of jazz as a vehicle for solo artistry, one so compelling that within a few years all the other competing types either adapted to the new standard or fell by the wayside. Armstrong's triumph, however, was not quickly or easily accomplished. He had to overcome many obstacles over a period of years.

As I have argued in another context, one of those obstacles had to do with rhythm. Before the Sunset, Armstrong was stymied by rhythmic clichés held over from ragtime. In trumpet solos on "Go 'Long Mule," "Cake Walking Babies," and "Muskrat Ramble," he seems to be struggling, unsuccessfully, to break out of the rhythmic straitjacket of previous decades. During and after the Sunset, however, his rhythms suddenly become liberated. His solos on "Big Butter and Egg Man," "Potato Head Blues," and "Struttin' with Some Barbecue" display a newly free and flexible rhythmic language, one that animated his melodies in turn. By the early 1930s Armstrong's improvisational ideas provided the main prototype for musicians of the Swing Era. What happened in 1926–1927 that put Armstrong—and jazz—on a new course? What happened, in particular, to change his thinking about rhythm?

One possibility is his close-up exposure, on a nightly basis, to some of the best tap dancers in the business. By an odd coincidence, three leading dance teams—Buck and Bubbles, Rector and Cooper, and Brown and McGraw—all joined the floor show at the Sunset within a few months of each other. Rector and Cooper appeared in January. They were a "class act," elegant in dress and movement. Eddie Rector, a tapper in the Bill Robinson mold, was one of the heavyweights who had laughed Bubbles out of the Hoofers Club in 1921. According to Marshall and Jean Stearns, he was "unquestionably the greatest soloist" of the low-key, soft-shoe tradition, tapping out "pure and beautiful rhythms." One night Rector and Cooper looked up to see the great Bojangles himself walking into the Sunset. He mounted the stage and the three of them danced an impromptu routine. The distinguished visitor was "feeling fine," observed a reporter, greeting "old acquaintances right and left as he strolled up the aisles."

Sometimes these encounters veered into friendly competition, right there on the Sunset stage. Recognizing an old sparring partner whom he had once fought "for hours" during a legendary duel at the Hoofers Club, Bubbles threw down the gauntlet again upon seeing Sammy Vanderhurst at the Sunset. Earl Hines remembered their battles vividly: "You can imagine the kind of tap dancing that was going on. They did things with their feet that looked impossible." Hines's language suggests that Vanderhurst belonged to the growing body of dancers aspiring to the high technical standards that Bubbles had begun putting in place five years earlier. Indeed, if he had the wherewithal to challenge Bubbles, it is hard to believe anything else. The same could be said of Brown and McGraw, a dynamic husband-and-wife team with a reputation for "very fast" and "difficult" steps. While Rector and Cooper stood for the polished perfection of the Bill Robinson school, Bubbles, Vanderhurst, and Brown and McGraw reveled in the groundbreaking complexities of rhythm tap.

For Louis Armstrong, an insatiable musical sponge, this powerhouse roster of dancers must have been hard to resist. He seems to have been especially fascinated by Brown and McGraw. They joined the Sunset in July 1926 and that fall began performing with Armstrong in a very unusual manner. Armstrong recalled it this way: "There was the team of Brown and McGraw.

They did a jazz dance that just wouldn't quit. I'd blow for their act, and every step they made, I put the notes to it." Fellow trumpeter Doc Cheatham added more detail: "[Armstrong] played every step they made. And he screamed the whole act, playing trumpet, and every movement that they made, Louis would make it on his horn, and that made Brown and McGraw one of the most famous dance acts in Chicago, at that time."

He played every step they made. These words, confirmed by other eyewitnesses, turn the standard relationship on its head. Instead of the dancers working out a routine to Armstrong's music, it was the other way around: Armstrong copied the rhythms of Brown and McGraw. This idea casts a provocative light on one of their likely collaborations, "Big Butter and Egg Man." Armstrong's recording of this piece in November 1926 is the first to give evidence of his rhythmic breakthrough. In this solo the old ragtime clichés give way to constantly changing patterns—the kind you'd expect from someone shadowing a pair of rhythm tappers. Thereafter it is as though a dam had burst in Armstrong's mind. His solos unfold in fresh and ingenious contours, both rhythmically and melodically.

The tappers' apparent influence went beyond Armstrong's solos. The act was so successful that Brown and McGraw had Armstrong's trumpet part arranged for full band. After they left the Sunset, they took the arrangement with them so they could recreate the act with other bands. According to Rex Stewart, cornet player for Duke Ellington, this stimulated a larger movement toward jazz bands playing the rhythms of tap dancers—again, contradicting the traditional assumption that the music came first:

> I wonder how many people realize how much modern orchestration owes to Louis Armstrong? It's quite a great debt—because there used to be an act called Brown and McGraw . . . Well, Louis is the fellow who started the idea of catching those steps as Brown and McGraw were doing it, and that's where they really got the idea of imprinting rhythm into arrangements.

Eager to credit his hero, Stewart inadvertently raises another question: If "modern orchestration" owes a great debt to Armstrong, what does it owe to his source: Brown and McGraw?

Assessing the role of tap in the 1920s is a bit like trying to see the dark side of the moon. We cling to fragments of indirect evidence—tantalizing recollections, changes in trumpet style—but in the absence of audio or video footage of the dancers it can be hard to know what it all means. Still, just as astronomers deduce the presence of celestial phenomena through implied evidence, so may historians use networks of circumstance to illuminate their own mysteries. On any list of places tap dancing *might* have influenced jazz, the Sunset Café in 1926–1927 must rank somewhere near the top. And in this scenario, although Brown and McGraw would appear to have been the most direct conduit, Bubbles himself must have played a non-trivial role—both as "father" of their art and through his own example.

3

Buck and Bubbles's time in Chicago was rich and profitable in just about every way—professionally, financially, socially, emotionally. But by April, Nazarro had discovered their whereabouts and extended the injunction to include the Windy City. Forming a plan to evade further detection, Bubbles asked William Morris to send them on the road. Morris booked a tour across the eastern United States. They arrived in Cleveland in late April, then after a couple of weeks moved on to the little town of Marion, Ohio, population thirty thousand. The good citizens of Marion were thrilled to receive the attentions of a big-time vaudeville act. The last week of May the local paper issued a friendly reminder: "Buck and Bubbles Held Over by Popular Demand!! The two most legitimate and pleasing entertainers ever appearing in Marion. Last opportunity to see Buck and Bubbles."

The team continued its tour all the way to Boston, where they got a note from the Sunset asking them to come back and perform again. Injunction or no injunction, they were happy to return to Chicago. Earlier in the year Buck and Bubbles had grown sweet on two chorus girls at the Sunset, Amber "Flash" Vincson and Viola Sullinger. Bubbles was alarmed, though, by how serious Buck suddenly seemed to be about his girlfriend. Within a few weeks he was talking marriage—and Bubbles didn't like it: "Flash had a lot of interest in Buck's future, and she never really understood that Buck and I were a team. Whatever he did would affect me, and whatever I did would have an effect on him. Whatever either one of us did would have an effect on the act. And that was the most important thing to me. It was to Buck, too, but he never realized it."

Of course, Bubbles himself had wanted to get married not too long ago. Yet now, with Buck and Flash, it was different. "I tried to tell her that she shouldn't marry him at that time," he said. "I told her that Buck didn't have any money, and that I didn't either. I thought it would be better for them to wait." But they got married anyway, and this provoked Bubbles to follow suit—for a truly frivolous reason. "It threw things out of balance," he said, "and it put more weight on his end of the expenses. I felt that Buck being married would be part of my expense. So I got married [too]. I got married so I'd have the same excuse he had for expenses." Buck married Flash Vincson in a "secret wedding" on August 23, 1927 (Flash's birthday), and Bubbles married Viola Sullinger four days later, on August 27. Buck's reception was held at the Nest Club, where Louis Armstrong, Jimmie Noone, and others "really had a jam session."

Bubbles with his first wife, Viola Sullinger, around the time of their courtship, winter 1927.

Source: L. Tom Perry Special Collections, Harold B. Lee Library, Brigham Young University, Provo, Utah.

Bubbles was right: Things would never be the same again. Since arriving in New York in 1920 Buck and Bubbles had been inseparable, sharing the same room, the same trunk, the same money supply, the same work schedule, the same leisure activities. Through good times and bad, they had comforted and confided in one another. Their loyalty was unshakable. "He was closer than a brother to me," Bubbles said. "I felt he was closer."

> We could understand each other. We had a whistle that we crossed to each other, know the whistle, you know. It was good. We would call each other Mike. He never called me Bubbles. I never called him Buck. I called him Mike. Oh, we were two, we were two—I don't think there's any other two Negroes in the world like Buck and Bubbles—no other two, uh-uh, impossible.

But now, that loyalty was divided. Flash would tell Buck that Bubbles wanted to be "better" than him. She said Bubbles was "jealous" of her. The gap would widen with time.

Back in Chicago, Bubbles remembered, they watched newsreels of the ticker tape parade welcoming Charles Lindbergh home from his transatlantic voyage. It was emblematic of their own solo flight, which was also coming to an end. William Morris eventually heard about Nazarro's contract and dropped them as clients. They couldn't work in Chicago theaters because of the injunction, and they couldn't go on the road again without an agent managing their bookings. They had been making a lot of money, but without more work it would soon run out. Knowing he had them cornered, Nazarro sent an olive branch from New York. He had just signed them up, he said, to appear in a new Broadway show called *Weather Clear—Track Fast*, starring famous monologist Joe Laurie Jr. If they would just come home, they could work everything out. Bubbles thought about it. He knew they had another year on their contract. They could go back to Nazarro and when their contract expired move permanently to William Morris. With no other options, he and Buck caught a train back to New York.

8

Alone

1

Buck and Bubbles's first gig after returning to New York, a horse-racing drama called *Weather Clear—Track Fast*, turned out to be a dud. Burdened by a weak story and financial troubles, the show barely lasted a few months, and Buck and Bubbles left in December. Having played a somewhat arbitrary function, popping up in the second act "apropos of nothing in particular," they nevertheless stole the show with their unrelated vaudeville antics. According to writer George Seibel, Buck and Bubbles "showed that they had more magnetism than Willard Mack's melodrama or [headliner] Joe Laurie's comedy work." More significantly for their future careers, *Weather Clear— Track Fast* provided their first opportunity to shine in "legitimate theater." For the first time they were listed separately in the cast, with their own stage names: "Joe Buck" played the role of Chicken Man, and "Jim Bubbles" played Baltimore Sleeper. "Buck and Bubbles can act with the most unusual naturalness for negroes on the stage," wrote one critic. "They are a certain 'find' for the legitimate."

In January 1928, Buck and Bubbles began a tour of the Loew circuit. Things were different now, though. Although being forced to return to Nazarro was a big defeat, Buck and Bubbles soon realized they possessed considerable leverage—and they used it to extract major concessions. First, within a year Nazarro would dramatically reduce his share of the act's income. Second, they no longer appeared under his name; they would have the chance to become headliners in their own right. Finally, they enjoyed freedom of mobility, traveling alone instead of under Nazarro's watchful eye. Rather than taking the train, they now drove from one performance to the next, often with their wives, in two separate cars.

For an engagement at Loew's State, with Nazarro no longer part of the act they were given the No. 2 spot, "the graveyard," where most Black acts spent their entire careers but where Buck and Bubbles, as far as is known, had never appeared before. Yet even from this lonely outpost they "stopped

Sportin' Life. Brian Harker, Oxford University Press. © Oxford University Press 2022.
DOI: 10.1093/oso/9780197514511.003.0009

the show after making every gag . . . register a 100 per cent score for laughs." Someone was impressed. By the end of the month, they had "won themselves a warm spot in the heart of the Loew booking office. As a result the pair will be featured over the circuit's houses." And featured they were—as "principal headliners," wrote the *New York Herald Tribune*. A new kind of tribute began rising out of the entertainment pages: In reviews of other acts, critics noted that some performers were imitating the jokes and dance steps of Buck and Bubbles. They were becoming popular enough to merit the ultimate show business compliment: being ripped off.

After hours, however, the old conflicts continued. For his $20,000 suit against Buck and Bubbles—which despite his peace overture he had *not* dropped—Nazarro won damages of only $1,100, not even enough to pay his legal bills, which he accordingly ignored. Eventually his lawyers' patience ran out, and in July 1928 they won a judgment against Nazarro for $2,500, and against Buck and Bubbles (as garnishment of wages) for the $1,100 they still owed their manager. While the team was performing in Chicago, a judge called them in and asked why they hadn't paid the money. They concocted a story for the judge, who found them in contempt for lying and sentenced them to six months in jail. Fortunately, some show business friends interceded on their behalf and persuaded the judge to show leniency. He gave them six months' probation, with orders to check in every week. On September 13 they finally paid the $1,100. But they were not about to sit around Chicago while they had a full tour schedule awaiting them. Besides, they had a very important engagement coming up in New York.

2

The fall season of 1928 was supposed to launch a "new era" in vaudeville. For years the Keith organization had been plotting its revenge against the upstart Loew, which by 1926 had nearly doubled the profits of Keith and Orpheum combined. In early 1928, after months of negotiations, Keith and Orpheum merged to form a mega-circuit: Keith-Albee-Orpheum. The new circuit would connect the theater chain of the East Coast with that of the West and—it was hoped—strangle the life out of Loew. But it was vital to roll out the merger with commensurate ballyhoo. Publicity notices went out. The matinee on Monday, September 17, at Keith's flagship theater, the New York Palace, they said, would mark "the opening of the 1928–'29 vaudeville season" and inaugurate "the nation-wide 'New Era' celebration sponsored by the Keith-Albee-Orpheum Circuit."

The bill was carefully designed to suit the loftiness of the occasion. There would be two headliners: Louise Groody, a musical comedy star famous for introducing the hit song "Tea for Two"; and Lucille La Verne, a grande dame of the stage best known today as the voice of the wicked queen in Walt Disney's *Snow White and the Seven Dwarfs*. In addition, the show would feature Frank Gaby, ventriloquist; Gaston and Andre, a man-and-woman gymnastic act; Arthur Petley and Co., acrobatics and aerials; Loma Worth, a one-woman-jazz band; Elsie Pilcer and Co., ballroom dancers—and Buck and Bubbles. The latter were spotted fourth, to be followed by La Verne, then Groody, then Gaby, next-to-closing. With all the newspapers watching, the stakes were high. Nazarro published an ad announcing Buck and Bubbles's true coming out. The Palace date, he fibbed, would be their "first appearance alone."

When the reviews came in, it was clear, even if politely framed, that the headliners had been overshadowed by another act. Despite worthy efforts by Groody and La Verne, the *New York Herald Tribune* wrote, "yesterday's matinee audience devoted much of its enthusiasm to a pair of Negro comedians, billed as Buck and Bubbles. . . . [who] won their audience completely with their casual humor, relieved by some remarkably fine dancing." Likewise *Variety*: "Despite the pomp and eclat surrounding the star attractions, Buck and Bubbles, colored boys, stopped things cold with songs, dances, foolery and stepping." Likewise *Billboard*: "Buck and Bubbles . . . were a sensation. . . . These boys, who have played everything Loew could give them, hit a homer both from the angle of laughs and applause." The most remarkable and insightful review appeared in the *Wall Street Journal*:

> With the opening of a new vaudeville season this week, the Keith-Albee-Orpheum Corp. is conducting an extensive national campaign in celebration of what it terms the "new era" in vaudeville. . . . The performance of the young negro team known as Buck & Bubbles in the present bill at the Palace in itself is worth a considerable campaign. Their foot work, the work of one of them at the piano, and their humor make them an exciting addition to our national supply of entertainment. . . . Their humor is delightfully native to them so that in its originality it has ease and warmth. It is in their feet and in their minds and on their finger tips. Their performance is breath-taking too in its skill. The taller boy of the two appears to depend considerably in

his dancing on the whimsical effect of the other's fingering at the piano. . . . Their talent is creative.

Buck and Bubbles's victory brought happy consequences. Most strikingly (though it may seem a small thing today), they were invited to return for a second week at the Palace—the only act on the bill to be so honored. To be held over for a second week was unusual at any theater, but especially at the Palace, and even more especially for a Black act. Black newspapers insisted it was unprecedented. "First time a colored act ever played at the Palace Theatre two weeks straight," crowed the *Pittsburgh Courier*. Keith-Albee-Orpheum offered a three-year-contract to Buck and Bubbles, guaranteeing them thirty weeks annually, with $750 a week the first year, $850 the second, and $900 the third. They signed, and with so much to lose, Bubbles had his ankles insured for $50,000.

Around the same time, they signed another contract, one that brought no joy. With their obligation to Nazarro coming to an end, Buck and Bubbles were determined to switch representation to William Morris. But Nazarro outfoxed them. Arranging to talk to Buck alone, without Bubbles around, he explained all the reasons why Buck should sign a new three-year contract. He played on his emotions. He played on his nerves. And when Buck went home, he got more of the same from Flash, who wanted the security of a known quantity. Under intense pressure from both sides, Buck caved. Without telling Bubbles, he signed—and their plan to be free of Nazarro died. When Bubbles found out, he was devastated. After dithering for a while, though, he signed too. He felt he had no choice. "If I didn't sign with him," he said, "then Buck and I would have had to split up. I didn't want that."

The new contract, dated September 28, 1928, essentially divided the act's income three ways, with Buck, Bubbles, and Nazarro each getting $250 a week for the first year. This represented a big improvement on their previous arrangement, but Nazarro's cut still far exceeded the industry standard of 5 percent. He justified it by claiming he would be not only the team's agent but also their personal representative, manager, and even their attorney (though he had no law degree). He would pay all their transportation costs and provide office space, free of charge, that they could use whenever they returned to New York. Moreover, it was understood, he would continue to help them out of financial jams as he had done in the past. There was, for instance, the time he bailed Bubbles out of jail after the dancer hit a pedestrian with Nazarro's car. And the time, by Bubbles's own admission, when Nazarro bribed a police chief after Bubbles was arrested during a brawl at Small's Paradise. No question: Buck and Bubbles were an expensive investment. But 33 percent was a lot to take.

Even more troubling was Nazarro's tendency to control, demean, and manipulate. To maintain the upper hand, he maliciously used race to drive a wedge between his prize employees. He'd say, "Buck, Bubbles said he didn't like working with you anymore because you're blacker than he is." Or: "Bubbles, Buck thinks you act smart about not being as black as he is, and he's going to quit you." Bubbles thought Nazarro was trying to keep the team from getting too big, for fear he'd lose them. And so he found subtle ways to undermine them. "He'd . . . plant bad reviews in the newspapers . . . [or] he'd forget . . . to get our publicity pictures in the papers." Worst of all, whatever the contract said, Bubbles was convinced he cheated them:

> He made all of the deals, and we never really knew just how much he was charging' for our act. He'd tell us one price, and then he'd take twice that for himself. On top of that, he kept us broke. Then we'd have to borrow money from him. Then he'd take the repay out of the pay we made at the theater, and usually there wasn't anything left, and we'd have to be borrowin' from him again.

"He kept us broke" sounds like a copout, as though Bubbles were blaming Nazarro for his own financial failures. But as Bubbles reminded Nazarro years later, "*You* taught me to borrow." When the boys first arrived in New York, Nazarro took advantage of their youth and country naivete, encouraging them to spend their newly acquired riches and teaching them to borrow—from him—to pay for it. That way they would always be in his debt and, crucially, unable to leave him. In the South they had a name for this sort of shell game: sharecropping. Bubbles resented it, and made up his mind that eventually he would find a way to escape. For now, though, he would just have to make the best of a bad situation.

Since performing without Nazarro, *Variety* declared in November, "Buck and Bubbles have become the best colored two-act on the white stage." Given the team's recent success, one might have expected Keith-Orpheum to send them on the road as headliners, just as Loew had done the previous year. But the vagaries of institutionalized racism, it seems clear in hindsight, intervened to prevent that from happening, for the first time putting the brakes on their rapidly burgeoning ascent. Instead, they were assigned to a traveling show headed by a singer and comedienne named Frances White. The tour would follow the old Orpheum route, heading west toward California.

Frances White had made her name during World War I by dressing as a child and singing the novelty song, "M-I-S-S-I-S-S-I-P-P-I." By the Orpheum tour she was still doing her nursery routine but now added adult characterizations to her repertoire. Yet her efforts, though applauded, did not live up to her billing. In February 1929 the troupe arrived in Los Angeles, where in a by now familiar pattern Buck and Bubbles were proclaimed "the hit of the bill" at the Orpheum Theatre, bringing out "one of the most tremendous hands ever heard here." "The pair casts a spell over an audience that some critics have called 'hypnotic,' " wrote the *Times*. Another reviewer was slyer: "Buck and Bubbles, mind you, are no sensations. It was just this: an audience which sincerely wanted to find somebody worth getting excited about, and wasn't making out any too well, reached a point of spontaneous combustion just about the time Buck and Bubbles came on to play the piano and to dance."

The pattern continued into the summer, even after Frances White had left the troupe. Reviewing another show at the Orpheum, this headed by Gus Arnheim, famous bandleader of the Cocoanut Grove Orchestra at the Ambassador Hotel, a *Times* critic dropped the dispassionate tone so assiduously cultivated by others of his trade: "In contrast to the color, harmony and glitter of the other offerings, however, it takes two lads of somber black to bring all activity to a standstill while they strut their stuff. Right the first time! Who else but Buck and Bubbles? Here are two real entertainers. . . . They could easily carry a show by themselves." In a reprise of September, the team was held over for a second week.

Buck and Bubbles loved California, and California loved them. In March, an admiring reporter published a rare glimpse of the team after hours:

Two very interesting lads are Buck and Bubbles. They are two happy-go-lucky chaps with a world of unaffected personality, and, oh, how they can dance, and, oh, how the audience tells them so. They have a wonderful act and spare no effort to please. Once their work is done, they are usually off on their tour of seeing California, as they are automobile fiends. It is a custom here for visitors to indulge in a "You Drive Yourself" car and one car was not enough for these boys. They commandeered one each and the beaches, studios and mountains have all had visits from these nimble lads.

They exude sunshine, and life to them seems one glad song, which is reflected in their work.

Many years later Bubbles confirmed the spirit of this report. "It must have
been sort of difficult traveling on the road all the time," offered an interviewer.
"It was nice," Bubbles replied. "It wasn't difficult. Nice."
"Why do you say that?"
"'Cause it was a pleasure. See the scenery, too. It was nice."

3

Successful though the Orpheum tour had been, it was only a prelude to Buck
and Bubbles's true purpose in California: to make movies. For all the fanfare, Keith's "new era" in vaudeville had turned out to be nothing more than
extremely wishful thinking, a last-ditch effort to preserve the old system.
With the popularity of Al Jolson's *The Jazz Singer* and the advent of "talking
pictures," such delusions were no longer possible. Barely a month after the
"new era" celebration in September, Keith-Albee-Orpheum had been sub-
sumed into yet another merger, becoming Radio-Keith-Orpheum (RKO),
a company prioritizing motion pictures over vaudeville. As one era passed
to another, a single question remained: Which vaudevillians would have the
requisite magnetism to make the transition to film?

The year 1929 was the big one for talkies, yielding the first fully synchro-
nized movies by John Barrymore, Clara Bow, Eddie Cantor, and the Marx
Brothers. Surprisingly, it looked like Black actors might benefit even more
than whites. The introduction of sound seemed ideally designed to capture Blacks' "native" strengths in singing, dancing, and comedy. "No sooner
had talkies come into vogue," writes film historian Donald Bogle, "than
two major studios, Fox Pictures and MGM . . . set out to put all that ole-
time natchel rhythm on dazzling display." The result was two early classics
of Black cinema: *Hearts in Dixie* and *Hallelujah*. Almost simultaneous with
the making of these films, Nazarro ushered Buck and Bubbles into the Pathé
Studio in Culver City, where the team completed six comedy two-reelers
in May.

The material for these films was taken from short stories published by
Hugh Wiley in the *Saturday Evening Post*. Better known today for his stories
about Mr. Wong, Chinese-American detective, Wiley began his career

imagining the lives of a different ethnic group—American Blacks. In the *Post* series (whose racist trappings won it a spot in a registry of "late Jim Crow-era literature"), a peripatetic young Black man named Wildcat Marsden "is yanked by Lady Luck and pushed by Old Man Trouble." Pathé cast Bubbles as Wildcat and Buck as his comic sidekick Demmy in adaptations of six Wiley stories: *Black Narcissus, Fowl Play, High Toned, Honest Crooks, In and Out,* and *Darktown Follies.* Scenarios included, for example, Wildcat fending off the advances of a two-time widow; the two friends finding a mysterious black bag in a haystack; and the police locking them up for a crime they didn't commit.

These were "race movies"—all-Black films (or nearly so) marketed principally to African American audiences. "The first thing I did," Bubbles recalled, "was to scout up the people who were going to be in the movie with Buck and me. I went down to Central Avenue," the main drag in L.A.'s Black district, "and I picked up all the people I thought would have character. . . . I got all

Wildcat and Demmy (Buck and Bubbles), Pathé's *Fowl Play,* 1929.
Source: Kurt Albert.

of them to come to the studio, and I loaded Pathé Studios down with people from Central Avenue."

Watching the filmmaking from the sidelines, Nat Nazarro wasn't impressed. He pulled Bubbles aside and asked him to tell the producer he wanted to be directed by Nazarro. Bubbles complied, to his later regret. The job of directing *In and Out* and *Darktown Follies* fell to Nazarro, who had never directed films before. Evidently determined to break some kind of production speed record, Nazarro made one film in twenty-six hours without a break, starting at 9 a.m. and finishing at 11 the next morning. To keep his actors awake, Nazarro plied them with whiskey. "Nat brought it in in a flask," Bubbles said, "and he poured it down Buck and me. . . . If one of us even looked like we were getting drowsy, here he'd come with the flask."

Later, Bubbles was incensed to discover Nazarro's reason for wanting to direct: For each film he got an extra $1,250 which he kept for himself. "That did it," he said. "I decided not to go to Nat to tell him he was a thief or a liar. I just decided to get at him in my own way. I decided to make myself unreliable. . . . I started drinking. I drank enough so that when I went on to do the work in the movie I couldn't stand up or talk."

How much this offstage drama affected the quality of the films is hard to say. The record shows only that early reviews were positive while later ones were more mixed. When the first film, *Black Narcissus*, came out, *Variety* applauded: "This short convinces that Buck and Bubbles are a bet. . . . Will hold up in any house." Even more enthusiastically, *Billboard* predicted that the film "will rank along with anything Laurel and Hardy have ever done." The movie "gets a big hand from the audience on the fadeout of the two Negroes running down the road when the widow's husband comes in to break up the wedding." By contrast, *High Toned*, the only extant film of the series, was faulted for "mumbled dialog and a flop finish," criticisms hard to argue with. The critics' biggest complaint, applying to all except *Darktown Follies*, lay in the movies' failure to showcase Buck and Bubbles's greatest strengths—their singing, dancing, and piano playing—a strange lapse, indeed, given the filmmakers' presumed purpose.

When *Hearts in Dixie* and *Hallelujah* came out, they won critical praise for their musical and dramatic power. But their box-office weakness dissuaded Hollywood moguls from their initial impulse to go big with Black talkies. Buck and Bubbles wouldn't appear in another Hollywood film again until 1937. In the meantime, white up-and-comers poured into the breach. One of them, an eighteen-year-old dancer and singer named Ginger Rogers, also made movies with Pathé in 1929. A year later she signed a seven-year contract with Paramount Pictures.

4

After the sunshine of the California tour, Buck and Bubbles entered a long period of storm and conflict. Some of their suffering was self-inflicted, but most stemmed from Nazarro's financial chicanery and mismanagement. It began with a stopover in Davenport, Iowa, where Buck came up short for his hotel bill. Flummoxed, he left his wife Flash as security on the hotel. From Madison, Wisconsin, he wired Nazarro in New York for an advance on his salary, then went back to Davenport and got his wife out of hock. This did not solve the team's money problems. According to *Variety* (which spoke with the Keith office), "Buck and Bubbles' salary has been mysteriously eaten up before conclusion of the dates played."

More trouble awaited them in Chicago, where Nazarro's former attorneys tried to garnish more of Buck and Bubbles's wages, this time for $1,464.12. This amount represented the difference between $2,500, the lawyers' original claim against Nazarro, and the $1,100 paid by Buck and Bubbles the previous year, plus accrued interest. It was Nazarro who owed the money, but since his income flowed from the earnings of his famous two-act, Buck and Bubbles became the attorneys' actual target. They stoutly resisted making payment, denying through their attorney "that the same [is] equitably due the plaintiffs."

The setbacks continued in August. While playing the Chicago Palace, they were suddenly yanked from the bill midweek and thrown in jail. The judge who had suspended their contempt sentence the previous year had heard they were in town, and saw his chance to sanction them for violating their probation. After two days RKO secured their release on a writ of habeus corpus, but two weeks later the judge jailed them again. He was sorry to do it, he said. He told Buck and Bubbles (according to a possibly embellished report by the *Chicago Defender*) that they "were the most accomplished comedians of the twentieth century," and that "they had been taken advantage of and persecuted by Jews because of their ability." He hoped that "after serving the contempt sentence, in lieu of paying their hard-earned money [to Nazarro or his attorneys], the pair [would] have the chance to sue civilly their white contractors." After the Keith office put up a $1,600 bond, Buck and Bubbles were released.

These adversities were but foreshocks of the coming earthquake—the stock market crash on October 29, 1929. Three days later, Nat Nazarro filed for bankruptcy. Owing $8,728 to his various creditors, he was forced to sell his belongings for pennies on the dollar at public auction. He moved quickly to protect his most precious possession, his contract with Buck and Bubbles, by transferring the title to his elderly mother. But the courts dismantled Nazarro's little artifice, and the contract was put up for sale along with every-thing else. Jacob Markus, co-owner of the Hotel Stanley and Nazarro's most aggressive creditor, bought the contract for a paltry $250. A month later he also bought Buck and Bubbles's RKO contract for $1,000. Stunned by his good fortune, he immediately set about ensuring the profitability of his new acquisition.

Nazarro, however, was not a man to be put off by mere legal formalities. Employing his standard MO of maximal defiance and intimidation, he plowed ahead as if nothing had happened. Three days after the auction, he went to the manager of the Capitol Theatre in Union City, New Jersey, and, still claiming to be Buck and Bubbles's manager, demanded payment for the team's performance that week. The manager refused, having already heard from the Keith office about the change of ownership on the contract. The next day Nazarro demanded payment for the same job from RKO attorney Robert Broder. Again, he was refused. Beating a strategic retreat, Nazarro tried a new angle, suggesting to Broder that Buck and Bubbles at least be paid the $600 they had coming to them. The agent's commission could be withheld until the claims of Nazarro and Markus were sorted out. Uncertain who really had the better claim, given Nazarro's unusual history with the team, Broder agreed.

Nazarro's apparent good faith, however, was just a distraction. Knowing he couldn't personally book the team anymore given the widespread know-ledge of his bankruptcy, he used William Morris as an intermediary to set up a job at the Scollay Square Theatre in Boston. When Broder found out, he notified Morris about RKO's continuing contract, and the theater manager in Boston stopped Buck and Bubbles from going onstage. Nazarro then turned to a different agency, Lyons and Lyons, and booked a job at Fox's Academy Theatre in New York. Frantically trying to catch up with Nazarro's relentless machinations, Jacob Markus paid a late-night visit to Lyons and Lyons and told them emphatically that he had not given his consent for these non-RKO engagements. Meanwhile, Bubbles met with Rosalie Stewart, manager of RKO radio, and requested payment for a broadcast Buck and Bubbles had completed the week before. She refused, indicating the money was "now in the possession of Broder awaiting the disposition of the court as to its [rightful] ownership."

Buck and Bubbles had had enough. As much as they despised Nazarro and wanted to be free of him, the prospect of working for Markus was even less appealing. As a fellow professional, Nazarro at least inspired a grudging respect. Markus was nothing more than a callow parvenu, a hotel man with a piece of paper in his hand. The idea of sharing with him a third of their income boiled their blood. Moreover, they were tired of being jerked this way and that by outside parties. Through no fault of their own, they were being denied the basic right of earning a living. Did they not have a say in their own fate?

With the disposition of the contract seemingly headed for the courts, Buck and Bubbles lunged for their freedom. On February 27, 1930, they filed an injunction against interference on "about everybody," as *Variety* put it: Louis H. Saper [trustee of Nazarro's estate], Jacob H. Markus, Radio-Keith-Orpheum Vaudeville Exchange, Inc., Nat Nazarro, William Morris Theatrical Exchange, Inc., Paul Dempsey [an agent for RKO], and even Nazarro's harmless old mother, Yetta Davis. "Each of these defendants," their attorney charged, "wrongfully, unlawfully, fraudulently, and maliciously are preventing plaintiffs from earning a livelihood."

Buck and Bubbles "are both colored men," he continued plaintively. Unschooled and inexperienced, they offered a ready mark for predatory patrons. Disturbingly, all this fighting over who owned the contract with Buck and Bubbles seemed, in practice, little different from the question of who "owned" the men themselves. The attorney's language is melodramatic and patronizing to his clients, but his argument goes to the heart of the case:

> Under the contract they became servants of Nazarro. Their sense of self-volition was entirely destroyed. . . . They were in financial difficulties at the time of the signing of the said agreement and . . . Nazarro told them if they did not sign the contract he would not help them out of their financial difficulties. . . . They are unbusinesslike; they are children in the hands of a smart, ingenious man as Nazarro proved to be. . . . At one time in their lives [they may have believed] they had been emancipated, but their present theatrical slavery is being used as a shuttlecock to satisfy the vindictiveness,

enmity and animosity between the said Markus, who now claims to be their master, and Nazarro.

The only just remedy, he concluded, was to declare both contracts—with Nazarro/Markus and with RKO—null and void and allow the actors to start afresh.

As the affidavits and depositions rolled in, the entrenched powers asserted their prerogatives. Finally (and predictably), the New York Supreme Court pronounced the contracts ironclad and denied the injunction. Buck and Bubbles now turned to their only hope for relief from the constant turmoil. Markus found out about it when he stopped by the team's dressing room to discuss matters "relative to their future work." Bubbles told him they would be leaving the country soon to play a two-week engagement at the Palladium Theatre in London, a booking arranged by Lyons and Lyons. An apoplectic Markus positively forbade them from going, pointing out that he had no financial interests in England and that the pair would be defaulting on RKO engagements already scheduled in the United States. Laughing, Bubbles declared that they would go to England nevertheless, and, turning to Markus, that "you could do what you damn please." (This bon mot so scandalized the hotelier that he produced an eyewitness to swear to it in an affidavit.) Markus filed an injunction to prevent Buck and Bubbles from leaving, but this time the court denied his request. On Friday, April 25, the two actors sailed for England, their first trip out of the country, on the S.S. Europa.

5

Then as now, London was one of earth's great capitals, and in the realm of entertainment the Palladium was the city's crown jewel. All through the twentieth century the Palladium, with its lofty neoclassical façade, discriminating audiences, and 2,300 seating capacity, challenged and sometimes terrified visiting American artists, from Danny Kaye to Judy Garland, and from Ella Fitzgerald to Bob Hope. By the time Buck and Bubbles opened the week of May 5, 1930, Nat Nazarro had been negotiating for their appearance for two years.

The team appeared on a bill with at least six other acts, including a troupe of Russian singers and dancers, a trick cyclist, a ventriloquist, an opera singer, and the house staple, the Palladium Girls. All very familiar. What the duo did not anticipate was the degree to which their American jokes might not fully "translate" with an English audience. This cultural misfire is alluded to in the first review of their act, in the British publication *The Stage*:

> Buck and Bubbles, a coloured couple from America who make their first appearance in England here this week, offer an act that is distinctly American and different from most already seen here. As a consequence it may be some time before an average English audience "gets" them. Thus it was Monday, but after a quiet opening they soon had the audience laughing at their quaint dialogue and unconventional methods, and applauding some particularly smart tap dancing, while the behaviour of the gum-chewing pianist with an expansive smile caused further laughter.

Bubbles later claimed they had to modify their act to match the British sense of humor. This was tricky to do on the fly, "'cause by the time you try to get the gags to fit the personalities, you could starve to death."

Despite these challenges, the pair ultimately seem to have won their usual bonanza of audience affection. "Buck and Bubbles made their English debut at the Palladium Monday," reported *Billboard*, "going over big with a colored act of a type new to English audiences." The following week they shared the bill with headliner Gracie Fields, a house favorite, repeating "the great success they made on their first appearance here last week."

One of the Palladium reviews stood out from the others. Writing for the British jazz magazine, *Melody Maker*, the critic took the point of view not of the typical music hall enthusiast but of what he termed the "average rhythm fan," meaning the ardent admirer of American jazz that had sprung up in Great Britain in the last few years. Rhythm fans, also known as "hot collectors" for their habit of collecting "hot" jazz records, were looking for more than entertainment in a musical experience. Like their counterparts in classical music, they wanted artistic transcendence. Thus, it was notable that the *Melody Maker* reviewer gave thumbs up to Buck and Bubbles, despite their obvious role as entertainers and comedians. Comparing Buck's piano playing to that of Earl Hines, he went so far as to suggest that some elements of their routine might actually be beyond the comprehension of the uninitiated:

> Londoners witnessed a new type of variety turn recently when "Buck and Bubbles," a coloured duo from the States, put over their act at the

Palladium. One of these performers is an excellent dancer and something of a vocalist. . . . His partner is a vocalist, a fine humorist, and a pianist almost of the Earl Hines degree, all rolled into one, so that it may be taken for granted that their show was of a kind to appeal very thoroughly to the musician, even if parts of it were probably not appreciated by an ordinary cosmopolitan audience. Both the boys indulge in some amusing and excellent "scat" singing, and although their turn is really primarily a humorous one, it contains, as already stated, material which will be found extremely palatable by the average rhythm "fan."

By shifting the focus from the team's vaudeville appeal to their jazz artistry, the critic anticipated developments of the 1930s and beyond.

After the Palladium, Buck and Bubbles played two weeks at the Holborn Empire. One night after the show, a wealthy socialite came backstage looking for Bubbles. She found him down on his knees, concentrating so fiercely on a game of dice he was playing with the stagehands that he didn't notice her until Buck interrupted him. The woman introduced herself and invited Buck and Bubbles to perform for a private party. Bubbles, figuring such a job wouldn't be worth their time, made some excuse and immediately returned to his game. "And the first roll I tried," he lamented later, "was craps. [The dice] had cooled off while I was talkin' to the lady." By the way, he asked one of the stage hands, who was she? "One of the richest ladies in the whole of England!" he exclaimed in disbelief.

Buck and Bubbles returned to the United States after a bit more than a month, arriving in New York on June 4 aboard the S.S. Majestic. They disembarked to find themselves once more enveloped in tumult. Buck and Bubbles kept "attempting to break away from Marcus and the big cut he's getting out of the act's salary," Markus kept insisting they dance to his tune, and Nat Nazarro kept flailing away from the sidelines. Finally, RKO pulled the plug. In July the circuit canceled the team's contract "on grounds that [they] have been more trouble . . . than they are worth." At this point, an exhausted Markus also surrendered, agreeing at last to arbitration before the Vaudeville Managers Association. Within two days a settlement was reached whereby Markus would give up Buck and Bubbles in return for Nazarro's payment of $2,250 (at the rate of $125 a week). Nazarro returned to his place at the helm, Markus returned to his hotel business, and Buck and Bubbles returned to the devil they knew.

But the extraordinary drama that had played out over the last two years should not be overlooked. Under contract to RKO the team was repeatedly denied headliner status, even though critics and audiences gave them top honors everywhere they went—and even though, when it appeared they might break their contracts, a battle royal played out for six months as managers, agents, theaters, and circuits used all the considerable legal means at their disposal to prevent this from happening. This was no ordinary act. And for Buck and Bubbles, the disconnect between talent and rewards was never more stark.

9

Dreams Fulfilled

1

In 1928, fifty-year-old Bill Robinson got the break he had been waiting for all his life. Although he had long prospered on the Keith circuit, often performing next-to-closing, he rarely worked as a headliner. And while critics praised his dancing, outside vaudeville he was virtually unknown to white audiences. Then an all-Black show called *Blackbirds of 1928* opened to lukewarm reviews. Desperate to inject some show-stopping life into his pet project, impresario Lew Leslie hired Bojangles as a special "extra attraction." Robinson's presence transformed the entire production. Weekly grosses jumped from $9,000 to $27,000. The show became the biggest Black hit since *Shuffle Along*, running for 518 performances (and introducing the McHugh-Fields classic, "I Can't Give You Anything But Love, Baby"). And Robinson, all of a sudden, became the toast of Broadway.

In the show, he performed his standard vaudeville routine, complete with his trademark Stair Dance. But now, for the first time, critics started paying close attention to his feet. Robinson encouraged their scrutiny by watching them himself. "He croons with his feet and laughs with them and watches them in wide-eyed amazement," wrote one reporter, "as they do things which apparently surprise him as much as they do the rest of us and please him, if possible, even more." With this seemingly innocent act of showmanship, Robinson began the process of educating critics in the subtleties of tap. They started to notice small differences in technique, and to compare individual dancers more discerningly. "After they had seen Robinson a few times," wrote the Stearnses, "the competence of drama critics reviewing tap dance improved noticeably." The same was true of vaudeville critics. Within a short time, they started publishing the first critical appraisals of Bubbles vis-à-vis his peers.

It began about a year after the opening of *Blackbirds*. Reviewing one of Buck and Bubbles's shows at the Los Angeles Orpheum, a *Variety* critic made a new but increasingly common claim—that the team "principally reaped

Sportin' Life. Brian Harker, Oxford University Press. © Oxford University Press 2022.
DOI: 10.1093/oso/9780197514511.003.0010

[applause] on Bubbles's taps." From there he went straight for the Robinson comparison:

> Bubbles is now on the short end of a six to five wager when coupled in conversation with Bill Robinson, and many are willing to take even money if it comes to a contest. Don't ever doubt that this lad has become one of the top hoofers of the country with not more than three equals. . . . Bubbles' syncopated rhythmic taps did nothing except tear this assemblage apart.

A week later another reporter stated that "Bubbles rates with the best tapsters, colored or white." A month after that, a third critic reviewed a bill at the Chicago Palace headed by white tap-dancing star Jack Donahue, who appeared next-to-closing. Buck and Bubbles "stopped the show cold without even exerting themselves," he wrote. Bubbles, in particular, "set a pace that had Donahue going the limit later on to substantiate his rightful claim as one of the best dancers of his kind." Despite the critic's pro forma defense of the headliner, he couldn't resist continuing with the comparison du jour: "Bubbles particularly cycloned with his double and triple taps that puts him down as Bill Robinson's only near rival. And when talking of Robinson's contemporary imitators, they can start counting from this chocolate kid, too."

Exactly *how* Bubbles differed from Robinson and others was rarely explained. Perhaps it took a fellow dancer to tackle the topic. In 1931 the *New York Herald Tribune* issued a lengthy profile of Johnny Boyle, tap dancer and choreographer for James Cagney, who voiced an opinion that tracks closely with the judgment of history—at least with respect to Bubbles:

> It's impossible to say who is the one best tap dancer in the game today. . . . In any list of outstanding dancers you couldn't possibly leave out Will Mahoney, or Bubbles of Buck and Bubbles, or Harland Dixon. They're all great hoofers. But they all rely on different things. Bill Robinson is probably the greatest showman of them all. . . . On the other hand, Bubbles, perhaps, does more difficult steps. Fred Astaire is great on syncopation. And Will Mahoney . . . always introduces a lot of comedy into his act—comedy and novelty stunts, like dancing on a xylophone.

It's helpful to know that by this time Bubbles had made the pantheon of great hoofers, and that others regarded him as a master of the difficult step. At

the same time (full disclosure), the preceding transcript contains an unauthorized correction of the original article: Boyle did not know Bubbles well
enough to get his name right. Like many others, he assumed the first name of
Nazarro's famous two-act belonged to the tap-dancing member of the team,
whom he accordingly called "Buck." Despite Bubbles's high achievements, he
still labored in semi-anonymity.

As his stock rose in white circles, Bubbles maintained his Harlem reputation
as a fearsome gladiator, approaching each new tap challenge "with blood in
his eyes." Jazz clarinetist Mezz Mezzrow recalled a common scene: "Many's the
time some hoofer would be struttin' his stuff in the alley outside the Lafayette
Theater, with a crowd around him, and Bubbles would wander up and jump
in the circle and lay some hot iron that lowrated the guy, then walk off saying,
'Go home and wrastle with that one, Jim.'" With his heavy touring schedule
Bubbles only occasionally showed up at the Hoofers Club during this period,
and when he did, he often went to gamble. But, as he once admitted, competition gave meaning to his whole life. He did what was necessary to protect his
crown: "There's not a dancer who has been in New York—if he was colored—
that I haven't watched, and if he thought he could dance, we've had it out."

One glaring exception was his most obvious antagonist, Bill Robinson.
As Bubbles and Bojangles came to occupy a similar place of honor in the
tap hierarchy, their relationship evolved into one of cautious mutual respect.
Neither had any desire to face the other in combat. At one time Robinson,
who was old enough to be Bubbles's father, saw the younger man as a potential usurper. Like others before him (Eddie Rector, for instance), Bubbles
had had the temerity to imitate Bojangles's signature Stair Dance. Word got
around that Robinson was carrying his famous gold-plated pistol—and
looking for Bubbles. "We were playing at the McVickers Theater in Chicago,"
Bubbles recalled, "and I used a high stool."

> I'd put it down between the lip of the stage and the orchestra pit. I'd jump
> from the stage to the orchestra pit, and then I'd do my step on the rounds of
> the stool. Bill heard about this, and I heard about him lookin' for me with
> a gun. But he never found me. He found my partner. Then I started lookin'
> for him. I finally found him, and I explained how my dance . . . was dif-
> ferent from his staircase dance. . . . Rather than bein' mad any more, he just
> smiled and said, "Don't worry about it," and Bill Robinson and I became
> great friends.

Great friends, let's say, with a healthy degree of mutually suppressed rivalry. A clear recognition of their fundamental differences—in philosophy as well as style—probably saved them from the need to lock horns. They could spend their energies fighting off the constant incursions of the rising generation.

Bubbles's interactions with white dancers were very different—less adversarial, more accommodating. Following the code of deference expected of Black artists, he gave tips and private demonstrations to white dancers with a generosity he would never have bestowed on his fellow Harlemites. From the undifferentiated masses he tried to hold back his secrets as long as he could. "The other dancers would sit four deep in the front of the theatre at Loew's State watching me, trying to steal my steps," he said. "I changed my steps four times. I did each one four different ways so they couldn't catch it." But when circumstances brought him face to face with an individual white supplicant, he couldn't say no. A jaw-dropping example is when Bill Robinson brought eighteen-year-old white prodigy Hal Le Roy around to the Hoofers Club, possibly the only time a white dancer was ever admitted to the place. Bubbles had been Le Roy's same age when he was laughed out of the club ten years earlier. No one knew better than he the strict rules of seniority and the fiery trials required to gain any measure of respect. Now this same club was extending the royal treatment to a talented white novice. After an ostentatious "test" of Le Roy's skills, the club habitués crowded around to congratulate the young man, awarding him an honorary pin. Bubbles, supposedly flattered by Le Roy's execution of some of his characteristic steps, gave the boy a gift of metal taps.

Bubbles dispensed his knowledge to greater historical effect when he crossed paths with two future tap icons: Eleanor Powell and Fred Astaire. He met Powell in 1931 when a new singing sensation named Bing Crosby was completing an unprecedented ten weeks at New York's Paramount Theatre. For part of that time Crosby, as master-of-ceremonies, shared the bill with Buck and Bubbles. "At every performance" when Bubbles was onstage, Crosby recalled, "we had visiting dancers in the wings, who had dropped in from other vaudeville circuits or motion picture presentation houses, who came over to watch and learn. People like Eleanor Powell and Hal Le Roy." Eighteen-year-old Powell found the experience of rubbing shoulders with Bubbles galvanizing. "I think Bubbles is fantastic," she later told vaudeville historian Anthony Slide. "When Bubbles was on [at the Paramount], I'd be in the wings, on my stomach, watching his feet, and it got so he was playing to me, not to the audience. . . . And after the show we'd go down to the basement and knock our brains out jamming around."

By the late 1920s Fred Astaire had become a big fan of Bubbles. Early on he admired Bill Robinson, but later he became disillusioned, seeing Robinson as "a one-trick artist." The improvising Bubbles, by contrast, was "always new, always fresh." Astaire also knew that Bubbles had staked out a place at the far edge of tap complexity. If Astaire did pay him $400 for that legendary tap lesson in the fall of 1930—at the Ziegfeld Theatre, shortly after Buck and Bubbles returned from England—he probably consulted one of the few dancers qualified to teach him skills he had not already learned. All their lives Bubbles and Astaire tiptoed around the true nature of their relationship. For five decades Bubbles kept the secret of the Ziegfeld lesson bottled up, for fear of embarrassing his more celebrated counterpart. Then in 1978, perhaps fearing that his time for setting the record straight was running out, he told the story to tap historian Jane Goldberg and repeated it several more times before he died. For his part, Astaire spoke of Bubbles positively, but in bland generalities. He could never bring himself to admit publicly to the extent of his admiration. But in his autobiography Bing Crosby lifted the curtain to disclose feelings his friend had expressed only in private. Fred Astaire, he said, considered Bubbles "to be the greatest soft shoe, buck and wing, or tap dancer who ever lived."

2

When Bubbles returned from England in the summer of 1930, he was twenty-seven years old and nearing the height of his entertaining powers. He and Buck had returned to the United States to begin rehearsals for Lew Leslie's latest all-Black extravaganza, *Blackbirds of 1930*. For this show Leslie brought together the best talent he could find. Reassembling half the brain trust of *Shuffle Along*, he hired Eubie Blake to compose the songs (lyrics by Andy Razaf) and Flournoy Miller to write the book. To this foundation he added a stellar team of headliners: Ethel Waters, Flournoy Miller, The Berry Brothers, Jazz Lips Richardson, Buck and Bubbles, and Eubie Blake and His Blackbirds Orchestra. Lesser lights included holdovers from *Blackbirds of 1928* Mantan Moreland, Blue McAllister, and Jimmy Baskette, and gifted newcomers Neeka Shaw, Broadway Jones, and Minto Cato. "Never before in the history of the revue has Mr. Leslie corralled so many finished performers under one banner," wrote one reporter. From the Black perspective there were promising innovations in the story—"no crap game [or] ghost scene," for instance. The show introduced one of Blake's greatest songs, "Memories of You," as well as a new Harlem dance called the Lindy Hop.

According to the program for November 3, 1930, Bubbles appeared in six of the numbers, including one entitled "A Few Minutes with Buck and Bubbles," next-to-closing. His big feature was a love duet with Neeka Shaw, singing "Lucky to Me":

> *Whenever you're near*
> *All my fears disappear, dear,*
> *It's plain as can be*
> *You're lucky to me.*
>
> *My only luck charms*
> *Are your two loving arms,*
> *Anybody can see*
> *You're lucky to me.*

"It was a lovely number," Bubbles recalled. "And I . . . did a harmony to the song and we did a dance together to close the song off, which was very good, very good." Eubie Blake was so impressed by Bubbles's manifold talents that he gave him a lifelong nickname: "Mr. Showman." In view of Bill Robinson's breakout success in *Blackbirds of 1928*, Bubbles had reason to hope for a "Blackbirds" moment of his own.

Yet for some reason—the particular combination of ingredients that produce a hit is famously elusive—the show didn't catch on. The reviews of the out-of-town tryout were positive, especially in the Black press. "It is the fastest, funniest, and most tuneful revue ever presented," raved the *Pittsburgh Courier*, "and has the highest payroll of any colored show." But when it opened on Broadway on October 22, the tone changed. Somewhat churlishly, *Billboard* called it "a stale production made up of storage-worn drops from last year's *International Revue*, the usual brand of stale humor Amos 'n' Andy purvey and some dull ditchwater Flourney [*sic*] Miller wants you to believe are smart Broadway sketches with a sepia twist." Ironically, the sheer accumulation of talent may have worked against the show's success. Even the *Amsterdam News* admitted that "Mr. Leslie has so many [headliners] . . . that he does not get the best results from some of his stars." Most of the praise went to the dancers. Buck and Bubbles, wrote *Billboard*, "show what a finished vaudeville act can do for an unfinished revue."

The box office seemed to justify the critics' complaints. After the first five New York performances Leslie cut salaries by 40 percent. Buck and Bubbles had trouble cashing some of their checks and finally left the show after nine weeks.

They resumed their vaudeville career, playing the Loew circuit. Bubbles later recalled making $1,750 a week. This is quite possible. With top artists leaving vaudeville for other opportunities, it was a seller's market. We know Loew offered $1,250 to Buck and Bubbles earlier in the year, and that by the fall RKO was again making a play for the team's business. It is easy to imagine Loew going $500 higher to outbid its key rival.

Nevertheless, despite this unprecedented affluence, in early 1931 Bubbles fell into a deep funk. Perhaps the legal battles of the previous year or the failure of *Blackbirds* weighed on him. But the biggest problem had been brewing for many years. He had long since resigned himself to the Black actor's daily slights and inequities—the segregated lodgings, the fourth-rate dressing rooms—but there was one thing he couldn't get past: the continued denial of headliner status. Ever since their New York debut in 1920, when Buck and Bubbles stopped the show four times at the Audubon Theatre, it had been clear they offered more entertainment value than most of their white competitors. The list of headliners they had upstaged was long: Herman Timberg, Harry Steppe, Bennie Kreuger, Joe Laurie Jr., Louise Groody, Lucille La Verne, Frances White, Gus Arnheim, Jack Donahue, and of course Nat Nazarro himself. It is hard to find a review that does not betray a clear preference for Buck and Bubbles. And yet, with the exception of a few months with Loew right after *Weather Clear—Track Fast*, they were rarely given the recognition of the biggest letters on a brilliantly lit theater marquee.

Bubbles knew the reason: "[It was] because we were Negroes. No one but a Negro performer knows how difficult it is to make it in show business." For all the applause and the critical praise, there were other feelings, deep buried or expressed only in private, that ultimately motivated the white decision-makers of the entertainment world. Occasionally such feelings made their way to the surface. Amid all the huzzahs over Buck and Bubbles's triumph during the "New Era" Celebration in 1928, one critic gave the team a patronizing pat on the head: "The colored young fellows are great entertainers *in their own little way*, and theirs is an act that is a decided asset to the big time." In other words, they had a contribution to make, but only if they didn't forget their subordinate place. Even now, as Bubbles was coming level with Bill Robinson and fielding dance questions from Fred Astaire, theaters wouldn't put his name up in lights. And that injustice was beginning to chafe.

His frustration came to a head in February 1931. The team was booked to perform at Loew's State, Loew's flagship theater and the "chief opposition" to the New York Palace. The Sunday before they opened, Bubbles bought a ticket and went to see the show from the previous week. The headliners were the Ritz Brothers, a white trio of knockabout comedians who later made a successful career in film. On this occasion, though, they failed to generate much enthusiasm from the audience. As Bubbles recalled years later, they "died the death of a dog" and had to "steal a bow." He knew Buck and Bubbles could do much better. And yet if history was any guide, they would not receive the billing given the Ritz Brothers. He walked home despondent. It was not just a matter of pride. Headline status led to better salaries and other opportunities. Success bred success. At one time Bubbles thought if they just worked hard enough, they could break through the barriers separating them from the highest rewards of their profession. Now he was not so sure. His thoughts grew very dark:

> I figured if we didn't get top billing at Loew's State that I'd stop being in show business. . . . I went home to my apartment, and I sat down to think about all Buck and I had been through. I knew in my heart that if I walked up Broadway for the eight o'clock rehearsal at Loew's State [the next morning], and if I didn't see our name up in lights . . . that I was through fightin' it. I sat down in the darkness of the apartment, and . . . I stayed up all night long thinkin' about my career in show business. I didn't sleep at all. I knew that tomorrow would give me the answer.

When the sun came up, Bubbles arrived at Loew's State and couldn't believe his eyes. Up on the marquee the words BUCK AND BUBBLES were emblazoned in big letters. In the lobby were big signs and posters trumpeting their appearance. He went backstage, and for the first time the stage manager addressed him not as Bubbles or John but as "*Mister* Bubbles." He and Buck were given the star dressing room with a telephone in it. Bubbles was dumbfounded. "Who could have told them that I was going to quit [show business]?" he asked himself. "Nobody. Because I didn't tell a soul. My manager didn't know and my partner didn't know." Yet the marquee didn't lie. After the first matinee Bubbles walked to a nearby coffee shop and took up his preferred ritual for celebrating momentous occasions. As he sat there, he wept and prayed: "Thank you, Jesus. Thank you, Jesus."

Despite the personal and even mystical nature of this experience, it is remarkable how much checks out with historical sources, confirming Bubbles's general reliability as a narrator. According to *Variety*, the Ritz Brothers did perform at Loew's State the week of February 16, 1931, and Buck and Bubbles did appear—as headliners, next-to-closing—at the same venue the following week. "Heading the program are Buck and Bubbles," wrote the *New York Herald Tribune*, "the Negro singing, dancing and comedy pair who have long been favorites at the State. . . . This team drew round after round of applause." One critic seemed taken aback by their promotion. "Buck and Bubbles get plenty of billing at the ace Loew house," he marveled, "and seemed to justify it by the reception." Then he took stock: "Nat Nazarro's protégés have come a long way to the status of a comedy standard, their position based on honest and spontaneous Negro comedy and entertainment and clean cut specialty."

Buck and Bubbles headlining at Loew's State, 1944.

Source: L. Tom Perry Special Collections, Harold B. Lee Library, Brigham Young University, Provo, Utah.

It takes nothing away from Bubbles's "miracle," as he termed it, to observe that in 1931 New York's leading vaudeville theaters were desperate for name acts. As top stars were leaving to take jobs in radio, film, musicals, or revues, even the vaunted Palace was struggling to sign "names" that would draw potential audiences. As a result, they began booking headliners as repeats. Whereas in earlier years a second week's booking represented an exceptional honor, now big draws were staying for three, four, or five weeks at a time. (Or in the case of Bing Crosby at the Paramount, *ten* weeks.) The "dearth" of name acts, as *Billboard* put it, made headlining Buck and Bubbles an easier task. This is not to say they didn't deserve it, rather that conditions finally made possible what they should have had all along.

For Bubbles, of course, the matter could be boiled down more simply: The universe had bestowed justice at last. And the angels weren't done yet.

3

As Bubbles tells it, on the same day as the Loew's State opening, as soon as he got back from the coffee shop, in fact, he walked into his dressing room and found Buck talking on their newly acquired phone. Wide-eyed, Buck put his hand over the receiver and whispered, "It's the Ziegfeld office." Bubbles took the phone and heard a voice on the other line asking when it would be convenient for Buck and Bubbles to have an appointment with Mr. Ziegfeld. That afternoon the mighty impresario had come to the matinee to see another act, but was taken instead by the headliners, Buck and Bubbles. He was putting together another "Follies" and needed talent. When could they meet? The childhood dream was coalescing before Bubbles's eyes. Cool as ice water, he said, "Call my manager," and hung up. After the next show Nazarro told him he'd indeed heard from Ziegfeld and that they had an appointment.

The meeting took place at the Ziegfeld Theatre at 54th Street and Sixth Avenue. In front of Ziegfeld himself and his assistant Gene Buck, Buck and Bubbles were asked to do something they hadn't done in eleven years: audition. Then the white men in the room began talking money. Ziegfeld proposed $500 a week—a big drop from their vaudeville salary. Nazarro countered with $750, then called Bubbles over to get his opinion. "Well, I never like to interfere with the business part," Bubbles said, "but if Mr. Ziegfeld can only pay five and you're asking for $750, I'll say $800." (It wasn't about the money, since, he later admitted, "we'd have played Ziegfeld for nothing." It was about self-respect: "I don't go for either one of their salaries and . . . *neither one of them bought or sold me, neither one.* The man who is going to hire me is going to pay me more money than what he said and more money than what Nazarro said.") At this point Ziegfeld turned to his assistant and said, "Give them a contract, Gene." And Buck and Bubbles became the first Black act to play the Ziegfeld Follies since Bert Williams in 1919.

By 1931 the Follies had been an American institution for twenty-four years. Florenz Ziegfeld, a child of German-Belgian immigrants, modeled his first Follies on the Parisian *Folies Bergère*. As such, the show revolved around a chorus of beautiful women, tall, statuesque, dressed in the utmost finery or little at all. The company slogan was "Glorifying the American Girl." Ziegfeld's productions exuded pomp and pageantry. Everything had to be the biggest and the best, the most elaborate sets, the most luxurious costumes. Some of the greatest performers of the day—Nora Bayes, Fanny Brice, Will Rogers, Bert Williams—won fame with the Follies. During the franchise's heyday in the late 1910s the shows took the form of a topical revue, presenting socially relevant songs, dances, sketches, and comedy acts. Often, the principals would lampoon prominent people of New York, many of whom were sitting right there in the theater in their tuxedos and furs laughing along with the rest of the house.

Like vaudeville, however, the Follies declined in the 1920s. After staging a new edition every year beginning in 1907, Ziegfeld skipped a year between 1925 and 1927. He turned to other projects, including the landmark musical *Show Boat*. Then at the beginning of the new decade he decided to launch one last edition, the *Follies of 1931*. This show made less of an attempt to capture the zeitgeist of the day. It was instead a misty tribute to a bygone era, filled with backward longings for a time before talkies, before radio, before the Jazz Age had obliterated the quaint fantasy of an American belle epoque. The show, indeed, was Ziegfeld's swan song; he would die eight months after it closed.

The cast was immense. In addition to seventy of Ziegfeld's "glorified girls," more than twenty-three chorus boys, three prize-winning beauties—Miss Universe, Miss America, and Miss Memphis—and a troupe of eight ballerinas, the *Follies of 1931* boasted up to twenty-seven principals (the number varied over the life of the show), including four headliners: Harry Richman, Helen Morgan, Ruth Etting, and Jack Pearl. In 1931 Harry Richman was allegedly making $25,000 a week, one of the highest salaries in show business, for his work as a singer, dancer, and master-of-ceremonies.

Sultry-eyed torch singer Helen Morgan was known for performing her popular nightclub act while sitting or reclining on top of a piano. Ruth Etting, an alumna of the *Follies of 1927*, had gained a reputation for an unusual singing voice, which some called a "female baritone." And vaudevillian Jack Pearl was an established "Dutch comic," getting laughs for his manufactured German accent.

Buck and Bubbles formed part of a large "supporting cast" that also included tap-dancing *wunderkinder* Hal Le Roy (the Hoofers Club pledge) and Mitzi Mayfair. Sixteen-year-old Mayfair, a discovery of indefatigable talent scout Gus Edwards, was "a cute, pug-nosed youngster whose limbs seem fastened to her body on loose strings." Another standout was the band of "mad musical maniacs" led by Frank and Milt Britton. This group specialized in prim performances of classical music that gradually degenerated into violent slapstick.

For its out-of-town tryout, the Follies opened at Pittsburgh's Nixon Theatre on June 15, 1931. Despite the midsummer heat, the theater was sold out for the entire week, including the standing section, which crammed in five hundred people on opening night. When "thousands" had to be turned away at the end of the week, Ziegfeld decided to postpone his New York premiere and keep the Follies in Pittsburgh for another week. The show, critics agreed, was a "gorgeous, sensuous, and magnificent spectacle," if in serious need of trimming. A leviathan in length, it lasted four and a half hours on opening night, starting at 8:30 and finishing after one in the morning. The scenery, the sets, the costumes, and of course the Ziegfeld girls were "eye-fetching," and the show "swept along on a roar of continuous approbation" from the audience. Especially stunning were the two big production numbers, the Buckingham Palace scene "wherein long rows of trained young ladies swung their kilties about and drilled with shiny, all-steel muskets," and the jungle scene that featured huge mechanical elephants "carrying draped maidens in their tusks." (For this scene Bubbles was enlisted to play the part of "Rumba, a servant.") The emotional heart of the show, however, was the sketch called "Broadway Reverie," a wistful tribute to the golden age of live entertainment in the years around 1910. Sitting in Rector's restaurant, a famous hangout for theatrical celebrities of that era, Ruth Etting impersonated Nora Bayes singing "Shine On, Harvest Moon" (1908) while Harry Richman portrayed Al Jolson on "You Made Me Love You" (1913).

Despite the exertions of the headliners (Harry Richman "worked and worked and worked," one critic said), they were not the audience favorites.

The only "legitimate show-stoppers" on opening night, according to *Variety*, were Hal Le Roy, Mitzi Mayfair, and the Frank and Milt Britton Gang. What about those compulsive show-stoppers, Buck and Bubbles? Surprisingly, the show business bible didn't have much to say about them. "Buck and Bubbles have a spot in the first act, in which they sell their old routine in style," the reviewer mused, "but it might be a good idea for Zieggy to dress the boys up in tuxes, same as his other principals. . . . Seemed as if their hoke get-up lowered the class of the revue immediately." It sounds like they didn't make much of an impression, as though they had a bad night.

The problem is, this review is not entirely representative. While the white press in New York low-rated Buck and Bubbles, newspapers from Pittsburgh and the Black community told a different story. During a postmortem at the end of the first week, for instance, Ziegfeld admitted to the *Pittsburgh Post-Gazette* that on opening night "Buck and Bubbles were given a wrong position; they stopped the show in a place where continuity was needed." The nerve of those guys, stopping the show in a place where—wait, they *did* stop the show? How did *Variety* miss that little detail? To be sure, that hoariest of all entertainment clichés could cover a lot of ground. "Stopping the show" might range from an act pausing slightly before going on with their routine, to a performer being called back for an extra bow. In the case of Buck and Bubbles on opening night in Pittsburgh, the team had finished their act, left the stage, and were cooling off in their dressing room—and *still* the audience wouldn't stop clapping. At least that is how a Black newspaper and Bubbles himself reported it.

During the month of rehearsal leading up to the Pittsburgh opening, Buck and Bubbles felt out of place if not unwelcome. Amid the elegant sets and sumptuous costumes, the team "stood out like a sore thumb" in their "vagabond clothes." No more star dressing rooms for them; the stage manager put them in the boiler room down in the basement. (Bill Robinson kept pestering Bubbles to ask for a better room, but Bubbles saw through this "generous" advice: "Bojangles was positive that he should be dancing in our place, [and] it didn't take a fortune teller to see that one squawk from us and we'd be fired.") Cruelest of all, in a show that lasted four-and-a-half hours, Buck and Bubbles were told at the last minute to cut their routine from fourteen minutes down to nine. Having honed their act over many years, this adjustment was not easily made. The team spent all day in the ballroom of the Penn Hotel, where Nat Nazarro was staying, trying to get the new sequence to flow smoothly.

At the opening the next day, their efforts were rewarded. As Bubbles danced over to the side of the stage, he recalled, the stage manager whispered, "Don't go over [nine minutes] or I'll put the lights out on you." Bubbles was furious at this act of disrespect. At the end of their turn, he and Buck made a quick bow and hustled downstairs to their dressing room. But the crowd wouldn't stop clapping. (According to the *Amsterdam News*, the uproar lasted a full five minutes.) They began to chant: "Buck and Bubbles! Buck and Bubbles!" In an attempt to quiet the audience, Harry Richman came out and explained that, regrettably, Buck and Bubbles had left for a speakeasy. Someone in the balcony shouted, "Well, go get 'em!" "So you know what happened?" Bubbles said, savoring the memory. "That same stage manager who said he'd put the lights out on us had to beg us to come back on." Recalling the event years later, Hal Le Roy remained awestruck: "I think they're still cheering in Pittsburgh."

Whatever happened that night—and the next two weeks—in the Nixon Theatre, it must have been powerful. When the Follies appeared in Manhattan for the official premiere on July 1, Buck and Bubbles were spotted . . . *next-to-closing*. Bubbles explained it was because the other principals didn't want to follow them. "They'd change the position of our act on every show until finally they got us down to where we could only go on next to closing and after us came the finale." They'd played next-to-closing many times in the past, but the weight of the position for this premiere was particularly heavy. "Luxurious limousines rolled up in endless procession," reported the *New York Journal*, spotlighting the show's high-class patronage. "Bejeweled society leaders and notables of the stage and screen, in Paris creations, stepped forth. Flashlights boomed, and police worked feverishly to keep back the throng of onlookers." Apart from the glamour of the event, there was the show itself. "Man, you talk about having to follow a tough act," Bubbles said, "just try following the whole Ziegfeld Follies." It was "a real challenge to Buck and me."

Reviews of opening night at the Ziegfeld again present a case of dueling narratives. "It was a mistake to spot Buck and Bubbles on next to closing," sniffed the *Variety* critic. "The colored boys got nice applause, but the second portion of the routine was wet, besides the brick wall drop used for them was much too drab." By vivid contrast, the critic for the *Amsterdam News* spun a tale of heroism worthy of the legendary John Henry:

Then, somewhat after midnight, following this prodigious list of stars, shuffled in a couple of Negro boys. It was the toughest spot on the program, just before the finale, when the audience had applauded their hands into calluses, were tired [of] laughing, and were ready to leave for the night clubs. But these youngsters—banging away at the piano, dancing feverishly, singing jubilantly—hit that opening house like a ton of granite, so hard that the Ziegfeld Theatre rafters trembled at the joints. In the hardest spot in the revue, with the most difficult audience in the country, those boys had stopped the show!

As the Follies continued performing in the months that followed, white critics turned their attentions elsewhere. But Black critics occasionally perked up to remind people of Buck and Bubbles's ongoing success. "In a plethoric age of dancers," one chortled, "Bubbles stands out as preeminently as a flagpole sitter on top of the Empire State building." He added dryly, "When an entertainer protrudes his personality and his wares above the Follies' magnificent ensemble he has nosed out Twenty Grand and left [championship sprinters] Eddy Tolan and Frank Wykoff still waiting for the crack of the starting gun."

After Bubbles died in 1986, his companion Wanda Michael got a warm condolence letter from one of his old friends, a dresser for the *Follies of 1931* named Wilhelmina Reavis. Hilariously, she recalled Buck and Bubbles twitting Ziegfeld, telling him "to put the piano in the lobby and they would do the act as an exit piece, because *no one* wanted to follow them on stage." The great showman eventually took such razzing to heart. By the time the Follies closed to begin touring in November, Buck and Bubbles had been added to the show's headliners, joining Harry Richman, Helen Morgan, Ruth Etting, and Jack Pearl.

It remains genuinely perplexing why *Variety* and other white newspapers would snub Buck and Bubbles on the biggest stage of their career. It was not to protect the headliners, since reviewers did not hesitate to shower praise on Hal Le Roy and Mitzi Mayfair. It might have been to protect the Follies, though. The reviewers seemed more concerned with Buck and Bubbles's lowdown appearance—their "hoke get-up" and drab painted backdrop—than with the substance of their entertainment. These complaints, in turn, may have stood proxy for other reservations. It is hard not to suspect that race had something to do with a critical reaction that contradicted eleven years of accolades for the team. The Follies, after all, epitomized the highest of high-class white fantasies involving sex, sentiment, and satire. In some unspoken way, perhaps, Buck and Bubbles posed a distraction if not a threat to that dream. The critics couldn't shove them down into a boiler room, so they did the next best thing: They ignored them.

The commentary of white critics laid the foundation for a skewed history of the *Ziegfeld Follies of 1931*. When telling the story of that show today, writers tend either to omit Buck and Bubbles entirely or to minimize their contribution. But as we have seen, they were much more an audience favorite than an asterisk. The strongest evidence comes from Bubbles himself. He cherished his time with the Follies: "We go in this show, man, and never look back. Never look back. It was the greatest show that we ever had in life." He had no recollection of failure. On the contrary, he recalled Buck and himself riding on wave after wave of applause, playing, singing, dancing—"tearing that building *down*, man."

PART III
MASTER (1931–1953)

Katie Sublett, Bubbles's beloved mother. All photographs courtesy L. Tom Perry Special Collections, Harold B. Lee Library, Brigham Young University, Provo, UT.

The Three Ink Spots, wearing the fancy clothes bought for them by their short-lived manager, Billy Maxie, 1918. Left to right: Sugar Bailey, Bubbles, Buck.

This early publicity shot captures Buck and Bubbles's playful antagonism and easy rapport. The photographer's New York stamp suggests a date no earlier than 1920. The boys would have been sixteen or seventeen, but they looked so young that the Gerry Society (The Society for the Prevention of Cruelty to Children) filed an injunction against their manager, Nat Nazarro, for child endangerment.

John "Bubbles" Sublett, a young man in his prime. The inscription is dated 1934, but the photo was probably taken several years earlier.

Ford "Buck" Washington, around the same time, here dated 1926.

Buck and Bubbles's moods were as varied as their headgear.

Buck and Bubbles, "the most consistent showstopper of all vaudeville acts," according to *Variety*.

Buck and Bubbles, Warner Bros.'s *Varsity Show*, 1937.

Pals—despite everything.

John W. Bubbles as the original Sportin' Life, *Porgy and Bess*, 1935.

Rhea Wright, Bubbles's mistress in the 1940s, and their daughter, Charlynn.

Aysha De Festa, Bubbles's third wife, ca. 1955.

On the Perry Como Show, January 25, 1958. Left to right: Pat Boone, Peggy Lee, Perry Como, Bubbles.

Bubbles in full opera dress for Judy Garland's *Judy at the Met*, May 1959.

Bubbles relaxing backstage.

Bubbles sang, Bob Hope said, with "a special brand of springtime in his larynx."

Bubbles reprising the role of Sportin' Life, mid-1960s.

Bubbles on the "supper club" circuit with Anna Maria Alberghetti, mid-1960s.

Bubbles on the same circuit with Eddie Fisher, mid-1960s.

Bubbles sharing a laugh with Bob Hope during a USO tour, early 1960s.

Bubbles with Judy Garland, 1967.

Bubbles giving a dance lesson at Foothill Elementary School, Riverside, California, 1967.

Bubbles reminiscing with Johnny Carson, the man who jump-started his career in 1962.

Bubbles with three leaders of the tap revival in the 1970s and 1980s: Jane Goldberg, Frances Neely, and Matia Karrell.

A volatile career, a complex man.

10

Jazz, Jazz, Jazz

1

On May 7, 1932, after years of stubborn resistance, the New York Palace became the last big theater in the country to supplement its live shows with films. Three years later, the legendary venue eliminated vaudeville altogether, becoming a dedicated movie house. For many, the repurposing of the Palace came to signify the death of vaudeville itself.

The reality was not so simple. For years a sizable number of theaters would continue to feature live entertainment. But the encroachment of film squeezed vaudeville bills smaller and smaller, until a show might consist of no more than two or three acts. Performers unable to graduate to radio or film would either fight their way onto these hollowed-out bills or, more likely, leave show business entirely. Consider a few of Buck and Bubbles's recent headliners. Harry Richman and Jack Pearl were fortunate enough to make the transition to new forms of media. Joe Laurie Jr. was not so fortunate, but as a consolation prize he took a job writing for *Variety*. Louise Groody lost everything in the stock market crash and faded from the scene. Frances White grew so destitute that in 1930 she was jailed for her inability to pay $3.50 in cabfare. (Her ex-husband, Frank Fay, bailed her out.)

Against this tumultuous backdrop Buck and Bubbles stayed in the middle lane, neither reaping the richest rewards of radio and film nor suffering the worst ravages of the Depression. Bubbles rented an upscale apartment in the fashionable Sugar Hill section of Harlem, and kept a separate residence for his mother. Buck lived a bit farther south on the sixth floor of another luxury apartment building. Both men owned expensive cars. (They paid for the privilege with unwanted police attention. "I guess the police didn't think Negroes were supposed to drive Cadillac cars," Bubbles said. "We'd get stopped anytime we drove anywhere. They'd make us get out of the car and prove that we were the owners.") Black reporters began tracking their private lives. Bubbles, one wrote, "is very nervous and very seldom can finish talking about any one thing before he has gone into half a dozen other topics. Just as soon as they

Sportin' Life. Brian Harker, Oxford University Press. © Oxford University Press 2022.
DOI: 10.1093/oso/9780197514511.003.0011

leave the stage, he wraps a Turkish bath towel around his neck, jumps into his car and dashes madly to any place in his mind." Buck, by contrast, was the quiet member of the team. "When at home he wears silk lounging pajamas and eats most anything. . . . Being one of our best pianists, you can always find him near one trying out some new tune." They still spent money prodigiously (Bubbles once admitted entrusting his paycheck to his mother, knowing he'd "go mad and just throw the whole thing in the jug house"), yet they could count on steady work. As proven vaudeville mainstays, they enjoyed the confidence of an industry desperate for a sure thing.

The theater district to which Buck and Bubbles returned after leaving the Ziegfeld Follies was very different from the one they had known as teenagers. In 1920 the leading vaudeville theaters in New York were the Royal, the Riverside, the Colonial, the Alhambra, and the Palace. By 1932 the center of gravity had shifted to the big presentation houses—places like Loew's State (capacity 3,200), the Paramount (3,664), the Capitol (4,000), the Roxy (5,920), and Radio City Music Hall (5,960). Also known as "movie palaces," these buildings oozed Hollywood glamour. Bookers rotated top-line acts in and out of these theaters, leaving untested performers out in the cold. Such acts included Bob Hope, Milton Berle, Eleanor Powell, Ray Bolger, as well as Buck and Bubbles. Sometimes the latter appeared as headliners and other times they didn't. Yet they were dependable crowd-pleasers, prompting more than one critic to call them "sure fire." Buck and Bubbles "guarantee breaking up any show and will follow anything," wrote *Variety*. "No question of these boys clicking every time." Once, when the team did have an off night, a critic expressed disappointment that such a performance should come from "the most consistent showstopper of all vaudeville acts."

Some writers wearied of the duo's standard routine, unchanged after so many years. "I wish Buck and Bubbles would get a new act," lamented a Black reporter. "I know those jokes by heart." But others were unfazed. "These boys are entertainers no matter how many times you see them," wrote one critic. They are still using the "same material," acknowledged another, "but it couldn't be bettered." It was hard to complain when the act offered "more entertainment value than half a dozen ordinary turns."

Audiences remained as combustible as ever. Buck and Bubbles "tore the house to shreds," *Variety* said of the reception at one of their Palace shows. Likewise, from the moment they walked onstage at Pittsburgh's Nixon Theatre, scene of their Follies triumph, "a near riot ensued in the audience" (which, the writer quipped, "may still be thundering for an encore"). After one of their shows at the Capitol, "they received the biggest hand . . . that has been accorded an artist at the Capitol in many weeks, and that's saying something, considering the feature names that have made up the stage show." By this time such ovations came from a base of loyal fans. On a different errand entirely, a film critic noted that his audience applauded for an antiwar movie, "thereby proving that peace is almost as popular as Buck and Bubbles."

Stories circulated about the team's casual relationship with money, time, and stimulants. Once, when they arrived late for a show, the theater manager yelled that they only had five minutes to get ready. "Don't worry," Buck yelled back, "we'll go on in white face." Sometimes they arrived worse than late. At Loew's Theatre in Jersey City they were unceremoniously dropped from a bill because "they were not in condition to do their act." A month later a sheriff stalked them for a week at the Palace. "Matter of back rent," wrote *Variety*.

Yet the public triumphs kept coming. In Bubbles's memory the sweetest success was when they appeared at Radio City Music Hall—the first Black performers to do so, he noted proudly. The largest and grandest of all the presentation houses, Radio City Music Hall opened December 27, 1932. The theater booked Buck and Bubbles three months later. "This week's show is given life and speed by Buck and Bubbles," wrote a *Billboard* critic. "Even in this tremendous house they drew down huge applause, which is a major feat." After a newsreel, a classical selection by the orchestra, and a fair amount of singing and dancing, including by the "Roxyettes" (they were not yet called "Rockettes"), Buck and Bubbles took the stage next-to-closing. "The house came down for them so hard," the critic exclaimed, "that for a while it looked as tho it would have to be rebuilt." For the fall season the team was invited to perform in the vaudeville "prologue" to the opening of the Hollywood classic, *Dinner at Eight*, at Grauman's Chinese Theatre in Los Angeles (where they had to "out-talk traffic cops daily to duck parking tags"). The headliners were an act called Harrison and Fischer, but every night Buck and Bubbles held down the next-to-closing spot, from the movie's premiere on August 29 to its close two months later.

Despite Buck and Bubbles's smashing success, Loew imposed a 25 percent pay cut due to dwindling box office receipts. The cut also affected five hundred other acts, including such white stalwarts as Milton Berle, Walter Winchell, Jack Pearl, and Belle Baker. Cold comfort to Buck and Bubbles, to be numbered among the best sailors on a sinking ship.

2

If there were rescue vessels on the horizon, they were captained by people like Duke Ellington, Cab Calloway, and Chick Webb. In January 1932 *Billboard* made the surprising announcement, given the Depression, that "colored performers are in vogue," "getting big breaks," and "playing the Times Square houses consistently." The reporter speculated that Blacks' willingness to work for less money was partly responsible, also "the cropping up of vaude houses catering to colored audiences." But the biggest driver, he guessed, was "the vogue for hot jazz, built up by Cab Calloway, Ellington, and other hotcha bands." The popularity of these groups allowed other Black acts—singers, dancers, comedians—to ride on the bandleaders' coattails.

Over the next three years Buck and Bubbles appeared with many of the era's top bandleaders, including Duke Ellington, Cab Calloway, Blanche Calloway, Chick Webb, Don Redman, Red Allen, Lucky Millinder, Eubie Blake, and Ben Bernie. In May 1933 they played the Capitol as part of a "Cotton Club Revue" led by Ellington and Ethel Waters and including sensational tap-dancing prodigies the Nicholas Brothers. Waters sang her current hit, "Stormy Weather," and Ellington's band played "Bugle Call Rag" and a new composition, "Sophisticated Lady," both of which the *Variety* critic figured were too clever for "average lay appreciation." As an aside, the critic commented that Ellington seemed "to relish Buck and Bubbles's nonsense considerably."

The irrepressible twosome eagerly embraced the jazz spirit of the times, even going so far as to buy a trumpet and trombone at a second-hand store and "learning to play 'em by ear." For a scat-singing contest at the Roseland Ballroom, they joined Bill Robinson and other notables as celebrity judges. Around the same time, they gave their act an apt title, "Rhythm for Sale," which Bubbles fashioned into a song (with lyrics by Nat Nazarro):

All the world is rhythm mad
All the world wants rhythm bad
Colored folks are mighty glad
'Cause they've got rhythm for sale.

Everyone will hum a song
How a tune can cheer a throng
Colored folks cannot go wrong
'Cause they've got rhythm for sale.

Buck and Bubbles with Duke Ellington.
Source: L. Tom Perry Special Collections, Harold B. Lee Library, Brigham Young University, Provo, Utah.

On December 26, 1933, Buck and Bubbles recorded this song (with "Oh! Lady, Be Good" on the flip side), their first in a handful of commercially released recordings. On this record, the voice long hailed in press reviews becomes audible for the first time. Bubbles's sunny tenor slides high and wide with just a hint of sandpaper while Buck accompanies with a jaunty stride (oom-pahs in the left hand). Buck and Bubbles, of course, had been selling "rhythm" for sixteen years. The difference now? Their niche market was suddenly and dramatically expanding.

The opportunities in New York attracted a new generation of Black dancers. As early as 1927, one-legged dancer Peg Leg Bates arrived in Manhattan from his home in Fountain Inn, South Carolina. Philadelphians Honi Coles and the Nicholas Brothers came in 1931, as did Indianapolis native Ralph Brown. Baby Laurence arrived from Baltimore in 1932, and Eddie Brown from Omaha in 1934. Their reaction to Harlem was typically one of awe. "Not seventh heaven, *first* heaven," remembered Bates. "You can't possibly visualize it," said Coles, recalling the ghettoization of later years.

Harlem was *the* show spot of New York then. Everyone in the world came to Harlem—the Prince of Wales, Jimmy Walker, everyone. Their chauffeurs would still be sitting out there when the kids were on their way to school. They'd go to the Cotton Club or to the thousand little joints where great people were working: the Nest Club, Small's Paradise, or Connie's Inn. You could hear music at all hours—daytime, nighttime—especially nighttime. It was a nighttime town. Just jazz, jazz, jazz.

Among dancers, this heady musical environment fueled a mass adoption of rhythm tap. "Everybody during my maturing period wanted to be like Bubbles," Coles said. Maybe not *everybody*. Bill Bailey was a faithful disciple of Bill Robinson. (Those clean, pristine patterns never lost their appeal.) But plenty of dancers—almost certainly a healthy majority—gravitated toward Bubbles's innovations. "When I first saw Bubbles dance," Fayard Nicholas recalled, "I was so amazed, because his was a new type of tap dancin'. Most dancers only danced on their toes. He brought this heel beat into tap dancin'—rhythm and syncopation!" Eddie Brown was similarly impressed. Bubbles's heel drops "changed everything," he said. "We had to learn to dance all over again. But it had more soul al-to-gether." Coles became Bubbles's most fervent evangelizer and his natural successor. Even before leaving Philadelphia, he had already mastered one of rhythm tap's key ingredients—constant change. He was fast, too. His dance partner, Cholly Atkins, called him "the creator of high-speed rhythm tap. He could do all of Bubbles's steps, but faster."

Another talented youngster came north the same year as Coles. His name was Samuel Green, and like the Nicholas Brothers and Baby Laurence he was a juvenile performer, only sixteen years old. After appearing in Georgia in an act called Slim and Shorty, he and his partner, James Walker, were sent to New York for a shot at the big time. (Their sponsor was a hard-driving white woman named Lucille Lucifer.) Nat Nazarro saw them in a dance studio on 46th Street and introduced them to Buck and Bubbles, who immediately took a paternal interest. After some training they folded the boys into their own act, billing them as Buck and Bubbles Jr. (aka "the vest pocket edition of Buck and Bubbles"). In March 1932 the youngsters made a good showing at the Capitol. "When they start to go to town," a critic wrote, "they reach their destination. Kids were always more effective than flags for bows and finishes, and when the kids are good, like this pair, it's so much better." But Bubbles wouldn't let them onstage when he and Buck played the Palace. "I want them to feel that the Palace is something to strive for," he said. "Many actors would give all they had to play this house just once." Eventually a more felicitous name was found for the duo: Chuck and Chuckles. Thus did Samuel Green become Chuck Green, a name that would shine bright in tap history.

As Brian Seibert has noted, Green became Bubbles's only protégé. Childless at the time, Bubbles even invited the boy and his partner to live with him. Although Bubbles's mother and his sister Carrie had their own apartments, frequently both were to be found at Bubbles's place. Green recalled the atmosphere within:

> Everybody in his house had a happy feeling, all for one and one for all, and he was the head of the house. . . . Everyone got up at seven in the morning and he started singing then. . . . He would sing a song—to his mother, to his wife, to his sister, his niece—a different one for each, also for my partner and I. In other words, he was making love to the house. It was like saying a prayer.

Despite the occasional turbulence of Bubbles's life in show business, "at home it was like a normal family," Green said. "They went to church, they cooked a lot. . . . [Bubbles] liked a meatloaf. He was an expert—he cooked that meatloaf wonderfully. He was very talented at everything. A piano get out of tune, he would tune that up. And he could repair anything." Bubbles overflowed with fatherly affection, but he also demanded respect: "What he said—he wanted it to be done and everybody to take him seriously."

In April 1933, right after the Radio City Music Hall gig, the first of two back-to-back calamities hit the family when Bubbles contracted a life-threatening case of pneumonia, a disease to which he would be susceptible all his life. "He liked to die," Green said. "He was in an oxygen tank for a while. Then he got better and he got up, but he did not convalesce properly and he had a relapse." He wouldn't recover fully until June. To save their bookings Buck teamed up with another entertainer, Willie Bryant, and the two appeared under the unfortunate name, "Butt and Buttons." Later in the year they got the devastating news that Bubbles's older sister, Annie Gertrude, had died at age thirty-three. He sent his mother to San Diego to pick up his sister's two children and bring them back to New York. Through all this Chuck Green continued to live in Bubbles's home.

Having been welcomed into the family circle, Chuck hoped he might get some instruction in rhythm tap. No dice. A lifetime of competition had taught Bubbles to guard his secrets jealously, even from a worshipful student whom he regarded almost as an adopted son. Then one day, Chuck says, "His sister told me, 'I know his ways. You should say, you didn't do that [i.e., perform that step]. That ain't the way you did it.' And Bubbles would say, 'You can't tell me what I didn't do.' So I'd tell him to repeat something. Finally, one day he laughed and said, 'If you want me to teach you, just ask.' "

He laughed because this was the same trick Bubbles himself had once used to steal steps from other dancers. Get them to repeat a step, watch carefully, and quietly pocket the knowledge. In Chuck Green, Bubbles saw his own younger self, just starting out.

3

The new crop of dancers entered into a long and lively dialogue with the jazz musicians of the city. Rhythm was the language that connected them. Female tapper Jeni LeGon recalled the musical conversations she had with pianist Fats Waller: "I'd do steps, and he'd say, 'Look at that little girl go, she really thinks she's something. I bet she couldn't do this.' And he'd play something on the piano, a rhythm pattern—and I would imitate it with my feet. Then I'd say, 'I bet he can't do this,' and I'd do one, and he'd answer on the piano."

It was Bubbles, LeGon said, who first took her to the Hoofers Club, by now a more ecumenical establishment attracting not only tap dancers but jazz musicians as well. (Just a block away was the Rhythm Club, the prime hangout for musicians. It was perhaps inevitable that clientele of the two places would mix.) Musicians were invited to cutting contests for a particular instrument, events they called "suppers"—trumpet suppers, trombone suppers, saxophone suppers. Amid these battles, recalled trombonist Dicky Wells, the tap dancers would still carry on as they always had: "All the musicians would be sitting around the walls, all around the dance floor. Maybe there would be forty guys sitting around there. The floor was for dancers only, and they would be cutting each other, too, while we were cutting each other on the instruments."

It may have been on these sorts of occasions that drummers and tap dancers began squaring off. "Sometimes we'd have jam sessions with just tap dancers, buck dancers, and drums," recalled Jimmy Crawford, drummer for Jimmie Lunceford's band. "And believe me, those rhythm dancers really used to inspire you." Bubbles had his own back-and-forth with a legendary drummer named Tommy Thomas, who, according to Louis Bellson, "paved the way for drummers like Gene Krupa, Buddy Rich, Cozy Cole, Jo Jones, and myself." In a letter from 1964, an old friend reminded Bubbles of how "you used to spend quite a bit of time with [Thomas] in the room underneath the stage [of Chicago's Capitol Theatre], where he taught you licks on the drums and you in turn taught him dance steps."

In these interactions, the drummers had the most to gain. Many of them, including such leading figures as Jo Jones, Cozy Cole, and Big Sid Catlett, had been tap dancers themselves before taking up the drums. Yet in the early 1930s jazz drumming was, from a rhythmic point of view, rudimentary compared with rhythm tap. As drum historian Theodore Dennis Brown has shown, most jazz drummers in the 1920s perpetuated ragtime rhythms, and even in the next decade they found themselves in a primarily time-keeping role with the big bands, to be "felt and not heard." Not surprisingly, when they set out to jam with rhythm tappers, they were often confused by the dancers' patterns, according to Honi Coles. As the drummers came to understand what was going on, their own art deepened. "We base all of our rhythms on [tap] dancing," said Louis Bellson. Big Sid Catlett, for instance, "learned by watching and listening to dancers like Teddy Hale and Baby Laurence." As bandleader Jay McShann summarized, "Tap dancers had a big influence on drummers, no doubt about it."

From Coles's perspective, that influence started with Bubbles—and now we are finally prepared to make sense of a quote already seen twice before in this book: "By using his heels," he said, "Bubbles added syncopation, changed the whole beat. Then the drummers listened to his feet, the other musicians listened to the drummer and a new style of jazz was born. All from him." As at the Sunset Café, it was probably not Bubbles personally but his disciples or like-minded competitors—other practitioners of rhythm tap—who had the most direct impact. Count Basie's drummer, Jo Jones, was one of the first to follow their example. Unlike other drummers of his day, Jones broke up the straightforward pattern of two- and four-bar phrasing to overlap "rhythmic ideas from one section to the next." Additionally, in his solos and fills, he deployed "varied rhythmic patterns," producing "a string of contrasting figures." Jones, according to Brown, was the key transitional figure leading drummers from swing to bebop. The first bebop drummers (who were themselves "influenced by rhythm tappers," according to dance historian Jacqui Malone) developed a reputation for "dropping bombs," unpredictable pops that broke up the time. This technique, Coles said, was the drummers' adaptation of tappers' heel drops: "I like to tease the musicians about it, but it's absolutely true; they got it from the dancers."

Coles overstates his thesis: Bebop involved much more than dropping bombs. But when Charles Mingus's drummer Danny Richmond confesses that as late as 1961 he learned about rhythm from watching the tapping of Baby Laurence—"night after night after night"—it suggests how durable Bubbles's legacy turned out to be.

4

A few weeks after Bubbles's siege of pneumonia, his contentious relationship with Nat Nazarro burst into the open. The *Baltimore Afro-American* reported that a complete break with the obstreperous manager—"a red-faced, busy-body sort of chap with a gift of gab and . . . a pair of the thickest glasses I have ever seen"—had finally taken place:

> The split between Nat and the boys has been pending ever since they joined forces 15 years ago. No team and manager ever fought more and stuck tighter than this combination. They quarreled every time they got behind closed doors. Nat and Bubbles did most of the quarreling, while Buck just looked on. . . . They quarrelled back stage, they quarrelled in the hotel and finally Nat would grab his hat and dash out or be chased out, or beaten up and thrown out and he would disappear for two or three days, only to show up on draw night and pay day. As he left the hotel he would always look up to make sure Bubbles would not bounce a flower pot or some other handy missile off his head.

The immediate source of the team's discontent was Nazarro's unwillingness to share in the 25 percent cut imposed by Loew three months previously. It was just another chapter in the same old story. If Buck and Bubbles did leave Nazarro (and it's not at all clear that they did), they were back together within six months.

More troubling was Bubbles's deteriorating relationship with Buck. "They were typical of what you hear about stage teams," said a friend. "The minute they walked off the stage, one went one way and the other went the other. They had different sets of friends, too." Buck's friends were people from the jazz world—promoters, fans, and fellow musicians. One was the Baron

Timme Rosenkrantz, a Danish writer and jazz aficionado. "Buck . . . often took me for hair-raising spins in Central Park," Rosenkrantz recalled. "The man must have been color-blind. He stopped at all the green lights and sailed blissfully through every red light." Another time the two friends were riding on a Harlem-bound subway late at night. As the passengers dozed, Buck whipped out his trumpet ("he was teaching himself to play," Rosenkrantz said) and "proceeded to blow, note for note, all of Louis Armstrong's solo choruses from 'West End Blues.' Up jumped the passengers—clapping in time, tap-dancing, scatting along as Buck blasted and the train sped uptown. It was like a scene from a movie musical."

One of Buck's favorite places to hang out was Louis Armstrong's. He and Satchmo would spend hours together, no doubt talking, jamming, and smoking marijuana, pastimes they both enjoyed. He also joined the lively bull sessions playing out daily on the streets of Harlem. His clarinet-playing pal Mezz Mezzrow (one of the few white musicians who *chose* to live in Harlem) recalled Buck's soft spot for the underdog and his distinctive manner of punishing people for their unkind words:

> If somebody passed a remark that wasn't in line, he'd start singing and beating on the offtime cat, catching the explosions on his head and back and every other part of his anatomy. You couldn't get away from him either. He slapped you easy enough, but the steady beating, with all eyes on you, made you stand there and take it. . . . This went on for as long as he felt you deserved it, and you either ran out of the place hot as a pistol or laughed till the tears came, but one thing sure, you never forgot it. . . . What a down-to-earth guy Buck was. If he was headlining at Loew's State at three thousand a week, he'd still walk up to the corner stand and eat his hotdog.

When Buck found out Mezz was hooked on opium he went out of his way to find the man some honest work playing in a pit band. No note-reader, Mezz was fired after two weeks, but he still cherished the memory of Buck's generosity. When one of Mezz's dear friends died suddenly, Buck came down to offer what comfort he could.

On nights his vaudeville schedule would permit it, Buck hit the clubs to participate in the cutting contests among Harlem's rich population of stride pianists. Like Bubbles, Buck was a ferocious competitor. Pianist Joe Turner remembered that he would "give all of us more trouble than we had the desire for." For a young and impressionable Mary Lou Williams, Buck was "the greatest inspiration"—before Earl Hines, before Fats Waller. "He showed me a run that Art Tatum stole from me. He said to me, 'When you're around Art Tatum and Count Basie, don't play this run.' And I forgot." In her opinion, Buck "played a lotta piano, especially when out jamming. Everything he did was unusual."

Especially when out jamming. Williams might have thought this qualification necessary in view of Buck's lackluster reputation in the recording studio. The handful of records he made without Bubbles were with the very best musicians: Louis Armstrong (1930), Bessie Smith (1933), and Coleman Hawkins (1934). But critics have generally dismissed his presence as regrettable or at best a poor man's Earl Hines. And indeed there is something strangely pedestrian about his work on these recordings. Perhaps the formality of the studio suppressed a creativity that came out more naturally in jam sessions, when "everything he did was unusual." Buck's recorded output is too small, in any case, to get a sense of his true capabilities.

5

Sometime in the fall of 1933 Bubbles ran into Chuck Green on the street. He later narrated in detail what happened next.

Chuck told Bubbles that Buck had been by his apartment.

"Oh yeah?" Bubbles said. "What did he want?"

Chuck hesitated. "He stopped by to see your wife."

"Oh?"

"And they had this argument. It was an argument about money, and that's all I know about it. Understand?"

Bubbles was driving Buck's birthday present, a 1934 Cadillac roadster on which he had made the first payment. When he got to the theater, he gave it to Buck. After the show Buck dropped Bubbles off at his apartment. Bubbles came through the door and confronted Viola: Were she and Buck having an affair? She denied it vehemently. But all day Bubbles had been devising a plan to find out the truth and, if necessary, punish Viola and Buck for their treachery—a scheme of gradually escalating cruelty. He now put it in motion.

Step one: Let's go to Buck's house, he said to his wife. "If he says you didn't have an affair, then I'll forgive you. If he says you did have an affair, then I'll never forgive you. That's the proposition, and those are the terms."

"Let's go," said Viola. "Give me a few minutes to get ready." But her bluff faltered at the door. She broke down and confessed everything through a torrent of sobs.

Step two: Bubbles drove back to the theater for another show. Upon returning home he saw Viola all dressed up with his favorite dinner on the stove. But he wasn't hungry.

"I want you to help me," he said. "Help me take Buck someplace. I killed him."

Crying uncontrollably, Viola followed Bubbles down the elevator. They took a cab to Buck's apartment. Bubbles whistled, and Buck stuck his head out the window.

"Wha'cha know?"

"I was close by, and I just thought I'd holler at you," Bubbles said, and told the cabbie to take them home. Bubbles turned to Viola. "See what could have happened?"

Step three: When they got back to their apartment, Bubbles pulled a knife and told a still weeping Viola to climb out on the window ledge.

"Now you're gonna have to jump out the window—or I'm gonna kill you." As she stepped onto the ledge, he relented. "That's all right. . . . Get down from there before you hurt yourself."

Step four: The next day Bubbles invited Buck to his apartment. When he arrived, Bubbles and Viola were standing there.

"Take your clothes off, Buck," Bubbles demanded.

"Huh? Take m' clothes off? What the hell for?"

"Take 'em off!" Bubbles shouted. Shaken, Buck stripped down to his underwear. "All of them," Bubbles said, and after some hesitation Buck obeyed. Then he turned and made the same demand of Viola. He forced them, now completely naked, to stand face to face. A long silence ensued. Finally, Bubbles turned to his wife.

"What is it about him that you want?" He turned to Buck. "What is it about her that you want?" Neither breathed a word.

The next day Buck came to Bubbles holding a bottle of Lysol. He would drink it and kill himself, he said, if that was necessary to balance the scales. Bubbles's response was chilling: "I told him if he was going to take that, there was no use me lettin' him live. I told him to forget all about it, and that ended it." They never spoke of the incident again. But their years-long friendship, already strained, was permanently wounded.

On January 2, 1934, Viola sent what she called "an humble New Year's present" to her husband—a notarized letter (with four copies):

> My dear one: In consideration of the past, this is the most happy moment of my life to extract my true feelings without force and without any obligation on my part. It is essential; I am of age, and I am sane . . . and old enough to know right from wrong. You have been both loyal and just to me, which makes me feel that all I can do would not repay . . . you for the loyalty you have shown me. . . . That is why I am giving you all that I possess and all that may ever come into my possession. . . . I sincerely hope that by doing this it will prove to you that my intentions are those of a faithful wife.

Whatever possessions Viola may have had or promised, they were not enough to secure Bubbles's trust or his own fidelity. If a gossip columnist for the *Pittsburgh Courier* is to be believed, by the end of the year Bubbles had a "sweet young thing pining" for him in Pittsburgh. She was probably not the first. She would definitely not be the last.

11

A Miracle of Racy Brilliance

1

Sometime in early 1935 Bubbles got a call from a man he had never met but knew by reputation as the most celebrated American composer of his day: George Gershwin. Gershwin explained that he had conceived an all-Black opera based on the best-selling novel *Porgy* and wanted Bubbles to play the part of Sportin' Life, one of the four principals. Bubbles agreed on one condition: that Gershwin find a role for his partner as well, so they wouldn't have to break up the act. Fortunately, Gershwin already had plans for Buck. He had apparently seen Buck and Bubbles perform at Grauman's Chinese Theatre in the fall of 1933, and on October 26 he signed a contract with New York's Theatre Guild to produce his opera, *Porgy and Bess*. Two weeks later his librettist, DuBose Heyward, proposed that the opera begin with a raucous jazz piano solo. At casting time Buck was enlisted to play two parts: Mingo, an inconsequential role, and Jasbo Brown, "the 'funky' piano player the script calls for," as the *Brooklyn Daily Eagle* put it.

For the first time since arriving in New York fifteen years earlier, Bubbles didn't feel entirely comfortable in a job he was contracted to do. In June or July, while Buck and Bubbles were on a tour of Texas, Gershwin sent them a copy of the newly printed vocal score so they could learn their parts. "When they returned to New York," Ira Gershwin recalled, "George asked if they now had a good idea of their parts. 'No, sir!' 'Didn't you get a copy of the score?' 'Yes, sir,' said Bubbles, 'I handed it to Buck and said: "Can we learn this?"'" The pages were flipped, the score hefted; then it was ruefully decided they couldn't. They thought the entire 559 pages were their parts." This account reveals just how alien were the basic conventions of opera to this pair of life-long vaudevillians, neither of whom could read music. George Gershwin, however, was undeterred. He had chosen Bubbles, he explained, because "it was my idea that opera should be entertaining—that it should contain all the elements of entertainment." He wanted Sportin' Life, a drug peddler, to be "a humorous, dancing villain, who is likable and believable and at the same time

Sportin' Life. Brian Harker, Oxford University Press. © Oxford University Press 2022.
DOI: 10.1093/oso/9780197514511.003.0012

evil." Bubbles, he decided from watching his vaudeville act, was "perfect" for the role. So Gershwin offered to teach him his part by rote. "I learned all of the numbers in Gershwin's apartment," Bubbles said. "He taught me all of the songs himself. We just sat side by side on the piano bench, and he played and I sang."

But when the cast came together in August, new problems arose. Day after day the singers felt their way toward a new kind of entertainment—part opera, part musical, part white fantasy, part Black reality. In this challenging setting, as the literature on *Porgy and Bess* tells us, Bubbles was a trouble-maker. He smoked marijuana on the premises. He hit on all the girls. Worst of all, he was constantly, incorrigibly, late. Recently discovered sources reveal Bubbles's side of the story—his reasons for causing trouble. As he explained, the other singers refused to accept him and Buck because they lacked classical training and experience:

> At the first call, everybody was there, and they bunched up in little cliques. There'd be two or three here, maybe five over there, and four or five some-where else. . . . They fixed themselves off so there'd be no way to have a con-versation goin' that would include either one of us. Remember, now, all of us are Negroes. And, man, that's a segregation of a different color. They seemed prejudiced that we hadn't finished a music school and that we were still in the show. We were . . . well known, even famous, in vaudeville, but they gave us the feeling that we weren't in their class.

Bubbles decided he would *make* them pay attention to him. The next day he showed up half an hour late. "When I came through the door, everybody had to turn and look. They'd been looking to see where Sportin' Life is since 1:00. I got everybody's attention. . . . The call for the next day was at 2:00. I come in at quarter to three. I was late to every rehearsal until I got it un-derstood that my part as Sportin' Life was important to the show." It took a while for the conductor, Alexander Smallens, to get the message. According to a famous anecdote, an exasperated Smallens finally threw down his baton and demanded that Bubbles be kicked out of the opera. Gershwin rushed down the aisle to defend him, using language the conductor could under-stand: "You can't do that. Why, he's—he's the black Toscanini!"

As for Bubbles's castmates, his behavior only increased their resentment. They had earned their roles, after all, in the usual painstaking manner. First, they had spent years studying voice in classical schools, mastering the techniques drilled into them by battle-hardened pedagogues. Then, as casting notices went out for *Porgy and Bess*, they had showed up to audition. Todd Duncan, an imperious voice teacher at Howard University, appeared with a sheaf of Italian and German art songs under his arm. Later, to complete his successful bid for the part of Porgy, he performed for a full hour for Gershwin and his friends. Anne Brown was a twenty-three-year-old graduate of Juilliard, the daughter of a Baltimore physician. She went through an audition and two call-backs, one with Gershwin's brother Ira and one with the entire Theatre Guild managing board, before receiving the part of Bess. By outrageous contrast, Buck and Bubbles didn't have to audition; Gershwin simply invited them to join the cast. Word may have leaked, too, that they were each paid $375 a week, $75 more than Duncan and $250 more than the fledgling Brown. (The only member of the company who earned more was Smallens, who received $400.) And now here was Bubbles, strolling in late by half an hour or more, every day. What was this vulgar upstart doing on the same stage with dedicated pros like themselves? And why was Gershwin so loyal to him?

Their contempt hardened as they watched him mangle his part, over and over, day after day. He may have learned the songs directly from Gershwin, but he didn't perform them with the rock-solid consistency expected of a seasoned opera singer. As Todd Duncan recalled, Bubbles tended to improvise—with disastrous results:

> He was not too particular about a musical score with symphonic accompaniment. The singer much preferred the "ad lib"; further, this individual would hold a particular note two beats on Monday night but on Tuesday night he might sustain that same note through six beats. Consequently, this very fine actor would conceive and reconceive Mr. Gershwin's score as often as he sang it.

As Bubbles changed his rhythms from one performance to the next, the orchestra parts didn't line up with the voices, the other singers missed their cues, and general chaos ensued. It seems he not only had a propensity for improvisation, but he also had a hard time simply remembering the correct melodies and rhythms. This must have been especially true of the recitative passages. Opera was a foreign language to him, and the vocabulary and grammar kept slipping from his head. His lapses led to another well-known contretemps with Smallens.

Bubbles had been in the habit of shamelessly kissing up to the conductor. He would apologize for being late and say he had tried to call but couldn't get through, or he had a flat tire, or his mother was sick. Now, after he missed yet another cue, Smallens asked sarcastically if there was something wrong with his conducting. Bubbles responded with the mother of all flatteries: "Mr. Smallens, if I had the money of the way you conduct, I would be a millionaire." For those who mistook his comment for contrition (and several writers did), Bubbles later set the record straight: "I just gave [Smallens] a little breather, you know, to let him know that I think he's a big man. . . . And it was right then that he realized that I was comin' in after the beat for a reason. He realized the importance of my experience on the vaudeville stage, and he knew that what I was doin' was helping the show—not hurting it."

Be that as it may, Bubbles finally learned how to be consistent. One day Gershwin (or the vocal coach—memories differ) suggested that he tap out the vocal rhythms with his feet. This solved the problem, according to Duncan.

> Gershwin taught him to dance his part; taught him everything—all the notes, all the rhythms, all the cues—with his feet. It was brilliant. And when he learned to dance it, he never made a mistake after that. . . . He had no education and certainly no musical education, and when you talked about a major or a minor third or a perfect fourth or go up the scale, well he didn't know what you were talking about. . . . But if he got the rhythm, and [you] would pat it out and let him dance it, he got it. He would never miss.

Hard-won congruence on technical matters, however, could not paper over the most fundamental division between Bubbles and his castmates. After widespread initial skepticism toward Gershwin, a white Tin Pan Alley composer, nearly the entire cast of *Porgy and Bess* quickly came to see the opera as a great and historic undertaking. Although Gershwin was putting music of his white imagination into the mouths of Black singers, somehow his work hit the mark. As choral director Eva Jessye recalled, "He had written in things that sounded just right, like our people." For a cast of performers doomed by their skin color to be denied admittance to standard opera companies, *Porgy and Bess* became a unique and precious opportunity. Moreover, the artistic depth of the work touched them to the quick. Anne Brown recalled the first complete run-through of the entire piece, with soloists, chorus, and orchestra: "When the echoes of the last chords of *Porgy and Bess* had disappeared into the nearly empty hall, we were—all of us—in tears. It had been so moving. Todd Duncan turned to me and said, 'Do you realize, Anne, that we are making history?'" Bubbles, meanwhile, couldn't understand what all the fuss was about. "To me," he said, "it was just another show."

2

Porgy and Bess opened out of town, in the manner of a Broadway musical, at Boston's Colonial Theatre on September 30. Buck and Bubbles sent a telegram to Gershwin that became one of the composer's treasured mementos: MAY THE CURTAIN FALL WITH THE BANG OF SUCCESS FOR YOU AS THE SUN RISES IN THE SUNSHINE OF YOUR SMILE BUCK AND BUBBLES. That night, a receptive house grew more and more enthusiastic as the opera progressed. When Gershwin, the director Rouben Mamoulian, and Smallens finally stepped up to take their bows, the audience applauded for fifteen minutes straight. But at almost four hours long, the work needed to be significantly cut before appearing on Broadway. One of the casualties was Buck's feature, the opening piano solo on "Jasbo Brown Blues." As Eric Davis has pointed out, the cut was fully justified. Buck's solo conjured the hot nightlife of Harlem, not the sleepy backwater of Catfish Row. By starting with "Summertime" instead of "Jasbo Brown Blues," Gershwin captured the opera's true setting and mood. Still, for Buck, the cut must have hurt.

As Buck's star dimmed, Bubbles's rose. Not that everything went smoothly for him. During the New York premiere on October 10, Bubbles stumbled badly. For the occasion he had bought a bright emerald-green suit. All went well until the penultimate scene, when Sportin' Life was supposed to entice Bess to accompany him to the big city, singing "There's a Boat Dat's Leavin' Soon for New York." But at the moment of his cue, Bubbles was sitting absentmindedly in his dressing room several stories above the stage. The long-suffering Smallens conducted Bubbles's entrance music over and over. A cast member appeared at his door: "Hey, Sportin' Life! You're on!" In a panic he raced downstairs and onstage—only to discover his fly was open and the zipper on his new suit was stuck. But Smallens couldn't vamp forever; Bubbles had to forge ahead. So he did his big number *with his back to the audience*. Kay Swift, one of Gershwin's girlfriends, still remembered the fiasco forty years later: "I was sitting between George and Ira, and we were dying. I was digging into their arms." Bubbles took it hard. "I went upstairs, and

I cried like a baby," he said. "If I don't make this part . . . it would kill the whole show." Nevertheless, he dried his tears and came down for the finale to introduce all the players. "I did it because I was the only one in the show . . . with the experience to do that. They could all sing, but none of them knew how to talk to the audience."

When the reviews came in, only two cast members were denied universal praise: Anne Brown (some critics considered her too genteel for the

Mingo and Sportin' Life (Buck and Bubbles), *Porgy and Bess*, 1935.

Source: L. Tom Perry Special Collections, Harold B. Lee Library, Brigham Young University, Provo, Utah.

drug-addicted Bess), and Bubbles. No one mentioned the zipper snafu. The reviewer for *The Wall Street Journal* simply thought a vaudeville performer didn't belong in an opera. (He added somewhat defensively that in their proper setting, Buck and Bubbles "are among my favorite knockabout entertainers.") Another critic grumpily bemoaned "the addition of the stale vaudeville routine which John W. Bubbles has been doing for too many years." But the majority who approved of Bubbles's contribution used superlatives rarely to be found in even the most admiring descriptions of the other principals. Writing for the *New York Herald Tribune* a day after the premiere, the famously dyspeptic Lawrence Gilman hailed "the ineffable Mr. Bubbles," whose "dancing reprobate, Sportin' Life, . . . makes praise impertinent." "His dancing," wrote another reporter, "is a kind of solo equivalent for the ballet of grand opera." Most effusively, the eminent theater critic Richard Watts Jr., also with the *Herald Tribune*, confessed his weakness for *Porgy and Bess* in general, and for Bubbles in particular:

> I would like to express some very restrained enthusiasm for a performance that seems to me the most completely soul-satisfying of the year in the theatre: the portrayal . . . of that worthless fellow called Sporting Life by the young man who is handsomely billed as John W. Bubbles. Here certainly is a performance that combines humor and heartiness and agility and grace into a rich and hilarious characterization that is a miracle of racy brilliance. . . . His, I repeat, is a really superb comic performance.

Bubbles was a special favorite with Black newspapers. After the premiere, the *Chicago Defender* called the dancer "New York's number one over-night sensation." The following month both the *Afro-American* and the *Philadelphia Tribune* claimed he was "stealing the show." In January the *Pittsburgh Courier* noted that the opera had "raised many of the race to starring positions, most noticeable among them being [John] Bubbles." Another critic for the same paper drew an implicit comparison with other cast members: "Bubbles, as 'Sportin' Life,' carries 'Porgy and Bess' in the palm of his hand. He snatches it from obloquy, gilds and furnishes it. He messes around with such genuine singers as Abbie Mitchell, Edward Matthews, Duncan, Miss Brown and Ruby Elzy and he messes them up." In April a reporter for the *Afro-American* was more forthright: "Seventeen weeks in *Porgy and Bess* gave some leads the swelled head," but Buck and Bubbles "took top honors of the show. Blame it on artistic ability." Such dispatches may suggest, at least in part, a bias in the

Black press for homegrown talent over conservatory pedigrees. On the other hand, even Bubbles's disgruntled castmates had to acknowledge his success. "I hated him," Duncan admitted later, but he was a "genius" on stage—"electric!" Gershwin, for his part, took great pride in his unconventional protégé, ever after calling him, affectionately, "my Bubbles."

During the company's stopover in Pittsburgh, a reporter caught up with Buck to find out what he thought about all the attention being lavished on his partner. He wasn't pleased. The cutting of his own feature had left Buck a minor role with only a few lines to sing. Now, he said, Bubbles was gobbling up all the publicity usually accorded to Buck and Bubbles the *team*. With gleeful sarcasm, Buck mused, "Maybe I have fewer lines because I am saving my voice for the Metropolitan Opera House. Now that I'm in opera anything can happen and I've got to be ready for it." Still, he bore no resentment toward Gershwin. Stories circulated that he had memorized the entire score to *Porgy and Bess* and could play it on the piano by heart. Gershwin's music, he told the reporter, was "the best he ever heard."

3

In the novel upon which *Porgy and Bess* was based, DuBose Heyward, a white author, wanted to recapture a "golden age" of Black life in Charleston, South Carolina, where he had grown up. Although paternalistic and condescending in his portrayals, Heyward also saw much beauty and goodness in the impoverished church women, street vendors, and roustabouts of Catfish Row. For him, Sportin' Life was a malevolent outsider, representing "all that [was] wrong with black life outside the cocoon" of this rustic Eden. Coming from New York, Sportin' Life enticed not only with drugs but also with money, fine clothes, and cosmopolitan ways. The richness of his experience made him a uniquely unstable threat.

Bubbles multiplied that instability with an equally rich performance. Some critics thought they saw a stereotype in his "brown dandy," as one put it. But the old minstrelsy character they had in mind, Zip Coon, was a figure of ridicule, a buffoon. Sportin' Life, though well dressed, was no buffoon. He was a wily operator, a Don Giovanni type that audiences loved and hated in equal measure. Other stereotypes were equally irrelevant. Sportin' Life bore a superficial resemblance to the classic "Buck," the hyper-sexualized Black man of so many white morality plays. But the true "Buck" of *Porgy and Bess* was Crown, a blunt instrument in the conventional mold. Sportin' Life, who matched Crown in sexual allure, was—in addition—sophisticated, funny, and visually dazzling in his terpsichorean pyrotechnics. "John was magnificent," Kay Swift recalled. "Just the right combination of attractiveness and evil." In a world that forced Black actors to play to type, Bubbles wouldn't be forced. The complexity of his portrayal is what captivated critics like Gilman and Watts and later persuaded such larger-than-life talents as Cab Calloway and Sammy Davis Jr. to take on the role for themselves.

It is possible to catch a tantalizing glimpse of Bubbles's Sportin' Life by watching the only extant footage of the cast in rehearsal, a home movie made sometime in September of 1935. The black-and-white image flickers silently, a lustrous ghost from a distant past. Bubbles is dressed in a dark suit and tie with a light vest and derby, and carries a wooden cane. Nimble as a deer, he is constantly in motion, bopping around the stage, flipping himself off a table—for two or three uncanny seconds he floats swiftly backward as if on skates. All the while he is selling his pernicious product, hands upturned, a wicked little shimmy in his torso, an irresistible smile lighting his face. To punctuate his sales talk, he tips his hat rakishly or twirls his cane. There are other striking moments in the film: Bess singing to Porgy, or a bespectacled Rouben Mamoulian pacing the stage with an untied bow tie hanging from his neck. One powerful scene shows the whole cast, in unison, throwing their arms repeatedly at something or someone in an upper corner of the set. But no one else has the drop-dead charisma of Bubbles.

Mamoulian had instructed Bubbles "to make no movement except in the pattern of dance," and it was principally by dancing that he took control of the stage. One might assume he tapped the whole time, but the film suggests otherwise. He struts, he glides, he spins, he marches, but only once, briefly, in thirty-four seconds of camera time, does he appear to actually tap. The footage shows him in dialogue with other characters, that is, singing recitative. It would seem logical to choose less formalized body movements for such scenes. At the same time, eyewitnesses attest that he did tap on his featured song "It Ain't Necessarily So," and indeed the 1935 published score shows a nine-bar sequence marked "Dance (Sporting Life)" that would have given him a perfect opportunity to do so. Similarly, during his other big number, "There's a Boat Dat's Leavin' Soon," Bubbles recalled that he was "supposed to be dressin' that stage with every dance step I know." Whatever the exact proportion between tap and more personalized moves, the sheer range and subtlety of dancing expression—of bodily movement—must account for much of his appeal. Put another way, Bubbles's "dancing" and his "acting" were indistinguishable from one another.

In view of the heated controversy over the true status of *Porgy and Bess*—was it an opera or was it not?—one might expect critics to have complained about Bubbles's singing, which lacked the firepower of classically trained tenors. But beyond general objections to the influence of vaudeville, few writers faulted his song interpretations or the weakness of his voice, the impurity of his tone, or the variability of his delivery. Is it possible these apparent defects could have actually heightened his dramatic power?

Consider "It Ain't Necessarily So," Sportin' Life's devilish ode to agnosticism. In this scene from Act II the god-fearing residents of Catfish Row have gathered for a picnic on Kittiwah Island. As their merrymaking brings them dangerously close to ungodliness (prompting a fierce rebuke from the pious Serena), Sportin' Life sees his opening. Suddenly he takes center stage to preach a spellbinding sermon on the unreliability of scripture. No recording of Bubbles exists from 1935, but on the "Great Scenes" recording of 1963 (featuring Leontyne Price and William Warfield) he matches the insinuating melody and incantatory lyrics of the song with a lazy rollercoaster of slides, scoops, and end-of-line fillips:

> *It ain't necessarily so,*
> *It ain't necessarily so,*
> *De t'ings dat yo' li'ble to read in de Bible,*
> *It ain't necessarily so.*

In the double-time sections Bubbles roars and growls the scat syllables in rollicking call-and-response with the choir:

Sportin' Life: *Wa-doo*
Choir: *Wa-doo*
Sportin' Life: *Zim bam boddle-oo*
Choir: *Zim bam boddle-oo*
Sportin' Life: *Hoodle ah da wa da*
Choir: *Hoodle ah da wa da*
Sportin' Life: *Scatty wah*
Choir: *Scatty wah*

To the extent that *Porgy and Bess* can be called a "jazz opera" (and even Gershwin used the expression early on), Bubbles's performance of this song justifies the term.

Just before the finale (next-to-closing), as Sportin' Life prepares to sing "There's a Boat Dat's Leavin' Soon," he is introduced by the same slinky accompaniment used on "It Ain't Necessarily So," a reminder that, though circumstances have changed, this old "rattlesnake" only ever has one objective: to seduce. Yet, this song has a different character, and Bubbles shifts gears accordingly, channeling the exuberant salesmanship of the melody and lyrics:

> There's a boat dat's leavin' soon for New York,
> Come wid me, dat's where we belong, sister.
> You an' me kin live dat high life in New York.
> Come wid me, dere you can't go wrong, sister.

The sunny buoyancy of his voice seems to forecast, for Bess, the excitement of New York's "high life," with "de swellest mansion" and "de latest Paris styles." Bubbles's final high notes, with his warm vibrato and surprisingly assured breath control, make for a stirring close. On this number, the *Chicago Defender* wrote, Bubbles "becomes a Barrymore of drama."

Nevertheless, it was his dancing that best defined the role. Inspired by his example, Bubbles's immediate successors Avon Long and Joseph Attles continued the dance emphasis. But after Sammy Davis Jr. played the role in 1959, Bubbles's operatic descendants mostly abandoned this aspect of his legacy. This shouldn't be surprising. Few performers today can sing and dance with equal confidence, and fewer still know how to tap.

4

Bubbles's indifference to *Porgy and Bess* melted away fairly quickly. The process began, he said, the first time he saw the work from the audience's perspective: "I didn't really know what I was doing for the show until one night I sat out front and watched my understudy do it; then I fell in love with it." Soon he could speak of little else; a Black reporter complained that Bubbles "has talked me sick" about it. Believing they could make more money in vaudeville, Buck and Bubbles didn't participate in the opera's early revivals, but they incorporated songs from the show into their act almost immediately. "It Ain't Necessarily So" became Bubbles's unofficial theme song, which the team often performed as an encore with delighted audiences joining in boisterously at the chorus. Bubbles became somewhat typecast, playing Sportin' Life–type roles in other jobs as well.

Bubbles liked his new identity. He had grown up in a Southern working-class culture that valorized underworld figures for their power, style, and masculinity, even if, like the church women in *Porgy and Bess*, not everyone approved of their illicit activities. Despite a traumatic upbringing in Nashville, Bubbles did not court trouble as a child. He wanted to please his beleaguered mother and ingratiate himself to local whites who had the ability to give him a leg up. But as he got older (and as the trauma caught up with him, perhaps), he developed a taste for drinking, gambling, and other vices. His life motto—"Live it up, as tomorrow you may die"—became more or less fixed. By the time he arrived on the set of *Porgy and Bess*, his personal reputation matched that of his character's. A month into the opera's run an otherwise admiring Black critic noted that "up to now, when this was going to press, Bubbles has been late twice and missed one performance. Not because of illness, my friends. Sportin' Life before the footlights is Sportin' Life offstage." Bubbles had to agree, though for different reasons. "You could tell I'd been around," he recalled years later. "And my characteristics of life are almost in the same category of Sportin' Life. Nearly all the parts I had, even way back to the . . . Hugh Wiley pictures for Pathé, were like Sportin' Life. I was supposed to be taking a girl away from someone, and I did. I was a sport. I *am* Sportin' Life."

In the years after Buck died, Bubbles headlined regional productions of *Porgy and Bess* as "the Original Sportin' Life." And as the opera ripened into one of the great masterworks of the twentieth century, Bubbles's 1935 performance likewise came to be regarded as legendary, "one of the classic performances of the American musical theater." Bubbles happily basked in the glow of history. When he died in 1986, his creation of Sportin' Life alternated with "Father of Rhythm Tap" as the first line of his obituary.

Over the years he kept in touch with various people associated with the opera. He was a faithful pen pal to Eva Jessye, the choir director, exchanging letters with her into his eighties. He also maintained contact with the Gershwins. Ira's wife Lee was especially solicitous of Bubbles during the lean years after his stroke. On a regular basis she sent the penniless retiree $1,000 checks, on one note adding, "For fun and recreation dear Bubbles."

Buck's post-*Porgy* connection was of a different sort. On July 11, 1942, five years to the day after George Gershwin's tragic death from brain cancer, Buck walked into a storefront recording studio in Hollywood and recorded two tracks on an acetate disc. On Side A he played a medley of "Jasbo Brown Blues," the piece that had been cut for the New York premiere, and "Summertime." On Side B he gave a personalized rendition of one of Gershwin's greatest love songs, "Embraceable You." As Eric Davis has beautifully demonstrated, Buck's purpose was twofold: to salute Gershwin, whom he idolized, and to commemorate for posterity the composer's original assignment to him in *Porgy and Bess*. Whereas Side A closely follows the opera's published score, Side B is a rich improvisational fantasy suggesting the distinguished career Buck might have enjoyed as a full-time jazz pianist. The most touching moment comes in his introduction to the latter. To make his intentions doubly clear on this fifth anniversary of Gershwin's death, Buck paraphrases the first few bars of Eubie Blake's "Memories of You."

12

Swing Is King

1

Porgy and Bess marked a turning point in Bubbles's career. To the great merriment of writers for the entertainment weeklies, he was for the first time billed as John W. Bubbles. This comically highfalutin moniker (as the critics saw it) rescued him from the semi-anonymity of "Buck and Bubbles" and gave him his own identity. For the rest of his life, he would be known professionally as John Bubbles or John W. Bubbles, rarely anymore to be confused with his partner (who continued to be known either as Buck Washington or, sometimes, by his *Porgy* billing: Ford L. Buck). For the first time reporters showed an interest in aspects of his biography. In interviews prompted by the opera, Bubbles addressed the matter of his birthplace. According to two accounts, he was born in Nashville; in one of them he added that he "was christened in a Methodist church." That in later years he consistently swore he was born in Louisville must reflect a conscious PR move, probably at Nat Nazarro's behest, to simplify the origin story of Buck and Bubbles: The two boys from Louisville!

As the team finished a brief East Coast tour with *Porgy and Bess*, new possibilities beckoned for both of them—but only if they were willing to split up. Five days before rehearsals for the opera had begun in Manhattan, pandemonium broke out at the Palomar Ballroom in Los Angeles. The hot jazz that for years had been so popular in Harlem and other places in the greater New York area suddenly went national as reporters spread the dramatic story of white kids surging around the stage at the Palomar, blissfully savoring every note by Benny Goodman and His "Swing Band." This event triggered the swing craze, a tidal wave that overtook Buck and Bubbles even before *Porgy and Bess* closed. The following March, the team joined forces with Benny Goodman himself at Chicago's Congress Hotel, performing in the floor show. Two months later they appeared in Gershwin's revue *Swing Is King* at Radio City Music Hall.

Sportin' Life. Brian Harker, Oxford University Press. © Oxford University Press 2022.
DOI: 10.1093/oso/9780197514511.003.0013

Vaudeville was declining, swing was rising. At this point, Buck might have been well advised to bid farewell to his longtime partner and become a full-time jazz musician, an occupation he appeared to covet in any case. Over the long run he may not have made any more money (since vaudeville paid so much better than jazz), but in riding the swing wave he may have enjoyed a more stable career and, possibly, avoided the sad end to which he finally came. As for Bubbles, *Porgy and Bess* had positioned him to pursue a promising career as a single in night clubs and on Broadway. His performance as Sportin' Life revealed a rare dramatic gift. Two weeks after the opera's premiere, a Black reporter claimed that "at least 50 playwriters are after [Bubbles's] services as lead in their next sepia play." Even if only a fraction of this statement were true, Bubbles would have had the basis of a new career.

But after almost twenty years with Buck, he couldn't envision any other route to success than the one he already knew. "I got plenty of offers," he admitted. "But they wanted to break up the act. I didn't want to break the act up. They were going to use me and not use my partner because of my dancing, you know. No, I don't want that . . . Couldn't see it." As a result, Buck and Bubbles continued as a team, even when conditions no longer favored a vaudeville-style duo. And over time, making a living became harder and harder.

2

One of the problems confounding bookers in the 1930s is that one minute vaudeville seemed ready to die and the next it would spring back to life. Was it a safe bet or not? In March 1936 the manager of the Chicago Palace tried presenting movies without a stage show. After five weeks the theater lost so much money he reinstated vaudeville the following month, including on the opening bill "the two never-miss boys," Buck and Bubbles. The weekly box office soared from $6,400 to $23,000, and the theater acknowledged in a publicity blitz that "the public demands the return of vaudeville." Over on the eastern seaboard, on the other hand, the "difficulty" of booking live attractions of sufficient drawing power caused the RKO Boston Theatre "to drop vaude for the summer." The inconsistency was maddening.

As the prospects of vaudeville rose and fell, so did those of Buck and Bubbles. Their big engagement of the fall season recalled the glory days of yore. In August they made their second trip to England to perform with a Ziegfeld-style extravaganza called *Transatlantic Rhythm*. Produced by Felix Ferry, a Romanian impresario known mostly for his revues in London and the French Riviera, the show combined American and British talent: twelve principals (including Buck and Bubbles), twelve showgirls ("Felix Ferry's American beauties"), and thirty-one members of a "British Chorus." The cast's "big three" were comedian Lou Holtz, singer Ruth Etting (who had appeared with Buck and Bubbles in the *Follies of 1931*), and Lupe Velez, a Mexican film star who specialized in doing impersonations of American film stars. The show was to open with the entire cast arriving in "a huge silver aeroplane," and the acts would perform on a revolving stage. Spectacle was the keynote.

Preparations for the tryout in Manchester did not bode well. "A lot of last-minute trouble including innumerable squabbles" delayed the opening by two days, and the last grueling rehearsal went on for forty-eight hours straight. More problems arose before the London premiere. Ferry announced that the production was $110,000 in debt and that principals' salaries would be cut by 25 percent. On opening night rumors flew that the show was in trouble even as celebrities filed into the theater and rubbernecking crowds pressed against cordons of police. Backstage, the cast received more grim tidings: There would be no salaries that night. Ferry begged the actors to appear for the audience's sake. Buck and Bubbles flipped a coin, which came down in Ferry's favor. The show went on a half-hour late.

Critics derided the production ("more sumptuosity than taste," wrote one), but the audience loved it. As "spectacle succeeded spectacle," and the stage revolved "like anything," "applause was heavy all around." On one point the reviewers were unanimous. As the *Guardian* described it, "Two easy Negroes, called Buck and Bubbles, appeared only twice and gained most of the applause.... The three stars seemed comparatively uneasy." The following day, Ruth Etting abruptly boarded a ship back to the States. A few weeks later, the *Chicago Defender* gleefully disclosed the reason: "Angered because she, as headliner, wasn't getting the same applause for her singing" as Buck and Bubbles, "Miss Etting was said to have quit the show in a huff and sailed for America." Buck and Bubbles took her place as one of the "big three." Despite the successful premiere, however, the money problems continued. Nazarro appeared before every show to collect the team's salary "on an or else basis." At the end of October Buck and Bubbles left the production.

Their success in *Transatlantic Rhythm* opened other opportunities. Making a bit of history, the BBC invited the team to appear in a telecast at Alexandra Palace on Monday, November 2, the event that officially launched "the world's first public TV service." The lineup was short. The show opened with a newsreel, which was followed by Adele Dixon, a popular British performer, singing a song called "Television." The next (and final) act on the program was Buck and Bubbles. Everything was "perfectly reproduced on the screens," wrote the *Guardian*, "and artistically faded in and out with close-up variations very much in the style of film technique. It seemed a mistake," however, "to provide a white background for the Negro artists, who were themselves dressed in white."

Buck and Bubbles next appeared in a movie short titled *Calling All Stars*, together with the Nicholas Brothers and a long list of British musical comedy acts. They also fulfilled theater engagements at the Manchester Hippodrome and two London venues: Shepherd's Bush Empire and the Holborn Empire. Reviews were positive, but several made the same complaint. In contrast to their first experience in England, when audiences could barely comprehend their exotic American humor, this time—six years later—Buck and Bubbles encountered a jaded public. As *The Stage* put it, some of their gags "are not so new."

Somehow Buck and Bubbles became acquainted with the Royal family. On one occasion they were driven to one of the Crown's many properties, probably Fort Belvedere in Surrey, to give a "command performance" for the Prince of Wales, his paramour, Wallis Simpson, and some of their friends. "There was this huge livin' room with a fireplace," Bubbles recalled, "and everyone was standin' around the fireplace." While the bluebloods drank and chatted, Buck and Bubbles performed at a baby grand piano about fifty feet away. Bubbles was annoyed that most of the time their audience didn't seem to be paying much attention to them, but the ride home was worth it. As the Prince himself drove them back to London in his big Rolls Royce, Bubbles said to his partner, "Oh, if I died [now], wouldn't that be something? All this royal blood we were mixed up in, you know . . . What could be sweeter?"

After four months in England, Buck and Bubbles returned in triumph to New York, arriving on December 28. Bubbles took with him a woman named Rhea Wright, with whom he'd had a whirlwind affair. In a few years she would impact his life in a major way.

3

Back in the United States Buck and Bubbles found themselves in a changed environment. Suddenly, it seemed, without any warning or preparation, they had to compete with newly minted celebrities in an age of burgeoning superstardom. In February 1937 they were booked to play RKO Boston with the Ritz Brothers, a trio of slapstick comedians appearing as the headliners, next-to-closing. Recall that six years before, Bubbles regarded the Ritz Brothers as Buck and Bubbles's unworthy predecessors at Loew's State, "dying the death of a dog." But in the last six months the brothers had appeared in no fewer than three movie musicals for Twentieth Century-Fox. By the time of the Boston engagement, the Ritz Brothers were "suddenly popular," according to the *Globe*. Their new fans "yelled, screamed, whistled, and shouted" as the trio "stopped the show again and again." Buck and Bubbles were reduced to being "secondary showstoppers," an unfamiliar role indeed. If they were to stand up to this sort of onslaught, they would have to acquire some of that Hollywood wattage for themselves.

Fortunately, Hollywood was in a mood to accommodate them. At that very moment, according to *Variety*, film companies were conducting "an unprecedented raid for talent" from the ranks of vaudeville. "Practically every one of the companies" was involved, "all of them with an eye to the numerous musicals on their production schedules." Filmmakers had used vaudevillians before, but never in such numbers. "This latest raid" was "probably the last as well as the biggest. It won't take long to exhaust pretty nearly all the film possibilities among the current crop of variety acts." The hunt started after recent musicals saw unexpected success with vaudevillians, "topper of 'em all" being the Ritz Brothers. New signings included comedian Red Skelton and ventriloquist Edgar Bergen. In February, the same month as the Boston gig, Warner Brothers recruited Buck and Bubbles for a movie called *Varsity Show*.

Bubbles was ecstatic. He had long been "crazy to go in pictures," by which he meant not comedy shorts but feature films by major Hollywood studios. *Varsity Show* was "the biggest (if not the best)" of its kind, one of twenty-five cinematic "college musicals" produced in the 1930s. The story involves a group of college students struggling to put on their annual "varsity show" against the outmoded opinions of their hopelessly square and dictatorial faculty advisor. Thwarted at every turn, they finally head to New York, and, with the help of a Broadway producer who also happens to be an alumnus of the school, stage a blockbuster revue under the bright lights of the big city. Swing music being one of their winning ingredients, a prominent role was given to Fred Waring and his Pennsylvanians, playing a student dance orchestra. Dick Powell and Rosemary Lane played the male and female leads, and Ted Healy a wise-cracking promoter. In line with other Black assignments in movies of the 1930s, Buck and Bubbles were cast as janitors, which grieved Bubbles. To give them such demeaning roles—however true to life on a white college campus in 1937—was "a sad thing."

Buck and Bubbles were given a little more than three minutes of performance time, divided into two set pieces. In the first, Bubbles does a tap dance to a swing arrangement played by Fred Waring's band (offscreen) and Buck, playing an upright piano. The setting is the basement of a fraternity house. Clad in his janitor's uniform, Bubbles serves up some impromptu entertainment for a small group of students sitting on the stairs in the background, while a fire flickers in the boiler. The dance strikes a miraculous balance between content and delivery, the former as extravagant as the latter is nonchalant. Bubbles taps out an L shape on the floor, going first one direction

Buck and Bubbles, Warner Bros.'s *Varsity Show*, 1937.

Source: L. Tom Perry Special Collections, Harold B. Lee Library, Brigham Young University, Provo, Utah.

then the other, varying both steps and rhythms every few seconds but rarely establishing a discernible pattern. His arms swing back and forth or bob erratically as though he were dancing on a tightrope. Throughout, he punctuates his steps with wordless singing, humming, and, once, a resounding hand clap on the upbeat. As the dance progresses, his tapping accumulates more and more complexities until the homestretch, when he switches to wide spins of the whole body and emphatic foot slaps on the basement floor. The effect is a shifting kaleidoscope of sound and image that builds in energy all the way to the end. A one-minute masterpiece, it is the first (and possibly the best) film documentation of Bubbles's tapping.

In the other set piece, Buck and Bubbles open the big Broadway show put on by the students. This number spotlights the team as well as director Busby Berkeley's elaborate production values. Dressed in white Prince Albert suits, Buck and Bubbles perform a highly abbreviated version of their vaudeville act on a fantasy set of glamorous props. Bubbles slides down a long, winding ramp and lands on top of a big white piano. The pair sings a medley of two of the film's original songs, "Love Is on the Air Tonight" and "Have You Got Any Castles, Baby?" While Buck accompanies, Bubbles dances on the piano top then sits at the keyboard himself as Buck does his dance parody. The scene lasts all of two minutes.

In the end, Buck and Bubbles didn't make much of an impression. (In *Variety's* review of the film, they aren't even mentioned.) Later, Bubbles bemoaned what he saw as the show's missed opportunities: "I think we should have had a different song to sing. We should have had different scenes to do. There were a lot of things that I thought could be done, that would get more out of us . . . than we got. We didn't get nothing, to my estimation." In comparison with their white counterparts, he was about right. In the Ritz Brothers' first feature film, *Sing, Baby, Sing* (1936), the trio got almost five times as much camera time—the length of an entire vaudeville act. At the end of the movie, before the credits, a written message filled the screen: "This picture has introduced to you three new Twentieth Century-Fox personalities— the Ritz Brothers." The studio immediately signed them to a long-term contract. Similarly, Red Skelton's feature film debut was followed by thirteen more movies in the next five years, and Edgar Bergen's with six more over the same period. Buck and Bubbles' contract, however, was not renewed.

This failure cannot be pinned solely on their race. Bill Robinson, Stepin Fetchit, and Eddie Anderson, it should be remembered, all succeeded in Hollywood despite the color of their skin. So what was the problem with

Buck and Bubbles? More than any other single issue, filmmakers were al-most certainly terrified by Bubbles's sexual potency. Once again, the example of Bill Robinson is instructive. For his breakout movie, *The Little Colonel* (1935), Robinson played the part of "Walker," an elderly Black retainer of a postbellum Southern house. His character was fully integrated into the story. Even Robinson's Stair Dance with seven-year-old Shirley Temple had a plau-sible (and charming) narrative justification. Such integration was possible because, as Joan Acocella has written, in his role as loyal and aged family servant, Robinson "did not have a lot of sexual allure." She added parenthet-ically, "The studio would not have let Temple dance with John Bubbles." No, it wouldn't.

It's not just that people still associated Bubbles with Sportin' Life, a demon he resurrected every night with "It Ain't Necessarily So." Bubbles exuded car-nality even on the programmatically neutral ground of his tap-dance spe-cialty, according to the great film critic Pauline Kael. As a teenager in 1930s San Francisco, Kael recalled,

> I thought I would die from pure pleasure when I saw Buck and Bubbles perform in the stage show that came on before the movie at the Golden Gate Theatre; I'd sit through the picture over and over so I could watch John W. Bubbles glide through his tap numbers, smiling crookedly, his eyes hooded, as if he knew that kids like me had never seen anything so slinky sexy. I thought he was evil, but I loved it.

In *Varsity Show* the director attempted to blunt Bubbles's magnetism. He tried to emasculate him with the role of janitor. He tried to infan-tilize him with his manner of speech, the "spacey singsong" required of all Black actors of the time ("When Chuck DAN-iel was puttin' on our shows, we NE-ver had no trouble. And they was GOOD shows."). During filming, the young women of the cast flocked around Buck and Bubbles during breaks; but when it came time for Bubbles's dance feature the director stuck him down in the boiler room of a frat house, where only male students would be there to see it. Bubbles did his best to play along, smiling broadly for the camera. But his actions—his white-hot tapping, his sub-rosa vocalizing—say: *I'm the baddest so-and-so on this lot.* Underneath the custodial trappings, he was still Sportin' Life. At the end he even snuck in his signature sportin' *line:* "Shoot the liquor to me, John boy."

For Clark Gable, sex appeal was a key to success; for John Bubbles, it was fatal. He and Buck wouldn't appear in white feature films again until the 1940s, and by then their on-screen presence shrank to almost nothing. With the exception of the all-Black *Cabin in the Sky* (still to come), *Varsity Show* would be the highlight of Bubbles's film career.

4

After bombing out in Hollywood, Buck and Bubbles—or, more likely, Nat Nazarro—turned to that other route to wealth and fame in the late 1930s: leading a swing band. Inspired by Benny Goodman's stunning triumph at the Palomar, hundreds if not thousands of young jazz musicians had started their own bands. The most successful attracted legions of ardent fans who knew all their song titles and soloists, bought all their records, and—when the bands came through town—waited in line for hours to see them. As early as 1932 the Duke Ellington and Cab Calloway organizations were each charging $5,000 weekly, and within ten years that number had more than doubled. If Buck and Bubbles were looking for a new source of income to replace vaudeville, a thriving big band might fit the bill.

In January 1938, they announced their intention to become bandleaders. Nazarro hired an outfit led by bassist Charlie Turner that had recently played for Fats Waller. Bubbles would "lead" the band in public; Turner would rehearse it behind the scenes. Bubbles would sing, dance, and m.c. while Buck played the piano; together, they would serve up a few vaudeville antics. After a rousing debut at Harlem's Savoy Ballroom—the established launching pad for new Black bands—Nazarro planned a Southern tour, to begin in March. This was not a good sign. Buck and Bubbles had never performed in the Deep South before. Their drawing power in Northern theaters was strong enough to insulate them from the danger and indignity of Southern routes. But Black swing bands could not afford this luxury. While white bands sewed up most of the plum location jobs in the big hotels and ballrooms of the North, Black bands had to subsist on one-nighters in Dixie. Buck and Bubbles's willingness even to consider this prospect indicates the seriousness of their predicament.

Yet the Southern tour never happened. Instead, Nazarro made a characteristically bold move. Rather than start small and build up gradually, he suddenly went all in on the swing project, adding to Buck and Bubbles and the Charlie Turner band a "girl singer," a "boy singer," and an all-Black floor show including contortionist dancer Jigsaw Jackson, three other acts, and "sixteen dancing beauties." With this expensive unit Nazarro staged a "huge extravaganza" at Harlem's Apollo Theatre. Billed as the "Prime Ministers of Rhythm," Buck and Bubbles mixed songs and jokes from *Porgy and Bess*, *Transatlantic Rhythm*, and *Varsity Show*. The Charlie Turner band was "much improved . . . since being under the personal management of Nat Nazarro," noted the *Defender* ominously.

After the Apollo, a warm-up in friendly territory, the unit kicked off "an extended tour of deluxe theaters" under the banner "Harlem Parade of 1938." On April 7 they opened at RKO Boston, where Bubbles introduced a new swing dance, the Kangaroo. Critics mingled gentle criticism with faint praise. Buck and Bubbles, the band, and the floor show "make up a company that will doubtless improve," wrote *Variety*. "A little more Buck-Bubble comedy near the front of the show would help." Similarly lukewarm commentary greeted the unit's opening at Hartford's State Theatre. The show "gives a good band a chance to show its semi-individual abilities," wrote the *Hartford Courant*. "A little more chance to cut loose as the show progressed, with a few hot popular numbers, wouldn't be a bad idea." *Semi-individual abilities?* It's hard to imagine a more devastating characterization of a jazz group, and this from an obviously sympathetic source. After the Hartford gig, Nazarro's experiment collapsed.

It's not hard to see why. Successful big bands had a strong leader, a few outstanding soloists, and a distinctive style. Floor shows were strictly optional. Judging from descriptions in the press, Nazarro presented to the public a confusing hodge-podge. Was it a vaudeville act or a big band? Was the music sweet or hot? (*Down Beat* said the band presented "sweet swing, a novelty for a colored band.") And who was in charge? Bubbles was the nominal leader, but with Turner and Nazarro both pulling strings behind the scenes the result had to be messy. Equally problematic was the band itself. By all accounts, the Charlie Turner band was just not very exciting. By pairing a first-rate vaudeville act with a second-rate swing band, Nazarro turned the proven formula on its head—and it didn't work.

The setbacks and humiliations continued. As the swing craze advanced, nightclubs, hotels, and resorts replaced theaters—the most profitable venues—as the prime spots for live entertainment. Buck and Bubbles's salaries fell accordingly. So did their prestige.

In June they joined an all-star bill of "super-vaudeville" at Billy Rose's Casa Mañana, a new club on 50th Street and Seventh Avenue. Headed by

Bert Wheeler and Frank Fay, the show also included the Three Stooges, Morton Downey, Gracie Barrie, Clyde Hager, and "Billy Rose's Depression Chorus." Bandleaders Louis Prima and Vincent Lopez took turns providing dance music for the patrons. On a bill no doubt bursting with egos, it isn't surprising that the only Black act was positioned badly. According to the *Times*, Buck and Bubbles were "made to suffer the rank injustice of being put on as the opening number without any introduction beyond mere announcement of their names." Not that it mattered a great deal. Like the Ritz Brothers at RKO Boston, but to a much greater extent, the Three Stooges brought with them the unfair advantage of having appeared in a recent spate of popular films. Sure enough, these "mad fugitives from Hollywood" got "the biggest laughs," leaving the rest of the bill, including Buck and Bubbles, in the shade.

The team hit the road again, crisscrossing the country to take whatever jobs they could, whether at a theater in Toronto, a nightclub in Los Angeles, or a hotel in Swan Lake, New York. In early 1940 they took a gig at the Cadillac Tavern in Philadelphia. This was a "neighborhood club" (a "nabe club" in *Billboard*-speak), a new type of venue "catering to neighborhood residents and located away from the bright-light districts" in the center of town. Patrons liked the convenience and no-cover no-minimum policies. For artists, the clubs offered "long engagements, direct bookings, and a chance to break in new numbers." But let's not kid ourselves. Nabe clubs paid less than clubs in the city, and far less than theaters. According to *Billboard*, most such establishments in Queens, Brooklyn, and the Bronx paid a measly $20 to $30 a week. Even if Nazarro were able to squeeze a bit more out of the Cadillac Tavern, Buck and Bubbles's wages would still have fallen abysmally short of their usual salary. Nevertheless, the team willingly played this club for twelve weeks straight.

The Cadillac Tavern episode crystallizes the dilemma of all but the most successful Black artists in 1940. By this time, as Scott DeVeaux has shown, the swing market had reached a point of maximum saturation: too many bands for the available gigs. Black bands suffered more than white bands, and Black dancers and comedians—the expendable ornaments of the swing industry—suffered most of all. By the end of the year, employment for Black entertainers had fallen by 25 to 30 percent. Buck and Bubbles hit bottom at precisely this moment. In November they were poised to begin a Southern tour with the Tiny Bradshaw band when the hosting auditorium in Atlanta mysteriously burned down. The team then entered a barren stretch of about one engagement per month. They did not work steadily again until June 1941.

5

Six months later, the United States entered World War II, prompting a major shift in the economic landscape. On the one hand, the rationing of gas and rubber made life harder for entertainers dependent on long-distance transportation. But on the other, the draft removed large numbers of performers to Europe and the Pacific, easing competition on the home front. At this point things began looking up again for Buck and Bubbles, who, in desperation, had finally started updating their routine with new jokes and patter. Critics were reminded how good they were. "Buck and Bubbles have a new routine," reported *Billboard*, but they "are as funny, if not funnier, than before." The team also benefited from a surprising development of the last few years: a calculated and determined effort to bring back the ancient joys of vaudeville.

In the late 1930s, as the whole swing phenomenon began drawing charges of shallowness and commercialism, artistic purists campaigned for a revival of past idioms: Dixieland jazz, boogie-woogie—and vaudeville. In 1938 almost five hundred vaudevillians crowded into the Club Sharon, intoxicated with nostalgia, to honor Henry Chesterfield with "a three-and-a-half-hour vaude show and as many hours of sentimental reminiscing. For the occasion old-time teams were reunited, old vaude routines . . . were exhumed, and a galaxy of acts was on hand to entertain and reminisce about the old days." Chesterfield was an old trouper and past executive secretary of the National Vaudeville Artists union. (He died a month and a half later while eulogizing another fallen actor.) Among those who performed in his honor were Buck and Bubbles. As some of the few old-time vaudevillians still working, the "two never-miss boys" provided consolation, and, for the diehards, perhaps a reason to hope for a comeback of the entertainment they loved.

One of those diehards was producer Kurt Robitcheck, who booked the Maryland Theatre in Baltimore the following February for his second attempt to "bring back" big-time vaudeville (the first, at New York's Majestic Theatre, having flamed out spectacularly). Called *Laughter Over Broadway*, the show featured ten acts, including Buck and Bubbles, next-to-closing. The show presented straight vaude, no film. However noble the organizers' intentions, however, this show, like the first, did not succeed. *Variety* deemed it "just fair vaudeville making up in quantity, at least, what it lacks in quality." Even the "never-miss boys" were only "okay." After an anemic first-week box office, the show folded. A deflated Robicheck declared himself "thru trying to revive vaudeville in America."

Yet as the years passed, others took up the cause. In May 1942 the *Los Angeles Times* reported another vaude revival, this time at the Biltmore Theatre under the title *Show Time*. Sparked by a surprising "fever" for vaudeville "rampant in the east and central areas of the country," the show would feature such marquee names as George Jessel, Jack Haley, Ella Logan, the De Marcos (ballroom dancers), Kitty Carlisle, and, naturally, Buck and Bubbles. Although several of the actors had had extensive Hollywood exposure, Buck and Bubbles had no trouble holding their own this time. Spotted in their customary position, next-to-closing, they thoroughly charmed the audience, ultimately having to "tear themselves off the rostrum to make way for Ella Logan, who has the tough assignment to close the show." In one of the earliest extant letters from Nat Nazarro to Bubbles, dated June 12, 1942, Nazarro congratulated his prize performer: "Am more than happy to know that you are such a big hit in the show, and keep up the good work and Buck and Bubbles will be on top again where they belong. . . . Give our bestest to Buck and of course yourself, and lots of luck, we all need it."

To widespread astonishment, *Show Time* took the first-week audiences "by storm," breaking attendance records and forcing the theater manager "to prolong its original booking of two weeks to accommodate crowds turned away each night." The publicity jump-started Buck and Bubbles's career, making possible one last legacy-defining appearance.

At some point during the Biltmore engagement, a Black reporter tells us, Bubbles "was spotted for a role" in Vincente Minnelli's upcoming picture for MGM, *Cabin in the Sky*. Presumably, as in *Porgy and Bess*, Buck participated at Bubbles's insistence. Whereas Bubbles played one of the starring roles, Buck received only a minor part as a messenger boy.

Unlike *Varsity Show*, a well-worn cinematic type, *Cabin in the Sky* represented a quite rare and special undertaking. As Minnelli's first feature film, it launched a distinguished career that would produce such classics as *Meet Me in St. Louis* (1944), *Father of the Bride* (1950), *The Bad and the Beautiful* (1952), and *Lust for Life* (1956). Moreover, as the first all-Black feature film by a major Hollywood studio since 1929, the movie generated a lot of excitement within the Black community. Its filming coincided with a remarkable concentration of Black talent in the Los Angeles area in the summer of 1942. With such luminaries on hand as Duke Ellington, Ella Fitzgerald, Jimmie Lunceford, Lester Young, Billie Holiday, Art Tatum, The Nicholas Brothers, and the Four Step Brothers, in addition to Buck and Bubbles, Minnelli had a rich pool to choose from when it came time for auditions. The time was right economically as well. The Black film industry, which had "grown to immense proportions" in recent years, was set to target Black audiences in the South, "a gold-rush territory" just waiting to be exploited. *Cabin in the Sky* had the potential to become a juggernaut.

Based on a successful Broadway musical, the film told the story of Little Joe Jackson (played by Eddie Anderson, better known to radio audiences as "Rochester," Jack Benny's valet), a likable and well-meaning fellow torn between a life of gambling and one of church-going piety. Wanting to please his long-suffering wife Petunia (Ethel Waters), he is at the same time bewitched by the seductive Georgia Brown (Lena Horne). During one of his sprees at Jim Henry's Paradise he gets into a fight with professional gambler Domino Johnson (Bubbles), who pulls a gun and shoots him. In response to Petunia's powerful prayers on his behalf, feuding emissaries from heaven and hell agree to prolong his life for six more months as a final test. But after a promising start he backslides, leading to another fracas with Domino, who again whips out his gun and shoots him and Petunia, killing them both. Despite his moral failings, Little Joe squeaks into heaven on a technicality. While climbing the stairs to his "Cabin in the Sky," arm in arm with Petunia, he awakens to discover the whole probation episode was a dream. He recovers from his gunshot wound a truly changed man.

When he wasn't busy unloading Domino's six-shooter, Bubbles got some choice screen time for a justly celebrated song-and-dance feature. The song he performed, however, was problematic, both then and now. Published in 1910 under the title "That's Why They Call Me Shine" (and more commonly known as "Shine"), the song had long stirred controversy for its lyrics, particularly their use of the epithet "Shine," seen by some as only slightly less offensive than the n-word:

> 'Cause my hair is curly
> 'Cause my teeth are pearly,
> Just because I always wear a smile
> Like to dress up in the latest style,

'Cause I'm glad I'm living
Take troubles smiling, never whine
Just because my color's shady
Slightly diff'rent maybe
That's why they call me Shine.

Many years after *Cabin in the Sky*, tap historian Jane Goldberg asked Bubbles if the song wasn't "just putting the Negroes down." Bubbles demurred. "The words are beautiful," he said, "*because I put the verse to the song, to the chorus.* It wasn't like singing the song, 'Shine,' [i.e., in its original form]." As his cryptic comments suggest, Bubbles had his own problems with the song. In other interviews he described his solution.

According to Bubbles, MGM initially wanted him to sing the song dressed in overalls while carrying a lantern by a train, a setting at least as humiliating as the janitor's outfit he wore in *Varsity Show*. He rehearsed "Shine" for two weeks, but when it came time to film, he recalled, "I had to refuse to do it because the song didn't fit the part I was playing. It was too good for a railroad background." In addition, "I didn't feel that it was a thing in which I could show myself off, and you got to do that. But I couldn't dance or anything to the way it was written, and I refused to do it." Fortunately for Bubbles, the top brass at MGM actually wanted to produce a film that wouldn't antagonize the Black patrons who would be their prime customers, and they took pains not to run afoul of the NAACP. Bubbles sat down with Louis B. Mayer, choreographer Busby Berkeley, and the writer, and had a conference. It was decided to move the scene to Bubbles's preferred setting, a cabaret. One problem solved.

But Bubbles also objected to the song's lyric. He wanted to substitute *Domino* for *Shine* (and sing "That's why they call me *Domino*"), but the studio wouldn't go for that. They did, however, allow him to replace the song's obnoxious opening verse:

When I was born they christened me plain Samuel Johnson Brown
I hadn't grown so very big 'fore some folks in the town
Had changed it 'round to Sambo, I was Rastus to a few
Then Choc'late drop was added by some others that I knew
And then to cap the climax I was strolling down the line
When someone shouted, "Fellers hey, come on and pipe the Shine."

As he later tried to tell Jane Goldberg, Bubbles composed a new verse (possibly with the help of some of the MGM pros) that transferred the focus from racially offensive nicknames to the supreme nattiness of this guy, Domino Johnson:

What is it about me that makes me feel well-dressed?
The same old clothes, shoes, and hat,
The same old things, rearranged.
It's very plain to see
Just how it happened to be.

I put some polish on my sky piece [i.e., his hat],
I made a shoestring into a tie,
I cut the corners off the end of my coat
So they wouldn't fly.
I got my shirt from a silver lining,
I got my cane from an old oak tree,
And that is just the reason why the folks all nicknamed me—

This introductory verse gave the song a new context, one that Bubbles could totally buy into: a celebration of sartorial splendor. Denied access to social and political levers of power, African Americans in Bubbles's day clung to the one lever available to them: economic power. The most obvious symbol of this power lay in fine clothes and expensive cars (two of Buck and Bubbles' favorite preoccupations). These trappings of wealth stood not only for financial security but, even more meaningfully, for high achievement in the face of withering opposition. Bubbles's new verse, drawing attention to his character's luxurious appearance, thus transformed a racist minstrel song into an anthem of race pride.

It would be a mistake to credit the quaint modesty of the lyric, with its lip service to making do ("the same old things, rearranged"). The man singing is Domino Johnson, but he is dressed like Sportin' Life after a big win— immaculate jacket, derby, vest, and cane. Domino, in a sense, *was* Sportin' Life, just a different incarnation. His connection with the forces of evil is here made even more explicit, both in the gravity of his sins (two murders) and in his unspoken legwork on behalf of the devils working to engineer Little Joe's downfall. Like Sportin' Life, Domino also loves the spotlight. In a film brim with ravishing performances—the singing of Ethel Waters

Domino Johnson (John W. Bubbles), MGM's *Cabin in the Sky*, 1943.

Source: L. Tom Perry Special Collections, Harold B. Lee Library, Brigham Young University, Provo, Utah.

and Lena Horne, the tap dancing of Bill Bailey, the sweltering ruckus of Duke Ellington's band—Bubbles doesn't exactly upstage his castmates. But his dance on "Shine" is a tour-de-force that stands out even in this august company.

Released from jail after shooting Little Joe, Domino makes his first visit back to Jim Henry's nightclub. He's dressed for the occasion, and beautiful women cluster around him. "My, you do look sharp *tonight*," one says. "Yeah?" Domino answers, and goes into his song. After the singing, the band kicks up and the dance begins—a virtuoso performance most striking for its *minimalism*. Bubbles doesn't execute a single tap. He himself called the dance "a strut," and that sums it up: Like a model on a catwalk, he dances to showcase his appearance. What fascinates is how he elaborates this simple concept into a panorama of expressive motion. As the Ellington band wails in the background, Bubbles struts, marches, skips, and spins, lithe as a young willow but with laser precision. His arms and hands are constantly busy, tilting his hat or swinging his cane. Periodically his legs blur, scissor-kicking or snap-stepping as he strikes a momentary pose then takes off to circle the floor again. His bearing is brash, haughty, audacious, foreshadowing the affect of a James Brown or a Michael Jackson. Finally, at a raucous drum break he runs over to a landing at the bottom of the stairs. For a moment he turns away—*to look at himself in a mirror hanging on the wall*. Then, with a final flourish of body, cane, and hat, he leaps up the stairs and vanishes through the door. It's the kind of sweeping performance that would have been impossible in the claustrophobic boiler room of *Varsity Show*: a true counterpart to the set pieces of Fred Astaire.

It's hard to know how Bubbles's performance was received. The movie itself did very well among Southern Black audiences but by Hollywood standards was otherwise only moderately successful. Most reviews mentioned Bubbles in passing or not at all, focusing instead on the three leads, Waters, Anderson, and Horne. For a young Black child in Baltimore, however, Bubbles's performance outshone them all.

André De Shields is best known today as a Tony Award–winning stage performer whose illustrious career began in 1975 with his Broadway debut in the title role of *The Wiz*. Growing up in the 1950s in a family of eleven children he harbored a dream none of his friends understood: that one day he would "escape those high, dense, impenetrable walls of racism and poverty" into which he had been born. The dream, as he recalled it many years later, took specific shape in an instant, during a Saturday matinee at Baltimore's Royal Theatre:

I'm watching Hopalong Cassidy, I'm watching Gene Autry, I'm watching Fred Astaire and Ginger Rogers, and then all of a sudden, Vincent Minnelli's *Cabin in the Sky* is playing. . . . *Cabin in the Sky* is featuring what at the time was every major black entertainer: Lena Horne, Eddie Rochester Anderson, Ethel Waters, Louis Armstrong, Bill Bailey, Butterfly McQueen, and others. There comes a scene when John Bubbles comes through the tavern doors and he's resplendent in white from head to toe. And he does this dance, and he slides across the bar, and he dances up a flight of stairs, and the way I remember it is that he was consumed into these glittering clouds—*and I knew right then*: That's what I want to do—forget *want* to do—that's what I'm *going* to do. So that was the epiphany, that was the dream, that's the dream I continue to carry with me. . . . It is John Bubbles, the pioneer, or one of the pioneers, of black males in this entertainment industry, that has been my inspiration right to today.

In actuality, Bubbles was not dressed in white for that scene in the club. He didn't slide across the bar. He wasn't enveloped in a mist of clouds. That De Shields remembered all these things suggests the mind-altering impact the scene had on an impressionable young boy. For him Bubbles came from another world, one heavenly in its implications. Although Bubbles's proud performance was quickly forgotten by his contemporaries, it held up a lamp for future generations, providing an ongoing source of inspiration and hope.

13

Black Bizet

1

After filming Bubbles's dance routine for *Cabin in the Sky*, an astonished Vincente Minnelli congratulated him on his agility. "I oughta be quick," the dancer replied, "'cause I'm just about the most excited man you ever did see!" Bubbles then announced he was the father of an eight-and-a-half-pound baby girl and began handing out cigars. The baby was named Charlynn Gertrude (after his late sister, Annie Gertrude). What he did not reveal was the identity of the mother, who was not Viola. For the past six years Bubbles had been carrying on a secret affair with Rhea Wright, the woman he had met in England in 1936, and the time was nearing to make their love public. Or so Rhea thought. So she hoped.

They had met in a London nightclub shortly after Buck and Bubbles arrived in the country. An American working in England as a sculptor's model, Rhea was a classical beauty with café-au-lait skin. Their mutual attraction was instantaneous. According to Bubbles's very specific recollection, they made an "agreement" on August 16, 1936, at 50 Carnaby Street, to find a way to make a life together. Bubbles brought Rhea back to New York with him, but they were both still married to other people and their relationship stalled. They decided to have a baby together, for Bubbles a lifelong dream that he had been unable to realize with Viola. After many failed attempts, Rhea finally became pregnant through artificial insemination. With Charlynn's arrival, they began planning their future.

A cache of letters from the period 1942–1943 attests to the difficulties they faced. As Bubbles traveled the country to fulfill his various engagements, Rhea sent letters to his projected destinations—the Earle Theatre in Philadelphia or the Clark Hotel in Los Angeles. She told him of her exhausting thirty-six-hour delivery, and of their beautiful baby: "She has eyes like yours, and a peach and cream complexion. She never cries since I have milk to feed her. . . . She is the headliner here." During the filming of *Cabin in the Sky*, when Bubbles's prospects for a film career looked momentarily bright, Rhea

Sportin' Life. Brian Harker, Oxford University Press. © Oxford University Press 2022.
DOI: 10.1093/oso/9780197514511.003.0014

yearned for the day she and Charlynn might join him in Hollywood. "I always heard that you had to experience a fact to recognize it," she wrote, "so now I know that it is sheer hell being away from you. Will we ever be together again?" It didn't help that Bubbles was oddly silent about his plans: "What about your work in future, will you stay there [in California] or come East? I do wish we could see each other and have all this out and understood. But with this way of communication there is only wonder this and wonder that. . . . You give me no clear picture to plan around. You ask only what are *you* going to do." Speaking of which: "Have you filed for divorce?"

Money problems exacerbated the tensions between them. Rhea had expenses, both for herself and for the baby, but she recognized that Bubbles also had to support Viola and his mother and occasionally his sister and her children as well:

> The shock of the cost of Charlynn's furniture and milk is so great that I still haven't recovered from it. And [it] makes me realize afresh the necessity of some work of my own. With your other families to keep I know that you do the best you can to help me but we aren't doing enough. Do you know that I never have the price of a Dr. if we took sick, have been unable to have my hair done, don't eat the necessary food for my well being—all because of insufficient funds.

Occasionally she admitted that she got money from a man named Hugh, her former husband, apparently, for whom she obviously still had feelings. She assured Bubbles he was first in her heart. But as an unwed mother in the 1940s, without money or a plan for the future, she felt vulnerable: "As I see my life now, I am standing in my own way, unsecure, unmarried and letting the grass grow under my feet." "Having burned my bridges behind me," she wrote in another letter, their long separations grew more and more unnerving. "I will stand it as long as I can," she said.

Bubbles did his best to pacify her. As Rhea acknowledged to her sister, he sent her a card every day. He also sent letters, packages, gifts of food and clothes, and money orders. But these installments came less frequently—clearly not often enough. In response to her specific complaints, Bubbles veered between empathy and defensiveness. "I must admit that you must be starved for everything pertaining to normal life," he wrote, "and please forgive me for not being on hand for the convenience human contacts." But when could they be together as a family? When would they buy a house in a nice neighborhood? When could Rhea count on a regular allowance? Bubbles didn't say. Instead, he focused on Hugh: "I asked you to get your business as far as Hugh was to be concerned straightened out before the baby was borned, and you said that it was all finished. . . . I ask you again not to be with him . . . until I have disappointed you in my utmost effort of your and Charlynn Gertrude's support." He pleaded for patience but also sounded a warning: "I don't want you or no one else that don't do as I say." Thus did Rhea suffer the fate of every other smart and independent woman in Bubbles's life: Without exception, sooner or later, he tried to bend them to his will.

In fairness, there was little Bubbles could do to end their agonizing separations short of bringing Rhea and the baby on the road with him. A life in show business required long months of travel, and after *Cabin in the Sky* Buck and Bubbles had plenty of work. The money issue was another matter. Although Bubbles wasn't making nearly as much as he used to, his salary from this period put him squarely in the upper-middle income bracket. In the spring of 1943, he personally averaged $825 a month. In 2020 dollars, that's over $12,000 a month, $144,000 a year. Not a fortune, but enough to support two small households at a modest standard of living. There's no reason Bubbles couldn't have taken care of Rhea and their baby while still satisfying his obligations to Viola and his mother. No reason, that is, other than his compulsive gambling habit.

According to financial records Bubbles kept in the spring of 1943, he was never out of debt to Nat Nazarro. In a two-week period in March, he requested no fewer than *six advances* on his salary:

Mar	17	Ft. Worth	$150
	23	Houston	$167.50
		Houston	$200
		Dallas	$20
	29	Houston	$20
			$174.79

Since Bubbles earned only $532.29 during the same period, he ended up owing Nazarro $200 for the month. The same thing happened in April. Despite earning $874.82, he still owed Nazarro $209.64 after eleven advances. In May he owed $397.51. In June: $122.36. July: $539.56. If Rhea had found out Bubbles was borrowing from his manager to send her those occasional life-saving money orders because he had frittered away his paychecks in riotous living, she might have left him then and there. But she didn't find out. So she stayed.

2

As it happened, Bubbles kept letters from Nat Nazarro during this period as well. The correspondence opens a window onto that strange, fraught relationship. As might be expected, the letters often deal with financial or logistical matters. "Please try to be economical," he implored Buck in one letter that somehow came into Bubbles's hands. In another he offered to wire Bubbles some money—but "take it easy," he urged. Sometimes just getting Buck and Bubbles to the same place at the same time was a challenge:

> Now, I want both of you to be on the same train, you already have your ticket—please see for your own good that Buck is on the same train, only on a day-coach, which he doesn't even deserve for losing his ticket, I want you both on the same train so that you won't have to look for each other in Chicago, this is very important. Let me know when you expect to leave so I can wire the money for Buck's coach ticket.

One note reveals Nazarro's Machiavellian turn of mind. He explained, conspiratorially, that even though a job at Chicago's Regal Theatre would only pay $1,300, he "asked for a contract for $1,500 and signed an IOU for $200 back to them." That way, he told Bubbles, he could show the inflated contract to the next booker and squeeze him for more money.

Sometimes Nazarro—or his secretary, Gertrude Quinton—would give Bubbles little pep talks to keep his spirits up or encourage good behavior. "We are negotiating a picture for you," Quinton wrote in July 1943, "also we have offers for several other things. . . . It looks as tho Buck and Bubbles are back in the Big Time and see that they stay there, hear me talking to you!" In return, Bubbles could address Nazarro with surprising warmth. He once signed off playfully with names from some of his past roles: "Domino, Skipio [sic], Wildcat." Inevitably, however, the latent hostility would flare up. During Show Time in 1942, Bubbles wrote that unnamed Hollywood types had been badmouthing Nazarro and seemed justified in doing so. Nazarro defended himself as an unappreciated drudge, striving only to serve the interests of his clients:

Now, Bubbles, while you were saying . . . what they were saying in California about Nat, your dear manager was busy day and night stopping at no expense whatsoever, including many long distance calls to California. . . . I might add, you will be able to make California your home if the entire deal comes thru as I am planning, so you see Nat is not so bad after all, and if I were stingy, these things would not be accomplished.

Love and kisses

Soon enough, however, Bubbles would be reminded once again why he did not—and could not—trust his manager of twenty-five years.

Back on the road, Bubbles and his partner again joined the service of those hoping to stage a comeback of old-time entertainment. In 1943 they appeared in George White's Scandals, a traveling "girl show" along the lines of the Ziegfeld Follies, where, according to one review, they were "the standouts of the show." After eight months with the Scandals, they were hired by the same impresario who produced *Show Time*, the vaudeville revival in Los Angeles, to appear in two sequels—*Laugh Time*, in New York, and *Curtain Time*, in San Francisco. The former featured Frank Fay, Bert Wheeler, and Ethel Waters as headliners; the latter, Chico Marx and Connee Boswell. These engagements, plus a late-night coda at the Club Zanzibar in Manhattan, kept them busy through the end of the year.

In the spring of 1944, the team appeared in a movie called *Atlantic City*, another product of vaudeville nostalgia. Set in 1915, the film depicts a small-time vaude tycoon who aspires to turn his beach-town resort into an entertainment mecca. At one point, the white leads pay an anachronistic visit to the Apollo Theatre (transplanted from Harlem to Atlantic City), where Dorothy Dandridge, Louis Armstrong, and Buck and Bubbles do a sequence called "Harlem on Parade." Bubbles sings "Rhythm for Sale" and dances, followed by Buck doing his comic shuffling. Like the other variety scenes, this "colored segment" feels tacked on to add vibrancy to a lifeless script. Only from a financial point of view was the movie worth anything: During filming Buck and Bubbles earned $2,500 a week.

Two months later, Bubbles received the toughest news of his life. On September 21, 1944, his beloved mother died of heart failure at age sixty-six. Having borne eight children of her own and helped to raise her youngest daughter's ten children, having indeed "scuffled herself to the bone" just to bring up Bubbles, Katie Sublett occupied an outsize role in her family's life. She was "my every whim, my everything," Bubbles said, to the point that he "could have almost went to the cemetery with her, really." Memories were his one consolation: "She was always good to me, though. I can't get over that. I don't want to get over that. I just want to remember that as long as I live. . . . Thank God I was able to take care of her until she passed away."

In arranging her burial, Bubbles did an odd thing. He bought a double gravestone marked SUBLETT. The left-hand side bore Katie's name; the right-hand side was left blank. Twenty years later he wrote the mortuary to ask if another body could be interred in the plot, apparently hoping to move his father's remains from Louisville, where he had died in 1921, to be reburied beside his mother in Queens, the two of them united at last in death. The plan, which must have been prohibitively expensive, was never carried out, and to this day the blank space on the stone remains, a forlorn emblem of unfulfilled hope. But the hope was there: At some level Bubbles wanted to redeem the man who had terrorized his childhood.

3

In the spring of 1945, Buck and Bubbles joined the touring company of *Carmen Jones*, an all-Black adaptation of Georges Bizet's beloved opera *Carmen*. *Carmen Jones* was the latest example of a trend toward all-Black reworkings of classic theatrical or operatic works, including *Voodoo Macbeth* (1936), a Haitian reading of Shakespeare's tragedy, and *The Hot Mikado* (1939), a jazz remodeling of Gilbert and Sullivan, starring Bill Robinson in the title role. As an all-Black opera, of course, *Carmen Jones* also harked back to *Porgy and Bess*, making Buck and Bubbles natural candidates to fill vacancies in the cast.

Produced by Billy Rose with book and lyrics by Oscar Hammerstein II, *Carmen Jones* modernized Bizet's tragic story of lust, obsession, and murder, transferring the opera's setting from early nineteenth-century Spain to wartime America in the 1940s. The cigarette factory where Don José first sees Carmen becomes a parachute factory in the American South. After her arrest, Carmen Jones seduces "Corporal Joe," a naïve Air Force pilot-in-training, and persuades him to go AWOL. Joe's rival for Carmen Jones's affections is transformed from the bullfighter Escamillo of the original into a brawny prizefighter named Husky Miller.

Carmen Jones was a big success on Broadway, notching 503 performances. Having turned his initial investment of $175,000 into a profit of over a million dollars, Billy Rose was eager to take his show on the road. The production had gelled so well, he told a reporter, that the New York cast and the touring cast were *almost* identical: "The only important change of personnel is that of the two comedians—the prize fight manager and his stooge assistant. In New York these two parts were played by two fairly competent people. On tour, Buck and Bubbles are playing these parts. I think they are far superior performers and, incidentally, much more expensive ones." Buck and Bubbles were contracted to play Rum and Dink (originally, the smugglers Remendado and Dancaïre), "who play right and left bower to the prizefighter." As Rose suggested, these were essentially comic relief roles, not major ones—a fact Buck and Bubbles tried to spin as a willing sacrifice for the sake of art. "They interrupted a highly successful vaudeville tour in order to take their present roles," wrote the *Cleveland Herald*.

The truth, as Bubbles admitted years later—and as contemporaneous news accounts confirm—is that they were just finishing a job at the Paramount and didn't have any more gigs lined up. *Carmen Jones* came as an unexpected boon. Billy Rose's secretary called Bubbles to inquire about the team's availability and as always he referred her to Nazarro, hoping the job would come through. When he didn't hear anything the next day Bubbles called Nazarro, who explained he had rejected Rose's offer because the producer wouldn't pay any more than $100 a week. Then Bubbles himself called Rose and got a very different story. According to Rose, Nazarro said Buck and Bubbles couldn't take the job because they were booked solid. As a substitute he had offered the services of one of the other Black teams he represented, a younger two-act called Heckle and Jive. Incensed, Bubbles asked for a meeting the following day, and Rose agreed. At the meeting, which Nazarro attended as well, Bubbles simply asked Rose if he had parts for Buck and Bubbles in the show. Rose said he did.

"When do we start?" Bubbles asked. Rose told him. "What salary?"

"Seven hundred and fifty dollars."

Nazarro never said a word. There was nothing to do but sign the contract.

Bubbles later saw Nazarro's stunt as part of an underhanded campaign to phase Buck and Bubbles out of the business and replace them with younger, hotter acts. True or not, *Carmen Jones* would be the team's last significant show together.

Although Hammerstein had updated the story of *Carmen* and translated the original French into his own conception of Black American patois, Bizet's

Rum and Dink (Buck and Bubbles), *Carmen Jones*, 1945.

Source: L. Tom Perry Special Collections, Harold B. Lee Library, Brigham Young University, Provo, Utah.

music was left essentially untouched with the exception of some Broadway-style reorchestrations and some crowd-pleasing drumming by celebrated swing drummer Cozy Cole. As in the original version of the opera, the singers used spoken dialogue instead of recitative. For Buck and Bubbles, this concession would have made *Carmen Jones* an easier show to learn than *Porgy and Bess*. Their most difficult assignment was the complex Smugglers' Quintet from Act 2 (renamed "Whizzin' Away Along De Track"). Reprising their method in *Porgy and Bess*, they learned it entirely by ear according to the *Los Angeles Examiner*:

> A pianist played the number to them over and over on the piano. Presently Buck, who has a rare ear and magic fingers, was able to play it himself. From then on it was just another song number, so simple, in fact, that Bubbles is tempted now and then to "take off" and supply some [improvised] variations. But he is firm with himself: "If you change one note it isn't any more Bizet."

The reporter claimed that, as he did with *Porgy and Bess*, "Buck can now play all the music of the opera, and more than that, he can reproduce at the piano any part for any instrument in the orchestra. Maybe he can't read notes, but he knows the score."

The tour lasted two years. The show opened at New York's City Center on May 2, 1945, spent the summer in California, and the fall—four straight months—at Chicago's Erlanger Theatre. From there the company traveled steadily through the spring of 1946, broke for summer vacation, then continued traveling through the fall and winter, closing with a week in Pittsburgh in mid-April 1947. Most of the tour covered New England and the upper Midwest with periodic forays into California, but the troupe also spent one month in Southern states east of the Mississippi and another month in Texas. Fortunately, given all this touring (and the Southern destinations), the company traveled in style, riding in "its own private train of eleven cars: five sleepers, a diner, a club car, and four baggage cars full of scenery and costumes." "To move such a tremendous show is extremely costly," wrote a reporter, "but since *Carmen Jones* sells out everywhere, the venture is financially as well as artistically sound."

As in New York, the critics swooned. The show was hailed in Los Angeles as "incomparably the most thrilling footlight event of the season," and in Chicago as "the best show to strike this town since 'The Glass Menagerie'" the previous year. Writing for the *San Francisco Chronicle*, the eminent critic Alfred Frankenstein praised the sets, costumes, and choreography as "magnificent," and the singers as "very nearly perfect for their assignments." Buck and Bubbles, wrote *Variety*, were "admittedly put into the cast . . . because of their [box office] draw." Though dressed in loud rickrack stripes, however, they did not stand out from their castmates. Reviewers appreciated them as "able comedians" who served as Husky Miller's "amusing retinue"—nothing more. Occasionally their operatic inexperience became a liability, as during their big quintet number, "Whizzin' Away Along De Track," "where the women's voices drown them out." Still, their presence "added a little luster to what last year was voted the Donaldson Award as top musical of the season."

The show was more controversial among African Americans. Some objected to the script's ham-fisted Black dialect, others to its perpetuation of stereotypes that placed Black characters in settings of vice and dissolution. And some criticisms were more dependent on geography. In Louisville, Bubbles noted in his daybook, the NAACP and the Kentucky Bureau of Negro Affairs picketed the show because although Black patrons were allowed onto the main floor of the theater—a shocking breach of racial etiquette in that town—they were still segregated from white patrons. The picketing went on for two weeks, until the show opened again in unambiguously northern country. According to a white newspaper with an obvious interest in discrediting the protesters, "Negro actors expressed no sympathy with the picketing, saying members of their race were not refused admittance and asking why the pickets did not protest against segregation in shows with white casts." Black patrons, in any case, freely crossed the picket lines to see the show. In St. Louis, Bubbles observed jazz musicians Ella Fitzgerald, Dizzy Gillespie, and Cootie Williams doing just that.

The references to picketing in Bubbles's daybook reveal for the first time his awareness of or interest in politics, and more specifically the nascent civil rights movement that rose from the ashes of World War II. Within six months, he would be clipping news stories about Jackie Robinson. The tenor of the times may have inspired a new seriousness in Bubbles's backstage conduct with *Carmen Jones*. At forty-two, he and Buck were among the oldest members of the cast. It was time to settle down, forsake the hellraising for which he became known in *Porgy and Bess*, and show some leadership.

He got a nudge from Billy Rose himself, when the producer asked Bubbles to serve as master of ceremonies for the show's "second birthday party" in October 1945. Before a large gathering of dignitaries and celebrities, Bubbles introduced dozens of people "for extemporaneous speeches and unrehearsed routines and appearances." The following year the Actors Equity Association, a theatrical labor union, appointed Bubbles to be its deputy with the *Carmen Jones* company. Even though this post usually went to a prominent member of the cast, Bubbles had won the confidence of his colleagues to such an extent that a majority were willing to vote for him. Although in private he continued playing the part of Sportin' Life, in public he now began primping for the role of elder statesman.

4

The first time *Carmen Jones* came through Los Angeles, Bubbles enjoyed a reunion with Rhea and Charlynn, who had moved to the West Coast in hopes of seeing him more often. A food reporter for the *Pittsburgh Courier* sat down with the little family for an interview, at the end sharing with her readers some of their favorite recipes: Buck and Bubbles Almond Chicken, Lucille's Salad (Rhea also went by "Lucille"), and "Charlyeen's Cornflake Cookies." "Little Miss Charlyeen Bubbles," the reporter added, "made her stage debut while here at the tender age of three. She was a great success and has all the promises of becoming a great star. Like father like daughter. Her ambition, so she tells me, is to be a doctor."

That was in July of 1945. Rhea and Bubbles still weren't married. Two years later, back in New York again and living in a house Bubbles had bought for them, Rhea grew tired of the waiting and the privation. When Bubbles finally returned home from the road, divorced from Viola at last and ready to settle down, he found himself a stranger in his own house. To make ends meet, Rhea had begun taking in boarders. Now, to Bubbles's consternation, one of the boarders, a man named Wilson, sat at the head of the table at dinner. That night Bubbles and Rhea slept in separate bedrooms. When he got up the next day, he called her name. She opened a bedroom door, and Bubbles could see she was with Wilson.

"Well, what are you callin' me for?" she said.

"I've been calling you for eleven years," Bubbles replied.

And that was it. There were no mortifying retributions of the kind he had inflicted on Buck and Viola. By his own account he simply crumpled and walked away—from Rhea, Charlynn, and the house—taking only a few personal items.

Some months later Bubbles went to visit Charlynn at Rhea's sister's house. He recalled the last conversation he had with his daughter.

"Here, darlin', throw the ball," he said to her. "Throw the ball to your daddy."

"Oh, my daddy's dead," she said.

Stunned, Bubbles asked, "Well, then, Charlynn, who am I?"

"Oh, you're my Uncle Bubbles. And my mommy says you're no good."

Rhea and Charlynn moved back to England, and Bubbles never saw either one of them again.

14

Requiem for a Two-Act

1

After the *Carmen Jones* tour, Buck and Bubbles came home to a live entertainment world in free fall. As millions of soldiers returned from the war and got married, the country took a sharp domestic turn, forsaking the hot nightlife of cabarets and ballrooms in favor of more family-oriented activities at home (especially watching TV). The swing ecosystem that had helped sustain endangered vaudevillians for so many years collapsed. Nightclubs took a "nosedive" (according to the American Guild of Variety Artists), and jazz-heavy thoroughfares like New York's 52nd Street were turned to other purposes, sending musicians, dancers, and comedians scrambling for work elsewhere. Reflecting on the scene in the late 1940s, Bubbles shook his head: "It was in a wander, man. Black entertainment was in a wander."

As for vaudeville itself, that "curiously lively corpse" that had "died" and risen again so many times before, the day of judgment was nigh at last. As always, there were conflicting signals. In late 1947 Loew's State, "one of the last bulwarks of vaude left in the country," ended its policy of live acts and went into straight pictures. "Vaudeville has failed to pay off," the management explained. And yet shortly thereafter, in a final spasm of diehard revivalism, the New York Palace *reinstituted* vaudeville for the first time in fourteen years. If vaudeville limped along into the 1950s—and can be found as a retro-niche commodity even today—the fact remains that as a living industry catering to a mass audience, vaudeville was through by Eisenhower's first inaugural, and probably long before then. This sad fact is evidenced by the gradual disintegration of Buck and Bubbles's career from 1947 to 1952.

Tap dancing declined as well, a reality symbolized by the death of Bill Robinson on November 25, 1949, at the age of seventy-one. More than thirty thousand people filed past his coffin to pay their respects. Buck and Bubbles took their place among 150 honorary pallbearers, including Louis Armstrong, Bob Hope, Joe DiMaggio, and Jackie Robinson. In his eulogy, the mayor of New York noted "the ending of an era," a sentiment with strong connotations

Sportin' Life. Brian Harker, Oxford University Press. © Oxford University Press 2022.
DOI: 10.1093/oso/9780197514511.003.0015

at that moment in history. Putting his finger on the key point, Congressman Adam Clayton Powell Jr. acknowledged "the general opinion that Bojangles was an 'Uncle Tom'"—but, he said, "anyone who had that impression did not know Bill Robinson." Maybe not, but the impression persisted nevertheless, powerfully shaping the public image of Black tap dancers ever after.

In tap dancing's heyday, a Cotton Club chorus girl recalled, "tap dancing was considered a very masculine thing to do." For Black dancers in the civil rights-conscious 1950s and 1960s, however, it became a symbol of *emasculation*. As veteran hoofers plied their routines on TV, one of the few forums still open to them, their smiling performances for the amusement of white hosts and guests beamed the apparent image of the unreconstructed darky, happy-go-lucky and eager-to-please, into the homes of millions of Americans. The tap-dancing Black man as Uncle Tom became a cultural cliché. This change in perception coincided with Bubbles's sense of his own mortality. When someone remarked, "You don't dance like you used to," the fifty-year-old gave a ribald rejoinder that became a running gag with him: "I don't do *anything* like I used to." Sure, he was being a good sport, but he was also joking about a constitutional weakness that dovetailed nicely with the newly neutered image of his profession.

Cut off from traditional sources of employment, most Black dancers faced various forms of hardship and dispossession. The Nicholas Brothers moved to Europe. Honi Coles opened a short-lived dance studio. Chuck Green would spend the next decade in a mental institution. And Buck and Bubbles underwent a series of crises, culminating in the fiasco that, after thirty-six years together, would finally split them up for good.

2

The first crisis started out as a joyous occasion. On May 28, 1948, Bubbles married his second wife, Mabel Roane, at St. Mark's Church (in-the-Bowery) in Manhattan. Having divorced Viola the previous year in preparation to marry Rhea Wright, he was left entirely alone when Rhea threw him over for another man. Mabel represented a departure from Bubbles's usual choice in women. Whereas Viola had been a chorus girl and Rhea a sculptor's model, Mabel, though not unattractive, had a somewhat matronly appearance. A year older than Bubbles and a divorced person herself, she was 5' 2" and "plump," a prominent socialite in Harlem and the executive secretary for the Negro Actors Guild. In marrying her, Bubbles elevated his social status, gained proximity to one of the professional organizations he admired, and secured for himself a second income—not an insignificant consideration given his chaotic finances.

Yet Bubbles's affection for his new wife seems to have been sincere. Their reception at a quiet restaurant in Harlem "included only their close friends, and it was more like an intimate party with everyone pitching in to make it a memorable occasion for two well-liked people." Bill Robinson tapped out a routine as Buck played "I'll Dance at Your Wedding," and Bubbles sang a love song to his bride. "From where I sat," a reporter wrote, "I could swear there were tears of happiness in her eyes." In the ensuing months, Bubbles and Mabel were seen at various professional meetings and social events. At the end of the year Mabel took a three-month leave of absence in order to ac-company Bubbles to the West Coast, where he and Buck appeared again with George White's Scandals in San Francisco.

When the couple returned to New York, however, the dream shattered. On February 17, 1949, federal agents arrested Mabel on charges of forgery and grand larceny. At the indictment, the story came out. From March 1944 to March 1948 (just before marrying Bubbles), Mabel had allegedly forged more than 226 checks worth over $20,000, drawing the money from the Welfare Fund of the Negro Actors Guild. To carry out her scheme she assumed the identities of dozens of prominent Black entertainers, including Rex Ingram, Avis Andrews, Hall Johnson, Bill Robinson, Tom Fletcher, Tim Brymn, Mamie Smith, Abbie Mitchell, Pigmeat Markham, and J. Rosamond Johnson. Mabel initially denied the charges but later confessed, explaining she had used the money—only $8,000 of the total—"to educate my daughter." In June she was sentenced to two-and-a-half to five years in Bedford Hills, a prison for women in southern New York state. She would be eligible for parole in sixteen months. In the mean-time, her lawyer said, she would make restitution for the money she had stolen.

The second crisis occurred simultaneously with the first. Eight days before his marriage to Mabel, Bubbles sought for the final time to divorce Nat Nazarro. This followed Buck and Bubbles's appearance in A Song Is Born, their last and most disappointing feature film. A showcase for Danny Kaye that also spotlighted a broad pantheon of jazz royalty, both white and Black, the film makes little effort to show what Buck and Bubbles could do. Cast as window washers, the pair serve mostly as racial props to authenticate the movie's cringey white-bread references to jazz. Looking back on the experience, Bubbles seethed: "It's a disgrace when you think about it. We had more talent than anybody in the whole picture but didn't get a chance to display it. Buck would play the piano and I'd just do a little shuffle, which was nothin', . . . and I didn't get to sing. *They smother you, they smother you.*"

Shortly after Buck and Bubbles returned to New York, the gigs dried up. Judging from the entertainment weeklies, the team went without work for almost five months. On May 20, 1948, an exasperated Bubbles sued Nazarro to be released from his contract, in which fortunately his attorney found clear illegalities. (Buck later joined the suit as well.) A review of the contract, the attorney argued, showed that Nazarro demanded 30 percent of the team's earnings while only promising to place bookings. This put Nazarro in violation of New York's General Business Law, which stated that a booking agent couldn't ask more than 5 percent (though most acts gave 10 percent as a courtesy). Nazarro tried to disguise his actions by referring to himself as a "manager" rather than an "agent," but Bubbles's attorney called this a subterfuge. The judge agreed. On November 4, 1949, he declared Nazarro's contract "invalid and void." After twenty-nine years of struggle, Buck and Bubbles were finally free.

The next step was to sue for damages, to recover the 25 percent Nazarro had illegally taken for himself after each gig. Due to the six-year statute of limitations, the judge put a cap at $28,492. Nazarro responded indignantly that any amount would be unjust, given all he had invested in the team:

> 28 years ago when the plaintiff and his partner came to New York City they were poor and hungry. . . . They were unschooled and uncouth and wanted to be musical performers, although they could not even read music and still cannot. Almost as a lark, together with a group of others, I auditioned them. The others laughed but somewhere beneath the extremely rough exterior, I discovered a spark of talent. I fed the boys, bought them clothes and rehearsed them for months, hammering into them the essentials of show business. I wrote an act for them and some special material and rehearsed them in these unceasingly until (still in spite of the laughter of my friends) I put them on the stage in a vaudeville theatre as part of my act. They were terrible, but I didn't give up hope.

Terrible? Was this the same act he had locked in their dressing room after that very debut? That stopped the show four times at the Audubon? That made a clean sweep of the top New York theaters, including the Palace? That Nazarro himself told his friends was "a find of finds"? No, the history of that act had to be preposterously rewritten. Far from stumbling upon a precious cash cow,

Nazarro lamented, he had found worse-than-amateurs who needed to be taught everything (Nazarro's most brazen fabrication is that he taught Buck to play the piano). And if the ungrateful performers were now allowed to seize his rightful earnings after he had built them up from scratch, "it would be a great injustice to me."

The judge didn't buy Nazarro's story, but he encouraged Bubbles to settle with him. At the urging of his lawyers, Bubbles reluctantly agreed to a mere $4,000, of which $1,550 went to the IRS, $1,800 to his attorneys, and $650 to a judge's assistant for "services rendered." According to this accounting (summarized by his lawyer), Bubbles didn't get a dime. "But I was out of the contract," he recalled. "I was free of Nat Nazarro at last, and there was some satisfaction in that. Yessir, some satisfaction in that."

Hardy as ever, Nazarro plugged on into the next decade, signing new acts and playing the angles. But he was getting old. In 1959, alone in his apartment, he passed away at age seventy-one. Bubbles took grim satisfaction in learning that it took three days for someone to notice he was missing.

Today Nazarro is remembered—and rightly so—as a "monster agent" who exploited, cheated, and manipulated his clients. But for all his undeniable flaws, he also helped to integrate a generation of Black artists into white show business. At one time or another he represented Bessie Smith, Pearl Bailey, Bill Bailey, Avis Andrews, Pigmeat Markham, Betty Carter, the Berry Brothers, the Four Step Brothers, the Three Rhythm Queens, the Six Spirits of Rhythm, and a host of duos inspired by Buck and Bubbles's success: Chuck and Chuckles, Stump and Stumpy, Red and Curley, Moke and Poke, Heckle and Jive, and many others. Someone, at least, was appreciative. Every year for ten years after Nazarro's death, an anonymous individual placed an ad in *Variety* that read simply: "In Memoriam NAT NAZARRO— Mar. 14, 1959."

3

Beset by legal headaches involving Mabel and Nazarro, Bubbles could find no respite. "Everything was tough," he said. "I had no money. Everything is hard when you ain't got no money." To make up the shortfall Bubbles took a job in a tomato-packing plant shortly after marrying Mabel. He separated the good tomatoes from the bad and drove a delivery truck. But as soon as a performing job came along, he took it. "When it was over, I went back to get my job back at the tomato place. The fellow said I was unreliable, and I didn't get the job." Bubbles realized that with show business it would be all or nothing.

It helped, at least, that William Morris became the team's agent in the summer of 1948. Morris took only 10 percent, leaving Buck and Bubbles to split the rest. The first Morris gig was a TV appearance, a hopeful sign. As we have seen, in London in 1936 Buck and Bubbles had appeared on the first television broadcast in history. Three years later they also enjoyed the distinction of becoming the "first colored act"—according to *Variety*—to appear on American TV. The Black press was elated. "This honor is the highest Negroes could achieve in the fast progressing field of radio transmission of both voice and pictures," wrote the *Amsterdam News*. The question was, what next? "Will the fate of the colored artist," asked the *Defender*, "be the same in television as it is now in radio? Or will it be a new day for the Race? . . . How will he be portrayed? . . . Will he be made to cut up and act like a fool or shall he portray himself as he is in everyday life?" Such questions could only be answered once television left the experimental stage and took off as a viable new medium, which it did, finally, in 1948.

Even more encouraging for Buck and Bubbles, many people saw TV "as a possible medium for the second blooming of vaudeville." In this spirit, on August 10, 1948, ABC opened its New York TV station with a vaudeville-themed extravaganza. The show was broadcast from the stage of the old Palace Theatre. Seats were reserved for elderly patrons who had regularly attended the Monday matinees back in the day. Outside, horse-drawn streetcars and high-wheeled bicycles evoked the turn of the century. And the show itself featured "vaudeville's famous stars": Carlton Emmy and His Mad Wags, Ella Logan, James Barton, Willie West and McGinty, Pat Rooney, Walter "Dare" Wahl, Mary Raye and Naldi, Beatrice Lillie, the Paul Whiteman Orchestra, and those vaude revival mainstays, Buck and Bubbles. Ray Bolger, master of ceremonies, appeared next-to-closing, and in a distasteful nod to the past, Buck and Bubbles were given the traditional slot for Black acts: the deuce spot, second on the bill. The show was advertised as "the Greatest Television Show You've Ever Seen."

Critics indeed found the program "electrifying," bringing "tears to lovers of old vaudeville." Buck and Bubbles were tapped again to perform for ABC's Chicago premiere. Then NBC hired them for its Midwest opening in St. Louis. *Billboard* congratulated the team for "being on every important video operation premiere in the past couple of months." They did "the best job" in St. Louis and proved "a smash hit" in Chicago. "[They] ought to do well in video for years to come," wrote the *Chicago Tribune*. Yes, you would think.

During this period, variety shows were the most highly rated on television, and some hosts, notably Ed Sullivan and Steve Allen, made a conscious effort to feature Black performers. Buck and Bubbles did appear occasionally on shows like Milton Berle's Texaco Star Theater, Arthur Godfrey and His Friends, the Perry Como Show, and the Cavalcade of Stars. But other forces worked against them. Sponsors feared antagonizing Southern viewers, and racist attitudes infected TV executives as well. As in vaudeville, early TV typically used no more than one Black act per program. With only three networks and other genres to produce, there just weren't enough variety shows to keep a single act working steadily.

In an attempt to boost racial equality on TV, Bubbles won a leadership role with the American Guild of Variety Artists (AGVA) and spoke out at union meetings. In 1951, during a debate at the Television Authority Convention over discriminatory hiring practices, he "delivered the most stinging and accurate speech of the convention," a delegate said, "though not everyone realized it at the time, because of the terrific laughs he incorporated." It was noble and painstaking work but not the kind that would yield immediate benefits. Between sporadic TV appearances Buck and Bubbles were forced to continue seeking live engagements, an increasingly rare commodity.

As if sensing the famous duo's career was winding down, critics began garnishing their reviews with valedictories. After a show at RKO Boston a *Globe* critic wrote, "While the routines of Buck and Bubbles seldom change, they seem to get better and better as the years roll by. . . . [They] have that magic gift for transporting their auditors into a state of pure delight." During a long run at the Capitol, a *Variety* reporter waxed similarly nostalgic: "Buck and Bubbles seemingly go on forever. There's no denying their ability to entertain. While they've been around a good many years, a last vestige of the old Palace theatre two-a-day heyday, there's barely any slowdown in their performance." And after an appearance at the Casino Club in Toronto, another critic put it succinctly: "Around for a long time, Buck and Bubbles are the marquee draw as the epitome of vaudeville."

The epitome of vaudeville. Such words might come as a surprise to vaudeville historians who barely mention the team, usually wrapping up their accounts in the late 1920s just as Buck and Bubbles's career was taking off. Yet as we have seen, the inexhaustible twosome played a dominant role in vaudeville's zombie afterlife. They were "surefire," the "never-miss boys," "the most consistent showstopper of all vaudeville acts." They may well have been the greatest act of their time. In 1958, feeling the tug of days long past, legendary sports writer Jimmy Cannon made a list of some of the things he would never forget—"the first time I heard Bing Crosby croon 'Stardust,'" for example. "Damon Runyon talking about the old red-light district in Denver." "Phil Rizzuto running into center field for a pop fly." And, not least: "Any vaudeville bill with Buck and Bubbles on it."

During their last two years together, the quality of their bookings plummeted. According to news reports they played major theaters eight times in 1950, five times in 1951, and not at all in 1952. (Their last show at the New York Palace opened the week of August 23, 1951.) Twice they headlined at the "Aquashow" in Flushing Meadow, an "outdoor water carnival." In May 1950 they toured briefly with the Harlem Globetrotters.

Frustrated by a long lay-off between March and July in 1951, the team left William Morris for Joe Glaser, Louis Armstrong's agent. Glaser found them work for a while (including two shows with Billie Holiday), but the slow pace resumed. In 1952 Buck and Bubbles played the smallest of small-time venues, often one- or two-night stands: Kiel Auditorium (St. Louis), Municipal Auditorium (Kansas City), Mechanics Building (Boston), Congers Lake Country Club (New York), and the Little Theatre at the Colorado State Fair in Pueblo. They even gave a private party for one "Charles Rapp." In July Bubbles turned down an invitation to join the historic 1952 production of *Porgy and Bess* because of "his unwillingness to break up the team." If that was his reason, he should have taken the job.

4

The final crisis hit during a two-week engagement in Toronto. Mabel, out of prison by this time, drove to Canada with her husband. On September 15, 1952, Buck and Bubbles opened at Bassel's Lounge performing four shows a night, from 6:30 to midnight. All went well until the end of the first week, when a squad of Canadian Mounties burst into Buck's hotel room and began ransacking its contents, looking for drugs. After discovering "a quantity of marijuana cigarettes," they raided Bubbles's room as well, finding more weed in his trunk. The police arrested Buck, Bubbles, Mabel, and one of Buck's musician friends, saxophonist Benny Winestone, for "possession of narcotics."

Bubbles and Mabel pleaded not guilty. At the time of his arrest Bubbles told the Mounties the pot wasn't his, that, as a friend, "he took it from his partner and intended to let Washington have the drug when he needed it." Was this craven self-preservation, pure and simple? Was it long-delayed payback for Buck's betrayal with Viola? Or was Bubbles just telling the truth—that whatever drug problem he had in the past was no longer a problem? Impossible to say.

Buck and Winestone, on the other hand, pleaded guilty. On the stand, Buck took the blame and exculpated Bubbles, explaining that he, Buck, had

The great Buck Washington.

Source: L. Tom Perry Special Collections, Harold B. Lee Library, Brigham Young University, Provo, Utah.

gotten the marijuana from a guy he met at Bassel's named African Joe, a merchant seaman from Montreal.

"What did you do with it?" the prosecutor asked.

"I put it in a trunk," Buck answered—the same trunk the police found in Bubbles's hotel room. On the strength of Buck's testimony, Bubbles and Mabel were acquitted "on benefit of doubt." After two months of incarceration (since they couldn't get anyone south of the border to pay their $3,000 bail), they returned home to New York. Buck and his friend were each sentenced to six months in a Toronto jail and fined $200.

In the spring of 1953 Buck was released and sent home. But something had happened in the interim. Maybe he'd heard Bubbles had fingered him to the Mounties. Maybe he was hardened by his imprisonment. Whatever the reason, he didn't want to have anything to do with Bubbles anymore. He wrote friends from Toronto that he planned to do a solo act when he got home. For the next year and a half, he played for the Timmie Rogers band, starting with an extended tenure at ex-prize fighter Bob Olin's nightclub.

On January 31, 1955, at age fifty-two, Ford Lee Washington died of pneumonia at Sydenham hospital in Harlem. The major New York dailies did not report it. His funeral drew "a host of old-timers": Noble Sissle, Red Allen, Bessie Dudley, Stuff Smith, Hazel Scott, Mary Lou Williams—and Nat Nazarro. Bubbles was in Europe at the time. When he heard the news, he recalled years later, "I cried all night." For all the setbacks, provocations, and betrayals, Buck had been for him the one indispensable ally, second only to his mother. For the rest of his life, whenever someone asked when Buck died, Bubbles often gave the full date: month, day, year. It was a rupture from which he would never fully recover.

PART IV
SURVIVOR (1953–1986)

15

Exile

1

In the summer of 1953, Bubbles's listing ship finally ran aground. At fifty years old, with few jobs and fewer prospects, he appeared washed up, a has-been. All the people he had once relied on for sustenance and support were either gone or compromised. His beloved mother was dead, his wife a convicted felon. His lifelong partner refused to work with him. Even the loss of Nat Nazarro must have stung when he realized no one was going to bail him out of jail in Toronto—not his new agent, not his friends, not his family.

There may have been a time, when his celebrity peaked after *Porgy and Bess*, when Bubbles could have made a prosperous career as a single. Now his turn as Sportin' Life was a distant memory. Many people had heard of Buck and Bubbles; far fewer knew "John Bubbles." Without Buck he would have to develop new jokes, new patter, a new routine. And he would have to sell it to contractors in an environment indifferent or hostile to his kind of entertainment. The challenge of restarting his career would be great.

He began the process immediately, even before leaving Canada. After being released from jail, Bubbles took a job at the Silver Rail, where he was "a big hit," according to *Billboard*. The management even put down a new wooden floor, the better to hear his taps. Once back in New York, however, the pickings thinned out. He spent a few weeks at a midtown club called Snookie's, sharing the bill with other hard-luck cases: drummer Sonny Greer ("formerly with Duke Ellington") and pianist Cliff Smalls ("formerly with Billy Eckstine"). The nadir came on the Fourth of July, 1953, for a job at Campbell Inn in Roscoe, New York. At 11 a.m. sharp, a couple called "the Norberts" picked him up in Manhattan and drove him two-and-a-half hours into the country. After a rehearsal at 3:00 and a show at 9:00, the Norberts drove him home again, ending a fourteen- or fifteen-hour day. For his trouble, he made all of $60.

Then in early August at an AGVA meeting Bubbles got a tip that, if interested, he could make a movie in Germany. The company would pay

Sportin' Life. Brian Harker, Oxford University Press. © Oxford University Press 2022.
DOI: 10.1093/oso/9780197514511.003.0016

$1,000 a week, plus expenses. Around the same time, he clipped a very interesting story in *Variety*: Entertainers were taking advantage of a loophole in the tax law that allowed them to write off foreign income if they remained abroad for at least seventeen months in an eighteen-month period. Gene Kelly, the article said, "was the first actor to go overseas to take advantage of the law," saving himself some $280,000. Once in Germany, could Bubbles find a way to stay a little longer than he'd planned? Despite anguished protestations from Mabel ("she busted out, started crying, you'd think I was going to fall off a roof somewhere"), he decided he had to try. He booked a flight to Frankfurt, arriving by the middle of the month. He would be gone four years.

2

On his first day in Frankfurt, Bubbles received bad news. The two men who had brought him to Europe sheepishly confessed that, because they had neglected to provide the film studio with a signed contract, the director had given Bubbles's part to someone else. But not to worry, they said, he could work for the Special Services—the American military's entertainment program for servicemen abroad—for $15 a show. No thanks, Bubbles said angrily. He went to the American Consulate, which compelled his would-be handlers to pay for his hotel, at least. But believing he was coming to Europe with all expenses paid, Bubbles had improvidently (but characteristically) arrived with only $5.35 in his pocket. A pang of terror hit him. Looking around the streets of Frankfurt, he felt like the only Black person in Germany who wasn't in uniform. "The Germans are lookin' at me," he said, "like I was some kind of strange animal." He didn't speak German. He knew no one. And he had no money.

Then, a lucky break. That night at the train station he was astonished and elated to see an old friend from America, jazz pianist Norman Thomas. After a joyful reunion, Bubbles explained his dilemma. Thomas urged him to seek work at the Special Services booking office.

"I was over there," Bubbles said, "and they only pay fifteen dollars per show."

"Then they don't know who you are," Thomas replied.

Bubbles's friend promised he would place a call on his behalf and gave him a card with the inscription, "Give bearer 100 Deutschmarks." Abashed,

Bubbles went back to his room and wept. He later claimed he didn't even re-deem the card, just kept it as a memento of his friend's kindness.

The next day Thomas's intervention became apparent. The booking office called and told Bubbles there was a job in Kaiserslautern, 118 kilometers south-east of Frankfurt, that very day. Thus began years of steady work performing for American servicemen in Europe, making around $45 a show. Most of his time was spent in five nearby cities in south-central Germany—Frankfurt, Wiesbaden, Kaiserslautern, Stuttgart, and Munich—with an interval in London and occasional holiday excursions to places like Berlin, Vienna, and Venice.

With a lifetime of experience near the top of the American entertainment pyramid, Bubbles towered over his fellow actors, mostly obscure itinerants from various European countries: singers, dancers, jugglers, contortionists, magicians, animal trainers and the like. Appearing initially as "Johnnie Bubbles" (later he switched back to John), for most shows he served as master of ceremonies and star of the bill. He advertised himself and dressed as the original Sportin' Life, capitalizing on Germans' familiarity with the role. (Whenever the Nazis made an official pronouncement during the war, "the underground radio would immediately question its validity by playing a recording of 'It Ain't Necessarily So.'") With trademark derby and cane, he would come onstage and do something like the following routine:

1. Entrance: orchestra plays introduction to "It Ain't Necessarily So"
2. Song: "Shine"
3. Song: "It Ain't Necessarily So"
4. Dance: "Tip and Tap Along" [one of Bubbles's own compositions]
5. Encore: "Lady Be Good"

Three numbers and an encore, reprising songs from his two biggest roles, Sportin' Life and Domino Johnson—these typified his act in Europe.

The venues he appeared in, nondescript "service clubs" strewn along the performance route connecting Frankfurt at one end to Munich at the other, and the long bus rides between stops, made the Special Services a definite grind. Looking back on it years later, one of Bubbles's colleagues cursed the "boring atmosphere of that broken-down merry-go-round over in Germany" and asked, "How much of one's life is it practical to spend in such sterile never-never land?" Bubbles himself was appalled by the reception his shows sometimes got from drunk and rowdy American soldiers. At one event a female performer, an older woman, was hit in the face by a flying beer glass. Bubbles interpreted the audience's disrespect as race prejudice directed toward *him*. He made a scalding speech and walked off the stage.

Everywhere he went Bubbles saw evidence, even in subtle ways, of the want suffered by Europeans after the war. For a shoestring performance he gave in London, local businesses had to loan the company stage furniture and phonograph records (to be played for the enjoyment of patrons before and after the show), since none of the theater people had the funds to provide such items themselves. Similarly, Bubbles recalled the disconcerting experience of eating in public during a brief trip to East Germany. "Nobody trusts anybody there," he said. "When you go into a restaurant and order dinner, you must show your identification card and pay for the meal before they serve you. Too many people there are hungry and would order and eat the food first and then admit they had no money, if they could."

Yet despite straitened conditions and occasionally unruly crowds, Bubbles bonded with fellow actors and audiences alike. He became close to the entertaining family of Caterina Valente, a twenty-four-year-old singer and dancer who had recently "managed to become Germany's No. 1 recording star," according to *Variety*. After performing in several live shows with the entire family, Bubbles appeared with Caterina in two films in 1955: *Ball im Savoy* and *Liebe, Tanz und 1000 Schlager*. On a signed photograph the family expressed their affection: "To our Big Friend, a Big artist, the best souvenir from Maria, Joseph and Piebro. All the best wishing you. Valente family." Later, following a show on a Canadian aircraft carrier in Naples, Bubbles got a warm thank-you letter that resembled others he received: "The 'John Bubbles' show will long be remembered by this ship's company as one of the best variety shows we have seen on board."

Another encounter was related by one Pete Chaney, an American living in Wiesbaden who opened his home to many "wandering and unique souls," such as "an unemployed English show girl or an expatriate piano player from Los Angeles." One night an out-of-work hypnotist took Chaney to see Bubbles:

> On the stage, he looked like a large man. His gray hair and misty eyes spoke of his age. But his personality was timeless. He didn't do any violent acrobatic dancing, but he held his audience spellbound with his easy, pleasant talk and shuffling dance. . . . During the show he offered us, he sang his song "T'ain't Necessarily So," and had his audience join in at the chorus. I'm

Bubbles with Caterina Valente, *Liebe, Tanz und 1000 Schlager*, 1955.
Source: L. Tom Perry Special Collections, Harold B. Lee Library, Brigham Young University, Provo, Utah.

no singer and usually move my mouth and pretend when I'm caught. But I added my hoarse baritone to John's audience. We were part of a legend.

I met John backstage after one of his shows. . . . In the dressing room it was obvious John was not a large man. His tee-shirt was torn and he chatted amiably, smiling at my hypnotist friend who was twirling his cane and tried on his hat. The hat was too big for him to fill.

On another occasion Chaney witnessed a performance for "a group of old-time officers" who remembered Buck and Bubbles from vaudeville. "They brought him back for encore after encore," Chaney said. "When he had just about exhausted his repertoire, the entertainer pulled out a container of sand and sprinkled it on the stage. The folks who remembered [this practice] came to their feet applauding. To a warm ovation, John did his famed shuffling sand dance."

Chaney, who may have known Bubbles in later years, misremembered his appearance; in the 1950s the dancer's hair had not yet turned gray. Yet even this flawed description highlights the nostalgia that was already beginning to shape audiences' perceptions of him.

3

In February 1954 Bubbles traveled to England to appear in "Memories of Jolson," an all-Black show that had almost nothing to do with its ostensible subject, old-time blackface star Al Jolson. "It wasn't a very good show," recalled Marie Bryant. "If we hadn't been playing the little tiny towns, you know, where they just hadn't seen anything at all, I don't think it would have lasted." Those "little tiny towns" may have kept the show alive, but they also upheld their reputation for narrow-mindedness. In March a hotel reservation fell through in Rotherham, South Yorkshire, and the cast began a nightmarish search for lodgings on foot, in "bitter weather," for hours into the night. As one hotel after another turned them down, it became painfully clear that the problem was their race. Bubbles was dumbfounded: "We did not believe such a thing could happen in this country." Some performers ended up sleeping at the theater, while others relied on a compassionate stranger who took them into her home.

Race flared up again when it emerged that one of the dancers, a white girl, had been "browning down" (darkening her skin) to appear in the show undetected. A minor scandal erupted, and the director faced pressure to fire her. But Bubbles took her side, saved her job, and became her mentor. He also became her lover. Aysha De Festa was not exactly "white" by the usual standards—her mother was from Kashmir, her father from Mexico—but she was considered "white" by her peers. At twenty-one years old, she was thirty years younger than Bubbles, an exotic beauty with olive skin and a muscular dancer's body. Despite her youth, she was canny and independent, no easy target for older men on the make. But like others before her, she was enthralled by Bubbles's charm, his dancing skill, and his professional stature. They soon began living together, so intimately that acquaintances mistook them for husband and wife. When Bubbles moved back to Germany later that summer, he took Aysha with him.

In the meantime, back in the States, Mabel had been working hard to keep track of her wayward husband. From the beginning of his European tour, she sent a steady stream of letters, and Bubbles had responded, sometimes with money orders enclosed. Yet her letters betray gradually rising anxiety about their marriage:

August 1953   "No other love have I—just the nearness of u."

April 1954   "Time [to] bring your behind home."

March 1955   "[I'll] never forgive you for leaving me."

December 1955   "Why the hell did you marry me—I was as broke as you."

By March 1956 she had evidently found out about Aysha: "I can't put myself in your place because I couldn't go to bed with a man if I have a husband." By July she seemed resigned: "Hope you are well and enjoying the life you have chosen."

And yet she *wasn't* resigned. She decided that whatever Bubbles was up to, she couldn't exert any influence as long as he remained in Europe. She began to focus on bringing him home. The only way to do that, she knew, was with the right professional enticement—a movie contract, a television show, something big. She had already tantalized him with rumors of possible film roles. There was talk in Hollywood of him playing the lead in a projected "Bill Robinson Story" and Sportin' Life in a film version of *Porgy and Bess*. Both would be major, possibly career-altering, roles, but nothing was definite and Mabel couldn't wait. On September 17, 1956, she seized the initiative with a bold letter:

This letter is sent by interested friends, family, wellwishers and the wife of John Bubbles, formerly of the team of BUCK and BUBBLES. . . . On the strength of the famous "comebacks" recently, we are appealing to you now. . . .

We are anxious to have him return to America and wonder if you would . . . engage him for anything you may have "in work" now. He is ageless, looks the same; his dancing is as fast and different; he sings in the same original and pleasing style. . . .

At the present time he is now playing Berchtesgaden, Germany, closing on the 30th of September. May we have any suggestion or encouraging word from you before then. Thank you.

Mabel sent this letter to all the powerful people she could think of, including Billy Rose, Peter Lind Hayes, Ed Sullivan, Ray Bolger, Jackie Gleason, and Steve Allen. More surprising than the letter itself is the amazing fact that someone answered her stone-cold appeal. In 1957 Peter Lind Hayes was a rising star in daytime television and a feature attraction at the Sands Hotel and Casino in Las Vegas. Conveniently, he considered Bubbles to be "the greatest entertainer that ever lived. That includes Jolson, Crosby . . . everybody you want to name." When he got Mabel's letter, he acted—and Bubbles returned to the United States.

16

Turn Back the Universe

1

On May 21, 1957, Bubbles disembarked from the Queen Mary in New York and made his way to Las Vegas, the adult playground that had sprouted up in recent years to replace the good-time cities of the past—New Orleans, Kansas City, Chicago, New York. Aysha, who would follow him two months later, issued a tart warning from Wiesbaden:

> But I want to say this. Should you live at the Long Island address [i.e., with Mabel in Hempstead], don't think of me, don't write, and don't bother to look for me. I will not want you anymore, and if I should come there, and find out you were there, you'll be saying where did she go! But you have your own mind, and this is a good time to think what you really want in life. I may only be 23, but I know what I want.

Bubbles nevertheless went to see Mabel, who found Aysha's letters in his trunk and excoriated him for his unfaithfulness. He used her snooping as a pretext to demand a divorce, summarily breaking her heart (after she had almost single-handedly engineered his return to a performing career in the United States) and clearing a path for his third marriage. Whether Aysha found out about this visit is not known, but when Bubbles sent her a telegram upon her arrival to America, with a train reservation and specific instructions how to get to Las Vegas, she made it to her destination on schedule. Bubbles and Aysha were married the following year, at the Monumental Baptist Church in Jersey City, New Jersey, on June 5, 1958.

At that time, mixed-race couples were still shocking if not scandalous in the United States, and Bubbles and Aysha faced hostility in Vegas, a strictly segregated city then known as "the Mississippi of the West." Simply finding a place to live was a challenge. They couldn't live in the Black section of town and were even less welcome in the white section. They finally settled on a humiliating compromise: Aysha rented a house in a white neighborhood and told the landlady

Sportin' Life. Brian Harker, Oxford University Press. © Oxford University Press 2022.
DOI: 10.1093/oso/9780197514511.003.0017

Bubbles was her servant. In addition to these problems, Aysha quickly became attached to Vegas and never wanted to leave, whereas Bubbles recognized the city as the worst possible home for a man of his proclivities: "I knew I couldn't get any money from my agent as long as I was in a place where it could be gambled away." As TV bookings increasingly took Bubbles back to New York, the question of where they would live, New York or Vegas, became a wedge. Thus were the seeds of their separation planted almost from the beginning.

Bubbles had gone to Las Vegas for one reason: Peter Lind Hayes invited him to join his show at the Sands Hotel and Casino in mid-June 1957. Twelve years younger than Bubbles, Hayes was a mischievous, wise-cracking entertainer who sang a bit and danced a bit but mostly excelled at improvised comic repartee. He remembered Bubbles from the times they had occasionally appeared together in vaudeville and especially from a more sustained encounter in 1937, when Hayes worked as a stand-in for Ted Healy on the set of *Varsity Show*. Now, Hayes and his glamorous wife Mary Healy (no relation) were rising celebrities in daytime television, having guest-hosted for the Arthur Godfrey Show for the past three years. Hayes had always considered Bubbles one of the best of the old-time song-and-dance men and now believed him to be, without exaggeration, "the world's greatest living entertainer." When he heard Bubbles needed work, he leapt at the chance to bring him back into the public eye.

The Sands provided a good springboard for a possible comeback. This venue is best known today as the principal hangout of Frank Sinatra and the Rat Pack. A famous live album from 1966, *Sinatra at the Sands* (with Count Basie), opens a window onto the tony ambiance of the place. Both the great singer's repertoire— "Fly Me to the Moon," "The Shadow of Your Smile"—and his sardonic but also slightly corny jokes about "boozing," Communists, and his fiftieth birthday indicate an audience of middle-aged, middle-class white people. The tinkling of glasses and warm applause evoke the comfortable materialism of vacationing Americans at mid-century. You can almost smell the cigarette smoke.

Las Vegas casinos had been cultivating this audience for more than twenty years. To spare their prime customers the inconvenience of having to associate with people of color, the city's masterminds imposed Jim Crow restrictions that would have gladdened the heart of the most rabid Southern partisan. Casinos on the Strip forbade Blacks from appearing anywhere but onstage. As Sammy Davis Jr., the only Black member of the Rat Pack, put it, "We were performing at the hotel, but we couldn't stay there. We couldn't eat there. We couldn't gamble in the casino. We couldn't walk in the front door." In 1960 legalized segregation in Vegas was finally abolished, but when Bubbles opened at the Sands the old rules still applied: He had to enter through the back and vacate the premises after the show. Once onstage, he experienced the old familiar sensation of acceptance from an audience that in any other context might not have given him the time of day. According to *Variety*, he performed a medley from *Porgy and Bess* and joined Hayes for some comic dialogue and a song and dance. Hayes was delighted. "Bubbles was a tremendous success," he recalled. "Even the people who didn't remember him, or, like the young people who had never known him, loved him."

After four weeks at the Sands and another stint at the Riverside Hotel in Reno, it was time to put Bubbles in front of the cameras. In late August, Hayes and his wife reintroduced him to the American public on the Arthur Godfrey Show. Bubbles soon became "a regular on pretty nearly everything Hayes [did] on TV." Other hosts took notice. Over the next year, Bubbles appeared on the Perry Como Show, the Steve Allen Show, and the Bob Crosby Show. (He was shocked and saddened to see old vaudeville theaters turned into TV studios. "I almost cried when I went to the Ziegfeld to do the Perry Como Show," he said. "Cameras, lights, etc., were all over the place; the first eight rows of seats were covered—I tell you, Ziegfeld would turn over in his grave.") In October 1958 Hayes started his own program, the Peter Lind Hayes Show, on ABC, Monday through Friday, from 11:30 a.m. to 12:30 p.m. Bubbles became first among equals in a rotating cast, second only to Mary Healy in importance. Hayes had him on every day, five days a week, through the rest of October, then two weeks straight for each month in November, December, January, and February. Black columnist Ziggy Johnson reckoned that Bubbles, if asked, would probably say: "Ziegfeld, this is a good gig."

Daytime television in the 1950s focused on one key demographic: housewives. Following in the path of such popular and telegenic personalities as Arthur Godfrey and Art Linkletter, Peter Lind Hayes represented a TV genre designed to beguile female viewers with music, comedy, and, in the attractive and charismatic male host, "an appealing but low-key sexuality," as historian Marsha F. Cassidy puts it. The electricity was heightened by the spontaneous, participatory format and by the knowledge it was all taking place before a studio audience on live television. Anything could happen, and often did. For instance, Bubbles used to spend a lot of time at a Harlem bar called the Shack, an establishment in which he had a token financial interest. After a long night

Bubbles with Peter Lind Hayes, late 1950s.

Source: L. Tom Perry Special Collections, Harold B. Lee Library, Brigham Young University, Provo, Utah.

at the Shack, when he arrived the next morning to appear on the Peter Lind Hayes Show, he would sometimes, literally, fall asleep on camera. On such days Hayes, an inveterate prankster, couldn't believe his luck:

> I'd say to Bobby, our camera director, "Shhh. Get a close up of Bubbles." He'd get a big close up of Bubbles. Now Bubbles is sound asleep on national television. . . . And I'd say, "Say, John, uh, how'd things go at the Shack last night?" . . . No response. He's sound asleep, and his face is filling the entire television screen. And I'd say, "Bubbles, tell me, were there lots of girls up there last night? Did you dance a lot?" Still no response, see, he's just dozin' away. Finally, I'd shout, "JOHN!" and he'd look up, and those big brown eyes would sparkle, and he'd say, "*Did* I?"

Daytime viewers delighted in such candid revelations of celebrities teasing and discomfiting one another. If it appeared that Bubbles was being bullied, to be sure, Black viewers may have reacted differently. Yet they could also take a sort of backhanded pride in their guy: Who else was so comfortable in front of an audience that he could fall asleep on live television?

Despite the on-camera practical jokes, Bubbles was seemingly overwhelmed by his new patron's generosity. In December 1957 he expressed his gratitude in a heartfelt letter:

> Dear Peter: . . . I must say that it has been more than the pleasure found, working with You, and your dear Wife, "Mary" . . . Words, fail me to express, and put together for understanding, ALL that the Words, "Good Wishes" Health, Success, & Happiness Emply . . . I am happy to say, After my association with you and your many friends including your Family, the darkness in my Biography can be with more Light.

Not that the darkness went away entirely. "In the many years I spent with Bubbles," Hayes said, "I was always getting very sinister calls from people giving different names. Actually, you'd find out they were from a finance company. They were always looking for Bubbles."

2

Despite Bubbles's successful return to television, his appeal in the late 1950s was considerably narrower than it used to be. When he arrived in New York after four years in Europe, he discovered a country in the early throes of a long-simmering cultural revolution. Elvis and '57 Chevys were the most conspicuous signs of change, but below the surface lurked a rift between young people and their parents that would eventually widen to society-shattering proportions. Already Americans who had grown up during the 1920s or 1930s were beginning to look back wistfully on the songs, dances, and ideals of those earlier times. It was to these older viewers that a resurrected John Bubbles appealed most strongly. Where once his dancing was prized for its own sake, now his greatest value lay in his ability to channel nostalgia.

"Turn back the universe and give us yesterday," cooed the dreamy author of one of many fan letters that greeted Bubbles's return to the public airwaves,

> at the Palace or the Colonial or even the Audubon . . . and your partner "Buck"—give us the piano—and Buck drowsily manipulating the ivories, with his fingers, as you sang—and when you went into your tapping routine . . . to the applause of a full house. . . . Do you remember?

"Helene," another longtime fan, wrote from St. Petersburg, Florida:

> Saw you on T.V. tonight. . . . My mother remembers you also from vaudeville. . . . Mom said, we'll have to be quiet now, this is Helene's idol. As I guess I've told you before in my letters, I often wondered what became of you, then when T.V. came in I knew you would be back. I hope someone somewhere starts a fan club.

To Rosemary O'Callaghan, a mother of preschoolers from Chicago, Bubbles brought comfort:

> My three children wait for your song and dance routine. They could be fighting screaming and breaking furniture, but the minute your name is announced a wonderful, peaceful calm comes over the room. . . . Thank you for all the wonderful moments you've given us.

For other viewers, Bubbles brought the opposite of comfort. A few months after his return from Germany, he watched in horror as angry whites violently protested the integration of Little Rock Central High School. He clipped a story of a Black reporter being hounded and beaten by a white mob as twenty policemen stood watching, and wrote in the margin, "Is this America, home of the brave? Land of the free?" It must have hurt Bubbles (if he saw it) that in that same week another Black reporter accused him of Uncle Tomism: "Daytime TV viewers have been expressing their annoyance with the Peter Lind Hayes presentation of John W. Bubbles on the Arthur Godfrey Show by flipping to other channels. Claims are that the 'handkerchief' is being waved!" In other words, with his old-time entertainment Bubbles transported his viewers not only back to the Jazz Age or Swing Era but also to a time when the complacency of white America would have never been pierced by such incidents as Little Rock. Nostalgia had a social as well as a musical dimension, comforting some but hurting others.

How, specifically, was "the handkerchief" being waved on the Godfrey Show? With Bubbles as his guest, Hayes couldn't resist recreating the old Buck and Bubbles comedy routines he had loved as a young man. These recreations, a white reporter wrote, were "charming oldtime vaudeville nonsense and had us misty-eyed." But it's not hard to guess the problem from a Black point of view. With no doubt good intentions, Hayes arranged for himself to play Bubbles's part—the domineering straight man. In any other context giving the punchlines to Bubbles would be an act of generosity, but in this circumstance the effect was to place Hayes, a white authority figure, in the position of ridiculing or belittling a Black subordinate on national television. Worse, some of the jokes reinforced Black stereotypes. Here, for instance, is one Hayes remembered doing (in his best Black dialect) on his show with Bubbles:

HAYES: You is a coward.
BUBBLES: I'm no coward.
HAYES: Yes you are. You're scairt t' death of lightnin' and thunder.
BUBBLES: I'm not scared of lightnin' and thunder.
HAYES: What are you talkin' about? The other day when there was lightnin' and thunder you went down in the basement and hid.
BUBBLES: Of course I did.
HAYES: Why?
BUBBLES: Well, if lightnin' is gonna strike me, then let it come lookin' fo' me.

In later years Hayes defended such jokes as harmless "ethnic humor," once commonplace but lately taboo. He may have been sincere in his belief that Bubbles was "the world's greatest living entertainer," but that generous encomium—and his corresponding patronage of Bubbles—must be understood within the context of Hayes's retrograde views on race.

The partnership with Peter Lind Hayes illustrates a fundamental change in Bubbles's post-European career. For thirty-six years it was Buck who had played second banana, butt of all the jokes. Going forward it would be Bubbles who assumed that role—in counterpoint to his more famous and successful white patrons.

3

One of the incentives bringing Bubbles back to the States was the possibility of making movies. Mabel had told him he was being considered for Sportin' Life in a film version of *Porgy and Bess*, and news accounts confirmed her report. But others were under consideration as well, including Cab Calloway, Sammy Davis Jr., even Sugar Ray Robinson, the boxer. If Bubbles were honest with himself, he would have realized that a man his age might not be the best candidate. Even so, when he found out thirty-three-year-old Sammy Davis had won the part, he was not happy. "George Gershwin would roll over in his grave," he fumed to a reporter. "All the roles are being done by people who are different from the original cast." (Years later he was more blunt: "They ruined that show with Sammy Davis.")

In the summer of 1958, while Sammy Davis was out west practicing his lines, Bubbles settled for joining a regional production of *Porgy and Bess* in the East. In negotiating his contract with Pittsburgh's Civic Light Opera, he demanded and received top billing—as the original Sportin' Life—over the two leads, Andrew Frierson and Urylee Leonardos. Critics rejoiced to see him return to the role he created. "The amazing John Bubbles, who was the first Sportin' Life back in the Thirties, cancels out all the carbons with a performance that is even better than his original, if that is possible," said one. Bubbles's return, however, prompted comparisons with more recent interpretations. In 1935 his Sportin' Life had seemed an out-and-out villain, but in the late 1950s, with drama and film tending toward gritty realism, that view had to be revised. Particularly when Sammy Davis unveiled his own portrayal, depicting "evil on an almost repulsive scale," Bubbles's original character seemed tame in retrospect—"a sort of droll and impious rascal with the bright, lively quality of a minstrel man." That reading was on display again at the Civic Light Opera, clashing with modern sensibilities. John Bubbles "gives us a rather mild Sportin' Life," noted one reviewer.

One earnest young fan, who saw the show at Valley Forge, wrote to assure Bubbles he was in tune with the times in the only way that mattered:

> After seeing you and listening to you, I felt I had to tell you that I think you are terrific. . . . To me, a white young man, you represent the wonderful traits of a wonderful race, although I feel it is wrong to make any distinction between races. There is only one—the human race. I hope you will agree with this. You and the entire cast are doing so much good for a slowly improving situation, as well as for our country.

In addition to *Porgy and Bess*, Bubbles hoped to play the title role in a projected "Bill Robinson Story" with Twentieth Century-Fox. Although Bubbles liked the idea ("I was number one on the list," he boasted), the irony of his situation is hard to ignore. When Robinson was alive, he often eclipsed Bubbles, especially in the number and stature of his roles in Hollywood. Now, as Bubbles came close at last to landing his own big role in a feature film, the subject was . . . his old competitor. That hardly seemed fair. "If I played Bill," he asked plaintively, "who'd play me?"

As it turned out, a strike in Hollywood scuttled plans for "The Bill Robinson Story." But Bubbles got another chance to play Bojangles when NBC hired him to appear in "A Toast to Jerome Kern," a TV special honoring the great songwriter—now fourteen years dead—on September 22, 1959. Bubbles was asked to do a sketch leading into the song "Bojangles of Harlem," and here the ironies multiply. Kern wrote the song for the movie *Swing Time*, one of the great Fred Astaire-Ginger Rogers collaborations of the 1930s. In "Bojangles of Harlem," Astaire dances in blackface as an ostensible tribute to Bill Robinson. Curiously, though, commentators have observed that he seems more intent on glossing John Bubbles, with a dance and wardrobe resembling Sportin' Life, whom Bubbles had introduced in *Porgy and Bess* the year before. So, to recap: In "A Toast to Jerome Kern," Bubbles was asked to re-create Fred Astaire . . . paying tribute to Bill Robinson . . . possibly in the dress and manner of Sportin' Life (i.e., Bubbles)—all in an orgy of nostalgia that showered glory on his rival but not Bubbles himself, who served as a mere vehicle for his memorial.

Occasionally Bubbles's old-school performance values served not just to re-call a golden age but also to motivate and inspire the rising generation. One of the new realities he faced upon returning to the United States was a newly vibrant popular music scene among young Blacks, pioneered by soul artists like Ray Charles and Sam Cooke. In this environment how could an old di-nosaur like Bubbles compete? Pretty well, as it turned out.

In November 1958 he was booked to appear at the Apollo Theatre, a po-tentially disastrous gig. For a largely youthful crowd the management put to-gether a bill heavy on rock 'n' roll, R&B, and soul, with B-list but still famous acts such as Larry Williams, Baby Washington, Ed Townsend, Joan Shaw, and the Teenchords. Notably off-center from this lineup were the Hines Kids, fifteen-year-old Maurice and twelve-year-old Gregory, who specialized in the old-fashioned art of tap dancing. And then there was Bubbles, a ghost from another era, who stole the show.

John Bubbles is "by far the best act on the current bill," wrote *Variety*. "He can still belt out a tune with a flair for showmanship and his numbers are marked by originality. His stepping is still to be admired and the kids on the show could learn a thing or two or possibly three from Bubbles." Nor was the stuffy old newspaper critic the only one taken by the ancient vaudevil-lian. Maurice Hines was astonished that "the rock and roll audiences were loving John Bubbles, who was singing songs like 'It Ain't Necessarily So.'" How could this be? Bubbles took the two brothers aside and explained: "You know why they like me? Because I come out there and I'm honest with them. Never pick a song, never do a step, unless you love it."

Completely smitten, the Hines kids grew up to become great tap dancers in their own right, galvanizing the tap revival of the 1980s and starring in major Hollywood films like *The Cotton Club* and *White Nights*. Bubbles, Maurice said, "had the most influence over us."

4

After two years of television appearances evoking a misty world from a dis-tant past, Bubbles caught the eye of a legendary performer, the queen of nos-talgia, Judy Garland. Tormented, needy, impossible, and wondrously gifted, Garland was well into the post-MGM phase of her career. In 1951, after being dropped by the studio for failing to meet her obligations, she reinvented her-self as a concert artist with the help of her manager and third husband, Sid

Luft. Now she lived to gratify a house of cheering, delirious fans, whether at the London Palladium, the New York Palace, or Carnegie Hall. But the demons that all but destroyed her movie career didn't relent and by early 1959 she had sunk into a deep depression fueled by inactivity and substance abuse. She was especially self-conscious about her weight. One night her husband looked at her and thought, "She looks like . . . an opera prima donna, at home for the evening." Immediately he knew what her next booking should be, one big enough and prestigious enough to bring her out of her funk: the Metropolitan Opera House.

For *Judy at the Met*, Luft put together a huge production, her biggest yet, with a cast of a hundred and an orchestra of fifty. Judy was flanked by Alan King, a fast-rising young stand-up comic, and Bubbles, whom she'd seen on the Perry Como Show. ("Who's that?" asked Luft. "That's the world's greatest dancer," she supposedly replied.) Although *Judy at the Met* started with a tongue-in-cheek nod to the lofty setting (Garland sang "What's going on at the opera . . . did Mr. Bing make up with Maria Callas?"), it quickly settled into a roll call of beloved favorites. Some came from her old movies: "The Trolley Song," "A Couple of Swells," "The Man That Got Away." Others had a much earlier connection to Al Jolson: "You Made Me Love You" (1913), "Rock-a-Bye Your Baby with a Dixie Melody" (1918), "Swanee" (1919). Everything built toward the final surging chorus, sung by Garland while sitting on the edge of the stage, in tramp clothes, without a mike: "Over the Rainbow."

Along the way King told acerbic jokes about marriage, television, and suburbia, and sang a duet with Judy on "A Couple of Swells." Bubbles did his nightclub act, including "It Ain't Necessarily So," and tap-danced with Garland on "Me and My Shadow," another Jolson number. But there was no plan, initially, for Bubbles and King to perform together. "All my life I'd wanted to do a number with John Bubbles," King said. "I knew every bit he'd ever done with Buck in the big floppy shoes." So he asked Garland if they could share a little comic dialogue while she was changing costumes during the second act. Bubbles and King auditioned an old Buck and Bubbles routine for Garland, who pronounced it "perfect." (Like Peter Lind Hayes, King played the straight man.) For King, a seminal practitioner of stand-up who would inspire such later comedians as Billy Crystal and Jerry Seinfeld, the chance to perform with one of his own inspirations was an unexpected pleasure. "It was lovely, it was show business. And I got to share a stage with John Bubbles, that beautiful, talented man."

After a tryout in Baltimore, the company performed a week at the New York Met, another week at the Chicago Civic Opera, eleven days at the San Francisco Opera, and a final week at the Shrine Auditorium in Los Angeles, the whole tour lasting, with breaks, from May to July. One critic fretted that "it might be well" for Garland "to think in terms other than nostalgia" if she wanted to win new fans. But the old fans arrived in such droves and with such ecstatic ardor that she hardly needed to. Nostalgia was her brand. Swamped by a colossus and her cheering idolaters, Bubbles and King sometimes struggled to break through. Still, Bubbles earned $1,000 a week, significantly more than his usual rate.

5

Bubbles's historical reputation was beginning to take on a gilded sheen. For several years Timmie Rogers, Buck's old employer, had been doing a sketch called "Bubbles, Bert, and Bo" that placed Bubbles beside long-canonized Bert Williams and Bill Robinson as a Black entertainer for the ages. He came to be regarded as a valuable gift on loan from the past. Hastening to get his story on record, documentarians in 1960 enlisted him for a TV series designed to educate viewers in a history of the performing arts.

Running for six seasons on CBS, the weekly *American Musical Theatre* foreshadowed the public television of a later era. The congenial host, Jim Morske, interviewed such entertainment stalwarts as Richard Rodgers, Betty Comden, Marc Blitzstein, Bob Fosse, Roberta Peters, Harry Belafonte, and Stephen Sondheim. On February 13, 1960, Morske recruited Bubbles for an episode on the "Jazz-Mad Twenties," then called him back six months later for one entitled "Broadway, I Love You," on which Bubbles sang "I Can't Give You Anything But Love" while the song's lyricist, Dorothy Fields, sat listening. Morske was so impressed that he made Bubbles the subject of a two-part biography airing February 5 and 12, 1961. In front of an on-stage audience of well-scrubbed high school kids, Morske conducted a free-wheeling interview, liberally punctuated with live performances by Bubbles and questions from the assembled students. Bubbles kept everyone laughing with his seemingly unscripted asides. During a lengthy tap dance, he kept up a running patter with quips like: "I want you to know I don't do this for a livin'—I just do it to keep from *starvin'* to death." Or: "Nobody likes this step. It looks too easy. I just do it for spite." When Morske asked about the touring life with Buck,

Bubbles provoked nervous laughter (given news stories of the time) with his response: "We did everything from one end of the United States to the other. Only missed three places out of the whole continent."

"Do you remember what they were?" Morske asked.

"Yes. Mississippi, Alabama, and Georgia."

Not everyone appreciated programs like *American Musical Theatre*. In late 1961 one critic complained that "nostalgia's hanging on TV like moss. . . . Never before has a nation been subjected to such a Niagara of frivolity about its more foolish years." But others couldn't get enough. Reviewing a special called "Music of the 1930s," featuring songs by Jerome Kern, Irving Berlin, and Richard Rodgers, one writer made an increasingly common observation: "There can be no doubt about it—they're not writing tunes like that anymore. . . . 'Music of the Thirties' made it more difficult than ever to bear the harsh new musical sounds of the 'Sixties.'" Harsh? The Beatles, at this point, were still more than two years away.

17

Bubbles Bounces Back!

1

For all the fanfare hailing Bubbles's comeback, it didn't take long for the excitement to die down. As the 1950s passed into the 1960s, he once again found himself in extremis. Even though the Peter Lind Hayes Show had wowed the critics, one of whom called it "undoubtedly the best entry in daytime TV this year," for some reason ABC did not renew his contract and Bubbles's gravy train dried up. After the Judy Garland tour, he went a whole year—all of 1960—without landing a single live gig of sufficient standing to warrant a news report. Things got so bad that at one point Bubbles was evicted from his New York apartment.

In the summer of 1961, he caught a promising break when he was asked to headline the opening of the Carver House, a new Black casino in West Las Vegas, co-sponsored by Billy Eckstine and Sammy Davis Jr. As the first serious attempt in several years to compete with white casinos on the Strip, the Carver House raised high expectations in the Black community. In July Bubbles premiered "Le Jazz Hot," featuring two female co-stars (including Nichelle Nichols, the future Lieutenant Uhura in *Star Trek*) and a topless chorus of "Carverettes." During his two-week booking he did four shows nightly, for which he was paid $1,000 a week and allowed to sleep in the Carver House Hotel for the length of his contract.

" 'Le Jazz Hot' seems to be getting off on the right track," wrote *Variety*. "Bubbles, the vet song & dance man, scores with firstnighters as he breezes through his familiar footwork and flavorful vocals." But Peter Lind Hayes, who was also present, witnessed a different reaction. One of Bubbles's songs was "Shine," which in the 1960s he had purged even beyond its considerable transformation in *Cabin in the Sky*. Instead of singing "That's why they call me 'Shine,' " he sang, "You'll make the whole world shine." Yet for a table of young Black journalists during the summer of the Freedom Rides, it wasn't enough. According to Hayes, "they wouldn't let Bubbles sit down with them. They were so sensitive about him being 'Uncle Tom,' that they resented the

Sportin' Life. Brian Harker, Oxford University Press. © Oxford University Press 2022.
DOI: 10.1093/oso/9780197514511.003.0018

image of John Bubbles. . . . It broke his heart." After the two weeks elapsed, Bubbles returned to a life of poverty and neglect.

Then, in a huge and unexpected stroke of good fortune, in the early months of 1962 the pace of TV gigs picked up again, this time with a crucial shift to late-night time slots. Bubbles appeared twice on the Mike Wallace Show, and in May he got his first booking on NBC's Tonight Show. Created by Steve Allen and further developed by Jack Paar, the Tonight Show was a hybrid talk/variety show with opening monologue, comedy sketches, and celebrity performances and interviews. By 1962 it had become a phenomenon, "the most talked about show in television history," according to Johnny Carson, the man who replaced Paar. Between Paar's last show in March and Carson's ascension to the throne on October 1 (when his contract with ABC ended), a long procession of guest hosts kept the program going. Happily for Bubbles, one of them was Peter Lind Hayes. In his rapid-fire, wise-cracking manner, Hayes plumbed his idol's comic depths, "feeding him straight lines ad infinitum":

HAYES: What have you been doing lately?
BUBBLES: Helping my brother.
HAYES: What's he doing?
BUBBLES: Nothing.

If Jack Paar had made the Tonight Show "the most prestigious . . . job in show business," Johnny Carson increased that prestige. With a hipness that set him apart from his avuncular predecessor, the thirty-six-year-old Carson offered the glamour of "a flashy New York City nightclub," featuring top-draw entertainers and whip-smart satire. On his first few shows, a rich parade of celebrity guests came and went: Groucho Marx, Tony Bennett, Janet Leigh, Mitch Miller, Dr. Joyce Brothers. As the ratings soared, the Tonight Show became a Holy Grail for unknown talent. Early appearances by Barbra Streisand, Woody Allen, and Bill Cosby helped launch their careers (though Joan Rivers had to wait an agonizing three years for a sit-down with Johnny, all the while "beat[ing] at the door until her fists were raw").

For those veteran performers lucky enough to get an invite, the show offered redemption and revival. On November 1, 1962, a month into his run, Carson added Bubbles to the guest list—and changed his life. It wasn't long, wrote the *Chicago Defender*, before Bubbles "got all kinds of offers to resume his nitery career." The same paper published a lengthy profile of him, debunking rumors that he was "shinin' shoes for a livin'" with the most extravagant of tall tales: "His own numberless pairs of shoes sometimes require shining. When they do, they are transported by airplane to England, where they are, if you please, boned, and hastily returned by airplane." Such hallucinations aside, Bubbles unquestionably saw a dramatic rise in his fortunes—the clear result, according to *Variety*, of Carson's "star-making" power.

Over the next three years, Bubbles appeared on the Tonight Show no fewer than twenty-seven times, roughly once (and sometimes twice) a month when he was in town. Part of his appeal, as always, was his status as a living relic of golden-age show business. On one episode Carson dug up some old footage of Buck and Bubbles. On another he asked Bubbles about the experience of making *Porgy and Bess*. Bubbles's story of coming onstage with his fly open sent the NBC censors into a brief huddle over the salacious comment. "Johnny Carson swallowed, looked out at his studio audience and said, 'This . . . may get you a spot on David Susskind's 'Open End'"—a program known for controversial topics.

It helped, too, that Carson and Bubbles enjoyed an easy, on-camera rapport. Having been coached by Peter Lind Hayes in Bubbles's comic dialogues, Carson made "a wonderful straight man" for the venerable comedian. He also took an obvious personal pleasure in Bubbles's song-and-dance routine. Looking back on the highlights of his first year as host, he lauded "the great John Bubbles, with more energy than 10 younger dancers." On one episode, annoyed by a long-winded guest's endless pontificating, Carson took Bubbles by the arm and the two of them walked off the set together in mock protest.

By 1964, Carson acknowledged, Bubbles had become "one of [his] most popular guests," especially among the old-timers. "The [Tonight Show] is always at its best when John Bubbles shows up," wrote a critic for the *Hartford Courant*. "I don't think the younger set has the background really to appreciate this song-and-dance man, but he is a truly great performer. . . . They just don't make them like that anymore." One elderly fan—signing off as "Three Score and Ten"—wrote Bubbles with some requests for old songs. "You have a large following of people of my age and I'm sure many of them would remember any or all of these songs. . . . Will be watching and listening whenever you're on Johnny's show." In her memoir from this era, writer Gayle Pemberton recalls watching the Tonight Show with her aged father, "a great fan of John Bubbles [who] told me many times about Buck and Bubbles." As they sat watching together, she says, "something about John Bubbles and that high, scratchy, liquid tenor voice and his soft, smooth tap [dancing] struck chords of sadness and delight in my father."

In the Black community, judging from notices in the press, any reservations about racially offensive content were apparently outweighed by pride in seeing a Black performer featured on the hottest show on television. Even so, one Black fan—"A Real John Bubbles Fan," he emphasized—closed his letter to Bubbles with a little constructive criticism:

> Last night with Johnny and Ethel Merman I winced every time you said "Miss Merman." I think when all of you are on a first name basis, then why not "Ethel"? . . . I'm sure many bigots in the South and North felt good about it but you don't have to cater to that kind of crowd. . . . Not any more. . . . Just remember when you're on with Doris Day, it's Doris; Ethel Merman, it's Ethel, or Eleanor Powell, it's Eleanor.

Actually, with Eleanor Powell it was "Ellie." At least, that's how she signed her correspondence to Bubbles from this time. After watching him on the Tonight Show in late 1962, she thought she detected subtle hints of un-specified distress in his banter with the other guests. She wrote to reassure him: "Keep your chin up Bubbles, I can read through those lines that you de-liver on the Carson show. We hoofers stick together so don't worry you have a loyal friend who admires and loves you dearly." A few months later Powell had her own Tonight Show debut, and Bubbles made sure he was there to see it. According to the *New York Times*, what followed was a moment of pure show biz magic: "Out of the studio audience, under Carson's prodding, came John Bubbles completely unprepared and wearing street shoes. In a matter of seconds Miss Powell and the well-known member of the team of Buck and Bubbles went into a superb tap duel and the screen suddenly achieved that distinctive warmth of real 'pros' hugely enjoying an impromptu ball."

After two seasons on the air, Carson took a break from the show to launch his "major nightclub debut," a monthlong engagement at the Sahara Hotel and Casino in Las Vegas. As his supporting cast he chose January Jones, "a statuesque songstress," and, out of all the comic foils he *could* have selected, John Bubbles.

Unfortunately, a little less than a month before the show was due to open on July 7, 1964, Bubbles tore a ligament in his right leg during a performance in Chicago and wound up in Wesleyan Memorial Hospital. The timing was terrible. Uppermost in his mind was the money he would lose if he missed the Carson gig. For the Tonight Show, Bubbles made scale: $320 a show. But at the Sahara he was contracted for $1,750 a week, for four weeks, plus $600 for travel expenses. If he didn't make it, he stood to lose $7,000.

Ignoring the advice of his doctors, Bubbles flew to Vegas in time for the opening and hobbled gingerly around the stage—singing but not dancing—for the first show. But the Carson people, concerned about the success of the show as well as a possible lawsuit, did not want him there. The next morning Bubbles learned his name was being taken off the marquee. He called his agent, who flew to Vegas to straighten things out. As everyone sat around the negotiating table, Bubbles was adamant: He was ready and able to perform. The Carson crew wasn't convinced. They offered him two weeks pay to just go home. "Either pay me the full four weeks or nothing," Bubbles said. They paid, and Bubbles withdrew to rest his leg.

2

Bubbles's success with Johnny Carson caught the attention of other big guns in show business. In the spring of 1963, he played an extremely old-fashioned job in San Francisco with Ted Lewis, a hugely successful jazz clarinetist in his day who liked to say he was "the Elvis Presley of the 1920s." The gig was by all accounts a debacle. *Variety* deplored Bubbles playing "Uncle Tom in a gaudy purple tux" while dancing to "Me and My Shadow" with Lewis. (Bubbles himself recalled someone yelling from the balcony, "Which one is the shadow?") Apparently, Bubbles quit after one engagement, sparking a "noisy" feud between himself and Lewis. Later in the year Bubbles appeared on the Steve Allen Show and the Jerry Lewis Show. In August he declined auditioning for the new Carol Burnett Show so he could attend the rally in Washington where Dr. King gave his "I Have a Dream" speech.

These connections were small-time compared to Bubbles's next patron, the man he considered "the biggest man in show business": Bob Hope. In the fall of 1963 Hope was planning his twenty-third annual USO tour and his twelfth such event at Christmastime. For years, dancer Amiel Brown had lobbied Hope to include a Black entertainer in his lily-white troupe, to no avail. But for some reason, maybe in response to the searing eloquence the nation had heard that summer in Washington, Hope decided this year to bring along a single Black performer. Given his natural inclinations, the choice was obvious: John Bubbles.

A lifelong political conservative, Hope nursed an abiding devotion to the past—a devotion that came through in the songs, dances, and jokes he performed year after year. If Judy Garland was the queen of nostalgia, then Bob Hope was the king. "His performances have hardly changed at all since World War II," wrote *Variety*. "In fact, they are ritualistic and somehow satisfying for it." The company replayed the tried-and-true Hope formula: funny comedians, great musicians, and gorgeous women as eye candy for the lonely servicemen. Hope even reenacted some of his old routines with Bing Crosby—with *Phil* Crosby, Bing's son, taking his father's role. It is certainly true that Hope told topical jokes about current events of the day. But much of the show had a retrospective slant, and Hope's theme song said it all: "Thanks for the Memory."

In recent years, however, the meaning of nostalgia in America had shifted. In the 1950s, youth culture had been merely annoying. By 1963—even before the Beatles, Vietnam protests, and "Black power"—the new generation was, for conservatives, starting to feel more like a threat. In this context, hiring Bubbles may have served two purposes. It provided political cover for outmoded racial views (along the lines of "some of my best friends are Black"), *and* it did so in a safe environment, recalling the very era that enshrined those views. Like Rosemary O'Callaghan, the letter-writing mother from Chicago, Hope could take comfort in Bubbles, the smiling and accommodating Black man of his youth. Surely he wasn't the kind of guy to stink up the place with political remarks—was he?

Over Christmas 1963 the Bob Hope troupe toured military bases in the Mediterranean and Middle East: Turkey, Libya, Greece, and Italy. Besides Bubbles, the cast included Hope's longtime sidekick, Jerry Colonna; straight man Peter Leeds; a dance team called the Earl Twins; sirens Tuesday Weld, Anita Bryant, and Michele Metrinko (Miss USA); and the Les Brown Orchestra, a doughty refugee from the Swing Era. The company left Los Angeles on December 19 and traveled 16,000 miles in twelve days.

During a flight between bases, Bubbles asked Hope if he could try out a new joke with him at their next show. Hope sat down and listened to the joke. Without saying a word, yes or no, he then excused himself and went about his business.

When the plane landed, the troupe walked onto the outdoor stage before the usual multitude of cheering soldiers eager for some world-class entertainment. Bubbles performed his act, and as the troops were applauding

Bubbles with Bob Hope, December 1964.

Source: L. Tom Perry Special Collections, Harold B. Lee Library, Brigham Young University, Provo, Utah.

Hope stepped to the microphone. "John, that was very good," he said, then, turning to the audience: "Y'know, we've been trying for six years to get John Bubbles with us, and we finally got him." As the applause welled up again, Bubbles couldn't help feeling irritated: Not only was this a lie—it was the opposite of the truth. Hope had resisted bringing *any* Black performer on his famous Christmas tours. Bubbles decided to spring his (as yet unauthorized) joke:

BUBBLES: I'd like to ask you a question, Bob.

HOPE: Why, sure.

BUBBLES: Do you believe in integration?

HOPE: [*pause, big smile*] Why, sure.

BUBBLES: Well, then, kiss me.

At this point, "everybody in that audience yelled and laughed," Bubbles recalled, and Hope swallowed whatever reservations he may have had about a joke touching such a hot-button topic. "It brought the house down," he later admitted. "We did it everywhere." Bubbles worked up a racist alternate. Hope would stand (or sit) uncomfortably close to Bubbles, who then asked if he believed in segregation. When he said yes, Bubbles shot back: "Well, then, move over."

In January, following tradition, highlights of the tour were broadcast on a Bob Hope Christmas special, and the rest of the country got to see what the troupe had been up to halfway around the world. Bubbles came off well. "Among the supporting acts," wrote one critic, "the best is the ageless song-and-dance man, John Bubbles." Actress Jessie Royce Landis seemed to agree, but she had personal reasons for doing so:

> I was so thrilled to see John Bubbles and hear him sing "It Ain't Necessarily So." It took me back to when "Porgy and Bess" was playing in New York [in 1935]. I knew the manager of the theater, and when I'd be making the rounds looking for a job, I'd go into every matinee and catch that number. The way Bubbles dances now, you'd think he wasn't a day older. He seems to be defying the laws of gravity.

Bubbles would do two more USO tours—one with Hope in 1964, and another with Eddie Fisher the following year. Both were to Vietnam, when most Americans still regarded that distant conflict as unquestionably worthy of their patriotism and support.

3

No sooner had Bubbles returned to the United States from his first Bob Hope tour than he began working with his most profitable post–Buck and Bubbles patron yet, a dark-haired, doe-eyed waif with a heavenly voice and a face that bore a passing resemblance to Audrey Hepburn. Her name was Anna Maria Alberghetti.

Born and raised in Italy by an operatic stage father, Alberghetti was a vocal prodigy who made her American television debut while still a child. She played leading roles opposite Dean Martin in *Ten Thousand Bedrooms* (1957) and Jerry Lewis in *Cinderfella* (1960), and won a Tony for best actress in the Broadway hit *Carnival* (1962). She discovered Bubbles at a nightclub in Los Angeles, just before the Hope tour. At her request they had a meeting, where he sang and danced for her for more than two hours. Captivated, she made a startling invitation: Would Bubbles like to form a duo with her, primarily for work on the nightclub circuit? His first contract stipulated $500 a week for rehearsals and $1,000 a week for performances. But by the end of the rehearsal period Alberghetti was evidently so pleased that she doubled his salary, to $2,000 a week. In addition to live performances, he was expected to do at least three joint appearances on TV, for which he would receive $2,500 a pop. Bubbles was about to enter his most consistently prosperous period since the 1930s.

When the twenty-seven-year-old Alberghetti put together her new act, a friend observed, "she was valiant in selecting John Bubbles, [who] could easily have stolen the whole show." In fact, as many critics noted, the team proved an inspired combination, marred by few if any bouts of egotism. The individual qualities of this "May-December alliance" were intrinsically complementary: male-female, Black-white, old-young—a singer who also danced, a dancer who also sang. The result was "a double tour-de-force." Their fifty-five-minute act began with Alberghetti alone, in diamonds and a floor-length gown, singing operatic arias and show tunes. Then Bubbles, with derby and cane, came on for his dance sequence, culminating with "Lady Be Good." Finally, Alberghetti returned, also with derby and cane (and black tux), for what virtually all critics called the high point of the turn: a joint medley of favorites from *Porgy and Bess*. She would sing "Summertime," for instance, while Bubbles scatted softly in the background. "Bubbles's raspy pipes and Miss Alberghetti's tonal clarity [were] skillfully blended" in an exhibition of "pure class."

Critics also praised the pair's "ancient and delicious minstrel show jokes," including repartee from old Buck and Bubbles routines. The specter of race, in other words, hovered over the proceedings, for good or ill, depending on one's perspective. Provocatively, one Black columnist saw the duo as "Bojangles and Shirley Temple brought up to date"—but in a good way! All the old minstrel tropes were "purified [and] cleansed, without the slightest trace of blackface." The act, in any case, represented a triumph for the Black member of the team. "After fifty-five years on stage, it's a new life, a new role, a new vitality for Bubbles."

The Alberghetti-Bubbles partnership lasted for more than a year. Performing two-, three-, and sometimes four-week stands, they played "the swankiest rooms in the land": the Empire Room at the Palmer House,

Bubbles with Anna Maria Alberghetti at the Fairmont Hotel in San Francisco, January 1965.

Source: L. Tom Perry Special Collections, Harold B. Lee Library, Brigham Young University, Provo, Utah.

Chicago; Harrah's Club, Lake Tahoe; the Cave Supper Club, Vancouver, Canada; the Royal Box at the Americana Hotel, New York; the Venetian Room at the Fairmont Hotel, San Francisco; and Harold's Club, Reno. Richly appointed restaurant-theaters with crystal chandeliers and mahogany walls, these intimate "supper clubs" were Middle America's refuge from the noisy and ever-intensifying rock music scene (the Beatles' first American tour began the same month Bubbles opened with Alberghetti). Bubbles delighted in the perks that came with such bookings. "Hugh Hefner has learned of your presence in Chicago," wrote the sex mogul's public relations manager to Bubbles at the Palmer House, a "Celebrity Key" to the local Playboy Club enclosed within. At Harrah's in Lake Tahoe, Bubbles was astounded to be given, free of charge, the use of a Cadillac convertible for the length of his stay. (Alberghetti got a Rolls-Royce.) "No other person in this business has ever treated me finer than Bill Harrah," Bubbles said. "No club owner, no hotel owner, no theater owner—no one. . . . You're working for him, sure. But he makes you [feel like] a *guest*."

In the fall, Bubbles was in a strong enough position to renegotiate his contract. Now he wanted $1,000 for each of the weeks the act *didn't* work. Alberghetti gave it to him.

The following January *Ebony*, the premiere Black magazine, told the story of his return to prominence in a celebratory article titled "Bubbles Bounces Back." Heavily illustrated with photographs from throughout his life, from a shot with the Three Ink Spots in 1918 to an action photo of Bubbles dancing with Alberghetti, the article contrasted the struggles of his recent past (bouncing "back and forth between bad periods and worse ones") with his present unlikely success. Asked to explain that success, Alberghetti responded, "We're the old and the new. Bubbles has a quality of old times which hardly any other performer has today. He's probably the last person with it, I'd say." For himself, Bubbles envisioned eight more years in show business—"if my health holds out. I have a job to do and I intend to finish it. I'm not thinking about dying; I have too much work to do."

For the first time in his life, that work included promoting a new album of sound recordings. In their heyday Buck and Bubbles had made a handful of 78s, notably "Rhythm for Sale," "Lady Be Good," and "Breakfast in Harlem." But none of them made the hit parade, and the team was not known for its records. Now, with Bubbles's name back in the news, there began to be calls for him to make an LP. Chief among the Bubbles boosters was Patrick Scott, a Canadian jazz critic for the Toronto *Globe and Mail*. While Bubbles was touring with Bob Hope in 1963, Scott wrote a "letter to Santa" with an unusual gift request: "A long-play album of vocals by the great John Bubbles, whose inestimable talents are the most neglected of our times." Later he refined and narrowed this assessment, calling Bubbles "the most underrated singer . . . in the history of jazz." "I would rather hear him," he said, "than Jimmy Rushing, Olive Brown and Louis Armstrong put together."

In the fall of 1964, "Santa" came through when Vee-Jay Records released *Bubbles: John W. That Is . . .*, a long-playing record of Bubbles singing to the accompaniment of a studio orchestra. The album consists of standards ("Indiana," "Someone to Watch Over Me," "Lady Be Good"), Bubbles originals ("Belittling Me," "Bubbles's Blues"), and a few quirky choices ("When You Wish Upon a Star," "My Mother's Eyes"). Surprisingly, though Bubbles sings "There's a Boat Leaving for New York," the album doesn't include his unofficial theme song, "It Ain't Necessarily So." The liner notes were written by Bob Hope, who credits the singer with "a special brand of springtime in his larynx," producing "more charm and warmth . . . than the Beatles have hair."

In his review of the album, Patrick Scott leads with a disclaimer: "It is by no stretch of the imagination a great jazz recording." But the fault, he insists, lies not with the singer but with the accompaniment, a lush Hollywood-style orchestra complete with "harp chorale"—"someone's idea," he speculates, "of a critically sick joke." (To this critique one might add that Bubbles is placed much too far back in the mix, as if he were accompanying the orchestra rather than the other way around.) And yet, "such are Bubbles's wondrous resources that he makes even the ensemble he is stuck with here swing on almost every number."

> The vibrance, the warmth, the wit, the ease of his delivery have yet to be surpassed by any other singer (and I feel it worth repeating that he is primarily a dancer), and the inherent, built-in feel of jazz in everything he does—you can almost hear the ribs sizzling on Without a Song, of all things—makes this the most important and most infectious vocal offering released so far this year.

Unfortunately, as Scott well knew, his was a minority opinion. Despite a big kick-off by the record company and Bubbles's own high hopes for success, the record did not sell well. It remains, at best, a curiosity in the history of jazz.

4

As she watched Bubbles's achievements from her home in Las Vegas, Aysha Sublett was convinced their marriage was at an end. The stresses of long-distance romance, of mixed-race coupling in a racist society, and of Bubbles's corrosive addictions to gambling and alcohol had worn away the bonds of hope and trust that had kept them together for the last ten years. It was time to pursue their dreams on separate paths.

Bubbles could sense what was coming and tried to head it off. "I regret that you would ever feel . . . that you are not most necessary in my life," he wrote from New York.

> God Knows that it was never in my heart or mind, to harm you, in any way. . . . However, I have realized all that I have done to irk you in many ways, I am with many regrets for so doing. . . . I have told you and this is for the last time, I will not do the things that I have in the past, I am not drinking or gambling, plus late hours, and what ever else that you do not like. . . . I Love you, more than words can say It is you that I Need Want and with every Willingness to Please you.

But the problems went beyond drinking, gambling, and late hours. Many years later, an elderly and cancer-stricken Aysha described a frightening Jeckle-Hyde personality in the man who had once been her benefactor. Bubbles would come home drunk, she recalled, and beat her viciously, thereby renewing the cycle of domestic violence begun by his father. On one occasion she retaliated by pouring scalding hot wax on his naked back and taking a hatchet to every piece of furniture in their apartment. They reconciled repeatedly, as such couples often do, but by 1964 Aysha had had enough. "I don't want to hurt you," she wrote, "I still have feelings but I know now that things will never be the same and that I can never return."

Aysha filed for divorce, charging her husband "with extreme cruelty, mental in nature, all without cause or provocation." (She misleadingly described the abuse as "mental in nature," probably because that was the only way Bubbles would agree to the terms.) While Bubbles was performing at Harrah's in Lake Tahoe, Aysha drove the seven-plus hours from Las Vegas, and he signed the papers. The divorce was finalized on May 22, 1964.

Bubbles finished his last job with Alberghetti a year later, at Harold's Club in Reno. For a while, things continued without a hitch. His next patron, singer and actor (and Elizabeth Taylor's fourth husband) Eddie Fisher, hired Bubbles immediately, almost as if awaiting his turn. Though not particularly well known today, Fisher was a hot commodity in 1965. According to one news report, he was the most highly paid nightclub singer in the country, bringing in $320,000 a year in Vegas alone. Perhaps surprisingly given his youthful thirty-seven years, Fisher—like Alberghetti—pushed old-time entertainment values. In recruiting Bubbles, a reporter wrote, Fisher "revives the bitter-sweet era of the two-a-day." He mixed newer songs with a lengthy Al Jolson medley, and "when [Bubbles] and Eddie sit down on the apron of the stage to sing some old songs, it makes for delightful listening. It is a rare treat for any audience." Bubbles played his part, joshing the crowd about his age and his finances: "I was supposed to retire at 65, but I forgot to save my money. Seriously, I believe work keeps a man young and I plan to keep working as long as my voice and my legs hold up."

For $2,500 a week—$500 more than Alberghetti paid—Bubbles teamed up with Fisher to play the same high-class circuit he toured with Alberghetti: the Riviera, Las Vegas; the Cocoanut Grove, Los Angeles; Harrah's, Lake Tahoe; Eden Roc, Miami Beach; Fontainebleau, Miami Beach; and the New Harrah's, Reno, a run that spanned a period of more than a year. During the breaks, Bubbles kept busy with appearances in *Porgy and Bess* (on the New England "straw-hat circuit") and on television: the Tonight Show, the Dean Martin Show, Art Linkletter's House Party, and the Hollywood Palace, hosted by Bing Crosby. In a nod to Bubbles's professional longevity, Crosby introduced him as a holdover from another era even though the two men were the same age. As they sang "Me and My Shadow" together, Bubbles played the shadow, walking in time behind Crosby, his hand on his shoulder. The great dancer had been in show business for more than half a century.

5

From the outside, Bubbles's 1960s career looks like an unqualified success. He appeared with the biggest stars of the day. He played the most opulent venues. He was a regular on television, including the hottest show on the airwaves. With Eddie Fisher he was making over $20,000 a week in today's money. And yet, judging from his offstage behavior, Bubbles was not a happy man during this period. One of his girlfriends observed that although he "could turn on all the charm imaginable at show time," he was "always high strung and cross after performing." With Aysha, as we have seen, his actions escalated into brutal, alcohol-fueled violence. Where did this rage come from? There are, alas, several possibilities.

To every patron, no matter how much younger or less experienced, Bubbles played a subordinate role. This might seem only natural; they were paying *him* after all. But this fact must have dredged up old resentments about headline status, particularly since we can be sure he considered himself superior to the people writing his checks. ("Do you understand what a Negro has to do to be recognized?" he once asked an interviewer. "I got to dance four times as good as Fred Astaire. . . . I can't sing *even* with Frank Sinatra, I've got to sing *better* than him.") His tap dancing, once his greatest pride, now evoked images in some quarters of shame and self-parody. Repeatedly, he had to play the fool in old Buck and Bubbles routines, suffering the scripted taunts of his white betters. Again and again, journalists brought his name together with the hated words "Uncle Tom." This humiliating connection seemed borne out by his partnership with Alberghetti, which reminded at least one reporter of Bojangles and Shirley Temple—the archetypal example of Tomism. A few weeks into this engagement, he suggested privately, bitterly, that white patrons hired Black artists "in order to look better to the audience."

He was almost certainly right. Not that Johnny Carson's or Bob Hope's enthusiasm for Bubbles was insincere. But in the civil rights era, entertainers—like people in other walks of life—faced pressure to integrate their ranks. Hope began with Bubbles, the safest possible choice. A couple of years later, he hired a slightly younger option: the Nicholas Brothers. In 1966, under mounting pressure, the USO recruited still younger and hipper acts, first Sammy Davis Jr., then the Supremes. This pattern suggests a generational reason for Bubbles's success. He was the sort of Black entertainer middle-aged white people remembered fondly from their youth—the same middle-aged white people who now attended the Palmer House or arranged USO bookings. Yet it wasn't only generational. The dirty little secret is that this audience applauded Bubbles in part because, in an age of racial protest, he rang bells they associated with subservience. Surely the proud Bubbles sensed this—and it drove him mad.

Bubbles's humiliation ended in the only way it could—with unemployment. As his last gig with Fisher came to an end in July 1966, everything just sort of stopped. No TV shows, no tours, no club dates to speak of, for about six months. His state of mind can be guessed from a flurry of letters he exchanged with a possible business partner. Bubbles had dabbled in entrepreneurship ever since returning from Europe in 1957, when he invested in the Shack. His big dream was to launch a talent agency called the American Federation for Improving Talent, which, though he signed up a handful of prospects, never really got off the ground. Now he started corresponding with one James Thompson about a "tremendous business plan" the latter had hawked to Bubbles the year before—a California restaurant called The Clam Shell.

In July, Bubbles, who now lived in California himself, sent Thompson a $1,000 down payment on the $5,000 required to place him among "the stockholders." By late September, however, he wrote to inform Thompson, sadly, that he would not be able to come up with the remainder and asked for the return of his down payment. When Thompson stalled, Bubbles sent a series of increasingly plaintive appeals:

Sept. 26: "I am OK in health, but very low in finance. . . . Therefore it will be necessary that you refund the One Thousand Dollars. . . . My trip East was not as fruitful as I expected it to be."

Oct. 3: "I have been in a turmoil trying to keep working as you know what this profession is like, these days. . . . If your check does not meet with my approval, there will be room for discussion."

Oct. 20: "I regret that I was not able to raise the amount necessary to meet with the Clam Shell Stockholders. . . . James you know that I don't have a thousand dollars to lay out in the Sun. Now . . . why don't you be a good boy, and send me your check before it is messed up."

The denouement of this particular dispute is not known, but over the next year Bubbles continued corresponding with Thompson about other schemes, none of which amounted to anything. His actions are indicative of an increasing unreality spreading over his life, as he tried to forestall the reckoning—on all fronts—he must have sensed coming.

18

This Unforgettable Passage

1

In the summer of 1967, America's long-simmering cultural revolution broke into a boil. Urban unrest exploded as race riots convulsed northern cities and antiwar demonstrators packed the streets of New York, Washington, and San Francisco. Hippies in Haight-Ashbury and elsewhere celebrated the Summer of Love, a Saturnalia of sex, drugs, and rebellion against "the establishment." Breaking through the din of dissent were groundbreaking sounds in popular music: the Beatles' *Sgt. Pepper's Lonely Hearts Club Band*, for instance, and Jimi Hendrix's *Are You Experienced?* Taken together, these disorienting crosscurrents seemed to augur a brash, youthful new world. The old world seemed at last to be giving up the ghost.

As with any revolution, there were winners and losers, conquerors and casualties. Bubbles was one of the casualties. As fate would have it, he made his exit not in growing obscurity but in a final blaze of nostalgia. In a reversal of fortune that may have surprised even him, he was offered supporting roles in gauzy, high-profile productions by three of the most iconic women of show business: Lucille Ball, Barbra Streisand, and, once again, Judy Garland. The nostalgia of these shows didn't mourn the loss of vaudeville alone but also of the world that gave it birth, now crumbling before onrushing events.

For Bubbles, the year began on an auspicious note. On January 9 he bought a two-bedroom house in Los Angeles for $23,200. Where he got the credit for the loan or the money for the down payment is not known, but according to an accusation made in writing some months later (to be detailed subsequently), a schoolteacher from back east, a white woman, provided the wherewithal to complete the purchase. This seems more likely than not. The woman in question was Beatrice Canning, with whom Bubbles had been having a torrid affair since 1963. One refrain of their correspondence is Bubbles's constant demands for money and her frequent acquiescence to his overtures (or, contrarily, her exasperated denials when the requests came too

Sportin' Life. Brian Harker, Oxford University Press. © Oxford University Press 2022.
DOI: 10.1093/oso/9780197514511.003.0019

often). Since Bubbles was dead broke, he would have needed someone to help him buy a house, and Beatrice is certainly a likely candidate.

Nevertheless, she was only one of several women that Bubbles had been seeing, even while he was still married to Aysha. His letters from the time of their divorce disclose a tapestry of liaisons as he weaved his way around one woman after another from one week to the next. The scattered residences of his numerous paramours—in New York, New Jersey, Buffalo, Boston, Cleveland, and Chicago—made it easier for him to hide their existence from one another. As a close friend later recalled, "All these gals thought they were in his future plans, for each one wanted him as a husband. I think he knew he could arrive in these cities, be met at the airport, have a good, free place to stay. Sympathetic type who fed him, bedded him, [provided] transportation for him and even bought clothes for him."

Despite her generosity and devotion, it was not Beatrice whose romantic prospects burned brightest in early 1967. For various reasons, Bubbles felt increasingly attached to a woman from out of the country. Ruth Redina Campbell was the thirty-five-year-old daughter of an aristocratic family in one of the recently founded African nations (the extant documentation doesn't make clear which one). She had grown up with every advantage, going to school in Switzerland and taking graduate studies in the United States. She had known Bubbles for some time, having given birth to his daughter the previous year. She would be pregnant with his second baby within a month. Although Bubbles did not quit his other girlfriends, Ruth would lay the greatest claim on his thoughts and finances as the year progressed.

2

Fortunately for all concerned, Bubbles began making money again in late January, when Lucille Ball hired him to appear on her popular TV show. Ball was nearing the end of her second decade of television stardom following six blockbuster seasons of *I Love Lucy* and six more seasons, less historic but still successful, of *The Lucy Show*. She signed Bubbles for two back-to-back episodes from the fifth season of the latter, "Main Street, U.S.A.," broadcast January 23, and a sequel, "Lucy Puts Main Street on the Map," the following week. "He's a real humanitarian," Ball said of Bubbles. "I never met a more human human."

From today's vantage point, "Main Street, U.S.A." comes across as an allegory of the times in which it was made. The show depicts a pure, wholesome slice of Americana threatened by the soulless forces of modernity. Lucy Carmichael and her boss, Mr. Mooney, a bank executive, have come to the fictional town of Bancroft on a business errand. "Oh, what a darling little town," Lucy gasps, "so old-fashioned and quaint." A brass band marches by, and a boy sells newspapers in the street. Lucy meets her friend Mel Tinker (played by jazz singer Mel Tormé), and together they go into the town drugstore for some strawberry ice cream sodas. "Mr. Bubbles" (played by himself) is playing chess with a couple of old-timers.

"Mr. Bubbles used to own a garage here," says Mel, "but he sold it and bought the livery stable."

"The livery stable?" says Lucy. "I thought horses were practically extinct."

"That gives you an idea of how the folks around here feel about 'progress,'" says Mel.

With this remark Mel exposes the problem now facing Lucy, who, after all, has come to Bancroft to put the finishing touches on a deal to build a freeway down Main Street. Conscience-stricken, Lucy conspires with Mel, Mr. Bubbles, and the town brass band to stage an act of musical propaganda strong enough to convince the political and commercial powers-that-be to abandon their project and keep the little town as it is.

It's not a very good show. The nostalgia is corny and heavy-handed, and Lucy brings none of the anarchic zaniness that made *I Love Lucy* so brilliant. Yet it provides an effective platform for Bubbles, who in the drugstore does a little song-and-dance that serves as a human counterpart to the antique coffee grinder and penny candies that have just plunged Lucy into a stupor of bygone yearning. (In the sequel, "Lucy Puts Main Street on the Map," Bubbles does a longer dance that strikingly recalls his set piece in *Cabin in the Sky*.) More interestingly, during the banter around the chess table Bubbles is actually quite funny. In another life, one can imagine him becoming a successful character actor in the mold of his friend Redd Foxx (*Sanford and Son*) or Sherman Hemsley (*The Jeffersons*).

As a pageant of nostalgia, Bubbles's next job—though more grandiose—was even less compelling. During a four-day period, April 26–29, he taped his small part in Barbra Streisand's third television special for CBS. At only twenty-four years old, Streisand was already well along in her meteoric rise to superstardom. Her first two CBS specials, "My Name Is Barbra" and "Color Me Barbra," had each been an enormous success. For her third, the thinking went, she needed to change things up a bit so as not to become predictable. Since the first two shows were basically solo concerts for TV, focusing on Streisand from beginning to end, the third would bring on a supporting cast, including actor Jason Robards Jr. and Bubbles as co-stars, and "more than 100 [other] performers and technicians." In another change, the show would reach back to the turn of the century to "recreate the good old days of vaudeville" (possibly to harmonize with the movie Streisand was making that year, *Funny Girl*, based on the life of Fanny Brice). The show would be called *The Belle of 14th Street.*

In turning to the vaudeville theme, Streisand explained, "We weren't looking to make fun of it or camp it, but to do it as they did." Her team spent a year in preparation researching the customs of this ancient entertainment, and Streisand herself interviewed veteran comedian George Burns to get the proper feeling and color. In the TV studio the designers built a full-scale mock-up of an old-time vaudeville theater and assembled an audience consisting of the sponsor's employees all dressed in period garb. In keeping with Streisand's famously high standards, every detail of the fin-de-siècle costumes and sets was crafted to perfection.

Unfortunately, in their quest for verisimilitude, the producers revived practices so esoteric that modern audiences came away more baffled than edified. The show opened with Robards doing a number with a head-scratching chorus line of "Beef Trust Girls," two-hundred-pound women who accurately mirrored their hefty historical counterparts in Billy Watson's burlesque troupe. To evoke the elaborate mechanical illusions of past sets, Streisand "flew," Peter Pan-like, during a parody of Shakespeare's *Tempest.* More confusing was the quick-changing of costumes as she and Robards became first one character, then another, over the course of the skit—all very authentic in 1900 but seventy years later unnecessary and bewildering.

The most egregious misjudgment, though, was what the director decided to do with Bubbles. Inspired by an old photo of Bert Williams in the 1910 Ziegfeld Follies, dressed as Chanticleer with rooster tail and feathers, he put Bubbles in the same preposterous get-up—without context or explanation—and had him sing and dance to an old Al Jolson song, "I'm Goin' South." That was the extent of his contribution.

When the show was broadcast in October, the critics howled. Far from taking viewers on a delicious journey into the past, the show was "an embarrassing outing, a concoction of deranged productions," wrote the *Times.* The beef trust scene was "a total and tasteless disaster," the Shakespeare parody "a burden" on the principals. Like the other acts, Bubbles's turn may have been authentic, added *Newsday*, but it was an authenticity that "should have remained buried. The caricature of the befeathered, dancing Uncle Tom happily singing 'I'm Goin' South' was a chapter out of our entertainment past that needed no resurrecting." The show, according to Streisand's biographer, represented her "first big professional misstep."

3

Back in California, Bubbles's personal life took a sharp and enigmatic turn. On June 6, 1967, at age sixty-four, he married his fourth wife, Ruth Redina Campbell, in San Bernardino, under the hand of a Baptist minister. We don't know much about the thinking that went into this decision or his commitment to it on that day. But he never saw Ruth again. In New York two months later, he told a reporter, "I've been married three times already, and I'm waiting for the fourth. For that will be the success of my intentions— true happiness." Was he denying the marriage had taken place? As we shall see from his excruciating correspondence with Ruth during this period, she sometimes wondered the same thing.

Immediately after the wedding, Bubbles returned to New York to appear again with Judy Garland. Since *Judy at the Met* in 1959, the luckless Garland had experienced further calamities, the latest occurring only a couple of months earlier, when she was fired from the film *Valley of the Dolls* and lost her Los Angeles home. In another attempt to salvage her life and career, Sid Luft booked her to play four weeks at the New York Palace, a venue that figured prominently in the Garland mythology. After she had lost her contract with MGM in 1950, her career came roaring back when she played an unprecedented nineteen weeks at the Palace the following year. For her return engagement in 1967, she called the show *Judy Garland at Home at the Palace*. The old theater had special meaning for Bubbles, too, of course. He played there for the first time in December 1920 and most recently in August 1951 (two months before Garland's debut). This engagement would be a homecoming for both of them.

During a weeklong run at the Storrowton Music Fair, where the Garland show was warming up before opening on Broadway, Bubbles received a cryptic letter—essentially a blackmail note—from someone close to Ruth's family who obviously abhorred the marriage that had just taken place.

The writer, one T. Yates from Tel Aviv (though the letter was sent from Los Angeles), wanted Bubbles to know he was being watched very closely:

What elderly sephia [*sic*], whose initials J.B., a song and dance man, is causing an African Embassy in Washington a colossal headache, and by his last act, a marriage on June 6 to one of this New Nation's most brilliant personalities, of ruling parentage and a reigning beauty by all opinions of those who have seen the young lady, now has America in a very touchy spot?

Ruth's family had thoroughly investigated Bubbles, the writer went on, and knew of all his vulnerabilities as a "notorious lady's man":

And the day after the wedding wasn't the aging Romeo seen in an old female friend's home in the Los Angeles area; and didn't they spend the weekend together when he was supposedly enroute to join the Judy Garland show in New England; and didn't a white school marm in Boston recently buy him a home in Los Angeles; and isn't she furnishing it for him; and isn't she expecting him as soon as school is over on the 23rd of July for their annual vacation together?

Apparently assuming that Bubbles had targeted Ruth for her family's considerable fortune, the writer made a point of telling him that her disapproving siblings in Africa had cut off her annual stipend of $75,000 and were in the process of trying "to have the will broken." But, Yates warned, while they knew of Ruth's illegitimate child, they did not yet know of her "secret" marriage to Bubbles, and "neither does the school marm in Boston."

Bubbles never revealed his thoughts about this letter, but it may well have influenced his decisions about his marriage later in the year.

On opening night at the Palace, when Garland entered from the back of the theater, walked down the center aisle dressed in the gold-sequined pantsuit she was to have worn in *Valley of the Dolls*, paused to kiss Harold Arlen, composer of "Over the Rainbow," and turned to face the audience, "the house went unquietly mad." Her occasionally erratic singing at the Storrowton concert a week earlier, her tripping over the mike cord, her stopping midsong to start over—none of that mattered to her enraptured fans in West Springfield, Massachusetts. "We love you, Judy!" they had screamed. After the show, "people who had barely restrained themselves for the hour of her performance streamed onto the stage to kiss her, shake her hand, give her flowers or just touch her." Similar displays now transpired at the Palace, where multiple critics compared her frenzied reception to Beatlemania.

In contrast to the limp productions of Lucille Ball and Barbra Streisand, the nostalgia in Garland's show was not only hugely effective, but it was also absolutely essential to her emotional connection with her fans. Yet while the show was advertised as "a comeback of bigtime vaudeville to the Palace," the nostalgia was not about vaudeville per se. It was about Judy and everything she stood for. As one critic put it, "To a vast segment of her following, Judy is the eternal Dorothy, the embodiment of a simpler and happier time."

To the extent that this "happier time" included vaudeville, however, the show was also about vaudeville—and this is where Bubbles and the other co-stars, stand-up comic Jackie Vernon and juggler Francis Brunn, found their opening. Bubbles tap-danced, led the audience in "It Ain't Necessarily So," and reprised his duet with Garland on "Me and My Shadow," this time with her two children, Lorna and Joey, bringing up the rear. In line with most reviews from this late stage of his career, critics praised Bubbles less for his art than for his old-school professionalism, the "old-school" part, as always, carrying more than one meaning. "Mr. Bubbles," wrote the *Times*, "is a veteran trouper from the uncomplicated, naïve, pre–Stokely Carmichael era." As for the audience, they didn't just sit on their hands waiting for Garland to reappear. "John Bubbles wins his own applause," noted the *Boston Globe*, and Bubbles reveled in it. "Makes you feel at home to hear that kind of applause," he said.

On the last day of the Palace engagement, with an election year around the corner, someone stood with a sign that said "Judy Garland for President"— and not far away was another sign: "John Bubbles for Vice President."

4

All summer long, as Bubbles performed with Judy Garland on the other side of the country, Ruth sent letters from her home in Riverside, California. To read this correspondence is to survey a deeply dysfunctional relationship, as Ruth struggled to understand the inscrutable man she married. Faced with money problems (since her family had cut her off) and illness requiring hospitalization, she tried one strategy after another to get an adequate response from Bubbles. Her letters are by turn scornful or flattering or pleading or

Bubbles with Judy Garland at the Palace Theatre, August 1967.
Source: L. Tom Perry Special Collections, Harold B. Lee Library, Brigham Young University, Provo, Utah.

sarcastic. She laments his "blood-curdling tirades" on the phone and accuses him of abandonment. She makes clear that she knows of his dalliances with other women, condemning "any one (especially a new husband) with a pregnant wife who leaves her on the day he marries her, and spends the rest of the summer with others and thoroughly enjoys himself (but for token calls and cards he sends by the dozen to all his Harem. [And this I know] because once you sent me the wrong card)."

Bubbles typically responds with oddly dispassionate, almost business-like missives—sometimes with a check enclosed—that profess not to know what she's talking about. In a stunningly tone-deaf reply to a threat she made at one point to leave him, he writes:

> I would like to thank you for your message for Father's Day, and all other mail that I have received from you. . . . I dont know why you are so set on running away, unless you are un-happy. I am sorry that you will not help me do anything about what is best for you. . . . No matter how you feel, I advise that you wait until after the baby is born before you do anything. . . . What have you done to be so afraid, and emotional about?

As angry as Ruth often becomes, however, she is clearly still in love and unable completely to forget the noble and generous attributes that attracted her to Bubbles in the first place. In one besotted letter she reminds him of these qualities, so often hidden, she claims, by a façade of outward indifference: "John I know the love of the inner you. I have seen the pain of a rude remark reflected in your eyes, I've seen you reach out to the helpless, the sick, I've seen the light in childrens eyes that love you." In mid-August, as Bubbles began garnering publicity for his appearances with Judy Garland, Ruth gave him a loving pep talk: "I again say your star has been re-lighted, and mark my word . . . will glow brighter than you ever dreamed." "The charisma of you is class," she continued, "that aura of confidence that comes with knowing you have the goods. . . . John Kennedy had it, LBJ doesn't. . . . Perry Como in abundance has it, Dean Martin doesn't. . . . and John Bubbles has it, Satchmo doesn't."

Spousal boosterism aside, the Garland show generated real momentum for Bubbles. Merv Griffin invited him to appear on his talk show shortly after the week at Storrowton, and called him back four more times in August alone. (Had things gone differently, Griffin might have become Bubbles's new Johnny Carson.) Even more significantly, Bubbles was signed for his first movie since 1948, *Finian's Rainbow*, starring Fred Astaire and Petula Clark. (With *Guess Who's Coming to Dinner*, a film taking a sympathetic view of interracial marriage, coming out in the same year, it was a new era in Black cinema.)

Among numerous requests for interviews, the most significant came from *The New Yorker*. Bubbles happily rattled off the important milestones of his career. "This unforgettable passage I've been through," he reflected in conclusion, "all the things I've had to do to be sitting here. . . ." He searched for the words. "You do your best; you do your utmost. You've got to be born with the spirit. It's the spirit that does it. Everything I do is by the spirit—nothing by the flesh." About his financial setbacks he was philosophical: "I've had a lot of problems, and I've been through a lot of money, but if I still had the money, then I wouldn't know what I know." His worn-out body was another matter. "These legs have been through the mill," he said. "I do too much dancing for the wind-power department nowadays."

Strangely, as the Garland Show wound down, Bubbles began hearing voices from his distant past. On August 22 he got a letter from a woman who had been present at Buck and Bubbles's debut at the Mary Anderson Theatre in Louisville, back in 1919. "When I read that you were to be on the Judy Garland Show," she said, "I thot it would be a good time to write you as I had often intended to." The woman and her husband had appeared on the same bill, creating pictures by throwing colored sand on easels. "You really worked your hearts out," she recalled. "The audience loved it." A week later Bubbles heard from even farther back in his history. A woman from Indianapolis wrote that her father had owned the Crown Garden Theatre where Bubbles had won so many talent contests as an eleven-year-old boy. "I can remember how fondly Dad always spoke of you," she said. "This was his life too . . . he never ceased talking, writing about the wonderful world of Show Biz until his death in '59."

By the time she sent her letter, Bubbles was already incapacitated.

After four triumphant weeks, the Palace show had closed on Saturday, August 26. The following Monday, Bubbles retired to his bed in the Americana Hotel. The next morning, he couldn't move his left arm. He walked to Roosevelt Hospital, and while there the paralysis spread down his entire left side, the result of a massive stroke. Needless to say, he would not go on tour with Judy Garland as planned, or fill any return engagements for Merv Griffin, or appear in *Finian's Rainbow*. And though on rare occasions in the coming years he would put on the old derby again to sing a song for appreciative fans, his dancing days were over.

19

A World of Mirth

1

John Bubbles spent the fall of 1967 in New York's Roosevelt Hospital, hovering between life and death. Two weeks after his stroke, he caught pneumonia for the third time in his life and was not expected to survive. Yet after a mighty struggle, he recovered, and on December 23 was released from the hospital and sent home to California, where he spent the next year in physical therapy at Cedars-Sinai Medical Center in Los Angeles.

In the immediate aftermath of his stroke, Bubbles was deluged with well wishes—"so many phone calls and visitors that his doctor gave orders—no phone calls." He got notes from his old friend and protégé Chuck Green, from patrons like Barbra Streisand and Merv Griffin, even from Robert F. Kenney on United States Senate letterhead (Ruth was friends with the Kennedy family). Bob Hope sent a telegram: "John . . . we're all thinking of you and pulling for you and hope you're up and out of there soon because the band is playing your intro."

He also heard from some of the women in his life, including his ex-wife Mabel, who was still concerned about him despite everything. Upon hearing of his stroke, Ruth wrote him right away expressing unflinching love and support. But during a phone call soon after, he raged at her so unmercifully that she withdrew in apparent surrender to an impossible situation—an impossible man. Whether in response to the blackmail letter or to his physically reduced capacity or to some other unnamed provocation, Bubbles contacted his lawyer and asked about the possibility of getting a divorce or annulment. A divorce eventually took place, and after giving birth to a son Ruth flew with her three children (one from a previous marriage) to San Juan, Puerto Rico, and entered a convent to take up the life of a nun.

When Bubbles arrived in California, he found Beatrice Canning there to get him settled ("she loved him no matter what condition he was in"), but her teaching job kept drawing her back east. Finally, in the fall of 1969, Bubbles met the person who would take care of him for the rest of

Sportin' Life. Brian Harker, Oxford University Press. © Oxford University Press 2022.
DOI: 10.1093/oso/9780197514511.003.0020

his life—a dark-haired, heavy-set white woman named Wanda Michael. Twelve years younger than Bubbles, Wanda grew up in a working-class family, the daughter of an auto mechanic. Over time she acquired a love of the performing arts and a fan's interest in show business. (Her brother was Henry Farrell, who wrote the best-selling novel *Whatever Happened to Baby Jane* and co-authored the screenplay *Hush, Hush, Sweet Charlotte*.) When she met Bubbles, she was supporting herself by selling patches—cloth emblems and insignia—at flea markets, and didn't have much to offer financially. But as an experienced bookkeeper she was well positioned to bring a semblance of order to Bubbles's fly-by-night existence.

The precise nature of their relationship is uncertain. A few months after meeting him, Wanda, who had been married before, wrote Bubbles a letter flush with twitterpation:

> You are my safe harbor, sanity, reconstruction, reason, kindness, principle, sweetness, light, knowledge and peace. You care about what is happening to me. You are the man I love sincerely. You are many thousands of things to me and it all blends into a beautiful aura surrounding everything. I hope you derive some of this feeling from your association with your acolyte, "me." I want to return the same good things to you.

For several years she lived with Bubbles in his house in Los Angeles. But if they did share intimacies early on, within a few years it seems clear their relationship became more practical and platonic. Wanda moved out to live on her own while continuing as Bubbles's all-purpose factotum—his housekeeper, his bookkeeper, his gofer, his nurse. In appreciation, in 1977 Bubbles bequeathed to her his house upon his death.

When Wanda entered his life, Bubbles's financial woes loomed even larger than usual. His four months in Roosevelt Hospital had set him back $13,757.99, and his year at Cedars-Sinai, though partly covered by insurance, added to this debt. As word of his troubles got around, several show business friends sent money, including Bob Hope, Bing Crosby, Johnny Carson, Lucille Ball, and Pearl Bailey. Hope helped Bubbles get a bank loan for $3,000, and when Bubbles, living on Social Security, proved incapable of anything more than the occasional monthly interest payment, Hope wrote a check to pay off the loan. Such measures ultimately proved inadequate. In 1970 Bubbles filed for bankruptcy.

Unable to resume his work as an entertainer, he set his sights on a new objective: to make sure his lifetime achievements were remembered and honored. That meant writing a book—a project, he hoped, that might even bring in some money. In September 1968 he signed a contract with an author named Jerry McGuire to write his biography, splitting the profits 60–40 in Bubbles's favor. McGuire would conduct lengthy interviews with Bubbles and be given access to his recent patrons, including Peter Lind Hayes, Judy Garland, Bob Hope, Johnny Carson, and Lucille Ball. Incorporating a wealth of new anecdotes and quotations, McGuire produced an invaluable document, at 276 pages the first extended narrative of Bubbles's life. Bubbles lived in a state of high expectation, regaling his friends with his hopes of prosperity in the wake of publication. But when he and Wanda saw the manuscript, they were deeply disappointed (Wanda called it "lifeless"), and, indeed, McGuire couldn't find a publisher.

Bubbles settled into a life of watching television (he especially enjoyed the Black comics Flip Wilson and Redd Foxx), clipping newspapers, and writing letters. Chuck Green, Eubie Blake, and Eva Jessye became faithful pen pals. Bubbles heard from old girlfriends, one of whom swore she would move to Los Angeles and marry him if he would only say the word. Letters even arrived from Eleanor Gross (née Heinemann), the white chorus girl from *Dancing Around* whom he had briefly hoped to marry back in 1923. In between letters to and from old friends and flames, Bubbles also set out to find someone to replace Jerry McGuire, another writer or collaborator to help him publish the story of his life. Several candidates showed real interest, and an anxious Bubbles exchanged letters with all of them. But for one reason or another, none of these partnerships came to fruition.

2

The idea of publishing a Bubbles biography wasn't ridiculous on its face. It actually fit into a larger movement in the 1970s to rediscover, and in some cases institutionalize, the Black performing arts of previous eras. Unlike similar efforts in the past, this movement was not primarily motivated by nostalgia. The idea was to reclaim Black music and dance for posterity's sake, not old-time's sake. In the case of tap dancing, the main impetus came from two energetic young white women. Their method was to hunt down the old-time Black hoofers, bring them out of obscurity, and learn from them, gaining knowledge directly from the source. Dancer-impresario Brenda Bufalino featured Honi Coles and other veterans in a documentary called *Great Feats of Feet* (1977) and set up new opportunities for them to perform live. Working independently of Bufalino, Jane Goldberg followed a similar path. But as an avid dancer who also happened to be a journalist, she took a more historically minded approach, interviewing tap's elder statesmen and squeezing them for as many occult secrets as she could.

Goldberg's conversations with dancers like Honi Coles and Chuck Green inevitably led her to the Grand Old Man of the art, John Bubbles. From her home in New York, Goldberg opened a correspondence with Bubbles, interviewed him, and ultimately made a trip to California to greet him in person. She encountered an irascible old man, resentful of all he was missing and all he had missed. "It was lovely talking to you on the phone last night," she wrote after one of their more amicable conversations, "especially since we weren't yelling at each other." Yet Goldberg, an idealistic, curly-haired romantic, also found a soft spot in Bubbles's crotchety old heart. He took a fatherly interest in her dancing career, and in between imperious outbursts offered advice, encouragement, even praise. "You've got to surpass me, darling," he said grandly. "Not just do me, but surpass me."

Most of the tap revivalists were women, but not all. In 1979 documentary filmmaker George T. Nierenberg completed *No Maps on My Taps*, a labor of love five years in the making. Although this beautifully expressive work focuses on three aging tap masters—Chuck Green, Bunny Briggs, and Sandman Sims—Bubbles's spirit hovers over the production. In one scene Sims and Briggs argue over who would prevail in a hypothetical contest between Bill Robinson and Bubbles—"like if Ali and Joe Louis had met," Sims muses. Briggs appeals to the evidence of history. "When Bubbles would come around Bill, Bill would go out. Because he knew Bubbles could whip him," he says matter-of-factly.

A few months after the film's premiere, Nierenberg sat down with Bubbles for a massive soup-to-nuts interview, eventually filling more than six hundred pages of transcript, all under the auspices of the Jazz Oral History Project at the Institute of Jazz Studies at Rutgers University. Bubbles, who misunderstood the scholarly nature of the undertaking, was disappointed that the final product had zero market value in and of itself. He apparently thought he'd found a new ghostwriter to tell the story of his life. Nevertheless, the interview joins the McGuire manuscript as one of two indispensable sources for Bubbles's biography. Despite Bubbles's efforts to project a

carefully crafted image for posterity, there are moments of startling frank-
ness. For example, when Nierenberg asks what he had been doing since his
stroke, Bubbles can't help but sputter in frustration: "Nothin', nothin', nothin',
just what you see me doing now, nothin'. Did that for 12 years, nothin'. You
understand? Nothin'."

<h2 style="text-align:center">3</h2>

For all Bubbles's adamance, this wasn't entirely true. In fact, at the time of
the interview, he was in the early stages of an odds-defying second career
comeback. It had started in August 1978 with a letter he received, out of the
blue, from the representative of Broadway performer André De Shields. In
childhood, as we have seen, De Shields had been inspired by Bubbles's performance in *Cabin in the Sky* to go into show business himself. Now he had
a red-hot solo act at the Reno Sweeney in New York, one that featured him
doing an impression of his youthful idol, John Bubbles. Would the subject
of that impression, the representative asked, like to come to New York to
see the show, all expenses paid? Bubbles was so excited that he and Wanda
went through seven drafts of his return letter to make sure he said everything
just right. He flew to New York to see the show in September (Chuck Green
picked him up at the airport and served as his faithful assistant) and loved
every minute of it.

In December Jane Goldberg published "Hoofer's Homage" in the *Village
Voice*, a landmark article bringing Bubbles back to the attention of arts-
minded people in New York. And at some point, all the scattered references
to Bubbles reached a critical mass. For an old hoofer confined to a wheelchair
the unimaginable happened: The following spring he was invited to come
out of retirement and appear in a new musical, *Black Broadway*, as part of the
Newport Jazz Festival in New York. He joined a lineup that included some
of his oldest friends in show business—Eubie Blake, Adelaide Hall, Edith
Wilson, and Honi Coles—together with younger performers like Bobby
Short and (when Coles fell ill) Gregory Hines, whom Bubbles had encouraged as a child at the Apollo Theatre back in 1959.

The show, opening June 24 at Avery Fisher Hall, took a very willing audience on a tour of Black musical history, recreating hits from old shows like *In
Dahomey* (1903), *Shuffle Along* (1921), *Blackbirds of 1928*, and *Porgy and Bess*
(1935). When it came Bubbles's turn he sang "It Ain't Necessarily So" from

his wheelchair, and, as he used to do in the old days, cued the audience to join in at the chorus with a wave of his gray derby. "His voice had vitality and presence," wrote the *Times*, "with little indication of the years that had passed since he first sang that song." Another critic considered Bubbles, who won a standing ovation and "a house lights-up tribute," to be the high point in a night of "emotional peaks." The show was reprised the following year at Town Hall, and again Bubbles enchanted the critics.

"When you're hot you're hot," Flip Wilson used to say, and in the summer of 1980 Bubbles was hot. In July he sat for an interview on *Good Morning America*. In August he appeared at the Hollywood Bowl in a concert titled "The Great Singers Sing the Great American Songs" on a bill with Joe Williams, Carmen McRae, and Mel Tormé. Producer Bob Sunenblick ushered him into the recording studio to make an LP called *John W. Bubbles Back on Broadway*. Most promising of all, Alfred A. Knopf offered him a book contract, seemingly the prize he had been waiting for all these years. A generous advance of $25,000 was to be split 50–50 between Bubbles and his two able ghostwriters, Robert Kimball and Sylvia Pancotti. In 1973 Kimball had co-written beautifully illustrated and well-received books on Sissle and Blake and the Gershwins. It would be hard to imagine more favorable terms for a potential autobiography. But for reasons unknown—did he hold out for more money?—Bubbles never signed the contract, and his last best chance to see his life story in print melted away.

In the meantime, Bubbles's role in the tap revival continued. During the week of October 13, Jane Goldberg hosted the first-ever tap festival, at the Village Gate in New York. An informal video documentary of the event was titled *By Word of Foot: 12 Tap Masters Pass on Their Tradition*. As the tape rolls, instruction and demonstrations are given by an illustrious faculty: Honi Coles, Peg Leg Bates, Bunny Briggs, Sandman Sims, Charles Cook, Ernest Brown, Gregory Hines, and others. Presiding over the whole proceedings is Bubbles, flown in for the occasion from California. Coles introduces him with due reverence: "In closing I say, uh, the winner and still champ, John W. Bubbles. Every dancer that you possibly know of has been influenced by this gentleman here." After warm applause, a white-haired Bubbles appears somewhat overwhelmed. "God bless you, and thanks for being such a fan of mine in years gone by," he says. "And I'm grateful with all the words can express. And I don't know how to say to all the folks that are here how good I feel about having such an amount of people being interested in this idea"— tap. "I didn't know that."

When Bubbles got back to California, he found himself inundated by students and admirers and would-be disciples. "His house is like Grand Central Station," remarked a friend. "People are there day and night. If they're not ringing the bell, they're on the phone." His name ricocheted through the country, sometimes in odd or unexpected ways. Rumors surfaced, for instance, that the hottest pop star of the day, Michael Jackson, had named his pet chimp after the great dancer. Bubbles's public performances quickly dropped off, but the demand for his appearances as a kind of living legend increased, as universities, dance studios, and arts centers requested his presence and his wisdom. He kept fan letters in a cigar box next to his pillow and read them for solace. One older fan reflected on the meaning of his act with Buck: "Perhaps you don't think of things this way—perhaps to you it was a way of making a living—but to me it was much more than that—to have the gift—to be able to take people for no matter how long or short a time out of their hum drum world (perhaps filled with sorrow) into a world of mirth. . . . I feel this will merit you and Buck a place high in the next world."

Bubbles in retirement.

Source: L. Tom Perry Special Collections, Harold B. Lee Library, Brigham Young University, Provo, Utah.

4

In October 1984, Wanda found an almost empty bottle of Irish Mist Whiskey in the sink, a little contraband smuggled in for Bubbles by a well-meaning friend. The next day he had another stroke. Convinced the liquor had caused it, Wanda was "angry as the devil himself." This time the effects were more severe, including aphasia (impairment of speech) and general deterioration across the board. Bubbles declined rapidly. At 10:30 p.m. on Sunday night, May 18, 1986, he died peacefully at home. He was eighty-three years old.

Previously focused on Bubbles's health, Wanda now turned with dismay to financial matters. His estate was deep in the red. How would she pay for a funeral? In a panic, she wrote letters to some of Bubbles's old friends and patrons pleading for help. And help came—immediately. Johnny Carson sent $2,004.70 to the funeral home and $958.50 to the florist. Lee Gershwin (Ira's widow) sent $2,000. Bob Hope, Danny Thomas, and Robert Guillaume each sent $1,000. Donations came from the famous and the obscure, from Lucille Ball, Liza Minnelli, and Pearl Bailey (Bellson), and from ordinary people who just wanted to contribute. Wanda had enough to pay for the funeral and then some.

Honorary pallbearers included Willie Covan, Fayard Nicholas, Chuck Green, Honi Coles, and Louis DaPron, hoofers all. A written eulogy by blaxploitation film star West Gale consisted mostly of career highlights, but it closed on a personal note: "I saw how beloved Bubbles was when on his 81st birthday an elementary school in the black community named it 'John Bubbles Day,' they sang 'Summertime' and it was one of Bubbles's finest moments." Little was said, apparently, about his character. As Wanda once admitted—and as his four wives discovered—he was an intensely private man who guarded his interior life with an almost pathological secrecy. His actions attested to a complex nature. He was haughty and imperious. He could be cruel, sometimes brutally so, to those closest to him. He could also be kind, generous, thoughtful, and above all, charming. "All of us who cared so much about Bub owe you a debt of gratitude for your love and devotion," a friend wrote to Wanda in one of many thank-you letters she received. He was buried in Green Hills Memorial Park in San Pedro, California.

Obituaries appeared in newspapers across the country, a phenomenon unlikely even ten years earlier. Most reporters emphasized Bubbles's groundbreaking roles as Sportin' Life and, in the field of dance, "the Father of Rhythm Tap," giving less space to his career with Buck and Bubbles. Whatever their correct historical weights, these are indeed the three contributions for which he will be most remembered. By themselves they constitute an impressive legacy. The nagging question is, could there have been more—*much* more?

David Hinckley of the New York *Daily News* was among the few obituary writers to broach this question, the inconvenient question of stature:

> He was also, at the end, frustrated—not only by a stroke which paralyzed his legs, but by the curse that said black entertainers could be "acts" but not "stars." ... There's no reason a man with his looks, talent and presence ... should not have gotten a share of the musical-romantic roles that went to the Astaires, Cagneys and lesser lights. "It was," [Honi] Coles simply said, "a tragedy."

The point is not that Bubbles was robbed of his rightful place in show business; the point is that we will never know. What we do know is this: Because of his skin color, Bubbles was artificially suppressed in vaudeville and never given a proper trial in radio and film. For promising white actors, by contrast, the doors of possibility were thrown wide open. Burns and Allen were mediocre vaudevillians, but they shot to the top in radio. Milton Berle achieved only a modest presence in radio, but when television came along, he became the greatest star of the new medium. These now legendary performers were able to experiment their way to success because the gods of entertainment were always willing to give them another chance. For Bubbles, the margin for error was impossibly narrow and even flawless performances were hemmed in by a thicket of race-based restrictions. Thus, while he might well have been the greatest song-and-dance man of his generation, we don't know what he would have done with his own starring role in a feature film. Judging from his performance as Sportin' Life, it could have been extraordinary.

After the funeral, Wanda, as executor of Bubbles's estate, began sorting through the frightful state of his finances. He had three outstanding mortgages on his house and many open accounts, the total running into tens of thousands of dollars—and, unfortunately, "the property was not in condition to rent or sell." For the first year, Wanda paid these bills every month, presumably from her own pocket. By early 1988 she had somehow managed to get things whittled down to the point where she could close out the estate. But she still had two rooms full of Bubbles's belongings, a packrat's paradise of professional memorabilia dating back to his childhood. When she moved to Tacoma, Washington, in the 1990s, she packed it all up—more than thirty boxes' worth—and hauled it along with her.

Wanda was motivated by more than simple loyalty to Bubbles's memory. Before he died, he made her promise to fulfill the goal they had conceived together when they first met—to present his story to the world in some form, whether as a book, play, movie, or musical. For such a project, those thirty boxes were raw material. She began writing, part stream-of-consciousness, part journal entry, part rough draft, for the work she hoped someday to complete:

> I had a very dear friend who passed on in 1986. His life should be recorded in a vivid manner. . . . I have photos, films, costumes, newspaper clips, books, music and many other personal items that have been in storage since the death of my friend in 1986. I have begun to sort through all these things and am in the process of dating when events occurred. This process is far from complete. . . . I need to combine what I know with existing taped interviews and bring it to life. . . . It is scary to do this but I promised my friend that it would be done. My promises are made to be kept.

Like the bookkeeper she was, Wanda began making long lists—of Bubbles's gigs, his letters, his cards, even signed photographs from fellow celebrities. She covered page after page of notes in yellow legal pads. As a side project she campaigned (fruitlessly) for a star for Bubbles on Hollywood's Walk of Fame, another final request he had made. But by this time, she was in her eighties. Then nineties. She died on February 3, 2009, at age ninety-four.

Wanda never finished her book, never really even started it. But she did something more important, without which *this* book would have been impossible. She preserved Bubbles's archive, kept it in excellent condition, and found it a proper academic home. No one was clamoring to save his personal effects in 1986. Another kind of person might have taken his physical items to the Goodwill and consigned his documents to the shredder. But Wanda was used to sacrificing on behalf of "her friend." Because of her, people can now examine Bubbles's derby, his cane, and his tap shoes. They can read his letters and scrutinize his contracts. They can view sepia-tinted photographs dating back to the 1910s and 1920s. Because of Wanda, future generations will glimpse the life and legacy, in all its richness, of a once-forgotten American classic. And that, in the end, was all Bubbles really wanted.

Acknowledgments

I am grateful to the many people who assisted me with this project. First thanks must go to members of the Bateman and Betteridge families. In 2014 Emily Bateman (now Pulham) informed me that my employer, Brigham Young University, had recently acquired the John W. Bubbles Papers. Her father, Michael Bateman, and her aunt, Merlene Betteridge, were instrumental in making the donation possible. Her younger brother, Christian, spent his Eagle Scout project making a preliminary organization of the archive. I am extremely grateful for their foundational role, so willingly played.

The dedicated staff of the Harold B. Lee Library helped in innumerable ways. Cindy Brightenburg, John Murphy, and the student employees in Special Collections made using the Bubbles archive a happy, pleasant experience. In Digital Initiatives, Abby Beazer and her student assistants performed outstanding work in digitizing the photos. Myrna Layton, David Day, Bob Kosovsky, and Brian Champion answered my many questions and helped me to find sources and databases essential to my task, often using library funds to purchase them.

Outside Utah, I benefited from the gracious and efficient service of many other librarians and archivists: Joseph VanNostrand and Ken Cobb (New York City Supreme Court Records), Catherine S. Medich and Bette M. Epstein (New Jersey State Archives), Erika Louis (Queens County Clerk's Office), Tad Hershorn and Elizabeth Surles (Institute of Jazz Studies), Megan McDaniel and Tiffany Hebb (DePauw University), Kathy Shoemaker and Courtney Chartier (Emory University), Lindsey Winstone (Archives of Ontario), John Lodl (Rutherford County Archives), Ed Byrne and Tom Kanon (Tennessee State Library and Archives), and the staffs at the Performing Arts Division of the New York Public Library, the Chicago History Museum, and the Cook County Court Records and Archives in Chicago.

I am thankful to the BYU College of Fine Arts and Communications and the School of Music for research grants making my trips to these institutions possible.

For sharing their firsthand knowledge of Bubbles and his art with me, I want to thank Jane Goldberg, Lance Bowling, Kurt Albert, Aysha De Festa, and Bubblesette Zeta Martine. Goldberg, Bowling, and Albert also shared rare and valuable items from their own personal collections. I am most grateful for their kindness and generosity.

Several fellow scholars and writers answered questions and graciously offered the fruits of their own research. Mark Cantor shared with me a copy of Buck and Bubbles's 1938 film short, *Beauty Shoppe*. Eric Davis sent his excellent AMS talk on Buck Washington. John Mueller patiently checked on a quote by Fred Astaire from forty years ago. Richard Zoglin gave me his expert perspective on Bob Hope's view of the civil rights movement. Dan Morgenstern traded emails with me about Buck Washington's piano playing. And the jazz research email list hosted by the estimable Michael Fitzgerald flooded the zone with erudite facts and opinions on many questions I posed to the "hive mind."

Especially while writing the early chapters I was lucky to have many friends and family members who were willing to give repeated readings and feedback: Steve Johnson, Michael Hicks, David Kirkham, Rand Harker, Kim Harker, Scott Harker, Lisa Middleton, and my closest readers, Sally Harker, Dan Harker, and Rob Harker. At various points several of them, especially Sally, saved me from despairing and giving up entirely.

On short notice Tom Brothers, the late Jean-Claude Baker, and Brenda Bufalino kindly and without complaint wrote me letters of recommendation. Emily Smith, Shawn Mikkelson, and Hannah CJ McLaughlin performed yeoman service as my research assistants at BYU. I am also grateful to Michael Thompson and my pen pal from Toronto, Dave Waite, for their friendship and good cheer at various points along the way.

From beginning to end the people at Oxford have been a pleasure to work with. I am especially thankful to my editor, Norm Hirschy, and his assistant, Lauralee Yeary, for their good-natured professionalism and patience through the ups and downs of this process, from proposal to publication. I would also like to express gratitude to Gary Giddins, editor of OUP's Cultural Biography Series (and, as a jazz writer, one of my great heroes), for his enthusiastic support, and to the outside reviewers whose criticisms made this a better book.

As always, Sally, Dan, and Rob deserve my deepest thanks. Without their love and solidarity even my most cherished endeavors would mean little.

Notes

The secondary literature on John W. Bubbles consists mainly of the information to be found in dance histories, notably the excellent work by Brian Seibert and Constance Valis Hill. The most valuable published sources are those, like *Jazz Dance* by Marshall and Jean Stearns, that include interviews with Bubbles himself or those who knew him.

Until recently, unpublished sources were generally unavailable or difficult to come by. But in 2012 Bubbles's personal and professional archive was donated to the Harold B. Lee Library at Brigham Young University, making available to the public a wealth of primary material: photographs, letters, contracts, and much else. The most important items for this book were an unpublished biography of Bubbles by Jerry McGuire and a copy of the lengthy interview by George T. Nierenberg for the Jazz Oral History Project at Rutgers University. McGuire mingled valuable first-person quotations with semi-fictionalized dialogue, the latter fairly easy to spot. I have only included dialogue in this book that seemed more or less dictated by Bubbles himself, whom McGuire relied on almost exclusively for the details of his account.

Combining the McGuire and Nierenberg sources to form the spine of my narrative, I have reconstructed the remainder of Bubbles's professional life largely through newspaper reports, which the advent of fully searchable databases in recent years has made possible on a scale hitherto unknown. Outstanding works of scholarship in associated fields of vaudeville, jazz, Broadway, film, and television have illuminated historical patterns relevant to Bubbles's career.

When quoting news accounts and other primary sources I have occasionally standardized spelling and punctuation for ease of readability.

Abbreviations

AA	*Baltimore Afro-American*
AN	*New York Amsterdam News*

BB	*Billboard*
BG	*The Boston Globe*
BS	*The Baltimore Sun*
CD	*The Chicago Defender*
CT	*Chicago Tribune*
DA	*The Daily American*
HC	*Hartford Courant*
IF	*Indianapolis Freeman*
IN	*Indianapolis News*
IS	*The Indianapolis Star*
JOHP	Jazz Oral History Project
JWBP	John W. Bubbles Papers
LAS	*Los Angeles Sentinel*
LAT	*Los Angeles Times*
LHJ	*Light and Heebie Jeebies*
MG	*The Manchester Guardian*
MM	*Melody Maker*
ND	*Newsday*
NJAG	*New Journal and Guide*
NY	*The New Yorker*
NYC	*New York Clipper*
NYDN	New York *Daily News*
NYDM	*New York Dramatic Mirror*
NYHT	*New York Herald Tribune*
NYPL	New York Public Library
NYT	*The New York Times*
PC	*Pittsburgh Courier*
PPG	*Pittsburgh Post-Gazette*
PT	*The Philadelphia Tribune*
SFC	*San Francisco Chronicle*
TGM	*The* [Toronto] *Globe and Mail*
VA	*Variety*
WP	*The Washington Post*
WSJ	*The Wall Street Journal*
WWD	*Women's Wear Daily*

Introduction

As Bubbles told the story: Bubbles told the story of giving a tap lesson to Fred Astaire in at least four different interviews near the end of his life: Goldberg

1978, 112; JOHP 1979, 591–92; JWBP, Box 6, Folder 5: Tom Johnson, "On the Hoof," *Minnesota Daily* [Student newspaper for University of Minnesota], Sept. 1980; and Fantle and Johnson 2004, 23.

As Astaire told the story: Astaire 1959, 164–65.

One interviewed: *VA*, Nov. 26, 1930, 58. **Another critic:** *NY*, Nov. 29, 1930, 33.

"I went to Harlem": Giles 1988, 5.

"He was our Louis"; "Bubbles was the greatest": JWBP, Box 1, Folder 11: David Hinckley, "John Bubbles Was a Tap Dance Giant," *Albuquerque Journal*, June 1, 1986, E7; reprint from *NYDN*.

"They were an act": Lamparski 1974, 61.

Mindful: *NYHT*, Oct. 27, 1935, D4. **As one critic:** *NYHT*, Oct. 20, 1935, D1.

Even his vaudeville: *NY*, Jan. 7, 1985, 69.

He is regarded: https://www.nytimes.com/2017/07/06/arts/dance/tap-dance-and-the-hard-work-of-making-it-all-look-easy.html (accessed Apr. 18, 2018).

1. Words to Live By

Dressed in a dark: "Bubbles," 21.

"I was born": JOHP 1979, 2. **Every census:** *PT*, Nov. 7, 1935, 10; see also *NYHT*, Oct. 27, 1935, D4. Bubbles's death certificate also indicates he was born in Tennessee. **As to the year:** *IF*, Mar. 21, 1914, 4; and *IS*, July 10, 1917, 9. **Judging from:** In the Nashville City Directory for 1904, John Sr. is listed as John W. Sublett, suggesting that his son's middle name, William, may also have been his own, and that the boy was a "junior" in the strict sense.

According to the city: Doyle 1985, 78–82; Lovett 1999, 102–3. **"In these sections":** Gumm 1904, 107. **Saloons, brothels:** Doyle 1985, 78–82; Lovett 1999, 90.

In these crowded: Lovett 1999, 89. **Of eight children:** U.S. Census, 1910, Nashville, Tenn., John Sublett (head). All citations of government records may be found on https://www.ancestry.com/. **A doleful entry:** Tennessee, City Death Records, 1872–1923, infant of John and Kate Sublett, Sept. 18, 1907. **His older sister:** U.S. Find a Grave Index, 1600s–current, Annie G. Jones, San Diego, CA; Tennessee, City Birth Records, 1881–1915, Mary [crossed out, replaced with "Carrie"] Sublett, Feb. 13, 1906. **But to the**

end: Stearns and Stearns 1968, 213; JWBP, Box 2, Folder 18: Bio of John Bubbles in program for the 1980 Hollywood Bowl, Jazz at the Bowl, Aug. 13, 1980.

Tall and thin: JWBP, Box 2, Folder 8: Wanda Michael's notes about Bubbles's upbringing; McGuire 1969, 17. **"helped me to do":** JOHP 1979, 191.

She grew up: U.S. Census, 1880, District 16, Rutherford, Tenn., Antony Brown (head); Tennessee, Compiled Marriages, 1851–1900, Ruthey Ann Taylor and Anthony Brown, Aug. 23, 1865; New York, New York City Municipal Deaths, 1795–1949, Katie Sublett, Sept. 21, 1944. Katie's death certificate says she was born Aug. 31, 1874, but this information was given by her son John. More reliable is the census of 1880, which gives her age as one year old in June of that year. **Antony was that rare ex-slave:** U.S. Census, 1900, District 16, Rutherford, Tenn., Antony Brown (head).

Two years later: Tennessee Marriages, 1796–1950, John Sublett and Katie Brown.

John Sublett Sr.'s: Allen 1985, 27/3–27/51. **George and A. C.:** Henderson 1929, 52, 75. **On the eve:** U.S. Census, 1860, District 15, Rutherford, Tenn., A. C. Sublett (head); Map of Rutherford County 1878. **When the war:** Sims 1947, 44. **George's son:** Lamb 2012, 211–12.

One of them: U.S. Census, 1870, District 16, Rutherford, Tenn., Albert Sublett (head). On Dec. 26, 1870, Myra married Joseph Sublett (Tennessee, State Marriages, 1780–2002), but by 1880 she was living with Robert. Although it is possible Robert was the father of her children, Myra, John, and H.C. all take the name of Bilbro in the census, suggesting that Myra had separated from Joseph and reclaimed for herself and her children the name of her former master, B. H. Bilbro: U.S. Census, 1880, Milton, Rutherford, Tenn., Albert Sublett (head). (Note: "Albert Sublett" has been mistranscribed as "Herbert Steckleford" on https://www.ancestry.com/.) See also Map of Rutherford County 1878. **As a breadwinner:** U.S. Census, 1900, District 16, Rutherford, Tenn., Robert Sublett (head); William S. Rhodes and W. M. Byrn to Peter Turney, Apr. 6, 1896, Tennessee State Library and Archives, Turney Papers, Microfilm roll 9, Box 28, Folder 1. **Unfortunately:** Robert Sublett married Amanda Francis on January 3, 1884; Tennessee Marriages, 1796–1950. **Whatever sorrow:** Death certificate: John Sublett, Mar. 7, 1921, Louisville, KY, No. 5767. (Note: For some reason there are two death certificates for John Sublett Sr. The other one, No. 5763, does not give the names of his father and mother.) U.S. Census, 1900, Nashville, Tenn., John Sublett (head). The 1900, 1910, and 1920 censuses all show John Sublett Sr. as illiterate.

One summer night: *Republican Banner*, Aug. 13, 1875, 4; *DA*, Sept. 11, 1878, 4; Sept. 27, 1878, 4; *NYT*, Sept. 27, 1878, 1, 4; *DA*, Feb. 21, 1880, 4. **In 1890:** Tuskegee University Archives: Lynchings by Year and Race, 1882–1968; Lynchings in Tennessee, 1889–1944.

On Sunday: *DA*, July 16, 1891, 3; *DA*, Nov. 13, 1891, 1. A conscience-stricken judge: William S. Rhodes to Robert Cantrell, Nov. 16, 1896, Turney Papers, Microfilm roll 9, Box 28, Folder 1. **Attempted murder:** In 1915 Tennessee passed a short-lived law banning capital punishment for murder—while retaining it for rape. Vandiver 2006, 162.

In a packed courtroom: *DA*, Nov. 13, 1891, 1. They found him guilty: State of Tennessee v. John Sublett, col. [colored], No. 19, Thursday, Nov. 12, 1891. Rutherford County Criminal Court Minute Book 8, pp. 548–49.

Given his race: Shapiro 1998, 48.

At Coal Creek: Shapiro 1998, 65. In such close quarters: Crowe 1954, 177. Conditions: Crowe 1954, 180–82, 188.

If the workers: Shapiro 1998, 66–67; Crowe 1954, 180–82, 186–87, 200.

Prison clients: Lomax 1993, 264.

The legendary ethnographer: Lomax 1993, 262, 259, 258.

He'll come down: Shapiro 1998, 255–56. As the men: Lomax 1993, 263, 260, 267.

Nevertheless: *VA*, Oct. 22, 1920, 19.

After five years: As Karin A. Shapiro has shown, the pattern of a draconian sentence followed by a state pardon happened to thousands of Black citizens in Tennessee in the late 1800s. Enthralled by Lost Cause fantasies of a past in which happy slaves were cared for by strict but benevolent overseers, white officials—and the white voters who elected them—grandiosely pictured themselves walking in the noble shoes of their slaveholding forebears. They too kept their Black folks "in line," they too dispensed mercy with all the magnanimity of enlightened monarchs. Shapiro 1998, 58–63; *Nashville American*, Dec. 15, 1896, 5.

As a transplanted field hand: Smart 1904, 109; Lamon 1977, 136. **Drifting:** *Nashville City Directory*, 1900–1909. **One day in December:** *Nashville Globe*, Jan. 11, 1907, 6.

Late in life: JOHP 1979, 190–91. He spoke more frankly: Telephone interview with Aysha De Festa, Mar. 9, 2015.

He made up his mind: JWBP, Box 2, Folder 3: Irene Norwitz to John Bubbles, Sept. 30, 1984; Isaiah 22:13 (King James Version): "Let us eat and drink; for to morrow we shall die."

2. The Soul of Minstrelsy

On the Fourth of July: *Nashville Globe*, June 17, 1910, 1. The newspaper called the theater a "skydome," but Bubbles used the more common term: airdome.

The inaugural attraction: *IF*, July 23, 1910, 6.

He begged his mother: Docs&Interviews on MV, "John Bubbles—Interview—7/6/1980—Town Hall Theatre (Official)," Youtube video, 15:56, Sept. 25, 2014, https://www.youtube.com/watch?v=uBsuYC2Zdi4.

One day: JOHP 1979, 3–5; "Bubbles," 21; McGuire 1969, 20–24.

At one time: McGuire 1969, 263. Every week: See, for example, *IF*, Feb. 14, 1903, 2. In 1904: Smart 1904, 109.

Why Louisville?: Wright 1985, 2–7.

The strain of the move: Louisville City Directory 1911, 1141. Tensions mounted: John Sublett vs. Kate Sublett, No. 70088, Petition in Equity, Jefferson Circuit Court, Chancery Branch, Sept. 25, 1911. Summons for Katie issued Oct. 2, 1911.

"I don't think": McGuire 1969, 275.

One bright spot: Louisville City Directory 1911, 1141; JOHP 1979, 448. One day: *Louisville Courier-Journal*, Jan. 3, 1911, 12.

In the past decade: Abbott and Seroff 2017, 3–55, 83.

A vaudeville show: *IF*, Feb. 14, 1914, 4.

For starry-eyed migrants: Weathers 1924, 3; Thornbrough 2000, 2–28.

Right away: *Directory of Indianapolis Public Schools, 1913–1914*, 46; McGuire 1969, 35; JOHP 1979, 8.

"I was ready": JOHP 1979, 454. Every morning: McGuire 1969, 29; JOHP 1979, 7–8.

Hard-pressed: "Bubbles," 22. Finally: McGuire 1969, 26–27; JOHP 1979, 5–7, 402–3.

Bubber: Allen et al. 1867, xxxi. James "Bubber" Miley, Duke Ellington's trumpet soloist, is the best-known example in show business. "Well, I'm gonna change": McGuire 1969, 28; see also JOHP 1979, 12.

Sensing the boy's disappointment: McGuire 1969, 28–29; JOHP 1979, 7; "Bubbles," 22.

Master Johnnie Sublett: *IF*, Mar. 21, 1914, 4.

According to John Jr.: McGuire 1969, 29–30.

And yet, paradoxically: Forbes 2008, 24–25; Shiovitz 2019, 20–21.

"I'm just out there": Rowland 1923, 88. During the 1917 season: Smith 1992, 184; Rowland 1923, 128; Charters 1970, 138.

A Black reporter complained: *IF*, Apr. 15, 1916, 4.

But it was during: McGuire 1969, 76.

"Little old Bubbles": *IF*, Jan. 27, 1917, 5. The actors' full names were Butler May Jr. ("String Beans"), W. M. Stovall, Henry "Gang" Jines, Billy Higgins, and Billy Mills.

A performer like String Beans: Abbott and Seroff 2017, 104.

Beans was a natural idol: Abbott and Seroff 2017, 67, 108–9. **Performing in blackface:** Abbot and Seroff 2017, 94.

The Subletts moved: Indianapolis City Directory 1917.

In 1913: *IS*, May 24, 1913, 1; May 17, 1915, 14.

John and J.B.: The following account is based on McGuire 1969, 38–46; JOHP 1979, 11–18; *IS*, July 10, 1917, 9.

Treating John: The newspaper mischaracterized the incident as a fight between two rival gangs. *IS*, July 10, 1917, 9: "The fight took place in Camp Sullivan [aka Military] Park at noon. James Pruitt, . . . the injured boy, was a bystander and had not taken part in the fight waged by the two gangs of boys, it is said. Sergt. McGee, who made the investigation, was told that John Sublett, colored, 14 years old, did the cutting. The Sublett boy was sent to the Detention Home charged with assault and battery. The fight started when the white boys found Sublett in a swing at the park."

If this was only a kid: JOHP 1979, 26–29.

3. Buck and Bubbles

Louisville in the summer of 1917: *See Louisville First*, Louisville Convention and Publicity League [pamphlet], 1917.

"My Louisville": Wright 1985, 284, 6.

"I wisht": JOHP 1979, 427.

"Tiny and Bubbles": *IF*, July 28, 1917, 5. **It was a role:** JWBP, Box 7, Folder 14: letters from Carrie to Bubbles, 1970s. On one of the envelopes, Wanda Michael, Bubbles's companion and assistant, notes that the nickname is pronounced "Tiny."

Bubbles met his partner: McGuire 1969, 47–52; JOHP 1979, 20–22; City Directory of Louisville, 1916; "Bubbles," 22.

As the boys: JOHP 1979, 22; "Bubbles," 22.

Ford Lee Washington: New York, Northern Arrival Manifests, 1902–1956: Ford Lee Washington, Border Crossing, June 3, 1953. Under a section titled "Remarks and Endorsements," the following note reads: "Subject presented birth certificate showing birth in Louisville, KY." On reverse side, Buck's DOB is given as 10/16/03 and his age as 49. This birthdate is confirmed in Feather 1960, 454. **His parents:** U.S. Census, 1910, Louisville, KY, Abe Washington (head); JWBP, Box 18, light brown album: "John Bubbles: An Era of Great Dancing," *LAS*, Feb. 28, 1974; JOHP 1979, 23, 346.

The only problem: McGuire 1969, 51–52.

The draft: Abbott and Seroff 2007, 202–3, 280, 300.

"Buck played": JWBP, Box 4, Folder 7: *Dance/Flash*, January/February 1983, 2; JOHP 1979, 25. **"We were as busy":** JOHP 1979, 23.

To fill out their repertoire: JOHP 1979, 431, 19–20; McGuire 1969, 54–56.

One of those fascinated observers: JOHP 1979, 24, 36–38; JWBP, Box 4, Folder 5: timeline of Bubbles's career.

"As long as you live": Armstrong 1999, 160. **"I enjoyed":** JOHP 1979, 39.

Another Louisville patron: McGuire 1969, 56–59; JOHP 1979, 24; JWBP, Box 4, Folder 5: timeline of Bubbles's career. The hotel was either the Seelbach or the Watterson, *not* the Claypool, as appears in McGuire, since that hotel was in Indianapolis.

Billy Maxie hatched: McGuire 1969, 59–60; JOHP 1979, 440.

During the week: *IN*, Feb. 16, 1918, 12; Feb. 19, 1918, 18.

After their debut: McGuire 1969, 59–64; JOHP 1979, 430–42.

Bubbles got his opportunity: McGuire 1969, 64–65; *Tallahatchie Herald* [Charleston, MS], Nov. 19, 1919, 1; *Cambridge City Tribune* [Cambridge City, IN], Sept. 11, 1919, 3. **The minstrel tent:** McGuire 1969, 66; *Tennessean*, Mar. 23, 1919, 28; "Bubbles," 22.

"dogs, chickens": *IF*, Dec. 8, 1917, 6. **Superior Shows:** *Tallahatchie Herald*, Nov. 19, 1919, 1; "Bubbles," 22.

After several months: JOHP 1979, 442, 39; McGuire 1969, 68–69.

Bubbles's first priority: JOHP 1979, 443.

Bubbles told the story: See, for example, "Bubbles," 22; McGuire 1969, 71–76; Smith 1976, 56–58; JOHP 1979, 43–53. **"We had to wear cork":** JWBP, Box 18, light brown album: "John Bubbles: An Era of Great Dancing," *LAS*, Feb. 28, 1974.

Opening night: "Bubbles," 22; "Mary Anderson," vertical file, Louisville Public Library.

Buck and Bubbles were first: JOHP 1979, 43–45; McGuire 1969, 71; JWBP, Box 6, Folder 4: *ASPP Newsletter*, Jan.–Feb. 1976, 1; JWBP, Box 2, Folder 20: Unsigned letter to John Bubbles, Aug. 22, 1967.

In the first news article: *Louisville Courier-Journal*, Dec. 29, 1919, 4.

H. C. Carter hired the boys: McGuire 1969, 72–73; JOHP 1979, 48–53.

Buck and Bubbles raced home: JOHP 1979, 51, 30.

Buck and Bubbles packed: *BG*, Aug. 27, 1967, A13.

4. A Find of Finds

Within a few weeks: McGuire 1969, 77–78.

"beyond question": Bloom 1991, 262–63. When the boys asked: McGuire 1969, 83. The ghosts of history: Bloom 1991, 392, 332.

"without a doubt": *VA*, Jan. 16, 1920, 22. One improbable act: *NYS*, Jan. 21, 1920, 9.

"Prices for admissions": *NYS*, Jan. 14, 1920, 12.

"having broken down": *NYS*, Nov. 26, 1919, 9.

Of some twenty thousand vaudevillians: Snyder 1989, 46; fn 12, 182. One of those: *VA*, Feb. 6, 1920, 20.

"The manner in which": *NYC*, Feb. 25, 1920, 8. This experience: According to McGuire 1969, 81–83, Bubbles thought union troubles were the source of the delay, but coming through the fictionalized voice of his 1969 amanuensis this theory remains questionable. In late January: *NYS*, Jan. 28, 1920.

Martin whipped out: McGuire 1969, 87–88; JOHP 1979, 54–55.

The boys returned: McGuire 1969, 89–91; JOHP 1979, 57–59. whom he later recalled: NYPL: *MGZR Buck and Bubbles vertical file: *New York Post*, May 29, 1942.

Nazarro followed: McGuire 1969, 92–93; JOHP 1979, 59–61. For almost thirty: Laurie 1953, 56. When Buck and Bubbles showed up: McGuire 1969, 94–96; JOHP 1979, 61–62.

Despite the theater manager's: *NYC*, Feb. 25, 1920, 8. Nazarro attempted: McGuire 1969, 96–97; JOHP 1979, 62.

The sight of the boys: *Lodi News-Sentinel*, Sept. 6, 1967, 15. "Bubbles," Nazarro called out: Fox 1983, 52–53.

After the show: Fox 1983, 53; McGuire 1969, 97–99; JOHP 1979, 62–64.

On Thursday: *NYC*, Feb. 25, 1920, 10, 11; "Bubbles," 22.

Suddenly an irate: *NYS*, Feb. 25, 1920, 15; *NYC*, Feb. 25, 1920, 8; *VA*, Feb. 27, 1920, 6. Helen Keller: *VA*, Feb. 27, 1920, 22.

After hearing the case: *NYC*, Mar. 3, 1920, 8; *VA*, Mar. 5, 1920, 7; *NYC*, Mar. 10, 1920, 8; McGuire 1969, 123.

"a heart of gold": JOHP 1979, 171.

Nat Nazarro was born: Declaration of Intention, Southern District of New York, No. 333922, for Nat Nazaroo, formerly known as Notel Itziksohn, August 5, 1932; Petition for Naturalization, Southern District of New York, No. 249063, for Nat Nazarro, formerly known as Nat Nazaroo, August 8, 1935. U.S. Census, 1900, Philadelphia, Harry Isaacson (head); U.S. Census, 1910, Philadelphia, Yetta Isaacson (head).

Possessed of unusual: *VA*, Feb. 5, 1910, 39. Critics especially: *VA*, Feb. 12, 1910, 30. The trick looked: *Los Angeles Herald*, Feb. 2, 1910, http://www.heatherlynegan.com/thevaudevillian (accessed Apr. 28, 2014). "one of the most startling": *San Francisco Call*, Jan. 23, 1910, http://www.heatherlynegan.com/thevaudevillian (accessed Apr. 28, 2014).

During a stopover: *NYT*, Mar. 25, 1911, http://www.heatherlynegan.com/thevaudevillian (accessed Apr. 28, 2014).

The reviews were glowing: *VA*, Apr. 6, 1912, 40. These quotes come from an ad with blurbs from other publications. Six months later: *VA*, Nov. 22, 1912, 27. "Nat Nazarro (an acrobat)": *VA*, Feb. 14, 1913, 2. In the same month: *VA*, Feb. 28, 1913, 5, 25.

There he received: *VA*, Nov. 16, 1917, 20. As their adopted son: *NYS*, Apr. 30, 1919, http://www.heatherlynegan.com/thevaudevillian. Recognizing: *VA*, Aug. 1, 1919, 55.

old sins: *VA*, Apr. 18, 1919, 6; Aug. 15, 1919, 11; Nov. 7, 1919, 3.

"two phenomenal": *Harrisburg Telegraph*, June 7, 1920, 8.

In September: *NYC*, Sept. 15, 1920, 8. The act is announced: *NYC*, Aug. 25, 1920, 12; Oct. 20, 1920, 9; *VA*, Oct. 22, 1920, 19; *NYS*, Oct. 27, 1920, 14; *NYC*, Oct. 27, 1920, 9; Nov. 24, 1920, 10.

"the raggedy": *NYDM*, Dec. 4, 1920, 1055.

If Nazarro: *VA*, Oct. 22, 1920, 19; *NYDM*, Oct. 30, 1920, 798; *NYC*, Nov. 10, 1920, 9; *NYDM*, Nov. 27, 1920, 1007; *NYDM*, Dec. 4, 1920, 1055.

"For those": Spitzer 1969, 46. "Only a performer": Stewart 2005, 160.

Kitty Doner: Slide 1994, 133–35. Jimmy Barry: Briscoe 1907, 202.

Marie Nordstrom: *The Argonaut*, Aug. 3, 1918, 74. Harry and Emma Sharrock: *The Argonaut*, Oct. 25, 1919, 267. Henrietta De Serris: *VA*, Dec. 10, 1920, 17.

Corinne Tilton: *VA*, Dec. 19, 1919, 18.

"There ain't": JOHP 1979, 74.

A couple of wobbles: *BB*, Dec. 11, 1920, 9; *VA*, Dec. 10, 1920, 17. The biggest: *NYS*, Dec. 15, 1920, 9.

"The Nat Nazarro act": *VA*, Dec. 10, 1920, 17.

One review: *BB*, Dec. 25, 1920, 29.

Bubbles's year: Death certificate: John Sublett, No. 5767, March 7, 1921, Bureau of Vital Statistics, Lakeland, Jefferson County, Kentucky.

A few days later: McGuire 1969, 121–22.

5. Reinvention

"I didn't dance": "Bubbles," 22.

"Bubbles sings": *Evening News* [Harrisburg, PA], June 8, 1920, 17; *NYC*, Feb. 25, 1920, 11; *NYS*, Oct. 27, 1920, 14; *VA*, Oct. 22, 1920, 19; *NYC*, Aug. 25, 1920, 12.

Buoyed by their success: *PT*, Feb. 19, 1921, 4; *BB*, Jan. 8, 1921, 30; *VA*, Mar. 25, 1921, 4; *LAT*, Sept. 27, 1961, n.p., Frank Fay obituary.

With a population: http://www.gothamgazette.com/index.php/demographcis/4077-harlems-shifting-population (accessed Apr. 2, 2019). Two doors down: *VA*, Mar. 2, 1927, 47.

The Hoofers Club was neither: Stearns and Stearns 1968, 173–74, 212; Frank 1994, 42; Seibert 2015, 21–25.

"and a bunch": Stearns and Stearns 1968, 212.

Chicagoans received them: *VA*, Sept. 9, 1921, 9.

Reviewing a show: *CT*, Mar. 29, 1922, 19.

Born and raised: Haskins and Mitgang 1988, 15–103.

According to a longtime friend: Stearns and Stearns 1968, 187; JWBP, Box 5, Folder 1: Richard Strouse, "At 70, Still Head Hoofer," *New York Times Magazine*, May 23, 1948, 50–51. Robinson took: Honi Coles said Robinson was "probably the purest dancer around." JWBP, Box 5, Folder 10: Mel Watkins, "That Vaudeville Style: A Conversation with Honi Coles," *APF Reporter*, Oct. 1979, 4.

It was the accompaniment: Speaking of Robinson and himself in 1912, George Cooper said, "My partner and I seem to be able to dance to ragtime and to sing to ragtime in a way that few white dancers or singers can." Seibert 2015, 132. "didn't change": Stearns and Stearns 1968, 187. "Bo's face": Haskins and Mitgang 1988, 102. His dancing: Stearns and Stearns 1968, 156, 187. For an excellent overview of Robinson's career and achievements, see Seibert 2015, 130–36.

As Bubbles recalled: Stearns and Stearns 1968, 215, 249. A few dancers: Stearns and Stearns 1968, 76.

"got crazy": Goldberg 1978, 63. **On the road:** JWBP, Box 18, Red Album: Julie Wheelock, "Bubbles, The Rhythm Tap King," *Los Angeles Times Calendar*, Dec. 19, 1982. **"One of the best":** McGuire 1969, 104. **"And I cried":** Town Hall interview, 1980; McGuire 1969, 105. **"Man, I was really":** Stearns and Stearns 1968, 213. **"Don't go in":** JWBP, Box 4, Folder 7: *Dance/ Flash*, January/February 1983, 2.

On one occasion: McGuire 1969, 105; JOHP 1979, 86; JWBP, Box 4, Folder 7: *Dance/Flash*, January/February 1983, 2.

"I didn't look back": Stearns and Stearns 1968, 213.

"By using his heels": JWBP, Box 1, Folder 11: David Hinckley, "John Bubbles Was a Tap Dance Giant," *Albuquerque Journal*, June 1, 1986, E7; reprint from *NYDN*. **"By combining":** Stearns and Stearns 1968, 216. **"I took the white boys' steps":** "Bubbles," 22. **According to Ralph Brown:** Frank 1994, 100; Seibert 2015, 186.

"always new": Mueller 2010, [iii]. **The great teacher:** Stearns and Stearns 1968, 215. **In his vaudeville act:** Goldberg 1978, 112; "Bubbles," 22; Stearns and Stearns 1968, 214.

Like ragtime composers: Harker 2008, 110; Seibert 2015, 135–36. **In a 1932 film:** Julien Vardon, "Bill Robinson—'Stair Dance'," YouTube video, 2:58, July 4, 2015, https://www.youtube.com/watch?v=tg7ZNg1-2As.

Now consider: Bill Green, "Rhythm Tap Dance 1937," YouTube video, 0:58, Apr. 10, 2017, https://www.youtube.com/watch?v=mq38QLBE6wM.

As dancer Baby Laurence: Stearns and Stearns 1968, 215. For another explanation of Bubbles's style, see Seibert 2015, 184–88.

Reviewing his dancing: *BB*, July 21, 1923, 50.

6. Beautiful Days

"no one played it": Snyder 1989, 62.

For more than a decade: Wertheim 2006, 254. **By building:** Wertheim 2006, 239–40.

Despite Albee's: Wertheim 2006, 242–43.

"among the leaders": *VA*, Sept. 29, 1922, 20. **As one reporter:** *BB*, Sept. 30, 1922, 16. **As if simply:** *NYC*, Dec. 13, 1922, 10. **Everywhere the show:** *BB*, Sept. 30, 1922, 16; *NYC*, Dec. 13, 1922, 10; *BG*, Jan. 23, 1923, 6; *BB*, Dec. 23, 1922, 15.

Through a combination: Wertheim 2006, 243–44. **When the *Frolics*:** *VA*, Apr. 5, 1923, 4.

Box-office receipts: Although Noble Sissle and Eubie Blake took only one quarter of the profits of *Shuffle Along*, the success of the production made them both "wealthy men." Kimball and Bolcom 1973, 123.

Hiring Jo Trent: *BB*, June 16, 1923, 33. Trent fashioned: *BB*, July 21, 1923, 50. "poor business": *BB*, June 30, 1923, 52. Whereas: *AN*, July 11, 1923, 5; *VA*, July 26, 1923, 30.

After only two weeks: *PC*, Aug. 11, 1923, 11.

As *Billboard* reported: *BB*, Sept. 8, 1923, 34. Buck and Bubbles were cast: *BB*, Sept. 1, 1923, 72.

Dancing Around consisted: *VA*, Dec. 20, 1923, 8. "the only really bright": *IN*, Aug. 27, 1923, 7. Another: *BB*, Sept. 8, 1923, 34.

She invited Bubbles: JOHP 1979, 565, 587.

Around the same time: Baker 1993, 71–72.

Bubbles bared: McGuire 1969, 111–21; JOHP 1979, 566–89.

At the party: JOHP 1979, 570–78; McGuire 1969, 111–21. After they broke up: Eleanor Heinemann is listed in the chorus for *Dancing Around* in *BB*, Dec. 22, 1923: 16. The 1930 U.S. Census shows her still living with her parents under the occupation "dancer," and her late-in-life letters to Bubbles recalling their time together in *Dancing Around* show Eleanor Gross to be, in all likelihood, the same person.

"Vaudeville acts": *VA*, Dec. 10, 1924, 7. Few bidders: *VA*, Oct. 21, 1925, 3.

Guided by Nazarro's: *IN*, June 10, 1925, 25.

Summing up: "Bubbles," 23. "It's funny": JWBP, Box 8, Folder 18: Morris Duff, "Sportin' Life Bets: 'Porgy Film Will Be Goldwyn, Not Gershwin,'" *Toronto Star*, Sept. 13, 1958. "usually on the top floor": Kimball and Bolcolm 1973, 80–81. "We just persevered": Fantle and Johnson 2004, 25.

"Their dress": *NYDM*, Sept. 10, 1921, 381. "We looked poor": Baker 1993, 71.

One critic said: *NYC*, Oct. 20, 1920, 9. Buck played along: List of United States Citizens, S.S. Ile de France, sailing from Plymouth, May 29, 1930, arriving at New York, June 3, 1930; List of United States Citizens, S.S. Berengaria, sailing from Southampton, Dec. 22, 1936, arriving at New York, Dec. 28, 1936. Later in life: Feather 1960, "Ford Lee Washington," 454.

Handsome: *PC*, July 7, 1928, A1.

Buck would come onstage: JOHP 1979, 130–31; Buck and Bubbles, *Beauty Shoppe* (Mentone 1938), 20 min.; NYPL: (S) MGZMD 72–26, "Chuck Green: Buck and Bubbles and Their Act," 9. This joke and those that follow are often composites of various retellings of them. I have tightened the text in places for readability and clarity. **"the familiar negro crossfire":** *NYC*, Aug. 25, 1920, 12.

"Get outta that hole!": McGuire 1969, 101; JOHP 1979, 129–30; Fantle and Johnson 2004, 24. **"I passed by":** JOHP 1979, 130. **"What was you runnin' ":** McGuire 1969, 231. Peter Lind Hayes misremembers Buck as the straight man here. I have restored Bubbles's known role as straight man in these dialogues. **"Am I blue?":** McGuire 1969, 232.

"They just acted": *BB*, Dec. 23, 1922, 15.

"I thought I'd fix": Stearns and Stearns 1968, 217. "Bubbles has a casual approach to the complicated steps he executes," said Paul Draper. "His nonchalant manner contradicts the incredible things his feet are doing." Stearns and Stearns 1968, 214. **"I pretend":** Sobel 1947, 10–11. **They switch roles:** Stearns and Stearns 1968, 214. **Surveying:** *MG*, Nov. 24, 1936, 13. Italics added.

When they saw: "Buck and Bubbles are fast becoming the modern Williams and Walker team," went one typical assessment. *BB*, Sept. 30, 1922, 16.

In their second: *VA*, Mar. 25, 1921, 21. **Their small-time tour:** *Scranton Republican*, June 18, 1924, 19; *VA*, Nov. 12, 1924, 37; *BB*, Apr. 11, 1925, 16; Apr. 18, 1925, 14; *VA*, July 7, 1926, 52; Oct. 13, 1926, 25; *BB*, Oct. 16, 1926, 12.

the "deuce spot": Stewart 2005, 87. **"the honor spot":** *VA*, Feb. 6, 1920, 20. **"They were an act":** Lamparski 1974, 61. **The honor:** When a Black act played that spot in 1921, *Billboard* went so far as to claim it was "the first time in the history of [New York] vaudeville that such a team has occupied such a position." *BB*, Dec. 3, 1921, 10. This wasn't quite true; Sissle and Blake had appeared next-to-closing in 1919. Kimball and Bolcom 1973, 81.

"Here is an act": *NYC*, Aug. 2, 1922, 9. **"Nazarro was on stage":** *BB*, Dec. 23, 1922, 15. **Perhaps stung:** *VA*, Oct. 13, 1926, 25; *BB*, Oct. 16, 1926, 12.

Bubbles had recently: McGuire 1969, 123; JOHP 1979, 188–89, 357–59.

Somehow: JOHP 1979, 107.

7. Dancing in the Dark

At the end: This anecdote comes from McGuire 1969, 132–41 and JOHP 1979, 101–15.

"We were right back": McGuire 1969, 137. **"We were dead broke":** McGuire 1969, 138.

"We got under": McGuire 1969, 141.

Calling up memories: *Suburbanite Economist*, Jan. 21, 1927, 5. "These two colored": *Suburbanite Economist*, Mar. 4, 1927, 6. **Buck and Bubbles asked:** McGuire 1969, 141.

The shows started: *LHJ*, Jan. 8, 1927, 18; Feb. 19, 1927, 35. My thanks to Tom Brothers for bringing this important publication to my attention. **To this lineup:** *LHJ*, Feb. 19, 1927, 35. **Over the next:** *LHJ*, Feb. 26, 1927, 21.

In late February: *LHJ*, Feb. 26, 1927, 21.

Marshall and Jean Stearns: Stearns and Stearns 1968, 48. **His faithful:** JWBP, Box 1, Folder 11: David Hinckley, "John Bubbles Was a Tap Dance Giant," *Albuquerque Journal*, June 1, 1986, E7; reprint from *NYDN*.

As I have argued: Harker 2008, 97–113.

"unquestionably": Stearns and Stearns 1968, 288, 290. **One night:** *LHJ*, Jan. 8, 1927, 16.

Recognizing: Stearns and Stearns 1968, 219. **"You can imagine":** Dance 1977, 48. **The same could be said:** Harker 2008, 93. **While Rector:** See Brothers 2014, 222–75, for a rich overview of Armstrong and dancers at the Sunset.

Armstrong recalled: Harker 2008, 86–90. Armstrong misremembers the collaboration taking place at the Dreamland Café, but Brown and McGraw were at Harlem's Cotton Club or touring in vaudeville when Armstrong was at the Dreamland.

These words: Harker 2008, 98–102. Hines recalled that "Big Butter and Egg Man" "was a number Brown and McGraw used to do" at the Sunset. Dance 1977, 49.

According to Rex Stewart: *Metronome* 75, no. 2 (Feb. 1958): 24. For another account of this dynamic between tap dancers and bands, see Dance 1977, 48.

But by April: McGuire 1969, 141–42; JOHP 1979, 115, 121–23. **Morris booked:** *BB*, Apr. 23, 1927, 34. **"Buck and Bubbles Held Over":** *Marion Star*, May 27, 1927, 5; May 28, 1927, 12.

The team continued: McGuire 1969, 142; JOHP 1979, 151. **Bubbles was alarmed:** McGuire 1969, 142–43. **"I tried to tell her":** McGuire 1969, 143. **Buck married:** Illinois Cook County Marriages, 1871–1920: Ford Lee Washington to Flash A. Vincson, Aug. 23, 1927; John W. Sublett to Viola Sulinger, Aug. 27, 1927. **Buck's reception:** *MM*, Oct. 24, 1936, 2.

"He was closer": JOHP 1979, 406–7. **Flash would tell:** JOHP 1979, 174, 192.

Back in Chicago: JWBP Box 4, Folder 5: several drafts of short memoirs of his time in Chicago, and of Louis Armstrong. **Knowing:** McGuire 1969, 143; JOHP 1979, 201.

8. Alone

Burdened: *VA*, Nov. 23, 1927, 49; *BB*, Dec. 3, 1927, 15. **Having played:** *VA*, Oct. 19, 1927, 56. **"showed that they had":** *AN*, Jan. 25, 1928, 9. **For the first time:** *BB*, Oct. 29, 1927, 10.

"stopped the show": *BB*, Jan. 7, 1928. **"won themselves":** *BB*, Jan. 28, 1928, 18. **"principal headliners":** *NYHT*, Jan. 29, 1928, F5. **A new kind:** *VA*, Feb. 22, 1928, 31; *BB*, Mar. 3, 1928, 25; Feb. 23, 1929, 16.

For his $20,000 suit: *VA*, Aug. 22, 1928, 61; Aug. 15, 1928, 31; Mishkin et al. v. Nazarro et al., 482585, Superior Court of Cook County IL, 1928.

For years: Wertheim 2006, 262. **But it was vital:** *NYHT*, Sept. 16, 1928, F8.

The Palace date: *VA*, Sept. 19, 1928, 30.

"yesterday's matinee": *NYHT*, Sept. 18, 1928, 22. **Despite the pomp:** *VA*, Sept. 19, 1928, 39. **"Buck and Bubbles . . . were a sensation":** *BB*, Sept. 22, 1928, 17. **"With the opening":** *WSJ*, Sept. 20, 1928, 4.

Most strikingly: *NYT*, Sept. 23, 1928, X2; *PC*, Oct. 6, 1928, A2; *AA*, Oct. 6, 1928, 8. **Keith-Albee-Orpheum:** *BB*, Oct. 6, 1928, 16; Washington et al. v. Saper et al., 6801, New York Supreme Court, 1930.

With their obligation: McGuire 1969, 144, 147; JOHP 1979, 117.

The new contract: Washington et al. v. Saper et al., 6801, New York Supreme Court, 1930. **5 percent:** *VA*, Mar. 19, 1930, 40. **There was:** *VA*, May 30, 1923, 6. **And the time:** McGuire 1969, 198–203.

Even more troubling: McGuire 1969, 132–33. **"*You* taught me":** JWBP, Box 14, Folder 2: John Bubbles to Nat Nazarro, Sept. 27, 1947. Italics added. **In the South:** In 1904 the President of the Mississippi Cotton Association said in a speech, "Every dollar I own those Negroes made for me. . . . They are just what we make them. By our own greed and extravagance we have spoiled a good many of them. *It has been popular here . . . to exploit the Negro by high store-prices and by encouraging him to get into debt. It has often made him hopeless.*" Baker 1973, 104. Italics added.

Since performing without Nazarro: *VA*, Nov. 14, 1928, 40.

In February 1929: *BB*, Feb. 16, 1929, 18. **"The pair":** *LAT*, Feb. 10, 1929, C12. **Another reviewer:** *LAT*, Feb. 12, 1929, A11.

Reviewing another: *LAT*, June 11, 1929, A11. **In a reprise:** *VA*, June 19, 1929, 45.

Two very interesting: *Vaudeville News*, Mar. 2, 1929, 6. **Many years later:** JOHP 1979, 164.

Barely a month: Wertheim 2006, 269.

Surprisingly: Bogle 2016, 21.

In the *Post* series: Drew 2015, 183. Pathé cast: Bradley 2005, 259, 263.

"The first thing": McGuire 1969, 124–25.

Evidently determined: *VA*, May 22, 1929, 7. To keep his actors: McGuire 1969, 125–26.

"This short convinces": *VA*, Nov. 20, 1929, 12. "will rank along": *BB*, Nov. 23, 1929, 25. "mumbled dialog": *VA*, Apr. 2, 1930, 18.

When *Hearts in Dixie:* Bogle 2016, 28.

It began with: *VA*, July 31, 1929, 31.

More trouble awaited: Mishkin et al. v. Nazarro et al., 482585, Superior Court of Cook County IL, 1928.

While playing: *VA*, Aug. 7, 1929, 211; Aug. 14, 1929, 35; Sept. 4, 1929, 33. He was sorry: *CD*, Sept. 7, 1929, 7. After the Keith: *VA*, Sept. 4, 1929, 33.

Three days later: *NYHT*, Nov. 2, 1929, 22; *VA*, Feb. 19, 1930, 35; July 23, 1930, 41.

Employing his standard MO: Unless otherwise noted, the following account of Buck and Bubbles's legal battles up to their trip to Europe comes from Washington et al. v. Saper et al., 6801, New York Supreme Court, 1930.

"about everybody": *VA*, Mar. 5, 1930, 42.

Finally (and predictably): *VA*, Mar. 12, 1930, 40. Markus filed: *VA*, Apr. 16, 1930, 55; Apr. 30, 1930, 57.

By the time: *VA*, May 7, 1930, 65; Apr. 2, 1930, 68.

What the duo: *Stage*, May 1, 1930, 8; May 8, 1930, 4. Bubbles later claimed: JOHP 1979, 244, 246.

"English debut": *BB*, May 17, 1930, 7. The following week: *Stage*, May 15, 1930, 3; May 22, 1930, 4.

One of the Palladium reviews: *MM*, June 1, 1930, 517.

One night: McGuire 1969, 151–53.

Buck and Bubbles returned: *CD*, May 10, 1930, 10; June 7, 1930, 7. They disembarked. *VA*, July 16, 1930, 39. At this point: *BB*, July 19, 1930, 9; *VA*, July 23, 1930, 41; *BB*, Aug. 2, 1930, 11.

9. Dreams Fulfilled

Although he had: Haskins and Mitgang 1988, 165–66, 170–71. For examples of Robinson being spotted next-to-closing, see *VA*, July 15, 1925,

13; Dec. 2, 1925, 15; Feb. 10, 1926, 46. **Then an all-Black:** Stearns and Stearns 1968, 181.

"He croons": Stearns and Stearns 1968, 155. **"After they had seen":** Stearns and Stearns 1968, 156.

Reviewing one: *VA*, June 12, 1929, 46. **"Bubbles rates":** *VA*, June 19, 1929, 51. **"stopped the show":** *VA*, July 31, 1929, 39.

In 1931: *NYHT*, Sept. 13, 1931, G4.

"with blood": JWBP, Box 1, Folder 11: David Hinckley, "John Bubbles Was a Tap Dance Giant," *Albuquerque Journal*, June 1, 1986, E7; reprint from *NYDN*. **"Many's the time":** Mezzrow 1946, 231. **With his heavy:** Frank 1994, 42; Stearns and Stearns 1968, 338. **But, as he once:** Goldberg 1978, 112. **"There's not a dancer":** Stearns and Stearns 1968, 218–19.

"We were playing": McGuire 1969, 105–6.

"The other dancers": Goldberg 1978, 112. **A jaw-dropping:** Seibert 2015, 25.

For part of that: *VA*, Dec. 15, 1931, 31. **"At every performance":** Crosby 1953, 332. **"I think Bubbles":** Slide 1981, 18.

Early on: Mueller 2010, 108, [iii]. **Fred Astaire, he said:** Crosby 1953, 332.

For this show: JWBP, Box 2, Folder 13: photocopy of program for *Blackbirds of 1930* at Royale Theatre; *AN*, Sept. 10, 1930, 8. **"Never before":** *AA*, Nov. 15, 1930, 9. **"no crap game":** *AA*, Sept. 13, 1930, 9.

"It was a lovely": JOHP 1979, 217. **Eubie Blake was:** JWBP, Box 4, Folder 17: Eubie Blake to John Bubbles, 19 December 1977.

"It is the fastest": *PC*, Sept. 6, 1930, A6. **"a stale production":** *BB*, Nov. 1, 1930, 33. **"Mr. Leslie":** *AN*, Oct. 29, 1930, 10. **"show what a finished":** *BB*, Nov. 1, 1930, 33.

After the first: *BB*, Nov. 22, 1930, 17.

Bubbles later recalled: McGuire 1969, 159; Stearns and Stearns 1968, 217. In 1931 $1,750 a week was a lot of money (almost $30,000 in 2020 dollars), but the highest earners of the day made much more: Eddie Cantor ($8,000), Marx Brothers ($7,500), Jackie Coogan ($5,000), Sophie Tucker ($3,500), James Barton ($2,500). *VA*, May 8, 1929, 53; *PC*, Mar. 19, 1932, A6. **We know Loew:** Washington et al. v. Saper et al., 6801 (New York Supreme Court, 1930); *CD*, Nov. 29, 1930, 5.

Bubbles knew: McGuire 1969, 154. **Amid all:** *BB*, Sept. 29, 1928, 17. Italics added.

"chief opposition": *Variety* (Mar. 19, 1930), 40. The Sunday before: McGuire 1969, 8–11, 154–56; JOHP 1979, 250–55; Smith 1976, 60.

"Heading the program": *NYHT*, Feb. 23, 1931, 12. One critic seemed: *VA*, Feb. 25, 1931, 43.

It takes nothing: *BB*, Dec. 6, 1930, 20.

As Bubbles tells it: McGuire 1969, 157–60; JOHP 1979, 256–61; Smith 1976, 60; Stearns and Stearns 1968, 217. That afternoon: *AN*, Aug. 12, 1931, 13.

It was instead: Farnsworth 1956, 165–66; van der Merwe 2009, 200–201.

The cast: *VA*, June 23, 1931, 50. Some sources, as here, list Gladys Glad among the headliners. Harry Richman: Slide 1994, 418. Ruth Etting: Lamparski 1974, 24.

Buck and Bubbles formed: *NYHT*, July 1, 1931, 18. Sixteen-year-old: *VA*, June 23, 1931, 50, 54. Another standout: https://travsd.wordpress.com/2019/07/08/the-britton-band-musical-maniacs.

For its out-of-town: *VA*, June 23, 1931, 50. When "thousands": *PPG*, June 19, 1931, 22. "gorgeous, sensuous": *Pittsburgh Press*, June 16, 1931, 34. A leviathan: *BB*, July 11, 1931, 61; *Pittsburgh Press*, June 16, 1931, 34. Especially stunning: *BB*, July 11, 1931, 61; *VA*, June 23, 1931, 54. For this scene: van der Merwe 2009, 204–5. The emotional heart: van der Merwe 2009, 202.

"worked and worked": *BB*, July 11, 1931, 61. The only "legitimate": *VA*, June 23, 1931, 50. "Buck and Bubbles have a spot": *VA*, June 23, 1931, 54.

During a postmortem: *PPG*, June 20, 1931, 4.

Amid the elegant: JOHP 1979, 261. Bill Robinson kept: Stearns and Stearns 1968, 217.

the uproar lasted: *AN*, Aug. 12, 1931, 10. They began to chant: Smith 1976, 60–61; McGuire 1969, 160–62; JOHP 1979, 262–67; Stearns and Stearns 1968, 217–18.

"They'd change": JOHP 1979, 262; Seibert 2015, 189–90. "Luxurious": NYPL, Flo Ziegfeld-Billie Burke Papers, Box 14, Folder 30: *New York Journal*, July 2, 1931. "Man, you talk": McGuire 1969, 160.

"It was a mistake": *VAR*, July 7, 1931, 54. By vivid contrast: *AN*, Aug. 12, 1931, 10. "In a plethoric": *CD*, Aug. 22, 1931, 10.

After Bubbles died: JWBP, Box 1, Folder 11: Wilhelmina Reavis to Wanda Michael, Oct. 17, 1986. Italics added. By the time: *VA*, Nov. 17, 1931, 52.

When telling the story: Farnsworth 1956, 165; van der Merwe 2009, 206. "We go": JOHP 1979, 261, 269. Italics added.

10. Jazz, Jazz, Jazz

On May 7: Stewart 2005, 249–50, 254–55.

Joe Laurie Jr.: Slide 1994, 304–5. **Louise Groody:** Obituary, *NYT*, Sept. 17, 1961, 86. **Frances White:** Slide 1994, 224–26.

"I guess the police": McGuire 1969, 171. "is very nervous": *PC*, Mar. 5, 1932, A6. **Bubbles once admitted:** JOHP 1979, 364.

"guarantee": *VA*, June 6, 1933, 46. "No question": *VA*, Apr. 24, 1934, 13. "the most consistent": *VA*, Feb. 20, 1935, 47.

"I wish": *PC*, Oct. 20, 1934, 7. "These boys": *BB*, June 3, 1933, 9. They are still: *VA*, Oct. 31, 1933, 15. It was hard: *BB*, Feb. 9, 1935, 15.

"tore the house": *VA*, Jan. 30, 1934, 62. "a near riot": *PPG*, Oct. 13, 1934, 18. "they received": *BB*, Mar. 19, 1932, 17. On a different: *BB*, Apr. 1, 1933, 16–17.

"Don't worry": *VA*, Nov. 8, 1932, 41. At Loew's Theatre: *VA*, Dec. 19, 1933, 49. A month later: *VA*, Feb. 6, 1934, 60.

"This week's show": *BB*, Apr. 1, 1933, 8. "out-talk traffic cops": *VA*, Oct. 3, 1933, 60. The headliners: *LAT*, Aug. 24, 1933, 11; *AA*, Oct. 21, 1933, 18.

Despite: *NYT*, Feb. 24, 1933, 14.

In January: *BB*, Jan. 23, 1932, 3, 55.

In May: *VA*, May 27, 1933, 14; May 30, 1933, 14.

The irrepressible: *VA*, Nov. 1, 1932, 39. For a scat-singing: *BB*, Jan. 30, 1932, 20. Around the same time: JWBP, Box 8, Folder [25]: orchestral parts for "Rhythm for Sale," some bearing stamp: "Property of Nat Nazarro." On the back of the conductor's score two versions of the lyrics are typed, both attributed to Nat Nazarro. This phrase may have been "in the air." In the winter of 1933 black theatrical producer Leonard Harper staged a show called *Rhythm for Sale* at the Grand Terrace Café in Chicago. Reid 2013, 189–90.

"Not seventh heaven": Seibert 2015, 177. "You can't possibly": JWBP, Box 5, Folder 10: Mel Watkins, "That Vaudeville Style: A Conversation with Honi Coles," *APF Reporter*, Oct. 1979, 3; Box 2, Folder 10: Robin Reif, "Coles to Broadway," *Playbill*, Nov. 1983, 32–37.

"Everybody": JWBP, Box 5, Folder 11: Marilyn Hunt, "Time Steps: Mr. Honi Coles," *Soho News Dance Supplement*, May 7–13, 1980, 42. "When I first saw": Frank 1994, 73. **Bubbles's heel drops:** JWBP, Box 5, Folder 13: *LAT*, July 4, 1986, 2. **Even before leaving:** Stearns and Stearns 1968, 305–6.

After appearing: There is some confusion as to James's last name: Some sources give "Walker" and some "Howard." In interviews, Samuel Green has used both. Likewise, their act is sometimes identified as Slim and Shorty and sometimes Shorty and Slim, including by Green. **Their sponsor:** *AA*, Jan. 23, 1932, 9. **After some training:** *VA*, Mar. 15, 1932, 36; May 8, 1934, 23. **But Bubbles:** *AA*, Jan. 23, 1932, 9.

Green recalled: NYPL: (S) MGZMD 72–27, "The Professionals—Samy Chuck Green," 22–23.

"He liked to die": NYPL: (S) MGZMD 72–27, "The Professionals—Samy Chuck Green," 23. **To save:** *BB*, Apr. 22, 1933, 7. **Later:** JOHP 1979, 360. Bubbles remembered that she died during the Radio City Music Hall job, but her tombstone in the Mount Hope Cemetery in San Diego gives a death date of December 21, 1933.

Then one day: Goldberg 2008, 18.

Female tapper: Frank 1994, 125.

Just a block away: There were two Hoofers Clubs and two Rhythm Clubs. After 1932 or so, the Hoofers Club had moved to the basement of the Lafayette Theatre and the Rhythm Club was located a block north on 133rd Street. **Musicians were invited:** Wells 1991, 24; cited in DeVeaux 1997, 210.

"Sometimes": Malone 1996, 97. **Bubbles had his own:** https://www.notsomoderndrummer.com/not-so-modern-drummer/2016/5/31/the-legend-of-tommy-thomas-1901-1995 (accessed Mar. 21, 2020). **In a letter:** JWBP, Box 2, Folder 6: Frank Murphy to John Bubbles, Oct. 29, 1964.

As drum historian: Brown 1976, 198, 350. **Not surprisingly:** JWBP, Box 5, Folder 11: Marilyn Hunt, "Time Steps: Mr. Honi Coles," *Soho News Dance Supplement*, May 7–13, 1980, 42. Chuck Green said, "dancers had rhythms that fascinated drummers." JWBP, Box 5, Folder 10: Jane Goldberg, "Tapping Back into View," *Jazz Magazine*, Winter 1978, 31. **"We base all":** Malone 1996, 95. **Big Sid Catlett:** Balliett 1996, 204. The speaker here is bass player John Simmons. **As bandleader:** Korall 1990, 139.

"By using his heels": JWBP, Box 1, Folder 11: David Hinckley, "John Bubbles Was a Tap Dance Giant," *Albuquerque Journal*, June 1, 1986, E7; reprint from *NYDN*. **Count Basie's drummer:** Constance Valis Hill discusses Jones's "indebtedness" to the great tap dancers in Hill 2010, 216. **Unlike other drummers:** Brown 1976, 453–54. **"influenced":** Malone 1996, 95. Max Roach told singer Jimmy Scott "he got many of his bebop beats watching [tap dancer] Groundhog's feet." Hill 2010, 217. **This technique:** JWBP, Box 5, Folder 12: David Hinckley, "A Honey of a Hoofer," *Sunday News Magazine*, Aug. 7, 1983, 15.

"night after night": Goldberg 1988, 11.

The *Baltimore Afro-American*: *AA*, June 24, 1933, 10. **If Buck and Bubbles:** *VA*, Jan. 9, 1934, 39.

"They were typical": Dance 1977, 146. "Buck . . . often": Rosenkrantz 2012, 108–9.

One of Buck's: Dance 1977, 146. "If somebody passed": Mezzrow 1990, 237–38. When Buck: Mezzrow 1990, 254, 296–98.

Pianist Joe Turner: Liner notes to *Joe Turner: Stride by Stride*. 77 Records, LA 12/32. Reprinted at http://thereisjazzbeforetrane.blogspot.com/2009/03/joe-turner-pianists-in-my-life-33.html (accessed Mar. 24, 2020). For a young: Gitler 1985, 104. In her opinion: Shapiro and Hentoff 1966, 295.

He later narrated: McGuire 1969, 165–71.

On January 2: JWBP, Box 7, Folder 3: Viola Sublett to John Sublett, Jan. 2, 1934. If a gossip columnist: *PC*, Oct. 20, 1934, A8.

11. A Miracle of Racy Brilliance

He had apparently: In a TV interview from 1961, Bubbles said he thought Gershwin had seen the act at Grauman's Chinese Theatre, where Buck and Bubbles performed in the vaudeville prologue to *Dinner at Eight* from late August to mid-October, 1933. Richard Glazier, "John W. Bubbles discusses and performs music from Porgy and Bess," YouTube video, 8:17, Mar. 7, 2017, https://www.youtube.com/watch?v=7nvKSRUZU2o. Two weeks later: Kendall 1987, 140. "the 'funky' piano player": *Brooklyn Daily Eagle*, Feb. 10, 1935, 35.

In June or July: Alpert 1990, 104; Gershwin 1973, 83. He had chosen: Wyatt and Johnson 2004, 218. So Gershwin offered: McGuire 1969, 174.

He smoked: Wyatt and Johnson 2004, 233; Alpert 1990, 105. Recently discovered: McGuire 1969, 174–75. According to: Jablonski 1992, 105–6.

Todd Duncan: Thompson 2010, 132–35. Word may have leaked: Davis 2015: Payroll sheet, *Porgy and Bess*, 30 September 1935.

"He was not too particular": Jablonski 1992, 105.

"Mr. Smallens": Alpert 1990, 105. "I just gave": McGuire 1969, 176.

"Gershwin taught him": Wyatt and Johnson 2004, 223.

As choral director: Crawford 2006, 711–12. Bubbles, meanwhile: McGuire 1969, 177.

Buck and Bubbles sent: Gershwin 1973, 83. That night: *NYT*, Oct. 1, 1935, 27. As Eric Davis has: Davis 2015, 2–3.

For the occasion: Rimler 2009, 111; McGuire 1969, 178–80; JOHP 1979, 306–11. Kay Swift: Kimball and Simon 1973, 188. Bubbles took it: McGuire 1969, 181.

When the reviews: Pollack 2006, 606. The reviewer for: *WSJ*, Oct. 14, 1935, 17. Another critic: *Spur*, Dec. 1, 1935, 62. Writing for: *NYHT*, Oct. 11, 1935, 23. "His dancing": *WWD*, Oct. 11, 1935, 11. Most effusively: *NYHT*, Oct. 20, 1935, D1.

After the premiere: *CD*, Oct. 19, 1935, 8. The following month: *PT*, Nov. 7, 1935, 10; *AA*, Nov. 23, 1935, 8. In January: *PC*, Jan. 18, 1936, A6. Another critic: *PC*, Feb. 15, 1936, A7. In April: *AA*, Apr. 4, 1936, 18. "I hated him": Jablonski 1987, 286. "my Bubbles": Ewen 1970, 230.

During the company's: *AN*, June 17, 1939, 17. Gershwin's music: *PPG*, Feb. 10, 1936, 8.

For him: Noonan 2012, 20.

Some critics: *WWD*, Oct. 11, 1935, 11. "John was magnificent": JWBP, Box 8, Folder 18: "Gershwin: A Lover Looks Back," *Sunday News*, Sept. 19, 1976, 1, 5.

It is possible: David Fletcher, "Porgy and Bess, 1935 silent home movie," YouTube video, 1:31, Sept. 14, 2011, https://www.youtube.com/watch?v=khX92Ctfh-k.

Mamoulian had: *NYHT*, Oct. 27, 1935, D4. At the same time: From the same article: "In the picnic scene, he does a tap-dance of his own—probably the first tap dance ever to make its way into an opera." Similarly: McGuire 1969, 180.

To the extent: Crawford 2006, 731–32.

On this number: Noonan 2012, 170.

"I didn't really": "Bubbles," 23. Soon he could speak: *CD*, Dec. 21, 1935, 8. A month into: *AN*, Nov. 9, 1935, 13. "You could tell": McGuire 1969, 183. "one of the classic": Jablonski 1987, 286.

"For fun": JWBP, Box 1, Folder 11: Lee Gershwin to John Bubbles, 31 May 1985.

As Eric Davis has: Davis 2015, 1–15.

12. Swing Is King

According to two accounts: *NYHT*, Oct. 27, 1935, D4; *PT*, Nov. 7, 1935, 10.

The following March: *AA*, Mar. 7, 1936, 11. Two months later: *NYHT*, May 22, 1936, 15.

Two weeks after: *CD*, Oct. 19, 1935, 8.

"I got plenty": JOHP 1979, 223–24.

In March 1936: *VA*, Apr. 15, 1936, 19. **The weekly box:** *VA*, Apr. 15, 1936, 49. **Over on the eastern:** *BB*, Apr. 18, 1936, 14.

In August they: *Stage*, Sept. 19, 1936, 9; Oct. 8, 1936, 12.

"A lot of": *VA*, Sept. 16, 1936, 14. **Ferry announced:** *VA*, Sept. 30, 1936, 14. **On opening night:** *NYT*, Oct. 2, 1936, 16; *MG*, Oct. 2, 1936, 10; *VA*, Oct. 14, 1936, 18.

"more sumptuosity": *Observer*, Oct. 4, 1936, 19. **As "spectacle":** *MG*, Oct. 2, 1936, 10; *VA*, Oct. 7, 1936, 12. **On one point:** *MG*, Oct. 2, 1936, 10; *Observer*, Oct. 4, 1936, 19; *Stage*, Oct. 8, 1936, 12; *VA*, Oct. 14, 1936, 62. **The following day:** *VA*, Oct. 7, 1936, 12; *CD*, Oct. 31, 1936, 25. **Nazarro appeared:** *VA*, Oct. 7, 1936, 12. **At the end:** *VA*, Oct. 28, 1936, 54.

Making a bit: Vahimagi 1994, 2. **The show opened:** *MG*, Nov. 3, 1936, 5.

Buck and Bubbles next: *MM*, Dec. 19, 1936, 9. **As *The Stage:*** *Stage*, Nov. 26, 1936, 14.

On one occasion: McGuire 1969, 193. **While the bluebloods:** JOHP 1979, 247–48.

After four months: New York, Passenger and Crew Lists, 1820–1957: S.S. Berengaria, sailing from Southampton, Dec. 22, 1936, arriving at Port of New York, Dec. 28, 1936.

By the time: *BG*, Feb. 26, 1937, 33.

At that very: *VA*, Apr. 14, 1937, 7, 60. **In February:** *VA*, Feb. 24, 1937, 27.

"crazy to go": JOHP 1979, 328. ***Varsity Show* was:** Hischak 2009, https://www.oxfordreference.com/view/10.1093/acref/9780195335330.001.0001/acref-9780195335330-e-1873? (accessed May 1, 2020); Dooley 1979, 436. **To give them:** JOHP 1979, 332.

Later, Bubbles bemoaned: JOHP 1979, 353.

Such integration: Joan Acocella, "Not a Pink Toy," *NY*, Mar. 18, 2014.

As a teenager: Pauline Kael, "The Current Cinema," *NY*, Jan. 7, 1985, 69. **"spacey singsong":** Naremore 1993, 67. Naremore uses this expression to describe Butterfly McQueen, but it applies equally to other Black actors. **During filming:** *CT*, May 10, 1937, 17.

As early as: *PC*, Mar. 19, 1932, A6; Berger et al. 2002, 239.

In January: *WP*, Jan. 21, 1938, X7; *PT*, Feb. 3, 1938, 15; *VA*, Feb. 9, 1938, 48. **While White:** DeVeaux 1997, 148–52.

Rather than: *CD*, Mar. 12, 1938, 18; Mar. 26, 1938, 19; *PT*, Mar. 17, 1938, 14.

After the Apollo: *VA*, Apr. 20, 1938, 45. **"gives a good band":** *HC*, May 14, 1938, 8.

"sweet swing": *Down Beat*, May 1938, 27.

As the swing craze: *VA*, Jan. 6, 1937, 195.

In June: *VA*, June 8, 1938, 47; *WWD*, June 10, 1938, 19. According to: *NYT*, June 13, 1938, 15. Sure enough: *WWD*, June 14, 1938, 23.

This was a "neighborhood club": *BB*, Apr. 6, 1940, 1, 62.

By this time: DeVeaux 1997, 147. In November: *PT*, Nov. 21, 1940, 14; *BB*, Nov. 30, 1940, 4.

"Buck and Bubbles have": *BB*, Jan. 17, 1942, 25.

In late 1938: *BB*, Nov. 26, 1938, 29. Chesterfield was: *NYT*, Jan. 12, 1939, 14.

One of those: *BS*, Feb. 25, 1939, 6; *VA*, Mar. 1, 1939, 42. *Variety* deemed: *VA*, Mar. 1, 1939, 42. A deflated: *BB*, Mar. 18, 1939, 23.

In May 1942: *LAT*, May 26, 1942, 17; *VA*, June 17, 1942, 47. In one of the earliest: JWBP, Box 14, Folder 2: Nat Nazarro to John Bubbles, June 12, 1942.

To widespread: *LAT*, June 30, 1942, A8.

At some point: *NJAG*, July 11, 1942, B19.

Its filming: *PC*, June 27, 1942, 21. The Black film industry: *BB*, Aug. 8, 1942, 26.

Many years after: NYPL, *MGZIC 9-5600: *By Word of Foot: 12 Tap Masters Pass on Their Tradition*, documentary film, 1980.

According to Bubbles: McGuire 1969, 205–6; Josephson 2009, 145.

But Bubbles also: McGuire 1969, 203–6; JOHP 1979, 492–96. Bubbles had initially composed a verse in praise of his new baby daughter (see Chapter 13), but MGM rejected all except two lines: "It's very plain to see / Just how it happened to be."

The most obvious: Referring specifically to the zoot suit phenomenon of the war years, Kathy Peiss argues that fine or distinctive clothes represented "significant political behavior by those who had little formal power or ability to represent themselves through speech or texts." Clothing style offered "the powerless a potent means to communicate resistance to or alienation from the dominant social order." Peiss 2011, 3–4.

He himself called the dance: JOHP 1979, 494.

The movie itself: Bogle 2016, 116, 119.

Growing up in the 1950s: Interview with André De Shields, New York, May 12, 2003. NYPL Performing Arts Research Collections, TOFT, NCOX 2152 videocassette 1. Italics added.

13. Black Bizet

"I oughta be": *PC*, Oct. 3, 1942, 21.

According to Bubbles's: JWBP, Box 18, dark brown album: John Bubbles to Rhea Wright (undated); Box 7, Folder 5: John Bubbles to Rhea Wright, March 1943. They decided: McGuire 1969, 185–203.

"She has eyes": Box 7, Folder 4: Rhea Wright to John Bubbles, Sept. 23, 1942. "I always heard": Box 7, Folder 5: Rhea Wright to John Bubbles, Apr. 13, 1943. "What about": Box 7, Folder 4: Rhea Wright to John Bubbles, Apr. 15, 1942. Speaking: Box 7, Folder 4: Rhea Wright to John Bubbles, Sept. 29, 1942.

"The shock": Box 7, Folder 5: Rhea Wright to John Bubbles, Jan. 7, 1943. "As I see": Box 7, Folder 4: Rhea Wright to John Bubbles, Oct. 20, 1942. "Having burned": Box 7, Folder 5: Rhea Wright to John Bubbles, Jan. 7, 1943. "I will stand": Box 7, Folder 5: Rhea Wright to John Bubbles, Jan. 20, 1943.

"I must admit": Box 7, Folder 5: John Bubbles to Rhea Wright, March 1943.

According to financial records: This data comes from JWBP, Box 14, Folder 2.

"Please try": Box 14, Folder 2: Nat Nazarro to Buck Washington, July 31, 1941. "Now, I want"; "asked for a contract": Box 14, Folder 2: Nat Nazarro to John Bubbles, Aug. 4, 1944.

"We are negotiating": Box 14, Folder 2: Gertrude Quinton to John Bubbles, July 20, 1943. "Domino": Box 14, Folder 2: John Bubbles to Nat Nazarro, June 1943. "Now, Bubbles": Box 14, Folder 2: Nat Nazarro to John Bubbles, June 17, 1942.

In 1943: *VA*, July 28, 1943, 46.

During filming: Box 14, Folder 2: undated telegram, Nat Nazarro to Buck and Bubbles [1943?].

Two months later: Death Certificate: Katie Sublett, Sept. 21, 1944, No. 7310, Bureau of Vital Statistics, Department of Health, City of New York. Having borne: JOHP 1979, 190–91, 404, 455.

In arranging: JWBP, Box 2, Folder 5: Flushing Cemetery to John Sublett, Nov. 19, 1964.

Having turned: *AA*, Feb. 10, 1945, 8. "The only important": *CT*, May 6, 1945, E3. "who play right": JWBP, Box 2, Folder 19: *San Francisco News*, June 26, 1945, 8. "They interrupted": Box 2, Folder 19: *Cleveland Herald*, Oct. 5, 1945.

Billy Rose's secretary: McGuire 1969, 207–8.

"A pianist played": Box 2, Folder 19: *Los Angeles Examiner*, June 14, 1945, Part II-5.

Fortunately: *Ottawa Journal*, Sept. 17, 1946, 9.

"incomparably": Box 2, Folder 19: Unidentified clipping: Harrison Carroll, "'Carmen Jones' Season's Most Thrilling Event"; *CT*, Sept. 2, 1945. "magnificent": Box 2, Folder 19: *SFC*, June 28, 1945, 10. "admittedly": *VA*, May 9, 1945, 44. "able comedians": Box 2, Folder 19: Unidentified clipping: Harrison Carroll, "'Carmen Jones' Season's Most Thrilling Event"; *San Francisco Examiner*, June 27, 1945. "where the women's": *VA*, May 9, 1945, 44. "added a little": *BB*, May 12, 1945, 33.

"Negro actors": *Lancaster Eagle-Gazette* [Lancaster OH], Nov. 16, 1946, 1. In St. Louis: Box 13, Folder 12: *Carmen Jones* itinerary in one of Bubbles's daybooks, November 1946.

At forty-two: *PC*, Feb. 2, 1946, 20.

He got a nudge: Box 2, Folder 19: Unidentified clipping: "Carmen Jones Celebrates 2nd Birthday," Oct. 27, 1945. The following year: Box 2, Folder 19: Certificate: Deputy Credential for Production, Oct. 16, 1946.

A food reporter: *PC*, July 7, 1945, 9.

When Bubbles finally returned: McGuire 1969, 209–12.

14. Requiem for a Two-Act

Nightclubs took: *AN*, Jan. 25, 1947, 1. Reflecting: JOHP 1979, 186.

"curiously lively": *NYT*, Sept. 9, 1943, 35. In late 1947: *PC*, Dec. 13, 1947, 17. And yet shortly: Stewart 2005, 256.

Tap dancing declined: Seibert 2015, 330; Hill 2010, 165–66. "the ending of an era"; "the general opinion": *PT*, Nov. 29, 1949, 1.

In tap dancing's heyday: Goldberg 1978, 112. "You don't dance": *ND*, Apr. 23, 1953, 54.

On May 28: *AN*, May 29, 1948, 3; JWBP, Box 8, Folder 15: Scrapbook, unidentified clipping. A year older: People vs. Mabel A. Roane Sublett, No. 427–49, State of New York, 1949, contains a photo of Mabel as well as a handwritten note describing her appearance.

Their reception: JWBP, Box 8, Folder 15: Scrapbook, unidentified clipping. At the end: *VA*, Dec. 22, 1948, 44; *AN*, Dec. 25, 1948, 21.

On February 17: *NJAG*, Feb. 26, 1949, 14; *AN*, Feb. 26, 1949, 1; *Atlanta Daily World*, June 7, 1949, 4; People vs. Mabel A. Roane Sublett, No. 427–49, State of New York, 1949.

"It's a disgrace": JOHP 1979, 507. Italics added.

On May 20: John W. Sublett, etc., vs. Nathan Davis, trading in business as Nat Nazarro, No. 13292, Supreme Court of the State of New York, 1948. On November 4: JWBP, Box 14, Folder 2: *New York Law Journal*, Nov. 4, 1949; *VA*, Nov. 16, 1949, 61.

Due to the six-year: JWBP, Box 14, Folder 2: Court documents for John W. Sublett, etc., vs. Nathan Davis, known in business as Nat Nazarro, etc., No. 5026, Supreme Court of New York, 1950.

At the urging: JWBP, Box 4, Folder 32: Bernard Grossman to John Bubbles, June 20, 1961. "But I was out": McGuire 1969, 146.

In 1959: *Stage*, Apr. 2, 1959, 3; JOHP 1979, 451.

Today Nazarro: Constance Valis Hill, "Chuck Green," *American National Biography* (New York: Oxford University Press, 1999), 9:212.

"Everything was tough": JOHP 1979, 146–48.

It helped: JWBP, Box 14, Folder 1: Contract with William Morris, July 21, 1948. Three years later: *VA*, June 14, 1939, 35. "This honor": *AN*, June 17, 1939, 17. *CD*, July 1, 1939, 19.

Even more encouraging: *WP*, Aug. 8, 1948, L1; JWBP, Box 2, Folder 13: Program for RKO Palace Theatre, Aug. 10, 1948; Box 3, Folder 8: Photo of ad billboard.

Critics indeed: *BB*, Aug. 21, 1948, 1. Buck and Bubbles were tapped: *VA*, Sept. 22, 1948, 26; *Broadcasting*, Sept. 27, 1948, 34. *Billboard* congratulated: *BB*, Oct. 2, 1948, 13; *CT*, Oct. 3, 1948, N14. During this period: Barnouw 1990, 117–18; MacDonald 1992, 4.

In 1951: *AN*, Dec. 15, 1951, 14; *PC*, Jan. 5, 1952, 20.

As if sensing: *BG*, Nov. 14, 1947, 20; *VA*, Oct. 6, 1948, 53; Dec. 20, 1950, 47.

In 1958: *ND*, May 10, 1958, 38.

Their last show: *VA*, Aug. 29, 1951, 56. Twice they headlined: *WWD*, June 28, 1949, 35; JWBP, Box 14, Folder 1: Contract to play Aquashow, Aug. 14, 1952. In May 1950: *PT*, May 20, 1950, 11.

Frustrated: *PC*, July 21, 1951, 24. In 1952: JWBP, Box 14, Folder 1: Contracts. In July: *AA*, July 1, 1952, 6.

On September 15: JWBP, Box 14, Folder 1: Contract to play Bassel's Lounge, Aug. 14, 1952. All went well until: *VA*, Sept. 24, 1952, 2.

Bubbles and Mabel pleaded: *TGM*, Oct. 10, 1952, 8; Oct. 18, 1952, 10; Oct. 25, 1952, 5; Oct. 29, 1952, 5; Oct. 30, 1952, 5; *VA*, Oct. 15, 1952, 50; Nov. 11, 1952, 1; McGuire 1969, 215–19; JOHP 1979, 369–72.

In the spring: *VA*, June 17, 1953, 48. He wrote friends: JWBP, Box 2, Folder 2: Unidentified clipping; Box 6, Folder 16: Unidentified clipping.

On January 31: *VA*, Feb. 16, 1955, 63; *BB*, Feb. 19, 1955, 55; McGuire 1969, 220. His funeral drew: *PC*, Feb. 12, 1955, 18. "I cried all night": McGuire 1969, 220.

15. Exile

After being released: *BB*, Dec. 13, 1952, 55. He spent: *AN*, Apr. 4, 1953, 14. The nadir came: JWBP, Box 14, Folder 1: Contract for Campbell Inn, Roscoe, New York, June 19, 1953.

Then in early August: McGuire 1969, 220. Around the same time: JWBP, Box 5, Folder 2: *VA*, Aug. 12, 1953. "she busted out": JOHP 1979, 532.

On his first day: McGuire 1969, 220–24; JOHP 1979, 378–89.

He advertised: JWBP, Box 3, Folder 1: Clippings; program for Empress Theatre Brixton, London, May 31, 1954. Whenever the Nazis: *NYHT*, Mar. 8, 1953, D1. With trademark derby: JWBP, Box 9, Folder 24: Parts for "Shine." On the back of one part, Bubbles outlines the show from his solo years.

Looking back: JWBP, Box 3, Folder 15: Schedule card for the Latin Casino, Route 70, Cherry Hill, NJ; Box 6, Folder 9: Redd Knight to John Bubbles, Jan. 31, 1958. At one event: JOHP 1979, 389–95; McGuire 1969, 224.

For a shoestring: JWBP, Box 3, Folder 1: Program for Empress Theatre Brixton, London, May 31, 1954. "Nobody trusts": JWBP, Box 4, Folder 7: *Courier-Post* [Camden NJ], July 9, 1958, 22.

"managed to become": *VA*, Feb. 15, 1956, 20. On a signed: JWBP, Box 3, Folder 15. Later: JWBP, Box 8, Folder 17: C. Bird, Lt., Entertainment Officer of the Royal Canadian Navy, to John Bubbles, Jan. 25, 1957.

Another encounter: JWBP, Box 8, Folder 18: Unidentified clipping: Pete Chaney, "Voice in the Crowd."

"It wasn't": McGuire 1969, 226. In March: JWBP, Box 3, Folder 1: "Colour Bar in Town is Alleged," *Star*, Mar. 4, 1954.

Race flared up: McGuire 1969, 226–27. Aysha De Festa: JWBP, Box 7, Folder 6: Aysha De Festa to Jerry Bloom, Paramount Pictures, Feb. 6, 1961. They soon began: JWBP, Box 3, Folder 15: Signed photograph from Jack Tiney.

Yet her letters: JWBP, Box 3, Folder 21: A summary of correspondence between Mabel and Bubbles, 1953–1956.

There was talk: McGuire 1969, 228. JWBP, Box 3, Folder 21: On January 4, 1955, Joe Glaser wrote Bubbles about the possibility of appearing in *Porgy and Bess* the movie. **"This letter is sent":** JWBP, Box 7, Folder 8: Mabel C. Sublett to Michael Todd (of Michael Todd Productions), Sept. 17, 1956.

Conveniently: McGuire 1969, 233.

16. Turn Back the Universe

On May 21: JWBP, Box 2, Folder 8: John Bubbles to Mabel Sublett, May 12, 1957. **"But I want":** JWBP, Box 7, Folder 10: Aysha De Festa to John Bubbles, June 21, 1957. **Bubbles nevertheless:** McGuire 1969, 235. **Whether Aysha:** JWBP, Box 7, Folder 7: Telegram from John Bubbles to Aysha De Festa (petname Shur), July 9, 1957. **Bubbles and Aysha:** JWBP, Box 7, Folder 10: Marriage booklet for John W. Sublett and Aysha De Festa.

They finally settled: McGuire 1969, 234–35. **In addition:** McGuire 1969, 237.

He remembered Bubbles: McGuire 1969, 231–32. **Hayes had always:** *CT*, Nov. 1, 1959, A4.

"We were performing": Land and Land 1999, 145. **According to *Variety*:** *VA*, June 19, 1957, 68. **"Bubbles was a tremendous":** McGuire 1969, 233–35.

Bubbles soon: *NYHT*, May 16, 1958, A1. **"I almost cried":** JWBP, Box 5, Folder 2: *NYDN*, Mar. 19, 1958. **Black columnist:** *CD*, Nov. 8, 1958, 19.

Daytime television in the 1950s: Cassidy 2005, 75–76.

For instance: McGuire 1969, 4–5.

"Dear Peter": JWBP, Box 1, Folder 8: John Bubbles to Peter Lind Hayes, Dec. 1957. **"In the many years":** McGuire 1969, 232.

"Turn back the universe": JWBP, Box 4, Folder 20: Joe Christie to John Bubbles, c/o Godfrey Radio Program, Mar. 26, 1958. **"Saw you on T.V.":** JWBP, Box 2, Folder 6: Helene to John Bubbles, Aug. 16, 1958. **"My three children":** JWBP, Box 2, Folder 6: Rosemary O'Callaghan to John Bubbles, c/o CBS, N.Y., Dec. 11, 1957.

"Is this America": JWBP, Box 5, Folder 2: *NYDN*, Sept. 24, 1957, 28. **"Daytime TV":** *PC*, Sept. 21, 1957, 21.

These re-creations: JWBP, Box 8, Folder 18: *New York Mirror*, May 21, 1958. **"You is a coward":** McGuire 1969, 231. **In later years:** Ibid., 232.

But others were: *CD*, May 18, 1957, 9; *ND*, Feb. 3, 1958, 4C. **"George Gershwin":** *Toronto Daily Star* (Sept. 13, 1958), 21. **Years later:** JOHP 1979, 337.

In negotiating: JWBP, Box 14, Folder 1: Contract: *Porgy and Bess*, Civic Light Opera, Pitt Stadium, Pittsburgh, May 12, 1958. **"The amazing":** JWBP, Box 8, Folder 18: Unidentified review of *Porgy and Bess*, Pitt Stadium, [1958]. **Particularly when:** JWBP, Box 8, Folder 18: *NYT*, Aug. 2, 1959. **John Bubbles "gives us":** JWBP, Box 8, Folder 18: Unidentified review of *Porgy and Bess*, Sept. 3, 1958.

One earnest: JWBP, Box 2, Folder 6: Lee Swan to John Bubbles, July 8, 1958.

"I was number one": JOHP 1979, 593. **"If I played Bill":** Kurt Albert personal collection: Robert Wahls, "Forever Bubbles," unidentified newspaper, Aug. 13, 1967.

But Bubbles got: JWBP, Box 2, Folder 1: NBC scriptbook: "A Toast to Jerome Kern," Sept. 22, 1959—John W. Bubbles.

John Bubbles is "by far": *VA*, Nov. 5, 1958, 61. **Maurice Hines:** *NYT*, Jan. 26, 1986, Section 2, Page 1.

"had the most": *AN*, Jan. 9, 1982, 19.

"She looks like": Frank 1975, 445–46.

"Who's that?": *CD*, Dec. 29, 1962, 10. **Although *Judy at the Met*:** JWBP, Box 2, Folder 2: Scriptbook for *The Show at the Met* (1959); Fricke 1992, 167–77; Shipman 1993, 387–89.

"All my life": King 1996, 79.

One critic fretted: JWBP, Box 4, Folder 33: *VA*, July 16, 1959. **Still, Bubbles earned:** JWBP, Box 14, Folder 1: Contracts for Baltimore, Chicago, San Francisco, Feb. 13, 1959.

For several years: *LAT*, Oct. 10, 1956, 21; *AA*, July 11, 1961, 12.

Running for six: *NYT*, Oct. 22, 1998, E1. **On February 13:** *AN*, Feb. 13, 1960, 9, 15; *VA*, Sept. 28, 1960, 36; Feb. 1, 1961, 66. **In front of:** I am indebted to Lance Bowling for providing me with video recordings of these episodes.

In late 1961: *WP*, Nov. 8, 1961, C10. **Reviewing a special:** *NYT*, Nov. 6, 1961, 75.

17. Bubbles Bounces Back!

"undoubtedly the best": *Broadcasting*, Oct. 20, 1958, 18. **Things got so bad:** McGuire 1969, 238.

In the summer: JWBP, Box 3, Folder 15: *Fabulous Las Vegas*, Aug. 5, 1961, 10. **As the first:** *Jet*, May 18, 1961, 5. **During his two-week:** JWBP, Box 14, Folder 1: Contract to play Carver House Hotel, Las Vegas, July 10, 1961.

" 'Le Jazz Hot' seems": *VA*, July 26, 1961, 61. **Instead of singing:** CBS television broadcast: *American Musical Theatre* (Feb. 12, 1961); my thanks to Lance Bowling for sending me a DVD of this episode. **According to Hayes:** McGuire 1969, 236.

Bubbles appeared twice: *NYT*, May 28, 1962, 58. **"the most talked about":** Smith 1987, 83. **In his rapid-fire:** *VA*, June 6, 1962, 29. **"What have you been":** *Victoria Advocate*, June 3, 1962, 5.

"the most prestigious": Smith 1987, 78. **With a hipness:** Ibid., 92. **As the ratings:** Leamer 1989, 159.

On November 1: *NYHT*, Nov. 1, 1962, 17. **It wasn't long:** *CD*, Dec. 13, 1962, 27. **The same paper:** *CD*, Dec. 29, 1962, 10. **Such hallucinations:** *VA*, July 22, 1964, 46.

Bubbles's story: *Back Stage*, Nov. 30, 1962, 16.

Having been coached: McGuire 1969, 235. **Looking back:** *Atlanta Constitution*, Aug. 12, 1963, 20A. **On one episode:** Galanoy 1972, 139.

By 1964: *New Pittsburgh Courier*, July 4, 1964, 16. **"The [Tonight Show]":** *HC*, July 5, 1964, 4G. **One elderly fan:** JWBP, Box 10, Folder 18: "Three Score and Ten" to John Bubbles, c/o Johnny Carson Show, WNBC TV, NY, Nov. 24, 1964. **In her memoir:** Pemberton 1998, 222.

"Last night with": JWBP, Box 2, Folder 6: R. Goode to John Bubbles, undated.

"Keep your chin": JWBP, Box 6, Folder 18: Eleanor Powell to John Bubbles, Jan. 8, 1963. **"Out of the studio":** Metz 1980, 218.

After two seasons: *LAT*, June 30, 1964, C7; July 7, 1964, C7.

Unfortunately: *CT*, June 26, 1964, 19; JWBP, Box 2, Folder 8: Partial medical history. **For the Tonight Show:** JWBP, Box 14, Folder 1: Contract for Tonight Show, NBC, May 31, 1963; contract for Hotel Sahara, Oct. 4, 1963.

Ignoring the advice: McGuire 1969, 250–55.

In the spring: *SFC*, Apr. 11, 1963, 40. **The gig was:** *VA*, Apr. 24, 1963, 66; JOHP 1979, 591; *ND*, May 16, 1963, 7C; *VA*, June 12, 1963, 70. **In August:** *Austin Statesman*, Aug. 29, 1963, A23.

"the biggest man": McGuire 1969, 245. **For years, dancer:** *AN*, Dec. 7, 1963, 18.

A lifelong political conservative: Zoglin 2014, 240. **"His performances":** *VA*, Jan. 22, 1964, 52.

Over Christmas 1963: *ND*, Dec. 20, 1963, 5C.

During a flight; "John, that was very good": McGuire 1969, 244. "It brought the house": Hope 1974, 173. Bubbles worked up: McGuire 1969, 245.

"Among the supporting": *HC*, Jan. 17, 1964, 20. "I was so thrilled": *CT*, Jan. 14, 1964, A4.

She discovered Bubbles: *AN*, Nov. 7, 1964, 11. His first contract: JWBP, Box 14, Folder 1: Contracts with Anna Maria Alberghetti: Dec. 19, 1963, Mar. 11, 1964, Apr. 10, 1964, Jan. 13, 1965, Feb. 2, 1965.

When the twenty-seven-year-old: *AN*, Nov. 7, 1964, 11. "May-December": *ND*, Oct. 16, 1964, 2C. "a double": *VA*, Oct. 14, 1964, 59. Their fifty-five-minute: *VA*, Apr. 8, 1964, 76; May 13, 1964, 59.

Critics also praised: *CT*, Mar. 8, 1964, F10; *VA*, Mar. 11, 1964, 50. Provocatively: *AN*, Nov. 7, 1964, 11.

"the swankiest rooms": *VA*, May 13, 1964, 59. "Hugh Hefner": JWBP, Box 4, Folder 42: Benny Dunn, Public Relations Manager, PLAYBOY, to John Bubbles, c/o Palmer House, Feb. 28, 1964. At Harrah's: McGuire 1969, 242.

In the fall: JWBP, Box 14, Folder 1: Contract (in the form of a letter): John Bubbles to Anna Maria Alberghetti, fall 1964.

The following January: *Ebony*, January 1965, 50, 52.

While Bubbles was touring: *TGM*, Dec. 21, 1963, 14; June 17, 1964, 10; Apr. 3, 1965, 20.

In his review: *TGM*, Apr. 3, 1965, 20.

Bubbles could sense: JWBP, Box 7, Folder 10: John Bubbles to Aysha Sublett, Jan. 2, 1962. Many years later: Telephone interview with Aysha De Festa, 9 Mar 2015. "I don't want": JWBP, Box 7, Folder 6: SHUR [Aysha] to Bubbles, undated.

Aysha filed: JWBP, Box 7, Folder 10: Complaint for Divorce: Aysha Sublett vs. John W. Sublett, Clark County NV, Mar. 20, 1964. While Bubbles was: McGuire 1969, 253. The divorce: JWBP, Box 7, Folder 10: Decree of Divorce: Aysha Sublett vs. John W. Sublett, Clark County NV, May 22, 1964, Case No. A 10909.

According to one: JWBP, Box 5, Folder 5: *Buffalo Courier-Express*, July 30, 1965, 12. In recruiting Bubbles: *Austin American*, May 30, 1965, 7. He mixed: *VA*, Feb. 9, 1966, 52. "when [Bubbles] and Eddie"; "I was supposed": *Austin American*, May 30, 1965, 7.

For $2,500: JWBP, Box 14, Folder 3: Contract for the Riviera Hotel, Las Vegas, Apr. 15, 1965.

One of his girlfriends: JWBP, Box 2, Folder 8: Wanda Michael's summaries of the correspondence between Bubbles and Beatrice Canning, 1964.

"Do you understand": JOHP 1979, 143–44. **A few weeks:** JWBP, Box 2, Folder 8: Wanda Michael's summaries, 1964.

In 1966: *AN*, Apr. 23, 1966, A17; *LAS*, Dec. 1, 1966, A7.

His big dream: McGuire 1969, 235; *Ebony*, January 1965, 52. **Now he started:** JWBP, Box 4, Folder 24: James Thompson to John Bubbles, Aug. 30, 1965.

In July, Bubbles: All these letters are in JWBP, Box 4, Folder 24.

18. This Unforgettable Passage

On January 9: JWBP, Box 4, Folder 14: Escrow supplement and insurance policy for house on 5723 Brushton Avenue, to Mr. John W. Sublett, 8439 Sunset Blvd., Hollywood, California. **One refrain:** JWBP, Box 2, Folder 8: Wanda Michael's notes of Bubbles's correspondence with Beatrice Canning, 1963–1964.

His letters: JWBP, Box 2, Folder 8: Wanda Michael's notes of Bubbles's correspondence with "Bea, Carmen, Bettye, Matte, Laurice, Chappie, M, Essie, Mabel, Aysha, W., Frances Neeley, and on and on," Feb. and Apr. 1964. **"All these gals":** JWBP, Box 2, Folder 8: Wanda Michael's summary of Bubbles's lifestyle and attributes.

Ruth Redina Campbell: Materials relating to Ruth Redina Campbell can be found in JWBP, Box 7, Folder 11.

She signed Bubbles: Sheridan and Monush 2011, 360–61. **"He's a real":** McGuire 1969, 6.

During a four-day: *AA*, May 13, 1967, 10; Spada 1995, 203–7. **"more than 100":** *NYT*, May 21, 1967, D23. **In another change:** *NJAG*, May 6, 1967, 14.

"We weren't looking": Spada 1995, 204.

Unfortunately: Mordden 2019, 39–40.

Far from taking: *NYT*, Oct. 12, 1967, 91. **Like the other:** *ND*, Oct. 12, 1967, 2A. **The show:** Spada 1995, 207.

On June 6: JWBP, Box 7, Folder 11: Marriage certificate, John William Sublett and Ruth Redina Campbell, June 6, 1967, San Bernardino CA, Riverside County. **"I've been married":** *Jet*, Aug. 24, 1967, 60.

Since *Judy*: Shipman 1993, 489–92.

During a weeklong: JWBP, Box 7, Folder 11: T. Yates to John Bubbles, June 28, 1967. Yates is confusing Bubbles's girlfriends. The white school teacher was Beatrice Canning, from Tonawanda, New York. Bubbles's Boston girl-friend was Essie Scott, a Black department store employee.

On opening night: Shipman 1993, 494; *ND*, Aug. 1, 1967, 3A. **Her occasionally:** *ND*, June 14, 1967, 3A. **After the show:** *HC*, June 28, 1967, 34.

Yet while: *VA*, Aug. 2, 1967, 50. **"To a vast":** *WP*, Aug. 2, 1967, B9.

Bubbles tap-danced: *AN*, Aug. 12, 1967, 20. **"Mr. Bubbles":** *NYT*, Aug. 1, 1967, 23. **"John Bubbles wins":** *BG*, Aug. 27, 1967, A13. **"Makes you feel":** JWBP, Box 4, Folder 7: *LAT*, May 20, 1986.

On the last day: *ND*, Aug. 30, 1967, 7A.

She laments: JWBP, Box 7, Folder 11: Ruth Campbell to John Bubbles, undated. (All correspondence between Ruth and Bubbles is in this folder.) **She makes clear:** Ruth Campbell to John Bubbles, July 29, 1967.

"I would like": John Bubbles to Ruth Campbell, June 21, 1967.

"John I know": Ruth Campbell to John Bubbles, Aug. 14, 1967. **"I again say":** Ruth Campbell to John Bubbles, Aug. 18, 1967.

Even more significantly: JWBP, Box 4, Folder 33: *The Celebrity Bulletin—New York Edition*, Aug. 22, 1967, 4; *Austin Statesman*, Aug. 25, 1967, 30.

"This unforgettable passage": "Bubbles," 23.

On August 22: JWBP, Box 2, Folder 6: Unidentified correspondent to John Bubbles, Aug. 22, 1967. **A woman from:** JWBP, Box 2, Folder 6: Helen Owsley Porter to John Bubbles, Aug. 30, 1967.

After four triumphant: JOHP 1979, 603–4; JWBP, Box 8, Folder 15: Unidentified clipping.

19. A World of Mirth

John Bubbles spent: JWBP, Box 8, Folder 15: Unidentified clipping; Box 2, Folder 8: Partial medical history. His second bout with pneumonia happened in Germany in the 1950s.

In the immediate: JWBP, Box 2, Folder 8: Wanda Michael's notes about Bubbles's life. **He got notes:** JWBP, Box 3, Folder 18: Robert F. Kennedy to John Bubbles, Oct. 18, 1967. **Bob Hope sent:** JWBP, Box 3, Folder 18: Western Union Telegram: Bob Hope to John Bubbles, Sept. 25, 1967.

He also heard: JWBP, Box 7, Folder 8: Mabel Sublett to John Bubbles, Sept. 1, 1967. **Upon hearing:** JWBP, Box 7, Folder 12: Ruth Sublett to John Bubbles, Sept. 2, 1967, Sept. 4, 1967. **Whether in response:** JWBP, Box 7, Folder 12: Bernard Grossman to John Bubbles, Oct. 27, 1967. **A divorce**

eventually: JWBP, Box 7, Folder 12: Ruth Sublett to John Bubbles, Nov. 4, 1967; Box 7, Folder 11: Ruth Sublett to John Bubbles, letter and photo, Aug. 1968.

"she loved him": JWBP, Box 2, Folder 9: Wanda Michael's notes on letter dated Apr. 27, 1968. **Twelve years younger:** U.S. Social Security Death Index, 1935–Current: Wanda Zay Michael; U.S. Census, 1930, Chowchilla, Madera County, Calif: Charles Myers (head). **When she met:** Interview with Lance Bowling, Feb. 8, 2016; U.S. Census, 1940, Madera, Madera County, Calif: Pauline Harrington (head).

"You are my": JWBP, Box 2, Folder 9: Wanda Michael to John Bubbles, Feb. 25, 1970. **In appreciation:** JWBP, Box 2, Folder 9: John Bubbles to Wanda Michael, Feb. 9, 1977.

When Wanda entered: JWBP, Box 2, Folder 8: Partial medical history. **Hope helped Bubbles:** JWBP, Box 3, Folder 23: W. N. Newton, vice president and manager of Bank of America, Hollywood, to John Bubbles, May 19, 1969; July 18, 1969; Box 4, Folder 15: United States District Court, Central District of California, Notice of First Meeting of Creditors and of Last Day for Filing Objections to Discharge, June 10, 1970. How Bubbles kept his house after bankruptcy proceedings is not known.

In September 1968: JWBP, Box 4, Folder 3: "Letter of Agreement" between John Bubbles and Jerry McGuire, Sept. 30, 1968. **But when he:** JWBP, Box 2, Folder 9: Wanda Michael's notes on yellow pads; Box 4, Folder 3: Judee McGuire to John Bubbles, May 9, 1972.

Bubbles heard from: JWBP, Box 4, Folder 20: "Chappie" to John Bubbles, Feb. 6, 1979; Box 2, Folder 3: "Eleanor" to John Bubbles, June 22, 1976.

In the case of: Seibert 2015, 375–93; Hill 2010, 215–41.

"It was lovely": JWBP, Box 2, Folder 4: Jane Goldberg to John Bubbles, early 1980s. **He took a fatherly:** Goldberg 1978, 112. See also Goldberg 2008, 93–99.

Bubbles, who misunderstood: JWBP, Box 4, Folder 18: John Bubbles to Bernard M. Wasserman, Nov. 8, 1982. **For example:** JOHP 1979, 607.

It had started: JWBP, Box 4, Folder 27: Merle Frimark, Myrna Post Associates, to John Bubbles, Aug. 4, 1978; John Bubbles to Merle Frimark, final draft: Aug. 18, 1978.

"His voice had": JWBP, Box 7, Folder 1: *NYT*, June 26, 1979; *Christian Science Monitor*, June 28, 1979.

In July: JWBP, Box 4, Folder 14: Thank-you note from John Bubbles to Karen Good, of *Good Morning America*, July 16, 1980; Box 2, Folder

10: Program for the 1980 Hollywood Bowl Jazz at the Bowl: "The Great Singers Sing The Great American Songs," Aug. 13, 1980. **Most promising:** JWBP, Box 4, Folder 19: Unsigned contract between John W. Bubbles and Knopf, undated but associated letters indicate the date as June 1980.

"His house is": JWBP, Box 4, Folder 7: *Dance/Flash,* Jan./Feb. 1983, 2. **He kept:** Goldberg 2008, 99. **"Perhaps you don't":** JWBP, Box 1, Folder 8: Agnes Lynch to John Bubbles, Jan. 25, 1978.

In October 1984: JWBP, Box 1, Folder 11: Tony Walker to Wanda Michael, Oct. 19, 1984; Box 2, Folder 9, Wanda's notes. **This time:** JWBP, Box 8, Folder 14: Death certificate: John William Sublett, May 18, 1986; Box 4, Folder 7: *LAT,* May 20, 1986.

And help came: JWBP, Box 1, Folder 10: List of checks from funeral donors.

Honorary pallbearers: JWBP, Box 1, Folder 9: Funeral program, John W. Sublett, May 24, 1986. **A written eulogy:** JWBP, Box 1, Folder 10: Eulogy by West Gale. **As Wanda once:** JWBP, Box 2, Folder 9: Wanda's notes. **"All of us":** JWBP, Box 1, Folder 11: Dorothy McCurry to Wanda Michael, Sept. 26, 1986. **He was buried:** JWBP, Box 1, Folder 9: Funeral registry, John "Bubbles" Sublett.

"He was also": JWBP, Box 1, Folder 11: David Hinckley, "John Bubbles Was a Tap Dance Giant," *Albuquerque Journal,* June 1, 1986, E7; reprint from *NYDN.*

After the funeral: JWBP, Box 1, Folder 11: Wanda Michael to Richard Sharpe, atty, Sept. 17, 1987; spreadsheet of expenses during administration of John Bubbles's estate. Even before Bubbles died Wanda claimed to have spent $150,000 of her own money on his "needs." JWBP, Box 1, Folder 11: Wanda Michael to Leonore Gershwin, Oct. 20, 1985. **By early 1988:** JWBP, Box 1, Folder 11: First and Final Account, Petition for Distribution and for Allowance of Compensation and for Instructions Re: Creditors Claims Payments and for Extraordinary Fees; hearing: Jan. 13, 1988.

"I had a very dear": JWBP, Box 2, Folder 9: Wanda's notes.

She died on: U.S. Social Security Death Index, 1935–Current: Wanda Zay Michael.

Works Cited

Abbott, Lynn, and Doug Seroff. *The Original Blues: The Emergence of the Blues in African American Vaudeville*. Jackson: University Press of Mississippi, 2017.

Abbott, Lynn, and Doug Seroff. *Ragged But Right: Black Traveling Shows, "Coon Songs," and the Dark Pathways to Blues and Jazz*. Jackson: University Press of Mississippi, 2007.

Acocella, Joan. "Not a Pink Toy." *New Yorker*, Mar 18, 2014.

Allen, Cameron. *The Sublett (Soblet) Family of Manakintown, Virginia*. Detroit: The Detroit Society for Genealogical Research, 1985.

Allen, William Francis, et al. *Slave Songs of the United States*. Bedford, MA: Applewood Books, 1867.

Alpert, Hollis. *The Life and Times of Porgy and Bess: The Story of an American Classic*. New York: Knopf, 1990.

Armstrong, Louis. *Louis Armstrong in His Own Words: Selected Writings*. Edited by Thomas Brothers. New York: Oxford University Press, 1999.

Astaire, Fred. *Steps in Time*. New York: HarperCollins, 1959; reprint, New York: Cooper Square Press, 2000.

Baker, Jean-Claude. *Josephine: The Hungry Heart*. New York: Random House, 1993.

Baker, Ray Stannard. *Following the Color Line: An Account of Negro Citizenship in the American Democracy*. 1904; reprint, Williamstown, MA: Corner House, 1973.

Barnouw, Erik. *Tube of Plenty: The Evolution of American Television*. New York: Oxford University Press, 1990.

Balliett, Whitney. *American Musicians II: Seventy-Two Portraits in Jazz*. New York: Oxford University Press, 1996.

Berger, Morroe, et al. *Benny Carter: A Life in American Music*, Vol. 1. Studies in Jazz, No. 40. Lanham, MD, and London, and Institute of Jazz Studies, Rutgers University-Newark: Scarecrow Press, 2002.

Bloom, Ken. *Broadway: An Encyclopedic Guide to the History, People and Places of Times Square*. New York and Oxford: Facts on File, 1991.

Bogle, Donald. *Toms, Coons, Mulattoes, Mammies, and Bucks: An Interpretive History of Blacks in American Films*. 5th ed. New York: Bloomsbury, 2016.

Bradley, Edwin M. *The First Hollywood Sound Shorts: 1926–1931*. Jefferson, NC: McFarland, 2005.

Briscoe, Johnson. *The Actors' Birthday Book*. New York: Moffat, Yard & Co., 1907.

Brothers, Thomas. *Louis Armstrong: Master of Modernism*. New York: W. W. Norton, 2014.

Brown, Theodore Dennis. "A History and Analysis of Jazz Drumming to 1942." Vols. I and II. PhD diss., University of Michigan, 1976.

"Bubbles." *New Yorker*, Aug 26, 1967.

Bubbles, John. Interview by George Nierenberg. Jazz Oral History Project, Institute of Jazz Studies, Rutgers University, 1979.

Cassidy, Marsha F. *What Women Watched: Daytime Television in the 1950s*. Austin: University of Texas Press, 2005.

Charters, Ann. *Nobody: The Story of Bert Williams*. London: Macmillan, 1970.

Crawford, Richard. "Where Did *Porgy and Bess* Come From?" *The Journal of Interdisciplinary History* 36, no. 4 (Spring 2006): 697–734.

Crosby, Bing. *Call Me Lucky*. New York: Simon and Schuster, 1953; reprint, New York: Da Capo, 1993.

Crowe, Jesse Crawford. "Agitation for Penal Reform in Tennessee, 1870–1900." PhD diss., Vanderbilt University, 1954.

Dance, Stanley. *The World of Earl Hines*. New York: Scribner; paperback edition: Da Capo, 1977.

Davis, Eric. "Buck Washington's Blues: A Private Recording in Homage to Gershwin and Its Implications for the Score of *Porgy and Bess*." Unpublished transcript of talk given at the annual meeting of the American Musicological Society, Louisville, KY, November 14, 2015.

DeVeaux, Scott. *The Birth of Bebop: A Social and Musical History*. Berkeley and Los Angeles: University of California Press, 1997.

Dooley, Roger. *From Scarface to Scarlett: American Films in the 1930s*. New York and London: Harcourt Brace Jovanovich, 1979.

Doyle, Don H. *Nashville in the New South, 1880–1930*. Knoxville: University of Tennessee Press, 1985.

Drew, Bernard A. *Black Stereotypes in Popular Series Fiction: Jim Crow Era Authors and Their Characters*. Jefferson, NC: McFarland, 2015.

Ewen, David. *George Gershwin: His Journey to Greatness*. Englewood Cliffs, NJ: Prentice-Hall, 1970.

Fantle, David, and Tom Johnson. *Reel to Real: 25 Years of Celebrity Interviews from Vaudeville to Movies to TV*. Oregon, WI: Badger Books, 2004.

Farnsworth, Marjorie. *The Ziegfeld Follies*. New York: G. P. Putnam's Sons, 1956.

Feather, Leonard. *Encyclopedia of Jazz*. Rev. ed. New York: Bonanza Books, 1960.

Forbes, Camille F. *Introducing Bert Williams: Burnt Cork, Broadway, and the Story of America's First Black Star*. New York: Basic Civitas Books, 2008.

Fox, Ted. *Showtime at the Apollo*. New York: Holt, Rinehart and Winston, 1983.

Frank, Gerold. *Judy*. New York: Harper & Row, 1975.

Frank, Rusty E. *Tap: The Greatest Tap Dance Stars and Their Stories, 1900–1955*. Rev. ed. New York: Da Capo, 1994.

Fricke, John. *Judy Garland: World's Greatest Entertainer*. New York: Henry Holt, 1992.

Galanoy, Terry. *Tonight!* Garden City, NY: Doubleday, 1972.

Gershwin, Ira. *Lyrics on Several Occasions*. New York: Viking Press, 1973.

Giles, Sarah. *Fred Astaire: His Friends Talk*. New York: Doubleday, 1988.

Gitler, Ira. *Swing to Bop: An Oral History of the Transition in Jazz in the 1940s*. New York: Oxford University Press, 1985.

Goldberg, Jane. "A Drum Is a Tapdancer." *Village Voice* [supplement], Aug 30, 1988.

Goldberg, Jane. "John Bubbles: A Hoofer's Homage." *Village Voice*, Dec 4, 1978.

Goldberg, Jane. *Shoot Me While I'm Happy: Memories of the Tap Goddess of the Lower East Side*. New York: Woodshed Productions, 2008.

Gumm, Charles Clayton. "A Study of the Negro as a Criminal in Nashville, Tenn." *Vanderbilt University Quarterly* 4, no. 2 (April 1904): 97–108.

Harker, Brian. "Louis Armstrong, Eccentric Dance, and the Evolution of Jazz on the Eve of Swing." *Journal of the American Musicological Society* 61 (2008): 67–121.

Haskins, Jim, and N. R. Mitgang. *Mr. Bojangles: The Biography of Bill Robinson.* New York: William Morrow, 1988.

Henderson, C. C. *The Story of Murfreesboro.* Murfreesboro, TN: News-Banner, 1929.

Hill, Constance Valis. *Tap Dancing America: A Cultural History.* New York: Oxford University Press, 2010.

Hischak, Thomas. *The Oxford Companion to the American Musical.* New York: Oxford University Press, 2009. Available online at https://www.oxfordreference.com/view/10.1093/acref/9780195335330.001.0001/acref-9780195335330-e-1873? (accessed May 1, 2020).

Hope, Bob. *The Last Christmas Show.* Garden City, NY: Doubleday, 1974.

Jablonski, Edward. *Gershwin Remembered.* Portland, OR: Amadeus Press, 1992.

Jablonski, Edward. *Gershwin.* New York: Doubleday, 1987.

Jazz Oral History Project: John Bubbles. Interviewed by George Nierenberg. Institute of Jazz Studies, Rutgers University-Newark, Dec 1979.

John W. Bubbles Papers, MSS 8026. L. Tom Perry Special Collections, Harold B. Lee Library, Brigham Young University, Provo, UT.

Josephson, Barney, with Terry Trilling-Josephson. *Cafe Society: The Wrong Place for the Right People.* Urbana and Chicago: University of Illinois Press, 2009.

Kael, Pauline. "The Current Cinema." *New Yorker,* Jan 7, 1985.

Kendall, Alan. *George Gershwin: A Biography.* London: Harrap, 1987.

Kimball, Robert, and William Bolcom. *Reminiscing with Sissle and Blake.* New York: Viking Press, 1973.

Kimball, Robert, and Alfred Simon. *The Gershwins.* New York: Atheneum, 1973.

King, Alan, with Chris Chase. *Name-Dropping: The Life and Lies of Alan King.* New York: Scribner, 1996.

Korall, Burt. *Drummin' Men: The Heartbeat of Jazz: The Swing Years.* New York: Schirmer Books, 1990.

Lamb, Barry. *The Rutherford Rifles and the Struggle for Southern Independence.* Nashville: Pollock, 2012.

Lamon, Lester C. *Black Tennesseans, 1900–1930.* Knoxville: University of Tennessee Press, 1977.

Lamparski, Richard. *Whatever Became of . . . ?* Fifth Series. New York: Crown, 1974.

Land, Barbara, and Myrick Land. *A Short History of Las Vegas.* Reno and Las Vegas: University of Nevada Press, 1999.

Laurie, Joe, Jr. *Vaudeville: From the Honky-Tonks to the Palace.* New York: Henry Holt, 1953.

Leamer, Laurence. *King of the Night: The Life of Johnny Carson.* New York: William Morrow, 1989.

Lomax, Alan. *The Land Where the Blues Began.* New York: Pantheon Press, 1993.

Lovett, Bobby L. *The African-American History of Nashville, Tennessee, 1780–1930: Elites and Dilemmas.* Fayetteville: University of Arkansas Press, 1999.

MacDonald, J. Fred. *Blacks and White TV: African Americans in Television Since 1948.* Chicago: Nelson-Hall, 1992.

Malone, Jacqui. *Steppin' on the Blues: The Visible Rhythms of African American Dance.* Urbana and Chicago: University of Illinois Press, 1996.

Map of Rutherford County, Tenn., D.G. Beers and Co., Philadelphia, 1878.

McGuire, Jerry. "Sportin' Life: The Story of John Bubbles." Unpublished manuscript. John W. Bubbles Papers, Box 11, Folder 8. Brigham Young University, 1969.

Metz, Robert. *The Tonight Show.* New York: Playboy Press, 1980.

Mezzrow, Mezz, and Bernard Wolfe. *Really the Blues*. New York: Random House, 1946; reprint, New York: Citadel Press, 1990.

Mordden, Ethan. *On Streisand: An Opinionated Guide*. New York: Oxford University Press, 2019.

Mueller, John. *Astaire Dancing*. New York: Knopf, 1985; reprint, Columbus, OH: Educational Publisher, 2010.

Naremore, James. *The Films of Vincente Minnelli*. Cambridge: Cambridge University Press, 1993.

Noonan, Ellen. *The Strange Career of* Porgy and Bess: *Race, Culture, and America's Most Famous Opera*. Chapel Hill: University of North Carolina Press, 2012.

Peiss, Kathy. *Zoot Suit: The Enigmatic Career of an Extreme Style*. Philadelphia: University of Pennsylvania Press, 2011.

Pemberton, Gayle. *The Hottest Water in Chicago: Notes of a Native Daughter*. Middletown, CT: Wesleyan University Press, 1998.

Pollack, Howard. *George Gershwin: His Life and Work*. Berkeley and Los Angeles: University of California Press, 2006.

Reid, Grant Harper. *Rhythm for Sale*. North Charleston, SC: CreateSpace Independent Publishing Platform, 2013.

Rimler, Walter. *George Gershwin: An Intimate Portrait*. Urbana and Chicago: University of Illinois Press, 2009.

Rosenkrantz, Timme. *Harlem Jazz Adventures: A European Baron's Memoir, 1934–1969*. Adapted and edited by Fradley Hamilton Garner. Studies in Jazz, No. 65. Lanham, MD: Scarecrow Press, 2012.

Rowland, Mabel, ed. *Bert Williams: Son of Laughter*. New York: The English Crafters, 1923; reprint, New York: Negro University Press, 1969.

See Louisville First. Louisville Convention and Publicity League [pamphlet], 1917.

Seibert, Brian. *What the Eye Hears: A History of Tap Dancing*. New York: Farrar, Straus and Giroux, 2015.

Shapiro, Karin A. *A New South Rebellion: The Battle Against Convict Labor in the Tennessee Coalfields, 1871–1896*. Chapel Hill and London: University of North Carolina Press, 1998.

Shapiro, Nat, and Nat Hentoff. *Hear Me Talkin' To Ya: The Story of Jazz as Told by the Men Who Made It*. New York: Rinehart, 1955; reprint, New York: Dover, 1966.

Sheridan, James, and Barry Monush. *Lucille Ball FAQ: Everything Left to Know about America's Favorite Redhead*. Milwaukee, WI: Applause Theatre & Cinema Books, 2011.

Shiovitz, Brynn Wein. "Mouth Over Matter." In *The Body, The Dance, and The Text: Essays on Performance and the Margins of History*, edited by Brynn Wein Shiovitz, 18–40. Jefferson, NC: McFarland, 2019.

Shipman, David. *Judy Garland: The Secret Life of an American Legend*. New York: Hyperion, 1993.

Sims, Carleton C., ed. *A History of Rutherford County*. Murfreesboro: n.p., 1947.

Slide, Anthony. *The Encyclopedia of Vaudeville*. Westport, CT: Greenwood Press, 1994.

Slide, Anthony. *The Vaudevillians*. Westport, CT: Arlington House, 1981.

Smart, Richard Davis, Jr. "The Economic Condition of Negroes in Nashville, Tenn." *Vanderbilt University Quarterly* 4, no. 2 (April 1904): 108–113.

Smith, Bill. *The Vaudevillians*. New York: Macmillan, 1976.

Smith, Eric Ledell. *Bert Williams: A Biography of the Pioneer Black Comedian*. Jefferson, NC: McFarland, 1992.

Smith, Ronald L. *Johnny Carson: An Unauthorized Biography*. New York: St. Martin's Press, 1987.

Snyder, Robert W. *The Voice of the City: Vaudeville and Popular Culture in New York*. New York: Oxford University Press, 1989.

Sobel, Bernard. "Comedy Dancing." *Dance: Stage and Screen* 21, no. 3 (March 1947): 9–12.

Spada, James. *Streisand: Her Life*. New York: Crown, 1995.

Spitzer, Marian. *The Palace*. New York: Atheneum, 1969.

Stearns, Marshall, and Jean Stearns. *Jazz Dance: The Story of American Vernacular Dance*. New York: Macmillan, 1968; reprint, New York: Da Capo, 1994.

Stewart, D. Travis [Trav S. D.]. *No Applause—Just Throw Money: The Book That Made Vaudeville Famous*. New York: Faber and Faber, 2005.

Thompson, Robin. *The Gershwins' Porgy and Bess: A 75ᵗʰ Anniversary Celebration*. Milwaukee, WI: Amadeus Press, 2010.

Thornbrough, Emma Lou. *Indiana Blacks in the Twentieth Century*. Bloomington: Indiana University Press, 2000.

Vahimagi, Tise. *British Television: An Illustrated Guide*. New York: Oxford University Press, 1994.

van der Merwe, Ann Ommen. *The Ziegfeld Follies: A History in Song*. Lanham, MD: Scarecrow Press, 2009.

Vandiver, Margaret. *Lethal Punishment: Lynchings and Legal Executions in the South*. New Brunswick, NJ, and London: Rutgers University Press, 2006.

Weathers, Nelda Adaline. "How the Negro Lives in Indianapolis." MA thesis, Social Service Department, Indiana University, 1924.

Wertheim, Arthur Frank. *Vaudeville Wars: How the Keith-Albee and Orpheum Circuits Controlled the Big-Time and Its Performers*. New York: Palgrave Macmillan, 2006.

Wright, George C. *Life Behind a Veil: Blacks in Louisville, Kentucky, 1865–1930*. Baton Rouge: Louisiana State University, 1985.

Wyatt, Robert, and John Andrew Johnson. *The George Gershwin Reader*. New York: Oxford University Press, 2004.

Zoglin, Richard. *Hope: Entertainer of the Century*. New York: Simon and Schuster, 2014.

Index